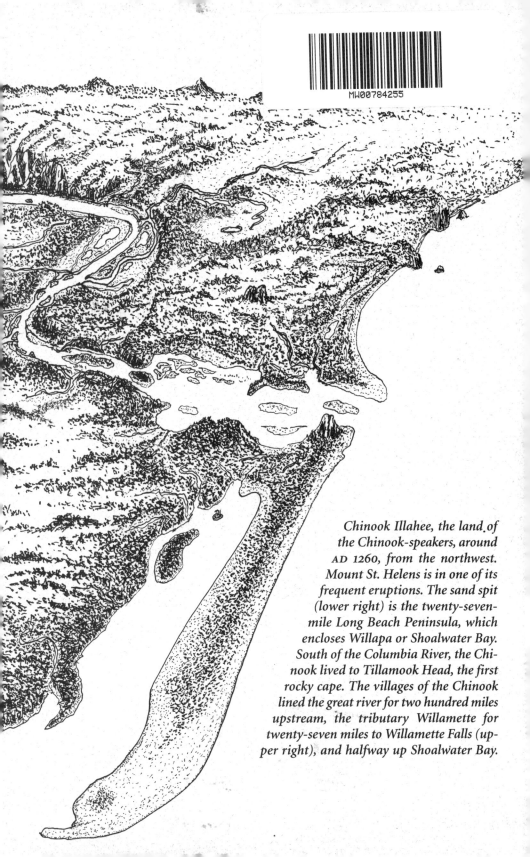

Chinook Illahee, the land of the Chinook-speakers, around AD 1260, from the northwest. Mount St. Helens is in one of its frequent eruptions. The sand spit (lower right) is the twenty-seven-mile Long Beach Peninsula, which encloses Willapa or Shoalwater Bay. South of the Columbia River, the Chinook lived to Tillamook Head, the first rocky cape. The villages of the Chinook lined the great river for two hundred miles upstream, the tributary Willamette for twenty-seven miles to Willamette Falls (upper right), and halfway up Shoalwater Bay.

Naked Against the Rain

Naked Against the Rain

The People of the Lower Columbia River

1770 – 1830

Rick Rubin

FAR SHORE PRESS
PORTLAND, OREGON

Designed by John Laursen at Press-22. Cover painting by Angelina Marino, after Paul Kane's "Mount St. Helens Erupting," 1847. End-paper illustration, "Chinook *Illahee* in 1260," by Rick Rubin, after a panoramic painting by Fred H. Routledge, 1915.

PUBLISHER'S CATALOGING-IN-PUBLICATION DATA
Rubin, Rick, 1931–
    Naked against the rain : the people of the Lower Columbia River 1770–1830 / Rick Rubin. —1st ed.
    p. cm.
    Includes bibliographic references and index.
    LCCN 93-72672
    ISBN 1-883287-00-6

    1. Chinook Indians—History—18th century. 2. Chinook Indians—History—19th century. 3. Chinook Indians—Social life and customs. I. Title.

E99.C57R83 1999   973'.049741
                            QBI99-900

For those who come after,
to live beside Big River.

And Charlotte, of course.

Acknowledgments

PROFOUND THANKS TO Bunny Doar, for editing and improving; John Laursen, for editing, improving, and designing; Dell Hymes, for aid beyond the call of duty; Charlotte Rubin, for unflagging support; and Kajira Wyn Berry, for manifesting the muse Clio.

Thanks also to Ron Abell, Jo Alexander, Carlton E. Appelo, Dale Archibald, George Barton, Bob Benson, Betsy Berry, Don Berry, Tom Booth, Tom Chamberlin, Hy Cohen, Ruth Dixon, Robert M. Drucker, Richard Engeman, Polly Eyerly, David French, Kittu Gates, Steve Halberg, Bill Holm, Jacqueline Hoyt, Mark Hughes, Franz Johnson, Craig McCroskey, Preston McMann, Norm Minnick, Margaret Moore, J. R. Moses, Thomas Newman, George Phebus, William Pilcher, Verne F. Ray, Sue Seyl, Michael Silverstein, Sieglinde Smith, Arthur Spencer, Chedwah Stein, Emory Strong, Wayne Suttles, Leon Tabor, Sharon Tiffany, Jane Van Cleve, A. C. Waters, and Henry Zenk.

Contents

NAKED AGAINST THE RAIN

Of the externals of savage life on the Oregon coast there are many graphic and full accounts; but an insight into their minds are not so easy to reach, and those who have most carefully sought it are likely to be most doubtful of their success.

—George Gibbs

The only human bones in this pasture would be those of the first comers, and they did not bury here, and left no tombs or tiles or shards or walls or coins behind them. If they had a town here it was made of what the woods and fields are made of, and is gone. One may listen, but all the words of their language are gone, utterly gone.

—Ursula K. Le Guin
Always Going Home

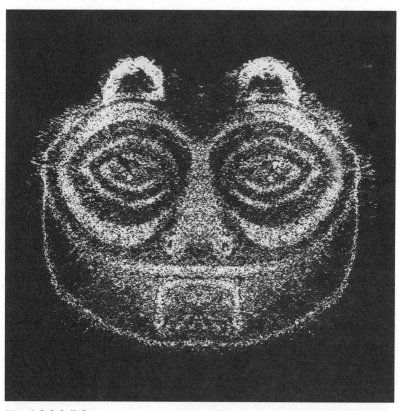

Tsagiglalal: "She sees you as you come, she sees you as you go." Reproduction of the rock image courtesy of the Bureau of Land Management.

She Who Watches

ONCE THERE WAS A PEOPLE so wealthy, plump, and sleek that they drank sea lion oil straight and didn't have to look for food all winter long. They danced and sang and recited stories instead. These people's upriver neighbors bent under ninety-pound packs. These people just carried their big boat down to their river, piled in several tons[1] of trade goods—cranberry preserves, smoked salmon, dried clams, six or seven kinds of vegetables, fur robes, and arrow-proof battle armor—and paddled a hundred miles or so up the river to trade.

They were not just rich but highly intelligent and comparatively sane. Their numerous villages of fancifully decorated houses lined the shores of the mighty river, from which they drew most of their living and much of their pleasure. That river—we call it the Columbia—was all they ever wanted. It provided them with more than they could use. Fish in profusion swam up the river—they called it *Wimahl*—salmon, sturgeon, smelt, and lamprey came, each in its season, to offer their flesh to the people.

What to call these people is a problem. The name *Wimahl* merely meant "Big River," and the people had no name at all for themselves. Each village had a name, and there were names for groups of villages that spoke the same dialect, but each village was really separate, indeed each family was separate, though inextricably connected by relationships to other families. A man might take his house planks and dependents, and paddle up to the next village, and then he was one of those people. As for a name for all those who spoke Chinookan languages, fifty or more winter villages strung along both banks of the lowest two hundred miles of the Columbia River plus twenty-five miles up the Willamette River and twenty miles north and south along the Pacific seacoast, for all those people the river people had no name, indeed hardly more than a memory that they were related.

When the first European ship sailed into the river and anchored eight miles above the mouth, offshore from proud Qwatsamts, a three-row village, the mariners wanted to know what to call the people. One sailor asked some sort of question, in some approximation of language, pointing at the village. Something like "What are these people called?" Pointing, by the way, was dangerous and ill-mannered among these people. A headman or spokesman responded *Chinoak* or *Tsinuk* or something like that.[2] Forever after, the white people called the people in that village, and three or four others along the riverbank nearby, Chinook or Chinooks. (The river people at first called the strangers *tlohonnipts*, "those who float—or drift—ashore.")

After a while, when they learned that the people upriver for a couple of hundred miles had roughly the same languages, the *tlohonnipts* called them Chinook too. Years later, all canoe-paddling Indians on the northern Pacific coast were sometimes referred to as Chinooks.[3] All that, based on no more than what some person answered when strangers impolitely pointed toward the village of long cedar-plank houses, row on row along the shore.

Later, explorers Meriwether Lewis and William Clark would put down as the name of a supposed tribe the response "he pointed at me."[4]

Tsinuk was what the Chehalis, who lived to the north and spoke an entirely different language, called that village, or some of the river people. And though it is probably only a coincidence, the suffix *ooks* or *uks* meant plural people in the Chinook language. So it

Naked Against the Rain

is possible that the people were really called the Chin, and Chinooks meant more than one Chin person. Of such shadows are names made, when strangers with no common language first meet.

The language is how we categorize them, and on that account we might call them Chinookans, if the word sounded better to the ear. During their at least three or four thousand years of living along the Columbia one language evolved into three or more languages, with relationships about like Dutch to German, or Portuguese to Spanish, and there were dialects and mutually understandable accents, but in all the world, only the people of the river spoke a Chinookan language.

CHINOOK OR CHINOOKANS OR CHIN, they were a singular people, far different from the stereotype "Indians." They were polite anarchists (in the classic, not the modern sense) with artificially flattened heads and a tendency toward red hair. They had a highly stratified society with many subtle variations of class. The Chinook had ritualized conflict into a maritime battle performance, where few were harmed and gifts were exchanged afterward. They were open to new people and ideas, true cosmopolites, and they loved more than anything to barter. They were good at it too. The Chinook bettered the canny Scottish fur traders again and again.

In trade they were very like ourselves, but in other ways they were utterly opposite. Our Western heritage contemplates a universe where there is one central God and all the subordinate creatures take their identities in relation to that overpowering One. The Chinook believed the world a multiverse where everything was alive and had its own spirit. The powers of the spirits differed widely but there was no central all-powerful one.[5]

The Chinook lived along the river for thousands of years. Then pale strangers floated ashore, and within forty years the Chinook were pretty much gone. All but a few in the center of their land disappeared, as did a great majority of those at the seacoast and Willamette Falls. A relatively smaller percentage was lost at the eastern edge, up the Columbia River Gorge. In much of their lands their culture was shattered.

Tsagiglalal saw all this happen, from her rock at the uppermost end of the Chinook-occupied river.[6] *Tsagiglalal* is a beautiful broad face, with luminous eyes and wide smile, her tongue thrust out, inscribed on rimrock at the easternmost edge of the Chinook land. Coyote, their Myth Age trickster-hero, put her there to watch the people. "She Who Watches" they called her. She became a symbol of conscience and of death. "She sees you when you come," they said, "she sees you when you go." We'll get to her story in a later chapter.

What, if anything, did the long persistence and swift collapse of the Chinook mean? They were living so nicely. They had all they wanted and nobody to bother them, were wealthy and respected. Then, because of the pelt of a sea mammal and a host of spirits too small to see, their culture crumbled and the survivors were sent away in a cruel diaspora.

BEFORE THESE HIGHLY INTERESTING PEOPLE come dancing into view in a whirl of myth and chanting, and with heroic feats of paddling, trading, sorcery, and over-eating, we need to establish a framework.

The word *Chinook* here denotes all groups up and down the river who spoke one of the Chinookan languages.[7] That makes the original Chinook at the river mouth Shoalwater Chinook, which is fair, for they lived half the year on the river, the other half on the banks and tributaries of broad Shoalwater Bay, a short portage to the north. Chinook subgroups include the Clatsop, Shoalwater, Wahkiacum, Kathlamet, Skiloot, Mahlnumax, Clackamas, Clowewalla, Shahala, White Salmon, Tlakluit or Wishram, and Wasco, plus several smaller groups.

But no tribes. Photographer Edward Curtis was correct when he concluded "to a remarkable degree they lack the tribal instinct."[8] A tribe is defined as having a unifying social organization, a common ancestor, a patron diety, and a leader with power.[9] The Chinook had none of those, but a family-centered society where each man had to encounter his own spirit helper and the leader had only the power of persuasion. Though much used by the *tlohonnipts*, the word "tribe" simply does not fit the Chinook.

ORTHOGRAPHY—writing down the sounds exactly—is a nasty tangle of worms we'd rather not get into. Linguists have evolved a code of special letters and symbolic marks for use with all languages, but few of us have mastered it. Any true approximation of the sound of Chinook is unlikely, and all those little marks make readers nervous. Give ear to Dell Hymes, the leading Chinook linguist, on one particular sound among many in Chinook:

> A third kind of sound common in western American Indian languages, [is] the so-called "voiceless l" and affricates based upon it. This sound is found in Welsh, where it is spelled with a double "l" and occurs in the native Welsh pronunciation of names we have borrowed into English, such as Lloyd and Floyd. The sound is somewhat similar to that of the sounds spelled "th" and "s" in English "thin" and "sin" but with the friction coming from contact with the side of the tongue. Early settlers and writers were bedeviled by this sound. The *tl*, *cl*, and *thl* in proper names like *Tl*ingit, *Cl*ackamas, *Cl*atsop, *Kathl*amet come from attempts to interpret it as a voiceless consonant plus an l. Close, but not close enough; both these words have a voiceless fricative in the . . .[10]

And so on, to considerable length. In all, Hymes listed forty-two sounds, further modified by glottal catches and stops. The sound is rendered as a capital, or barred L in anthropological literature. Linguistics is the theoretical physics of anthropology. We shall not attempt it. We print the words as they were first written, or most often written, or are most easily scanned; a row of letters stolid as soldiers, unmodified by accent marks, with no regard for the different alphabets the ethnologist or linguist used to capture the sound, little attempt to fathom the proper pronunciation. The exceptions are the barred L, rendered *hl*, and a ch sound as in the German *ach*, shown here as *x*, both on the suggestion of Dr. Hymes.[11]

THE GENERAL INTENT of this book is to treat all the Chinook as a single cultural experience, a people like the widely dispersed Celts, the Kurds, the Magyar, or the Hmong. For that purpose, differences between the various groups is sometimes minimized, and the similarities emphasized. In fact, each village was somewhat different from its neighbors, and the differences from seacoast to eastern reaches were often considerable.

Further, the book is an attempt to recreate the world at the center of the Chinook land; the thickly populated Wapato Lowlands, eighty river miles of villages thick on every shore, which was almost entirely obliterated in a terrible catastrophe in 1830. Of that center, almost nothing is known. Yet it was among the richest, most thickly populated regions in America north of Mexico. Out toward the Chinook frontiers, at the seacoast, up the Columbia River Gorge, and around Willamette Falls, some Chinook survived and a considerable amount is known. Thus, we have attempted to stretch the skein of knowledge inward, to salvage a glimpse of a world long gone.

THEY DIDN'T SIGN AWAY their rainy Eden or sell it, die in warfare, or move to reservations, not until twenty-five years after the catastrophes that swept most of them away. It wasn't smallpox that laid them low. Suddenly most of them were simply gone. The Wapato Lowlands in particular were empty and silent. Did *God* call them home? The few survivors walked away dazed. Took to speaking other languages. Were replaced by strangers. After a few decades hardly anyone remembered that they had ever been there.

This book is meant to remedy that lapse of memory.

Aunt Susan, the mother of Johnny Skanown. Photographer unknown.
Courtesy of Ye Galleon Press.

1

The People of Olden Times

1770

"Soon now people will come into this land," Coyote announced. "Listen!" And the people could be heard, "du'lulu-lu," like thunder rumbling from afar.[1]

MANY, PERHAPS MOST, peoples have an origin myth, a story about a place, or a set of circumstances or emergent forces or creatures, or a God, from which the tellers of that myth were created. The beginning of earth, or land, or tribe, or place. The Chinook were no exception, and being very diverse they had several such stories from one end of the river to the other.

The *Gitlapshoi*, "People of Sealand," who lived on the broad, twenty-eight-mile sand spit north of the river's mouth, had an origin story, which one of them, called Matil, related to one of the early settlers, Isaac H. Whealdon. Matil interspersed his account with words from a Chinook trade language, translated here in brackets.

A long, long time ago there was no peninsula or bay or Indians, but one day there came from the *siah cole ilahee* [far cold country] a big canoe with a hundred warriors with their *klootchmen* [wives] and papooses [babies]. They tried to enter the Columbia, but *hiyu* [strong] winds, *hiyu skook-*

um pe-wake yaka charco copa [great strong winds prevent-ed an entrance]. So they paddled ashore just where the hill and rocks terminate at the south end of what is now the [Long Beach] peninsula. Here they moored their big canoe, tying the stern to the rocks at the south and anchoring her bow to the north. Caching their paddles and other things in a cave in the rocks, they took the old Indian trail for the Co-lumbia river and what is now old Chinook.

After many moons they returned, *charco miami, halo, kanim. Yaka nanich okok kanim yaka clatawa keekwulee icta tenas sandspit.* [No, there was not a sign of their canoe, only they found a little sandspit] with a clam bed and the ocean on the west. A few small pine trees grew on top. At the east there were some bushes with *hiyu olallies,* [many berries] of a bright red color. These were cranberries. A little farther out to the east, *tenas siah mitlite tenas chuck.* [this was only a little water], but 'tis now Whealdon's Pond or Black Lake. When the Indians saw this they built a house on their sand sunken canoe and their children grew and multiplied and as the tribe grew so grew the tiny sandspit and a little bay [Shoalwater Bay] was formed which became a mighty water. So from the big canoe grew the peninsula and the bay and from the one hundred Indians grew the Shoal-water tribe.[2]

Those were the *Taanewatiks,*[3] "People of Olden Times," ances-tors of the Chinook. The growth of the sandspit, called the Long Beach Peninsula now, is geologically speaking true, and Chinook-speakers, over many generations, watched it happen. This was so because as the most recent Ice Age began to come to an end the melting waters of the great continental glaciers poured into the oceans, causing them to rise from their Ice Age level of about three hundred feet below our present sea level. The sea rose from about fourteen thousand years ago to about three thousand years ago, and as we shall shortly see, the Chinook were in place along the Columbia by then. They almost certainly remembered a wide shallow bay to the north of the great river, but it was open to the sea, lacking a sandspit to protect it from the force of the Pacific. Then, as the sea level stabilized, the sandspit would have begun to grow. The floats-ashores would have said it grew from Cape Disappointment, a series of rocks on the north lip of the river's mouth, but whether it originated from some big, rough pebbles or from a tied-down canoe is not important. Origin myths are, and perhaps will always be, enigmatic montages of group memory and elaborated fantasy. The sandspit stretched out, protecting the bay, and the Chinook grew to be a great people, known in all directions.

Another account, heard by pioneer author James Swan, told of an old woman and two young girls who came down from a country "far to the north." The girls wished for husbands, so they might have children. A man told them he would show them another world where they would see their husbands. They looked through where he made the earth open, and saw two young men, apparently made of fire. They were frightened, and told their mother, who was also alarmed. At night, the men came and stayed with them. In the morning, the fire men went to the sky and became stars. The girls followed, but their children became the Chinooks and peopled the country.[4] Upriver, the Wishram Chinook told of star men lovers too.

The Shoalwater Chinook told a story, about a bird, a wind, and an ogress, which James Swan, who recorded it, believed they probably learned from their neighbors to the north, the Chehalis.

South Wind—called Toolux—was coming north in the springtime when he encountered Quoots-hooi, a giant ogress. He asked her for food and she gave him a net to catch fish. Toolux caught a small whale, and started to cut off a nice piece with his flint knife when the ogress stopped him. She instructed him to cut the fish with a shell knife, and lengthwise down its backbone instead of across.

Ignoring her, South Wind hacked off a steak. Instantly the fish transmogrified into an enormous bird, called Hahness. Thunder crashed as she flapped her great wings, which blotted out the sun. Hahness flew north, with Toolux and the Quoots-hooi in futile pursuit.

Later, when the ogress was out berrying on Swallalochast, Saddle Mountain, she discovered the Thunderbird's nest. It was full of eggs, which she began to eat, tossing the shells down the steep mountainside. As they came to rest those bits of eggshell became people, the Chinook or Chehalis, or perhaps the original people.

When Hahness returned and found her nest ravaged she sought out Toolux and together they went to search for the ogress. Each spring the great bird and the south wind returned north to seek her.[5]

THE CHINOOK WERE PROBABLY LIVING by the river at least three or four thousand years ago. Tools and other remains dating from around 615 BC, found twenty miles south of the Columbia River, as well as near Cape Disappointment at the mouth of the Columbia, Skamokawa at the head of the estuary, and upriver on Scapoose Bay and Sauvie Island, are of the same riverine mix and style as those of the later river people.[6] Though such findings give no clue to what language was spoken, the similarity of style implies that it was the Chinook who were living in those places, as they were when the Europeans arrived. Before that the sea and river were still rising, inundating and destroying even the traces of earlier village sites.

There had been no fundamental change in the basic way the people of the river lived over the last three thousand years.[7] That is

Naked Against the Rain

not to say things didn't change—the bow and arrow came, arrow point chipping, all sorts of new spiritual practices, hair styles, and stories to tell—but the people lived in rectangular wooden houses, and fished the river with nets for all those thirty centuries and more.

WIMAHL, THE RIVER the Chinook had found, was a great torrent. There was a two-mile rage of combers, breakers, and chop all across its five-mile-wide mouth. A broad, shallow estuary occupied the lowest forty miles, above which was a thirty-five-mile passage through the low, thickly forested Coast Range. Above that, the eighty-mile-long Wapato Lowlands widened out to fifteen miles across. The river was still a mile wide 145 miles from the sea at the Cascades, its lowest falls and rapids. Its flow was immense, second only to that of the Mississippi River on this continent.

The prodigious stream was their cornucopia. In addition to fish that lived in the river all year long, many kinds of sea-going fish—called anadromous—returned to Big River to spawn. The Columbia is thought to have been the most fecund anadromous-fish river on earth. Five kinds of salmon came up, half-ton sturgeon, schools of smelt (called eulachon by scholars) so dense they wanted walking on, and lamprey in profusion. Sea lions and seals followed the fish up; otters, beaver, deer, and elk abounded; ducks and geese were so loud and thick in autumn that people couldn't sleep; the river's floodplain was blue with camas flowers; and giant cedar trees stood about, from the trunk, bark, roots, and branches of which the Chinook made most of the things they needed. The banks of Wimahl were a fair approximation of paradise most years, though their myths still reminded them of famine.

So large a river was scarcely useful without two elements of technology: canoes capable of withstanding its powerful currents, winds, and tidal flows, and nets to fish so huge a stream. Without those, it was better to live on a little tributary stream or bay. Any tribe could spear fish, or build a weir across a creek, but who could fish Big River? It seems likely that the Chinook brought the technologies of seine nets and seaworthy canoes with them, and that the nets made it possible for them to wedge in between the Salish-speakers who already occupied the seacoast. Thus, the Chinook could harvest the river. North or south along the coast the Salish had canoes but not seine nets, though there were small seines on Puget Sound.

Chinook canoes were excellent, but not exceptional. They bought and built the several styles of the Pacific Northwest coast. Their largest were fifty feet long and six feet wide, their smallest light enough for a woman to pick up and carry under her arm. They handled these boats with exceptional skill, as did the other fisher-folk of the northern Pacific coast. (Upriver of the Chinook, canoes were less developed.)

SEINE NETS ARE RIVERMEN'S NETS, called after the French river. They are merely big rectangles, the largest Chinook ones six hundred feet long by sixteen wide.[8] The mesh was precisely calibrated for the kind of fish they sought. Tied with wooden floats above and rock sinkers below, the nets stood upright in the water.

Three or four men loaded their big net in a canoe. One held the shore end at the top of the drift, a smooth sandbar or river beach clear of snags, and the rest pulled out from shore, paying out the net behind them as the boat drifted down. At the bottom of the drift they pulled hard for shore. The fish were trapped and soon gasped and flopped in shallow water. The men grabbed them by their tails and threw them up on the beach, a hundred or more in a single lay of a medium-size net.[9] Since the taboos allowed three lays during a single incoming tide, and the salmon weighed forty to eighty pounds, a few men could theoretically catch six or eight tons of fish a day.

Naked Against the Rain

IN A MYTH about net-making and fishing taboos, Coyote teamed up with his younger brother Snake, and their female cousins Frog and Newt, to make nets.[10] Frog and Newt were paid to spin rope; Coyote and Snake shared the net-tying and float- and sinker-making. There was a lot of humorous by-play between Coyote and Snake about who was working hard and who was just crawling around.

"Quick, quick, make your net. You make me wait," Coyote claimed, but Snake finished his net first. "Oh brother, you got the better of me," Coyote admitted.

It was hard work. "When a person makes a net he shall get tired before he finishes it," Coyote announced. "It would not be well if he would not get tired. Even I, Coyote, even I got tired!"

Then he announced the taboos—the Chinook word was *tge-lau*[11]—for catching salmon at each place, how many and when and how to throw them ashore, and how to cut them, an almost endless list of rules, different for each location. To disobey meant no more fish would come and offer the people of the village their luscious pink bodies for the taking and eating.

Those taboos that Coyote brought were stringent, exacting, and complex. At Clatsop, for example, the fisherman must not jump or step over the net, or cut the first-caught salmon of the year until the afternoon. The salmon had to be split at the sides and roasted belly and back on separate double spits, with four sticks vertical in the ground and two horizontal sticks across them. On top of this frame the cook must put the back with the head and tail still attached.

The Clatsop fisherman was forbidden to strike the salmon with a stick or to break the salmon's backbone. He must strew sand on its eye and press it with a fist. When many salmon were killed on the first day they must be eaten in the same house they were roasted in, not carried outside. Even leftover parts had to be kept at the same place. Salmon drying must begin when the flood tide set in the day after the fish were caught. When ebb tide occurred early in the morning the fisherman must not lay his net before sunrise. When a crow took a salmon, then the fish could be carried outside, but it must be distributed raw. No fire was allowed until daylight; the breast must not be eaten before the second day; the fire had to be put out with water. Prohibited in addition were a regular cast of taboo persons: murderers, those who prepare corpses, girls just at puberty, menstruant women, widows, and widowers; none of those might eat of the salmon.[12] A bafflement of rules, though a lot of them applied only to the first of that kind of salmon caught each year in the village, in celebration of which the villagers enacted a ceremony.

"Even I got tired," Coyote repeated, farther upriver, concluding the taboos for the Kathlamet drifts. "When men work on their net and make a small mistake, they shall not catch anything. When a louse is on a net, the owner shall not catch anything."[13]

FOR ALL THEIR CONCERN with workmanship and rules, the Chinook were equally attentive to something we would misunderstand to be luck, as illustrated by the Shoalwater story, the Four Cousins Legend:

> There were three brothers and their younger cousin, an orphan boy covered with lice, who lived with his grandmother. The grandmother spun willow bark into rope for people. Nipping off a little for herself each time, she finally made a long rope which she sent with her grandson and his three cousins when they went to trade and gamble with the Chehalis at the other end of the big shallow bay behind the long peninsula north of the river.
>
> "Take this rope and trade it for groundhog blankets," she told him.
>
> One Chehalis man had a sea-otter pelt that everyone wanted to trade for, but the man had eyes only for the boy's

rope. An advantageous trade, but it made his oldest cousin jealous. On the way home the cousin stole the valuable pelt while the youth slept, and the three brothers paddled off.

The lad awoke deserted, his fur gone. He started home on foot, swimming creeks as he came to them. He came to a small river and waited to swim across at slack water. He heard sounds in the water. "Tummm" he heard, and then "dulll." They were repeated, and then "gummm" he heard, and five black bears stood up out of the water.

The youth threw off his elkskin. He threw it ashore. "Now I shall die," he thought, and began to swim across. He passed the first, the second, and the third bear. When he reached the fourth bear it looked at him. It looked that human right in the face and he became unconscious. Itcixyan carried him to his house. Behold, he saw Itcixyan!

Itcixyan was the Chinook water spirit. At his house beneath the water, supernatural beings spoke one language on one side, another on the other side, and in the middle of the house they spoke still a third language. The boy understood them all.

"These women whom you hear now on both sides of the house will be your wives," the water spirit told him. "Thus will you live among the people. This will make you a chief." Then he gave that lousy boy a little bird arrowhead made of mere bone, and the youth awoke, ashore, on the other side of the river, his elkskin beside him.

When the orphan boy with lice reached home, the people were gambling at disks. They jeered at him because he had been abandoned. He stood watching them guess the pattern of the disks, tossing his bird arrowhead in his hand.

"How pretty is your arrowhead," one gambler said. "I will stake a stone arrowhead against yours." So they gambled and the boy won. He won ten times in a row. He understood the

language of both sides of the disk, and of the middle—the all-
important edge, about which they bet—as well. Then he went
home to sleep.

The next day a man came and asked him to play, mean-
ing to win those arrowheads back. "I have no disks," the youth
told him, but the man said he would provide them. "I have no
mat to play on," he told him, but the gambler said he would
provide it. So they gambled, and the boy won everything from
that man.

"That one with the lousy head is getting hopeful," anoth-
er gambler said. "Tomorrow I will play with him." He beat
that man. He won and won. He won the property of all the
gamblers. He won over all the common people, he won over
the chiefs, he won slaves, canoes, wives. He won everything
from the cousin who had stolen from him. The Chehalis came,
the Quinault came; he won their property and their slaves.
The Tillamook, the Cowlitz, all the Chinook who lived up the
river came. He had many wives and everyone ate at his house.
He became a chief.

If his cousins had not taken the sea-otter from him he
would not have seen the supernatural being, the tale conclud-
ed. He saw Itcixyan![14]

THERE WERE MANY WAYS in which their world view differed from
the European one. Some were simple, like the Darkness Woman's
box, described in a myth called Basket Ogress Took the Child. The
hero had ascended to the sky world, where he encountered and
transformed various fleas and lice, who before that had been capable of killing people.

Then as he went along again he saw an old woman approach-
ing. She was carrying something. He met her. He said to her,

"What are you taking along with you?" She said to him, "No, dearie! I am of the Darkness Ones." He said to her, "In spite of that, give me what you are taking along. I am hungry."

Then she again said to him, "Oh no. I am a Darkness One, my dear!" So then he went around to the rear of her, he saw where the plug was, he pulled it out. It became total darkness. She said to him, "Plug it back in so that it will become daylight! Plug it in." He sought unsuccessfully for her plug. He did not see it. So he merely pulled out grass, he plugged it in, it became daylight. Then he said to her, "But it will not be like that in the future. The people are close by now. They will not see you. It will merely become dark then, and then it will become daylight. But you yourself will not be going around." [15]

DID THE CHINOOK BELIEVE that light is the absence of darkness? That would have been a different thing indeed. Different too was their idea of the relative importance of landforms, as described in a story of the Earth's first battle. James C. Strong heard of it:

> As to the formation of mountains, rivers, etc., they believed that, in the long ago, the surface of the earth was quite smooth and level; that after dwelling long in harmony the different spirits quarrelled, and the water spirits were strong enough to sink portions of the surface for the rivers to run in, and larger portions for the lakes and seas to lie in; that the spirits of the levels had power to hold their own in the contest; while the mountain spirits were vanquished and pushed up out of the way, and there obliged forever to remain. [16]

The Chinook may not have thought darkness came from a box, but clearly the relative value they placed upon water, lowlands, and mountains was far different from our own. For us, mountains often have spiritual resonance; and until recently we held our waters in such low esteem that we routinely polluted them.

THE CHINOOK HAD FOUND their luck—their spirit helper—lurking beneath the water. With river and nets and boats, with plenty of hard, careful work, they prospered, spread, and multiplied. Became the wealthiest people around. Claimed every fishing drift on every bank of rivers and sloughs for hundreds of miles inland.

Fur trader Gabriel Franchère recalled of the Chinook:

> I believe them closer to a civilized state than any of the tribes living east of the Rocky Mountains. They do not seem to me so bound by their customs that they could not easily adopt those of civilized men. They possess to an eminent degree those qualities opposite to idleness, improvidence, and stupidity. The chiefs in particular distinguish themselves by their good judgement and their intelligence. Generally speaking they have quick minds and tenacious memories.[17]

They were even reported to be happy. Franchère's fellow trader Alexander Ross, admitted:

> On a fine day it is amusing to see a whole camp or village, both men and women, here and there in numerous little bands, gambling, jeering and laughing at one another, while groups of children kept in constant motion, either in the water or practicing the bow and arrow, and even the aged take a lively interest in what is passing, and there appears a degree of happiness among them which civilized men, wearied with care and anxious pursuits, perhaps seldom enjoy.[18]

Naked Against the Rain

FOUR DECADES before either of those men ever saw a Chinook—it was around 1770, but the Chinook did not know that—a son was born to wealthy and well-connected parents. His father, Komkomis, was a headman among the Quinault.[19] His mother, Tamaitamai, was of noble family, her father the headman of the village Qwatsamts, the three-row town Gray's sailors heard called Chinoak. Tamaitamai was said to have served for a time as headwoman of that proud, ancient village.[20] The baby was placed for a year on the cradleboard, then named Comcomly, an ancient, family-held name, probably most recently held by his mother's father.

They could neither know that the Chinook had lived three or four thousand years beside the river nor guess that they had only sixty years more to do so. That newborn babe would watch it happen, and play a larger role in the drama than any other individual. Comcomly. Remember his name.[21]

A Wasco man. Photograph by Benjamin Gifford, courtesy of the Columbia Gorge Interpretive Center, Stevenson, Washington.

2

Tlohonnipts Float Ashore

1780

THE *TLOHONNIPTS*, "those who float ashore," weren't all that new. A group were shipwrecked on the beach at Nehalem once. They made a village separate from the Tillamook-speaking Nehalem, who lived in the misty little river valley next south from the Clatsop. The sailors took wives from among the people, which was all right with the Nehalem until one of them tried to steal a headman's wife. Then the Nehalem rubbed them out. Ethnologist George Gibbs, who heard the story around 1855, deduced they were Japanese, from their distinctive offspring, whose "complexion is yellower than ordinary, and their eyes more oblique and elongated."[1] Nor was that the only such shipwreck along the coast.

AN EXCITING EVENT occurred around 1735. An old Clatsop woman had been mourning her dead son in Neahcoxie, one of their winter towns at what is now Gearhart. She was walking up the fifteen-mile beach toward Neahkeluk village on Big River when she encountered a monster that looked like a whale with two trees growing out of its back and ropes dancing from the trees. She beheld a bear with a human face on top of the whale. It beckoned to her. She ran for home. She feared that it was her son's ghost, or some other spirit.

At Neahkeluk, a big three-row town near Point Adams, she told the people, but they thought she was merely delirious from mourning. Finally they armed themselves and accompanied her back toward the monster. When they reached it, they found two of the bear-like creatures had climbed down, and brought a box in which a third one lay dead, as though ready to be put up in a tree like a person. The two carried kettles of copper, and signalled their need for water. Another kettle they placed in the middle of the fire they had built. They placed seeds in it, which after a time made popping noises and changed into much larger white objects, later known to be popcorn.

A chief inspected the bears and found that their hands were like those of people. Their faces were likewise human but grown thick with hair. The Chinook had little facial hair, and generally plucked that out, though a few old men might let a wispy growth occur. They plucked their scant body hair as well. One daring Clatsop youth climbed up onto the whale. The sides were covered with sheets of copper. The Chinook had already traded for copper and knew its value and uses. The youth entered the whale. Inside he found strings of brass buttons half a fathom long. He went out to tell his relatives the news, but found that the whale had begun to burn. He fled it.

The whale burned like fat. After it had cooled the people collected brass and iron for the first time, which were lying where the whale had been. Two fingers of copper long enough to go around an arm had the value of one slave. An iron spike was likewise worth a slave, a nail would get a cured deer skin or several *haiqua*, money beads.

Headmen and nobles came from all around to see the bear-like men. Shoalwater, Chehalis, Willapa, and Quinault from the north; Klickitat, Cowlitz, Multnomah, and Shahala from upriver. The floats-ashores' heads being round, they were enslaved. There was much discussion about who would own them. Finally, it was decided that one would remain with the Clatsops and the other would be carried off by the Shoalwater.

The one the headman of the Clatsop kept called himself Konapee and had the power to shape iron spikes and nails. He heated and pounded out knives. There was a traditional club the Chinook liked, made of bone or wood, slightly resembling a short sword. The iron clubs he made in that pattern were highly prized. At first, the Clatsop chief made his *tlohonnipts* work all the time, but Konapee produced so many valuable things that the chief became ashamed and perhaps frightened, and freed him. It was not wise to own a man whose spirit helper was so powerful. Konapee moved off a little upriver and built a place of his own.

After he had been free for awhile Konapee and the other *tlohonnipts* said that they wished to rejoin their relatives. They went inland, up Big River. Konapee fathered a son, probably among the Multnomah in the Wapato Lowlands. He called the boy Soto and refused to let his wife flatten the infant's head. He may have had a daughter as well. Konapee continued on and disappeared beyond the Wishram. That he should come from the sea but depart inland is said to have puzzled the Chinook.[2]

ANOTHER OF THE *TLOHONNIPTS*, who called himself Jack Ramsay (the Chinook pronounced it Lamsay), survived a shipwreck and was living somewhere south among the Tillamook around 1780. He had red hair, as did the first of his two sons. He would not let his wife, who was said to have been Nehalem, flatten the head of that boy and he tattooed the name Jack Ramsay on the child's arm. The second son, whose dark hair resembled their mother more closely, had his head properly flattened. He was named George Ramsay. The father died around 1790, but his sons, particularly George, would play important roles during the ensuing years.[3]

AT THE CASCADES, the Shahala already knew that white people were coming. Long ago an old man had dreamt it at night; he saw strange people, who spoke to him and showed him amazing new things. In the morning he spoke to the people. Everyone gathered to hear him—women, men, children, old men. They were made glad by his stories, and they danced.

> Soon all sorts of strange things will come. No longer will things be as before. They will bring us everything strange; they will bring us something which you just have to point at anything moving way yonder, and it will fall right down and die. There will be brought to us a bucket for boiling purposes. No longer will you use your old-fashioned bucket made out of stone.
>
> No longer will you make fire by drilling with sticks as before. Certain small pieces of wood will be brought to us with which you will make a fire.
>
> Strange people will bring us such things. White people with mustaches on their faces will come from the east. Do you people be careful!

The old man described axes, hatchets, knifes, stoves, cattle, and horses. The people danced with energy. "Thus long ago did it happen to the people dwelling along the river," the account concluded, "long before the coming of the first whites."[4]

BEFORE THOSE WONDERS reached the river people, another new thing came. It must have seemed a malignant spirit of a distinctive sort, for which their shamans and curers knew no remedy. Like a *yuhlma*, a wild spirit, it was invisible, and passed through the air from person to person. These spirits traveled not individually, as did *yuhlma*, but in a swarm. In 1781-1782, before the Chinook had encountered any Europeans except those shipwrecked *tlo-*

honnipts, an awful pestilence laid them low.[5]

The victims were wracked with fever for from one to five days. Many died of fever alone. Others went blind. Those who survived became covered with blisters all over their bodies, particularly on their hands and faces. After a while these blisters opened, oozed pus, then scabbed over. When the scabs dried and fell off they left a shallow round pock. Scabs and pus were how the Chinook described low-born commoners. The survivors' pocked faces shamed them so that many committed suicide. Historian John Dunn heard of this malady:

> They at first tried their medicine men, or conjurors. Then, when their medicines and charms were found unavailing, they adopted various expedients, which were as fatal as the disease itself; such as bleeding, blistering, steam, and cold baths in quick succession. Then they became desperate. The wretched sufferers were deserted and left to rot and perish, unaided and unpitied. The more hardened and courageous of those who escaped the attack fled. Others, more desponding, committed suicide, to save themselves from the horrors which they saw the sufferers enduring. The bodies of hundreds of men, women, and children used to be seen afterwards, suspended from the trees, close to depopulated villages, whilst the ground was strewed with putrid and moldering remains. Numbers of tribes were totally swept away; or reduced to a few scattered and powerless individuals."[6]

It was indeed a most ancient spirit that had attacked them. The first description of smallpox was of an epidemic in Arabia in 370 BC. For centuries it swept back and forth across Europe, Africa, and Asia, but was relatively mild. In the seventeenth century its deadliness suddenly increased.[7] One-tenth of all the deaths in Europe during the eighteenth century were from smallpox, particularly the deaths of children, and most of the blindness as well. In America it was deadly from the moment it rode ashore in Mexico with Hernan Cortes' conquistadors in 1520. By killing half the people it helped the Spaniards topple the mighty Aztec empire.[8]

Smallpox, now extinct, was untreatable to the end. Once established, it ran its course. Only vaccination, which eliminated the disease, stood between our ancestors and the writhing horrors of this deadly, disfiguring pestilence.

Few of the Chinook showed pocks, which Hudson's Bay Company physician John Scouler thought might mean the death rate was particularly high.[9] Even twenty-five years later the river was still spotted with empty houses and deserted villages: Nosqwalakal, down the beach from Qwatsamts, abandoned entirely; Neahkaltounalthe, on Young's Bay, a large village until smallpox smote it; Mahlnumax in the Wapato Lowlands, greatly reduced; Nechacokee, at Blue Lake, abandoned and a new, smaller village built in front of the old.[10] In 1806, when the explorer Captain William Clark asked what had happened to the abandoned village behind Nechacokee, the headman brought out a pockmarked woman of around thirty and indicated she had suffered the disease as a child.[11]

Recent studies suggest epidemics of various European diseases may have swept across the continent to the Chinook earlier still, but no accounts of them survive. The smallpox epidemic of 1781-1782 we know from the traces that remained, on faces and on villages. The virulent epidemic came either from Spanish ships exploring the coast in 1775, or spread up the Missouri River, decimating countless bands, wiping out some tribes entirely, then down the Columbia to the sea.[12] Being great traders, the Chinook were particularly at risk.

THEN THE EPIDEMIC passed, and those who remained alive moved a little way off and built new houses.

The cavernous winter houses of the Chinook resembled Viking halls more than tepees or hogans. They ranged to more than 120 feet long, and were twenty-five to fifty feet wide. The central ridge-pole of the gabled roof was twenty feet above the floor. Even poor commoners built sixteen-foot by twenty-foot houses. They were not fly-by-night affairs. One house near Scapoose was continuously occupied for four hundred years. Archaeologist Kenneth Ames estimated the 114-foot by 45-foot structure required fifty-five thousand board feet to build just the walls, roof, and floor, not counting partitions, about five times as much lumber as a three-bedroom contemporary house. During those four centuries the Scapoose house was totally rebuilt once and altered or repaired at least twenty-seven times. Timber and planks had to be replaced every twenty years or so. The builders were aware of this, and placed stones under posts to minimize contact with the soil. It required between 480,000 and 1.1 million board feet of lumber in all, the largest timbers being three-foot-thick house-posts. Ames concluded that building and maintaining a Chinook plank house was a labor-intensive activity.[13]

Houses were dug into the ground three or four feet at Sealand, quite shallowly in the Wapato Lowlands, and as much as eight feet upriver in the colder Columbia River Gorge. A framework was created of posts and beams, ridgepoles and rafters, with logs or boards holding up the ridgepole, all lashed together so that the building could work in the wind. Western red cedar was easily split with sets of elk horn or wooden wedges, forming planks two to five feet wide and twenty or more feet long. Wall boards were three or four fingers thick; roof boards were thinner. Often the roof was of bark.

Planks were placed vertically into the ground, forming walls that rose eight feet above the floor of the excavation. The eaves of the gabled roof extended eighteen inches beyond the walls, almost touching the ground in deeply entrenched houses. The roof boards were lapped horizontally. Roofs were lashed, and strong enough to climb on.

The entrance was usually at one end, an oval hole through which one person at a time could pass, cut about thirty inches above the ground outside. The end planks were generally decorated with paintings in red, black, green, and white, sometimes of a giant face with the doorway as mouth, sometimes of a giant spirit figure, representing the house owner's spirit power, between whose legs one entered crawling.[14] A mat or board hung inside as door and a log with convenient knots for steps descended into the interior.

Around three sides stood tiers of wooden bunks with platforms in front to sit or lie upon. Some houses had double bunks. The house was floored with planks except around the row of fire pits, where a timber-enclosed sandbox a foot or two deep extended down the center of the house. The fire pits had fire-hardened clay liners. In the ancient Scapoose house, numerous layers of clay liners reveal the house's history. Floor boards and walls were covered with reed mats, and the bunks were enclosed with mats, which the women made in great numbers, crimping their seams nicely with ornately decorated creasers. Many houses had dirt-floor work areas as well as board- and mat-floored areas.

Bunks, which were sometimes three to six feet above the floor, were entered by moveable post-and-rung ladders. Often, goods were stored in or under the lower bunks. Mats were bedding, piled with furs in the cold season. From the rafters hung baskets and bags of food and other things. The Chinook also stored food and goods in pits under the floorboards. Fur trader Alexander Henry visited a chief's house at Wahlala, a Shahala village above the head of the Cascades on the north, and recorded:

> The front planks of the beds are carved and painted in various styles. At the end of each range are some broad upright planks erect on which figures are rudely carved, somewhat

resembling fluted pillars. At the foot of the chief's bed are planted in the ground at equal distances four figures of heads, about two feet high, adorned with a kind of crown, and rudely carved and painted. Beside these figures are erected in the ground two large, flat, painted stones. On the side of each partition, facing the fireplace, are carved and painted on the planks some very large rude uncouth figures of eagles, tortoises, and other animals, some of them four feet long. The colors used are white, red, black, and green; the sculpture in some instances is not badly executed; they are rude but striking resemblances.[15]

There were a lot of architectural variations. Sometimes a partition screened the door, sometimes the whole back half of the house was walled off as a storeroom. Areas were partitioned off to seclude initiates at spirit dances, or girls when first menstruant. Many villages consisted of a long range of houses with roofed passageways between. Captain Clark described one with four-foot-wide passages between.[16] It had seven apartments in a row, each with a separate entrance. Another house, 160 feet by 40 feet, was built entirely inside a fully framed and planked outer house. Houses in the Wapato Lowlands tended to be larger than those up or downriver.[17]

Out back of the long houses the Chinook built small houses, sometimes round, where women went when menstruant, or to do women's craft work, or merely to be with other women. Only women could enter, and only there could the women be naked if they wished.[18]

The winter house was a great dark cavern. The dirt of the excavation was piled against the walls for insulation, so only cracks in the roof or high on the ends let in light and air. The peak could be opened in either direction to let the smoke out, but when the wind was wrong, the smoke billowed. People gravitated toward where the nobles lived, sometimes at the center and sometimes at the end farthest from the door. They lounged around the fires while dogs and children romped about. Poor dependents and slaves also lived in the house.

Three to ten families lived together, mostly related by blood or marriage; generally thirty to sixty people, including slaves. Eighty inhabitants was the most anyone counted.[19] Chinook houses were smoky, warm, and familiar. Fleas and lice multiplied, but home-like odors and social relations proliferated as well. Fur trader David Thompson recalled such houses as "comfortable to naked people, but to me intolerably close and warm. I was glad to breathe fresh air."[20] (It would not have occurred to a European to take off his clothes.)

CHINOOK LIFE revolved around their villages. Wilson Price Hunt noted in 1812 near Wishram, "The Indians give a special name to each village that has more than one lodge in it. They loved to talk about them to strangers."[21] (Wishram, he noted, "resembles one of the small fishing ports of the eastern coast of the United States.") Anthropologists used to classify peoples as stone age, bronze, or iron, but the Chinook classified them by whether they lived in villages or not. When their headman gave a dance they invited the people from wherever there were villages.[22] Seldom did a single house stand alone. Four or five was a small village; a big one had thirty or more buildings, laid out in one to three long rows parallel to the water and the prevailing winds. Along Lake River, for example, there was a row of twenty-five-foot-wide houses eighty-five, one hundred and twenty, forty, and ninety feet long, separated ten to fifteen feet from each other.[23] Walamt, at Willamette Falls, was a range of eight houses 350 feet long. Towns of twenty-eight, eighteen, and fourteen structures were recorded by Lewis and Clark.[24]

A five-row town was the Chinook idea of a metropolis, but no one ever saw one. Locations were dictated by wind and flood, the availability of fish and food plants, the shape of the beach and how far the canoes must be carried, the current off the beach, and exposure to the winter sun. In the estuary a village needed a source of fresh water, but above that the people could drink Big River, colored and somewhat hard, but not too bad when allowed to settle.

The inhabitants might move a house or village at the death of a headman or to escape the fleas, because of a flood or to be near a better fishing drift or wintering place, or because their shaman said they ought to, or their headman that he'd like to. Some villages carried their house boards with them to summer fishing camps, returning them in the fall. Others lived in mat houses during the summer.

The river people were proud to live in villages of cedar-plank houses. When asked what kind of leader she was, *Tsagiglalal* told the mythological trickster-hero Coyote that she had been teaching the people to live well and build good—meaning wooden—houses.[25]

"Stum-Ma-Nu, A Flathead Boy." Called William Brooks and said to be Chi-nook, he was orphaned at two, went east with a missionary, and died there before he was twenty. The blanket is not Chinook. Lithograph by George Catlin, courtesy of the Oregon Historical Society.

3

The Geography of Chinook *Illahee*

1790

THEY HAD FOUND THEIR RIVER, and spread along it, taken every good seine-net drift and built their villages where they liked. There were about fifty winter villages in 1790, clumped in geographic groups of eight to fifteen villages, and several of those groups were made up of subgroups of three or four villages.[1] There were also many seasonal camp sites.

In the following gazetteer, we use north and south for the banks of the Columbia, east and west for the Willamette, though for short stretches of both rivers the direction is incorrect. Miles are above the sea, or a tributary river's joining with a larger river. The places and groupings are as the Europeans found them, and thus a lot are from Lewis and Clark, who first traversed the entire Chinook-settled river, downriver in autumn, 1805, and upriver in spring, 1806.

THE *SHOALWATER* CHINOOK occupied *Wimahl*'s north bank from the sea up sixteen miles to Deep River. These were the original Chinoak, Tchinouk, Tsinuks, Chenoux, Chinucs, Chunnuks, Chinhook, Chonukes, etc. They were *Aladshush* to the Salish-speaking Nestucca; *Thlalah* to the Clackamas; *Hlakouk*, "People Below," to the Cowlitz; *Idaqwim*, "They'll Give You Food," to the Wasco. (All of the names of all of the subgroups depend on who is speaking of whom.)

The Shoalwater fished Big River from February or March to September or October, then most of them retired to winter villages on or up the little rivers draining into more-temperate Shoalwater Bay, north over any of three portages. Some wintered up small Columbia tributaries. We call them Shoalwater here, but *Tsinuks* might be more appropriate, for that was the sharper, shorter Chehalis word which the sailors flattened to Chinook.

Atsmitl, "People of the Enclosed Bay," the Chinook called the Salish-speakers, southern *Chehalis,* with whom they shared Shoalwater Bay. Villages halfway north up the bay were part Chinook and part Chehalis, and whoever was wealthy and wise might be headman. The Chinook lived in at least a dozen winter villages there. Inland lived the *Kwalhoikwa,* Athabaskan-speaking hill people who had arrived later. Their principal village, *Wilapahiu,* gave Willapa River and Bay their names. The shallow southward reach is still sometimes called Shoalwater Bay, the old name.

Along Big River, the Shoalwater summer villages began just behind the rocky cape on the north of the river's mouth and were scattered around Baker Bay and halfway up Grays Bay, at least half a dozen villages, one or two occupied year around. *Qwatsamts,* located near Chinook Point, came to be the premier village.

Qwatsamts, Comcomly's village, was variously described as twenty-eight or thirty-six houses and outbuildings, which were arranged in three long rows facing the shore. This was the village that the sailor on the *Bahsten* ship pointed toward, when he asked for the name of the people, and heard the man say Chinooks, by one or another spelling or pronunciation. A big village, and one of the two most famous (from a European-American standpoint) Chinook-speaking villages on the big river. It was a place of mighty winds, where ocean surf broke frequently on the shore, for it faced the Pacific Ocean across eight miles of bay and the five-mile-wide

Columbia Bar. Qwatsamts stood naked against the storm winds from the southwest.

ACROSS THE BOISTEROUS ESTUARY the *Clatsop* occupied Big River's south bank from the sea at Point Adams seventeen miles inland to Tongue Point, and twenty miles south along the seacoast to just beyond Seaside. They called themselves *Tiakelak*, "Dried Salmon,"[2] and were in no significant way different from the Shoalwater. Their farthest southern reach was one-thousand-foot *Nahseusu*, Tillamook Head. Beyond that for many bays and rivers south lived Salish-speaking *Tillamooks*, who came to visit and with whom the Clatsop intermarried. That name was another amusing misunderstanding. Asked who lived next south along the coast, the Clatsop told explorers Lewis and Clark "*Telemuks*," meaning "People of Elem," a village called *Nehalem* on the first river to the south.

Captain Clark waxed poetic, looking north from Nahseusu's summit at Chinook *illahee* (country):

> From this point I beheld the grandest and most pleasing prospect which my eyes ever surveyed. Immediately in front is the ocean, which breaks with fury on the coast from the rocks of Cape Disappointment as far as the eye can discern to the northwest. To this boisterous scene the Columbia with its tributary waters, widening into bays as it approaches the ocean, and studded on both sides with the Chinook and Clatsop villages forms a charming contrast; while immediately beneath our feet stretches the rich prairies, enlivened by three beautiful streams, which conduct the eye to small lakes at the foot of the hills.[3]

That was Clatsop Plain. Coyote made it on his way north to weave his net and announce the taboos. He had announced the methods and taboos for catching silver salmon at *Neahcoxie*, the village where Clark's three streams came together and entered the sea. Coyote started up the beach toward Big River, but the surf kept forcing him back into the spruce forest, where the needles prickled his nose. Again and again the surf drove Coyote inland, until at last he scooped up sand, and throwing it down, announced that henceforth there would be land there for the people to walk upon.[4] The grassy, stream- and lake-dappled plain extended seventeen miles from *Negotat*, now Seaside, to the Columbia. The Clatsop could canoe from Neacoxie or Negotat to the Columbia with only a single portage.[5]

Clatsop villages lined the Columbia, starting at *Neahkeluk*, "Place of Dried Salmon," and extending up the south bank around into Young's Bay, eight or more villages. Many of them wintered to the south, at Negotat, or at Neahcoxie.

UP THE COLUMBIA ITSELF, starting midway up the estuary, lived the *Kathlamet*, "People of the River." When Coyote reached the Kathlamet he found the fish would not enter his net again. He complained bitterly to his excrement sisters, who lived in his stomach and told him everything he knew. Those little shits were the real source of the taboos. Coyote only announced them.

"Ah, you lean-flanked one," his excrements told him, "did you think the custom is the same here as downriver? This is a different country, these people speak another language. Untie your net, take out two meshes, and turn around the buoys." Thus the recital began again, different rules for a different place, until it made Coyote tired.[6]

Kathlamet was a Chinookan language, and perhaps a loose political grouping. The Kathlamet Chinook language differed from Sealand Chinook as does Portuguese from Spanish.[7] Generally grouped together as Kathlamet were five subgroups, called the *Wahkiacum, Kathlamet, Cooniac, Skilloot,* and *Kalama.* They spoke alike and lived in about fifteen villages along the river from Tongue Point, mile 17 on the south, and Harrington Point, mile 24 on the north, up both sides of the broad estuary through the Coast Range to Deer Island, mile 80. The Shahala called them *Gahlamaht*, "Their River."

Kathlamet itself was a nine-house town on the south bank of the eight-mile widest part of the estuary, much of it tidal channels and sandbars revealed at low tide. There were two or three allied villages around Cathlamet Bay. They caught sturgeon and smelt off *Tenas Illahee*, "Little Land," an island just at the head of the estuary, and harvested roots on Puget Island, next above.

ON THE NORTH BANK lived the *Wahkiacum*, from Deep River to Abernathy Creek, about thirty-five miles of river. Their two most prominent winter villages were *Chahulkilhum*, "Winter Town," at the present Skamokawa, mile 34, and *Waqaiyaqam*, at Alockman Creek, mile 37 behind the Hunting Islands, reed-grown marshy jungles rich in wildlife. Wahkiacum met Kathlamet at about mile 35, where Cathlamet town now tiers up the hillside above the island-clogged river. But in fact, they were the same people in all but name, as those across from each other along the river were the same, for the river was a highway, not a barrier.

Behind Wallace Island the *Clatskanai*, "People of the Region of Little Oaks," came down to the banks of the Clatskanie River to trade with the Chinook. Those Athabascan-speakers lived in the Nehalem Hills and hunted elk, deer, bear, and beaver. Tradition had it that they had migrated across Big River not long before, when elk became scarce in the Willapa Hills.[8]

The *Cooniac* lived on the south bank in several villages, around Oak Point, mile 54. They said the Cooniac had once been the *Kolnit* with another band that later moved to the mouth of the Cowlitz River, mile 68, and made a village called *Seamysty*, "People of the

Beaklike Mouth." Those people and other villages were identified by Lewis and Clark as the Skilloot, so in all likelihood the Cooniac were actually Skilloot. Mount Coffin, *Yeehmastee*, was a basalt knob around two hundred feet tall, located beside the river two miles below the mouth of the Cowlitz, upon which the canoes of the dead were thickly placed. They called such places *memaloose illahee*, "country of the dead," in the Chinook simplified trading language.

Chinook lived up the Cowlitz River for four or five villages, increasingly mixed with the *Cowlitz*, who spoke a Salish language. The Chinook living up the Cowlitz River were called *Kullowith*. Far up at the headwaters of the Cowlitz River lived a Klickitat band, the *Taitinapam*, who were thought wild mountain people by the Chinook. The river people claimed they ate children and could travel unseen. The Taitinapam traded with no one, not even the Klickitat proper.[9]

A mile or so up the Kalama River, mile 73, lived the *Tlakalama*, "People of the Rock." Fur trader Gabriel Franchère described their town:

> The situation of this village is the most charming that can be, being built on the little river we had ascended, and indeed at its navigable head, being here but a torrent of numerous cascades leaping from rock to rock in their descent to the deep, limpid water, which then flows through a beautiful prairie enameled with odiferous flowers of all colors and studded with superb oak groves.[10]

The farthest Kathlamet village was on Deer Island, mile 80 on the south bank. Then the Wapato Lowlands opened out, and that was another country again, and a different language.[11]

THE WAPATO LOWLANDS extended along the river from where it emerged from the Cascade Mountains to where it entered the Coast

Range. The river bent round to flow north for thirty-five miles, among a maze of tidal bores, sloughs, swamps, lakes, and low islands grown to oak, cottonwood, and poplar. The land along the river was moist, temperate, and protected. Much of it was a seasonal flood plain. The marshes there grew a peculiarly delicious bulb-like root—it tastes like a cross between a fine baked potato and a roast chestnut, or like breadfruit—which came to be called *wapato* and later indian potato. The fifty-mile by fifteen-mile lowland has no established name today, though Wapato Valley used to crop up, and the Portland Basin is used by some scholars. It is not in any true sense a valley, and there was no Portland in those times, so we shall call it the Wapato Lowlands. This is the lost heartland we seek, the center of Chinook *illahee*.

The Chinook who occupied both banks and all the rivers, sloughs, and waterways of these lowlands are generally called "Multnomah," after an important village on the south (really west) bank of the Columbia at mile 97, where Sauvie Island shores Big River. The name of the dialect they spoke was *Nakwaiih*,[12] taken from the name of the earliest village in the region, but Multnomah was what explorers and traders were told as the name for the island, the people of the area in general, and even the lower Willamette River. This suggests a shift of importance between an original village and another that separated off over the centuries.

The lowest Multnomah village on the Columbia was *Kasniukatnai*, at Columbia City, mile 84 on the west. *Nayagogo*, "Where There are Blows," was at St. Helens, two miles above.[13] The name probably referred to the basalt cliffs, from which people viewed nautical battles, fought in the broad water where Multnomah Channel, Scapoose Bay, the Lewis River, and Lake River join the Columbia, just below Warrior Rock, the toe of Sauvie Island. Sauvie Island was the delta of the Willamette as it joined the Columbia, a watery expanse of meadows and groves. During low water the main flow was on the lower Willamette, now called Multnomah Channel, while at flood time everything might be awash except the highest ground. There were four villages on the Columbia side, six more on Multnomah Channel and a village across the upper Willamette three miles above the channel's upper mouth.

We know less about those people than we do about any other Chinook group, yet it is the one we seek. Early explorers hurried past; the epidemics hit hardest in this flood plain; but it was almost certainly the most populous area the Chinook occupied, and thereby perhaps the most thickly settled land in all of America north of Mexico.

On the other side of Big River on the north was *Quathlapootle*, a large village of fourteen houses, near the mouth of sluggish little Lake River, which parallels and flows into the Columbia from the east. Lake River isn't much of a stream but was heavily populated at one time or another with at least four villages. Those villagers became known as the Shoto when Lewis and Clark perhaps misunderstood someone trying to tell them that Konapee's son Soto lived over in that direction.[14]

Most famous of the Sauvie Island villages was *Mahlnumax*, "Closer to the Water," at Reeder Point, mile 97, a town of eight hundred in 1805–1806, even after being decimated by the smallpox. That is our Multnomah. Mahlnumax faced Big River, there a mighty flood a thousand yards wide, flowing implacably right to left. Behind the forested far shore towered three snow-capped strato-volcanoes. Fur trader Alfred Seton wrote,

> We coasted the beautiful shores of the Multnomah Island, without forgetting to pay the village a visit, famous as it was among our voyageurs for the fat dogs the old squaws always provided to make an excellent stew.[15]

The upriver end of Sauvie Island is formed by the upper mouth of the Willamette, mile 101. They called a place there *Wakshin*, "Little Dam." The opening was occluded by low islands and some years may have nearly shoaled closed.

In all there were perhaps fifteen winter villages in the Wapato Lowlands. The Chinook lived safe, wealthy, and contented there. The Kalapuyan-speaking *Tualatin* trudged over the mountains from their valley to trade. The better-class Tualatin people flattened their children's heads. Klickitat trailed down from the mountains to the north sometimes. Cowlitz and Kathlamet paddled up to trade, Shahala down, even Tillamook walked over the mountains for wapato. The Multnomah were surrounded by their flathead cousins.

Beyond *Nemalquinner* in the St. Johns area of North Portland, up the Willamette through what is now Portland and twenty miles to the Clackamas River, no villages are known. There were floodplain marshes scattered along that stretch of river, at Guilds Lake and Couch Lake, Mocks Bottom and Oaks Bottom, where the women must have dug roots, and the great cliff above the river called Elk Cliff, over which oral tradition has the Chinook driving herds of elk to their death, but the Chinook seldom made villages where we make ours now.

THE CLACKAMAS, who called themselves *Qimas*, "Vine Maple," lived up the river of that name in what Lewis and Clark heard to be twelve villages. The downriver Chinook, in a myth at least, treated the Clackamas as "notoriously dumb." [16] They fished the Clackamas River and *Ekeesati*, Willamette Falls. [17]

The Willamette takes its name from a location just below the falls, *Walamt*, perhaps "Green Water," from which came *Gitlawalamt*, "People of Green Water." [18] The sometimes forty-one-foot-high falls at Willamette River mile 26.5 marked one boundary of Chinook *illahee*. The *Clowewallas* are identified as living just below the falls on the west, in a town of six houses a hundred feet above the river. There were villages both top and bottom on both sides of the falls. [19] Lewis and Clark heard the people called Cushhooks.

South of the falls, no one lived along the river for six miles. The banks were rocky and steep to where the Willamette Valley opens out, at river mile 32. Kalapuya-speakers occupied that broad, fertile valley in a number of roving bands. The Chinook traded with them, but would not let them fish the falls. They lacked good canoes and their heads were round. In the foothills of the Cascades lived the *Molala*, who may have rather recently come across the mountains from the east. They did not live in proper villages of wooden houses, nor flatten their children's heads.

THE PEOPLE WHO LIVED from the Portland Airport, mile 110, to beyond the first rapids at the Cascades of the Columbia, mile 153, called themselves *Katlagakya*, "People of the Cascades," but the name that has come down, heard by the first explorers, was *Shahala*, said to mean "Above" or "Upriver." Their lowest village was lower than the highest Nakwaiih or Multnomah village, and the people lived at peace with each other.

The lowest Shahala village, evidently a seasonally occupied lowland outpost, was one large wooden house and, in season, numerous mat summer lodges, where many small women's bulb-gathering canoes were left during the winter. Another lowland village was a little up the Washougal River. There the Wapato Lowlands end, and at about mile 123, begins the steep-walled Columbia River Gorge. There were six or eight more Shahala winter villages up there, most of them on the north side of the river where it was sunnier in the winter and more eroded, rendering access to the high country behind easier.

They occupied the four miles of boiling water called the Cascades, where the river dropped about forty-five feet in three rapids. The top rapid was not canoeable, the lower ones could be run down but not up, so there were trails on either side. The *Clahclellah* wintered at the foot of the portage, the *Wahlala*, "Their Lake," at the top, and some villages were shared. The highest Shahala winter village was a few miles above, for though deep in the Gorge, they remained a lowland people, in moist coastal weather. It rained more there than in the Wapato Lowlands. The exceptional south-bank village was *Swapapani*, tucked in out of the wind at Eagle Creek, but other villages moved to the south bank in the summer. Also, a lot of Shahala went to Willamette Falls for the spring chinook fishery.

Five miles above the Cascades the climate began to change. At Wind Mountain, mile 156, the moist temperate Chinook winds battled the always dry and seasonally cold or hot Walla Walla winds. Fir and cedar ceased, oak and pine began. Within forty miles those too gave way, to sagebrush and grass, with trees only beside tributary rivers.

THE LITTLE WHITE SALMON, who lived at the mouth of the stream of that name, mile 162, were the most downriver of the White Salmon people, who called themselves *Itkauanbam idelxan*, "Dried Salmon People," referring to *itkilak*, a dried and pounded salmon pemmican everyone desired. Downriver the air was not dry enough to make it. White Salmon villages on the north bank extended to the mouth of the Klickitat River, mile 180. *Namnit*, at the mouth of the White Salmon River, mile 168, was their principal village. It was there that Lewis and Clark heard *chilluckittequaw*, "he pointed at me," and took it for the tribal name.[20] There were eight or more White Salmon villages. Across on the south lived their cousins the *Kigaltwalla*, at the mouth of the Hood (or Dog) River. *Smakshop* Lewis and Clark heard them called. Dog probably referred to dog salmon, which ascended the tributary river.

There was a *Klickitat* village at the mouth of the river bearing that name. That was probably the only village peopled by other than Chinook on Big River below the Dalles. Klickitat meant "Beyond the Mountains" in Chinook Jargon. They spoke a dialect of

Sahaptin, another language which bordered the Chinook on the east, flattened their children's heads, and had good relations with the Chinook, who are sometimes said to have hired them to fight for them.

Next upriver were the *Tlakluit*. Lewis and Clark heard *Echeloot*, meaning "I am Tlakluit." They came to be called the *Wishram*, the Yakima name for them. They had four or five winter villages and other villages for every season, winter fishing, summer trading, sturgeon and salmon. One of them bore the euphonious name *Tchipan-Tchick-Tchick*. Their lowest village was a mile below the mouth of the Klickitat River, mile 179, and they occupied the north bank to a mile or so beyond the head of the Long Narrows, which was at mile 195.

Nixluidix, the premier Wishram village, was famous for trade. The name was sometimes translated "At Once Your Flesh Came To-gether," from a village-origin story in which a monster destroyed the village and a daughter of East Wind restored it from five piles of flesh and clothing.[21] Other interpretations include "A Smooth Level Place," "The People are Heading for It," and "Fleas."[22] It consisted of more than twenty wooden houses, not in line but scattered about, at the head of the Long Narrows, where the river, once blocked by a massive lava flow, turned on edge to cut its way through. In places the main channel of the Columbia was 300 feet deep and only 160 feet wide. From this desolate, treeless place a trail led north over Satus Pass to the *Yakima* country and beyond. That trail helped make the Wishram rich. Washington Irving made Nixluidix famous as Wishram in his 1836 best-seller *Astoria*.

Wakemap, just above Nixluidix, is a village of mystery, aban-doned before the first whites arrived.[23] The final Chinook village, about a mile above, was the farthest inland Chinook village and the eastern frontier of Chinook *illahee*.

The *Wasco*, who called themselves *Gatlasqo*, "People Who Have the Cup," lived across the river on the south, but as elsewhere were hardly different from their cousins on the far bank. They took their name from a spring that fell into a basin. The Wasco occupied the river in season, but moved inland to protected places in winter. Their principal summer town, *Wasqo*, was opposite Nixluidix and they had at least three other towns, perhaps more.

Beyond lived Sahaptin-speakers in bands called *Wayam*, *Tygh*, and *Tenino*. The Chinook called the Sahaptin-speakers *Ilkaimamt*. Their heads were flattened[24] and they were on friendly terms with the Wishram and Wasco, but built only mat houses and hunted game more.

To the south of the river roamed the Northern Paiute, whom the river people called *Iltuanxayuks*, "Enemies," or *Shoshone*, "Inlanders." They were desert nomads with unflattened heads. The Chinook and Wayam united to wage intermittent slave raiding and ambushes against those Uto-Aztecan-speakers.

Petroglyph of a Coyote-like creature spewing at the mouth. Sometimes described as a water spirit, it looks like Coyote raving. Originally in a canyon near Nixluidix, it is now at The Dalles Dam. Rendering by the author from a photograph.

4

Chinook As They Spoke It

THE BASIS of the preceding Chinook geography is language, as though that were the most important way of identifying people, which it certainly wasn't to the Chinook. Yet, the Chinook language was a singular one; it shaped their hearing and their seeing and through it they experienced their lives. It recalled their history as it accompanied their board houses up the river.[1]

Though Chinook was unique, it sounded a great deal like all the other languages of the Northwest coast. From northern California to the Alaska panhandle, the canoe fishermen all spoke in a voice that sounded, to English ears, harsh and guttural, with many consonants, few vowels, and other similarities of sound. The sound visitors mentioned most often, described by linguist Dell Hymes and quoted in the introduction to this book, was the "tl," "cl," or "thl" sound, made by forcing air out between tongue and palate, on both sides of the mouth.[2] This expressive sound was prominent in most if not all of those languages. Yet the languages spoken along those two thousand miles of coast represented a dozen language phyla, languages as unrelated as Mandarin Chinese and Bantu, which is to say scarcely related at all.

This similarity of the sound of languages was most noticeable from neighbor to neighbor, for example, Tlingit sounded very like Tsimshian next door, though considerably different from Chinook; but all three sounded much alike when compared to the California languages, or those east of the Cascade Range of mountains.

Why they should sound alike is a puzzle. Beyond the Cascade Mountains, the languages were of soft and gentle sounds. The Wasco and Wishram must have sounded foreign indeed there. Why should Tlingit, a Nadene-phyla language; Salishan, Kwakiutl, and Nootka, Mosan-phyla languages; and Chinook, a Penutian-phyla language, sound anything alike? Somehow, regardless of meaning, it had become the accent of the region, called by scholars a phonological area. A slave from inland sounded as well as looked foreign. Among other reasons proposed, the languages may have sounded alike because those people married and traded together. Bilingualism was widespread, indeed multilingualism was common.[3]

In this too the Chinook occupied a boundary, for to the south and east, the phonetics changed. The Kalapuya, down the Willamette Valley, spoke softly in nasal and indistinct accents. The Paiute language, on the high desert and beyond, was monotonous, unstressed and unglottal, with high central vowels. The Californians, regardless of family affiliations, spoke in soft, mellifluous tones. Upriver too, the Yakima, Walla Walla, Cayuse, and others of the Plateau occupied an intermediate position, featuring considerable glottalization but less clustering of consonants and dropping of vowels.

None of the coastal languages sounded sonorous to European ears. Paul Kane wrote:

> I would willingly give a specimen of the barbarous language of these people, were it possible to represent by any combination of the letters of our alphabet the horrible harsh sputtering sound which proceed from their throats, apparently unguided either by the tongue or lips.[4]

"Decidedly the most unpronounceable compound of gutturals ever formed for the communication of human thought," someone maligned Chinook.[5] James Swan described "a guttural sound which to a stranger seems a compound of the gruntings of a pig and the cluckings of a hen."[6] Charles Pickering recalled "the slow deliberate manner in which they seemed to choke out their words, giving utterance to sounds, some of which could scarcely be represented by combinations of known letters."[7] "The Chinook appear actually to labor in speaking," claimed Horatio Hale.[8]

It was a throaty dance of rasps and glottals, irregular pauses, sibilant hisses, explosive climaxes, and throat-clenching contractions. Picket fences of consonants were separated by pauses and inflections instead of vowels. But there were whispers too, and mellifluous strings of vowels. A hesitating, almost stuttering diction, in a language rich in tonal interpretation, further confused the ear. The Chinook laid heavy emphasis on clear, exact enunciation.

ONE OF THE SINGULARITIES of the language, according to anthropologist Franz Boas, was its use of onomatopoeic words. These are words that imitate the cries of animals or sounds of actions. English words such as tinkle, pop, and chickadee are onomatopoeic. Boas heard more onomatopoeia in Chinook than any other language he had encountered. Among the words he said imitated sounds were the Chinook for wind, slap, the sound of dancing, strong, round, light of weight, to boil, and to be tired, afraid, or lazy. Almost all bird names were clearly onomatopoeic, naming the bird by its call. But the founder of modern anthropology decided their words for colors were too, an amazing concept, as were such abstractions as unlucky, foggy, and "to give payment secretly to a shaman."

Boas found all sorts of onomatopoetic words. For example: actions or processes accompanied by noise (he listed forty-four): *hemm*, noise of wind; *kumm* (repeated), noise of dancing; *teq*, to slap; *qalqlal*, to beat time; *tsex*, to break a piece of wood. Descriptive words (sixteen): *qel*, strong (*qelqel* meant hard); *lolo*, round; *lep*, to boil; *temen*, empty, clean. Words expressing states of mind or body (twenty-two): *tell*, tired; *tsxap*, to hesitate; *qam*, lazy; *la*, fear. Color terms (seven): *leel*, black; *kas*, yellow; *tkop*, white; *ptcix*, green; *lpil*, red. Miscellaneous words (forty-five), some of them imitative: *panic*, to give payment secretly to a shaman; *pax*, unlucky; *wuk*, straight; *pox*, foggy; *timm*, waterfall. Boas theorized,

> it seems likely that, in a language in which onomatopoeic terms are numerous, the frequent association between sound and concept will, in its turn, increase the readiness with which other similar associations are established, so that to the mind of the Chinook, words may be sound pictures which to our unaccustomed ear have no such value.

He noted however that onomatopoeic words are not pronounced as imitations of the sound, but flattened, like our clatter, snarl, whine, waft, or whir. Their words reported the sound of experience as information, news, a way of knowing and naming what was going on, as our language describes the look of things.[9]

THE LANGUAGES of even the most primitive peoples are no less complex than those of technologically advanced societies. In each there is a maze of grammatical rules awaiting only a grammarian. The grammar of Chinook was exceedingly complex. Whole strings of six or seven prefixes might lead the way, modifying a tiny central word, then two or three suffixes behind.

A breakdown of the word *tctalota*, "he will give them to her," illustrates:

> *tc* meant he (the subject);
>   *t* meant them (the object);
>   *a* meant her (the indirect object);
>   *l* signified to;
>   *o* the direction from the speaker;
>   *t* was the root, "to move" (*lot* meaning "to give");
>   *a* signified future tense.[10]

A Chinook speaker would not have been aware of this process. As Boas put it: "The laws of language remain entirely unknown to the speaker. . . . Linguistic phenomena never rise into the consciousness of primitive man."[11]

CHINOOK PRONOUNS were much more informative than ours. They told gender, number, near or far, and, in the case of duals or plurals, whether the hearer, or some third party, was included with the speaker or not included. The word also told whether the person was visible or invisible (invisible might be in the past, a myth, a person's spirit power, or his soul). The word informed whether the object or person being spoken of was closer to the speaker, the listener, or some third party. Our pronouns are stick-figures by comparison.

Chinook described events rather abstractly and had few words for emotions. On the other hand, their words for kin relationships were as rich in meaning as their pronouns. The word for cousin or uncle always distinguished on which side of the individual's family the relationship occurred. There were special terms for addressing one's own parent or child, and the words for brother and sister included whether the person was older or younger than one's self. They had words for relationships we describe only grossly, for example, a specific word for a boy's mother's sister's daughter, which we lump under cousin.

Kinship terms proliferated, perhaps in part because the Chinook were unwilling to speak personal names. That was improper and dangerous; to know a name gave power over the person named. One said the word "your older brother's wife's sister's son," instead of the boy's name.

Anyone old they called grandfather or grandmother, and Chinook had no words that went back further than great-grandparent. Earlier forebears were merely ancestors, *taanewatiks*, "people of olden times," the original ones.

Their plurals for humans were different from other plurals. There were two suffixes, *uks* and *max*, that denoted plural people. Everything was alive: rocks, trees, birds, fire, and clouds, but humans were distinct, and therefore *uks* or *max*.

The Chinook were polite. "It would be good if you would . . ." they'd say. "Please, just try to . . ." or "Since this is so, let us . . ." and "Oh, if only he would . . ."[12]

The order of their sentences had a certain charm to English-speakers. "It came, a person." "Dead was their chief." "He utters his song, that first one." "They watch it, a soul, the ghosts."

Though they may not have been aware of the rules of their language, they had stories about words, and humor about slang. One myth told how Blue Jay's sister Ioi caused trouble with her use of slang. Blue Jay was young and naive. When his older sister Ioi told him to "make a hole in a rotten log," meaning carve a canoe, he followed the literal meaning of her words.[13] She became angry when the rotten log fell apart. In another story, she sent him off to bring back money beads, but called them "widow's shit." In a little comedy of manners she told Blue Jay to hitch a free ride in a canoe by saying "hang down in the water and be dragged along," then told him to "throw pounded salmon behind yourself," meaning to gift the canoemen with food. The paddlers were surprised to find Blue Jay tied to the stern of their boat throwing salmon pemmican at them. He returned with baskets of human excrement instead of the long dentalia she'd sent him for.[14]

In addition to ordinary vernacular they all knew a more formal style, spoken in the recital of myths and formal speeches. The village crier spoke the classical language, as did the headman's announcer. It was archaic, perhaps related to daily Chinook as Elizabethan English is to American.[15]

AROUND FIFTEEN HUNDRED YEARS AGO,[16] after they had expanded to the Wapato Lowlands but not into the Columbia River Gorge, Chinook began to evolve into at least three languages.[17] Coast Chinook was spoken only by the Clatsop and Shoalwater. The Kathlamet groups spoke Kathlamet-Chinook. A third Chinookan language, called *Kiksht*, was spoken upriver by the Clackamas and by those later in the Columbia Gorge. The villages of the Wapato Lowlands probably spoke Kiksht too, but no one ever recorded their language. If they had spoken their own language, the Clackamas and Wishram, 125 river miles apart, would have been less likely to have spoken the same language.

A language changes constantly, as slang, invention, and pronunciation styles are taken up by one group of communities but fail to reach another. After many centuries speakers from different areas may come not to understand each other.[18] The elongated shape of the Chinook-occupied river made changes less likely to reach the farthest away Chinook-speaker. On the other hand, their trading propensities and marriage customs made changes more likely to spread. American and English are still mutually comprehensible after 370 years, but Jamaican English is a foreign tongue to an American-speaker. Kathlamet and Coast Chinook became different languages, though their life ways were similar and they lived side by side.

In all three Chinookan languages the words for numbers remained the same, but about a third of the other words were different, and a speaker of one language could not understand a speaker of the next one. They were as different as German and Swedish, or Holland Dutch and High German.[19]

One story had it that a chief of the Wahkiacum became angry at his Shoalwater relative and broke away.[20] The Wahkiacum were lowest downriver of the Kathlamet-speakers. Actually, many people in any village spoke more than one language. A dozen or more languages might be spoken daily or occasionally in a large village, for the Chinook were highly cosmopolitan and bought their wives from afar. Further, the region was among the most linguistically polyglot on earth. The balance needed only shift a little, or the headman favor one language more, and they were another country. Not that it mattered much, for the Chinook dealt with language as do the multilingual Swiss, and made their nationhood by using their heads (as we shall see).

THE CHINOOK LANGUAGE is associated with the Penutian phylum of languages, a made-up word combining the number "two" in two California languages.[21] The ancestor of Penutian may have been spoken by people living in the northern Great Basin ten thousand years ago when the basin was crowded with lakes watered by a thousand-mile rain plume extending south from the Ice Age glaciers. It is possible that the sagebrush sandal-makers who lived in caves at Fort Rock and along the Catlow Rim of eastern Oregon during those post-glacial times spoke Penutian.[22] When the glaciers melted and the lakes of the inward-draining Great Basin dried to dust, band by band, century by century, the Penutian-speakers dispersed in all directions.

This is all very speculative stuff, but romantic, for the tale it suggests. The Chinook of the Columbia, the Takilma of the Rogue River, the Coos, Siuslaw, and Yakonan of the southern Oregon coast, the Kalapuyan of the Willamette Valley, the Sahaptin, Molala, Cayuse, Walla Walla, Nez Perce, Klamath, and Modoc of the dry country inland, the Miwok, Costanoan, Yokuts, Maidu, and Wintun of the central valleys and the coast of California, may have constituted the core of the Penutian peoples.

Farther off, the Tsimshian of the British Columbia coast are thought to speak a Penutian language by some scholars, and far to the south, the Mixe-Zoque and the Huave of southern Mexico have at times been included in the Penutian family, though many

Naked Against the Rain

scholars dispute this. In Mexico, some anthropologists have written that Purepecha, spoken around Lake Patzquaro, is related to Wintun, a Penutian language, as well as to Totonacan, on the Gulf of California, all of which relate to Mayan, and even to Quichua (originally from Lake Titicaca), the language adopted and spread by the Incas in South America.[23]

Recently, linguist Joseph Greenberg has posited an AmerInd language family, comprising all aboriginal American languages but Eskimo-Aleut and Na-Dene as the descendants of a single language root. In the AmerIndian sub-group Penutian, he includes all of the above peoples plus a branch in the southeastern United States on the Gulf of Mexico coast plus a language or two in Mexico and the Zuni of the Southwest.[24] Some or all of those diverse peoples constitute the Penutian diaspora, which happened so long ago it was not remembered even in myths.

"Cascade Indian, Columbia River." Watercolor by Paul Kane, courtesy of the Stark Museum of Art, Orange, Texas.

5

Mountains Eat People

1260

ONE HUNDRED AND TWENTY MILES from the sea the mighty river poured out of the great U-shaped Columbia River Gorge through the Cascade Range. Those sixty-five miles of jagged basalt splendor, flood-carved and volcano-punctuated, are a wind, weather, and water passage, between ramparts four thousand feet high with perpetually snow-draped peaks of eleven thousand feet and twelve thousand feet behind.

Through the mountain range the river ran virtually at sea level. Until about AD 1260 there were, with the possible exception of a low-water rapid below the mouth of the Klickitat, no obstructions downriver of The Dalles.[1] There, from river mile 190 to 195, a basalt shelf obstructed the Columbia for five miles, just above the present city of The Dalles. The name Dalles comes from the French-Canadian word for water chute, downspout, millrace, or gutter, which describes the runnels at The Dalles.[2] People from downriver may have been able to paddle to the foot of The Dalles without portage. Nixluidix was five miles above.

For more than ten thousand years people had been drawn to The Dalles, and Celilo Falls ten miles above it, by the profusion of salmon. They met for ceremonies, to trade, gamble, and find mates. The salmon enabled it.[3] Nowhere else could feed so many so well.

This being so, Chinooks visited The Dalles, but evidently kept their winter villages in the Wapato Lowlands. In the lower Gorge and out a little way into the lowlands, from Bonneville, mile 145, to Fisher's Landing on the right bank, mile 115, lived another people, in round houses, scattered without plan.[4] Anywhere upriver of the Cowlitz River, rectangular wood houses in rows along the shore meant Chinook. None of their neighbors above the Coast Range lived so. So those round-house builders were possibly another people.

For their use in summer at The Dalles, the Chinook traders of more than a thousand years ago may have begun to frequent a place called *Wakemap*, at the head of the Long Narrows.[5] It has been suggested that Wakemap may have been a colony of the Multnomah village *Wacomap*.[6] People must have camped there for centuries, and a high mound accumulated out of their refuse. After a while, in about AD 900, Chinook-style rectangular houses began to be built on the mound. They seem to have been covered with mats.[7] The mound was abandoned by the time the first Europeans passed.[8] Probably those Chinooks canoed up for the trading season, and returned home in the autumn, when the fish, and people, stopped coming.

THEN ONE YEAR—around AD 1260—the earth shook. Animals fled, birds flew up crying, a great roar was heard, and the south sides of two mountains six miles north of Big River calved like glaciers, sending half a cubic mile of earth and stone roaring down a water-slicked layer of clay. That boiling mass slid to the river at mile 145, and crossed it to crash against the far mountainside. The landslide was five miles wide and 270 feet high where it came to rest.[9]

Anything living in its path was obliterated. Outside the swath the world was much the same, except that the river had stopped flowing! The dam created by the slide completely blocked the Columbia, perhaps for several years, backing up a vast lake, possibly all

Naked Against the Rain

the way to Idaho. When the water finally overflowed (or broke through) the dam, it did so a mile south of its previous bed, creating a narrow passage around the far end of the slide. What exactly happened when the water began flowing again is unclear. A single six-foot layer of silt that covered a village on Sauvie Island has been offered as proof that the dam came apart swiftly, inundating the lowlands below all at once.[10] Villages all over the lowlands seem to have moved around that time. Had the dam dissolved more slowly, the waters of the Columbia would have become dark with mud and impossibly steep for fish to ascend, eliminating the salmon runs upon which the people depended, for decades if not centuries.

If the dam took several years to fill, the salmon runs would have been severely depleted anyway. Salmon operate on a cycle of four years, five at most, from birth to spawning and death. The Plateau people—the ones in the round houses—were more attuned to hunting and less to fishing. Perhaps frightened by the slide, they apparently withdrew from the river. After the slide, round-house pits ceased being dug and another kind of house began to appear: proper, rectangular, wooden, Chinook houses, lined up neatly in rows instead of just higgledy-piggledy like the *Ilkaimamt* to the east built their houses.[11] That dates the expansion of the Chinook to the Cascades. The Shahala occupied much the same river miles as the round-house people, who may have been the ancestors of the Klickitat, for it was those Sahaptin-speakers who recalled the slide in a famous myth, "Bridge of the Gods," though by the time Europeans arrived the nearest Klickitat village was thirty-five miles upriver.

The "Bridge of the Gods" myth, of which several versions were recorded, was a violent love triangle. It told of two powerful young nobles from opposite sides of the river fighting over a beautiful woman. There was a place to walk dryshod across the river there, guarded by an old crone tending a fire. The youths hurled stones, breaking down the bridge. They were transformed by the Great Spirit into Mount Hood and Mount Adams, while the unmarried girl became supine Squaw Mountain. The blameless crone was given the youthfulness she desired, as Mount St. Helens, a young active volcano.[12]

There was neither word nor concept for "bridge" in the Chinook Jargon, the pidgin language in which the story was probably told to European settlers. The myth said the people walked dryshod across the river, and the pioneer imagined the water rushing beneath. "Great Spirit" isn't much of a translation either, there being no such idea as God until the missionaries brought it.[13] The story might describe what happened when another quake, or eruption of one or more of the volcanoes, destroyed the dam, spilling its contents on the lowlands.

Five and a half centuries later, when the first Europeans passed, Big River's narrow passage through and around the rubble was studded with rocks and dropped about forty-five feet in four miles, a powerful rapid given *Wimahl's* enormous flow. The Chinook always portaged their goods the whole way up or down, but sometimes paddled an empty canoe down the lower Cascades.

Forty-five feet represented how high the rubble-dam remained above the river's original level. In the pool behind, a drowned forest extended nearly fifty miles. Tree trunks stood upright where they had grown, in water even when the river was at its lowest.[14] It is from a carbon dating of those trunks that the year AD 1260 has been derived.[15] Traces of a village by the former river bank were also to be seen at lowest low water near the White Salmon River.

CHINOOK VILLAGES soon appeared at the bottom and top of the new Cascades portage, and afterward at the mouths of tributaries in the Gorge, the Little White Salmon, White Salmon, Hood, and Klickitat rivers. Those small openings were isolated places for inlanders to live, but good village sites for people with canoes and nets. A permanent village began at Nixluidix, and eventually replaced Wakemap. Or, the abandoned village may have been of up-river Salish, as some authorities contend.[16]

The Chinook brought their rectangular houses with them to establish permanent houses covered with cedar planks. Cedar didn't grow more than a few miles above the Cascades in the Gorge, though there was some in the high country around Mount Adams. To build a wooden house at Nixluidix the Chinook had to cut the cedar and split out planks, then transport them by canoe. If the tree grew below the Cascades they had to portage board by board and post by post across the five miles of the slide, then canoe up another fifty miles of river, then three more miles overland to Nixluidix.[17] The Chinook paid a heavy price to build proper houses.

After they arrived, coast-style objects began to appear at the Long Narrows in greatly increased quantities. They brought highly developed fishing equipment; a hundred-foot seine-net drift fronted their highest village. Soon they had several villages, on both sides of the river. After a while, that place where people had been coming and going seasonally for ten thousand years was occupied winter and summer by the Chinook, though there were seasonal camping trips after food.

It was a queer place for the lowlanders to build their houses. Between the Cascades and The Dalles annual rainfall diminished from rainforest to treeless desert in less than forty miles. It was hotter in summer and colder in winter than the lowlands, and populated by tall, leggy people with little shovel-nosed boats hacked out of the wrong kind of tree. The land by the river was bare rock, runneled with channels.

THE WISHRAM AND WASCO told a story about a dispute:

> *The Wishram were dwelling at Wakemap and at Nixluidix. A duck flew over their heads, making a noise "shu'lululu." A*

man said, "It made the noise with its beak." "Not at all," another man said, "it made the noise with its nostrils." A third said, "Beak." They got to arguing. Their relations joined in. They seized their weapons, they fought, both parties killed each other. They fought and fought. After a while when a man went to fish with his dip net two men had to stand nearby with weapons to protect him.

After three years of fighting one party of the Wishram said, "Being in some way disgraced, let us now go off somewhere."

They traveled up Wimahl past many villages. At length they stopped somewhere, but found the country too small and had to travel on. Each place they stopped seemed too small, but they encouraged themselves, saying, "Far away somewhere there is a country and there we will dwell."

Finally, they took a country to themselves where there were lots of salmon and lots of deer. To this day they dwell there and they are just nothing but Wishram. They would recognize me, straightaway they would kill me. To this day they hold the land where are many salmon and many deer, but we people have not seen them.[18]

IS THAT A MEMORY of how the Chinook moved stage by stage up the river? Or of why Wakemap was abandoned? Several people heard it related, always by a Wasco or Wishram, perhaps the last to move up. The Wishram said the people at the Cascades were more noble than themselves, for they were more ancient along the river.[19] The Wishram had a village-origin myth about a father and his daughters coming up from below when the Chinook didn't live up there yet. "They passed many attractive places, but did not stop until they came near to where Nixluidix is. At that place grew many fine roots, so they stopped at sunset and made their camp."[20]

IT WAS MORE LIKELY TRADE than roots that attracted the Chinook to the head of the Long Narrows. Where two so different peoples touch, good trade is always possible. The Chinook coming caused a cultural flowering.[21] From the lower end of The Dalles, mile 189, treeless rimrock with a cracked basalt pavement for ground, to Celilo Falls, mile 201, where Big River dropped twenty-five thunderous feet, culture and commerce flourished. Many dissimilar peoples met and traded and learned from each other.

Downriver, the Shahala villages at the Cascades would lend canoes to their trading partners or cousins, saving them from having to portage their boats. They expected gifts from those using their portage paths.

To the Wishram on the right bank each year came Spokane, Nespelem, Moses-Columbia, Wenatchee, Topenish, Yakima, and Klickitat. Some years Palus, Spokane, Nespelem, and Nez Perce are said to have come. To the Wasco across the river on the south came Umatilla, Walla Walla and Cayuse, Klamath, Molala, and Kalapuya. Multnomah and Shahala from downriver came, but seldom Kathlamat, Clatsop, or Shoalwater. Some of the same visitors may also have traded upriver at Celilo Falls, but the head of the Long Narrows was the greatest mart. Celilo Falls would last longer, and was more picturesque, so it is remembered. The area was one of the great aboriginal centers of North America. In season three thousand persons might visit there at once.[22]

The Klamath, after the coming of the horse if not earlier, came 250 miles north carrying Pit River bows, lily seeds, beads, and Modoc, Paiute, and Pit River slaves. They desired *parfleches*—hairless rawhide bags—dentalium shells, dried salmon, sturgeon, and lamprey. Sometimes the Klamath stayed six months; some even wintered over. They carried back things to trade onward with the Modoc, Takilma, Shasta, and Pit River people. Northward, the Wenatchee and Moses-Columbia traded things onward to the Sanpoil and Okanogan. The Walla Walla traded onward to the Nez Perce, who brought things back from beyond the Rockies after they got horses around 1720 or 1730. Yakima and Klickitat traders packed goods across the Cascade mountains to and from Puget Sound.

Among items famed for their quality were Klickitat baskets, Nez Perce *parfleches*, smelt oil from the Kathlamet or the Cowlitz, Sauvie Island *wapato*, bison robes from the Great Plains, dried clams from Shoalwater Bay, dried and pounded salmon manufactured in the Columbia Gorge, and dog-wool blankets from Puget Sound. Stones traveled farthest, or perhaps stones just last longer and can be traced. Native copper and nephrite came from Alaska, jadeite from British Columbia, galena and graphite from Montana, red pipestone from Minnesota, olivella shells from the California coast, and always dentalium, called *haiqua*, from beds off Vancouver Island in British Columbia.

Porcupine quills and embroidery, beargrass, silkgrass, and other basketry materials were exchanged, a dozen kinds of bulbs and roots, fish and sea-mammal oil, meats, berry cakes, mountain-sheep and goat horns, elkhide armor, feathers, seashells, clothing, furs, arrowpoint stones, abrasives, and rare earths and powders for paint.

Slaves from California, the Washington coast, and the Great Basin were carried there, frightened little Pit River children, or some unlucky Shoshone berry-picker, seized and carried off. The Chinook moved slaves both directions through the Gorge in their canoes. Once on the other side the stolen child lost all hope of running away.

Strangers came and went. Men spent the summer trading and gambling. When one got hungry he would bum a salmon. He signalled by slapping his rump when a fisherman netted a fish. Unless the fisherman had a good reason, he would give the fish to the bummer, who would cook it with his people. If the fisherman didn't want to donate it, he patted his own rump.[23]

Big traders and simple mountain people mingled. The Topenish and Wenatchee were just poor—the Chinook described them as of the "supposedly first class"—and managed only a few trades until the Klickitat took them in hand.[24] Everything valuable was in great supply. Wishram houses were typically half storeroom.

CHINOOK RULES OF TRADE were well established. A purchase might be returned in an hour or two and the deal called off, for whatever reason.[25] Negotiations for the same item at a different price might immediately begin. A slave, wife, or canoe was guaranteed for some months against sickness, defect, or death.[26] The Chinook traded repeatedly with the same people.

They bargained hard, at least with strangers, and enjoyed the activity greatly. Hear Captain Lewis on their trading propensities:

> They are great higlers in trade and if they conceive you anxious to purchase will be a whole day bargaining for a handful of roots; this I should have thought proceeded from their want of knowledge of the comparative value of articles of merchandise and the fear of being cheated, did I not find that they invariably refuse the price first offered them and afterwards very frequently accept a smaller quantity of the same article; in order to satisfy myself on this subject I once offered a Chinook my watch, two knives, and a considerable quantity of beads for a small inferior sea otter's skin which I did not much want; he immediately conceived it of great value, and refused to barter except I would double the quantity of beads; the next day with a great deal of importunity on his part I received the skin in exchange for a few strands of the same beads he had refused the day before. I therefore believe this trait in their character proceeds from an avaricious all-grasping disposition. In this respect they differ from all Indians I ever became acquainted with,

for [other Indians] dispositions invariably lead them to give what ever they are possessed of no matter how useful or valuable, for a bauble which pleases their fancy, without consulting its usefulness or value.[27]

The Chinook offered deferred payment when convenient, in one case selling early spring sturgeon but awaiting payment until the fish run was over and they could come to inspect the trader's goods.[28] At the Cascades, there was a system of canoe load, so that a boat need not be portaged along with goods.[29] They used a number of standardized packages, and their money beads offered a basis of comparison. Trade was based on mutual respect, and there was small, but not large, theft along the river. Canoes could be left lying around; houses full of household goods were closed but not locked; trade goods stored over the winter in someone's house were returned intact. No canoe floated away on *Wimahl* but someone caught and returned it.

On the other hand, the Chinook were expert petty thieves and liars. Carrying off some small item was a sign of friendship and a test of skill versus alertness, as it was among the Spartans. If caught, the thief denied everything. If exposed, he laughed, while his friends made fun of him. "He is the best fellow who can tell the biggest lie, make men believe it, and practice the greatest deception," historian Gustavus Hines concluded.[30]

A visitor might trade with whoever offered the best price. The Tillamook called that "throwing your money beads on any old woman's lap."[31] A better way was to know someone. Menait, anthropologist Edward Sapir's Wishram informant, said:

When one has a friend in another country, he comes to see you, or you go to see him. Both are glad to meet each other; one gives the other something valuable, the other gives something in return. Such are each other's *iellpet*, trading friend.[32]

Naked Against the Rain

MONEY BEADS, *haiqua*, were a major means of comparing value. The brilliant white, tusk-shaped dentalium shells were strung end to end in fathom lengths. (A fathom, the distance between one's outstretched fingers, averaged around five feet, seven inches among the Chinook.[33]) *Haiqua* were harvested by the Nootka along the west coast of Vancouver Island, and gained value in proportion to the distance from there. From southeast Alaska to northern California, and inland to the Rocky Mountains, everyone prized *haiqua.*

The Chinook valued them by number to the fathom. In 1811 a standard fathom contained forty shells. A fathom of fifty stubby little shells was worth less than half as much, a fathom of only thirty long, elegant shells was worth two or three times as much.[34] The shells ranged from a quarter of an inch to three inches long. The Chinook said they were gathered by a tiny people with little mouths, who sucked out the creatures inside for food, then allowed their slaves to string the shells as a pastime.[35]

Haiqua were sewn to clothing, dangled from headdresses, hung from the ears, or pushed through the nose. People engraved some with geometric designs, ground up others for medicine, buried them in the ground for safety, took them out and examined and counted and admired them, restrung them, and hid them away again.[36]

Haiqua provided an almost-standard unit by which the value of things could be compared. Standardization was well developed. Several basket sizes existed, for example specific baskets for hazel nuts, acorns, and dried huckleberries. The basket was part of the purchase. *Itkilak* salmon, an important item of trade, was packed in baskets a foot across and two feet deep, a ninety-pound backpack load. Tobacco was sold in small rush bags of a standard size, smelt side-by-side in fathom lengths, dried clams by the two-foot stick. Dried Shoalwater Bay butter clams were indeed an exotic delicacy to carry home to the Wallowa Mountains.

THE DALLES wasn't the only Chinook trade center. Clatsop and Shoalwater traded north and south on the coast. Quinault and Chehalis came down in summer with Nootka canoes, northern slaves, dentalium, baskets, and a kind of coarse grass prized for basketry. At Willamette Falls Clowewalla and Clackamas bought and sold with Kalapuyans. Klamath, Kalapuya, and Shasta slaves were brought north up the Willamette and passed on to Puget Sound up the Cowlitz.

Wealthy Chinook nobles journeyed to visit villages along the coast, and sent their wives to their home villages equipped with goods to trade.[37] Most goods moved from village to village; the Makah bought from the Nootka, then bartered to the Quinault, who traded to the Chehalis, who carried things along to the Shoalwater Chinook, who started them up Big River by trading to the Wahkiacum.

Along the river the most frequently traded item was said to be *wapato*. The Chinook diet was low on carbohydrates, and the flavorful little bulbs were the finest available to them. The river also moved large quantities of camas, bitterroot, kous, wild onion, and wild carrot, some for trade, some for gifts, some as a result of self-gathering.

AT ANY OF THE TRADING PLACES, but especially at the Long Narrows, a lot of goods changed hands through gambling, a great passion with the Chinook. There were always contests going at the trading sites. Since the Wasco and Wishram mostly awaited guests, they enjoyed the house advantage, upon which casino gambling is based. The house can weather long losing streaks by borrowing from nearby kinfolk if necessary, and still be in the game when the cards or bones turn. The visitor, far from home, is wiped out by a bad losing streak and goes home empty handed. Fur trader Alexander Ross described gambling, which alone draws so many vagabonds together at this place; because they are always sure to live well here, whereas no other place on the Columbia could support so many people together. The Long Narrows, therefore, is the great emporium or mart of the Columbia, and the general theater of gambling and roguery . . . all the gamblers, horse-stealers, and other outcasts throughout the country, for hundreds of miles round, make this their great rendezvous during the summer.[38]

It was trade the Chinook talked about. Fur trader George Simpson called them "the most acute and finished bargain makers I have ever fallen in with."[39] They always paid attention to details. They asked two or three times what an article was worth, and did not lower their prices except in response to their opponent's bargaining. They never sold lower than the real value of an article, which they knew perfectly well by the time they sold it.

YET MORE THAN JUST TRADE was going on at the Long Narrows. Utterly dissimilar cultures—Finnish and Italian might be comparable among Europeans—were meeting. The Chinook's neighbors up there were half a foot taller, but skinny, with long legs. They had different ways of living. A melding of techniques and ideas and images occurred, particularly between 1400 and 1600.[40] The Chinook brought wood-carving, stone-grinding, and head-flattening. Upriver they learned fine stone-chipping, the making of human effigies with revealed ribs and backbone, and how to grind images into rock.

Tsagiglalal was one of the images that came from that flowering. Her broad face, which blends features of river and plateau, appeared on objects large and small. She is identified by her wide grin, her tongue protruding or sometimes tucked back under. Sometimes she had bear ears, sometimes elegantly styled hair. Her eyes were concentric ellipses, joining to form her nose. Sometimes she wore elaborate earrings. Her forehead always slanted back. Images of this type have been found from above Celilo Falls to Sauvie Island.[41]

The finest image of "She Who Watches" was on the rimrock above Nixluidix; her face, three feet across, was abraded through red-painted rimrock. The curves around her eyes are sublime.

TSAGIGLALAL, THE ROCK WOMAN

A woman had a house where the village of Nixluidix was later built. She was chief of all who lived in this region. That was long ago, before Coyote came up the river and changed things, and people were not yet real people. After a time Coyote in his travels came to this place and asked the inhabitants if they were living well or ill. They sent him to their chief, who lived up in the rocks, where she could look down on the village and know all that was going on. Coyote climbed up to her home and asked: "What kind of living do you give these people? Do you treat them well, or are you one of those evil women?" "I am teaching them how to live well and to build good houses," she said. "Soon the world is going to change," he told her, "and women will no longer be chief. You will be stopped from being a chief." Then he changed her into a rock, with the command, "You shall stay here and watch over the people who will live in this place, which shall be called Nixluidix."

All the people know that Tsagiglalal sees all things, for whenever they are looking up at her those large eyes are watching them.[42]

PHOTOGRAPHER EDWARD CURTIS, who published the story, heard that it had been customary for several generations to invoke the image's aid in getting supernatural help. Offerings of baskets, mats, weapons, beads, and feathers were left. People asked for health, long life, or wealth. Women asked that they might have children, or for their children's health; young women asked that the man of their desire might love them.

Tsagiglalal, with her emphasis on witness, may have been a symbol of conscience. Though Coyote was endorsing male dominance as he announced a patriarchal future, the eyes, the watching, were central. Another interpretation was offered by an elderly Wishram woman shaman, who told archaeologist Robert Butler, "*Tsagiglalal* is for death. People grin like that when they're sick. When people look at you like that, you get sick."[43] This seems to imply a memory of one of the pestilences that were killing them, though no known disease is associated with such a grimace.[44] At least one archaeologist believes *Tsagiglalal* is always connected with death, and found exclusively at cremation sites,[45] which were new among the Chinook, and found only at the uppermost edge of Chinookia. Another archaeologist believes that *Tsagiglalal*'s protruding tongue illustrates a shaman's transition to power and is the same as images found farther north along the coast.[46]

Witness and death are not incompatible. There had always been a morbidity to the Chinook consciousness, which archaeologist W. Duncan Strong described as a "Ghost Cult."[47] For centuries, their art, most likely borrowed from an even older style at the Long Narrows, featured ribs and backbone. Long before the epidemics it reflected an awareness of skeleton, perhaps heightened by the bones of their ancestors, in their ever-present mortuary canoes and charnel houses.

THERE WERE MANY OTHER IMAGES. Coyote appears up and down the river, here clinging to the bow of a canoe four feet high, there carved on a mountain sheep horn ladle three inches long. On

Sauvie Island there were vesicular lava carvings of monumental design, a two-foot frog sitting comfortably with hands across belly, a massive owl, a *Tsagiglalal* head twenty-three inches high. Turtles and beavers held paint pots on their backs. The Wishram carved protruding rocks to represent what appear to be the heads of seals at The Dalles, modelled after the seals that followed the salmon up from the sea that far. Near Nixluidix there was a canyon the walls of which were incised with hundreds of images of birds, animals, and spirits.[48] The Chinook pecked and ground such images into the rock downriver as far as Willamette Falls and St. Helens, but nowhere in such profusion as at The Dalles. The Chinook learned rock art late and upriver.

No one knows for certain what the images mean. The petroglyphs—ground or pecked—and pictographs—paintings on rock—may have been inscribed by spirit seekers trying to attract a supernatural helper, as warnings of a dangerous water spirit, to mark a good fishing spot, or to commemorate an event. Some may have been just elaborate doodles. Many meanings have been suggested. At the Cascades and below the Chinook carved wood more than stone. They made spirit batons and shaman boards, which had great power. Their woodwork was finely polished, but wood does not last long. Their stonework was painted, but paints fade, and the vesicular lava they used, easier to sculpt than basalt, is full of pits and does not read well without color.

THE WISHRAM AND WASCO wore Plateau clothes. They put on moccasins and tailored shirts. The women wore brimless twined-basket hats, shaped like an Arab fez, as did the Plateau women. They wore skin dresses, leggings, and moccasins. They put on the skin of the head of a coyote or deer as a cap and made coyote-fur mittens. It got far colder upriver than west of the mountains, so they required such clothes. Yet, though scholars have taken to classifying the upriver Chinook as a Plateau people, they seem in most important ways to have remained a salient of coastal culture until the end. Their rectangular wooden houses, superior canoes, woodworking skills in a treeless land, gutteral coastal language, and desire to marry their daughters downriver show their essential Chinook identity.[49] In April 1811, when fur trader David Thompson and party were confronted by the Wishram, he recalled that the besiegers "were all men from thirty to fifty years of age, and were from near the sea."[50] He did not mean they had paddled up two hundred miles to attack him. He meant they were Chinook. Coastal people.

The Columbia River Gorge passed valuables, ideas, art forms, and customs in both directions. Through the Gorge the Chinook became sophisticated and shrewd. The Gorge may even have made them taller. At the mouth of the river, the Chinook were two inches taller than their coastal neighbors.[51] Perhaps marrying downriver was gradually bringing the *Ilkaimamt* tallness to the sea. The Gorge was the making of the Chinook; the Long Narrows was their wild frontier, their Alaska.

Caw-Wacham, of unidentified affiliation (some said Cowlitz), sketched by Paul Kane at the Cowlitz Farm portage in 1846. The head-shaping board is in the released position. Reproduced from a color lithograph printed in London in 1859.

6

The Skulls of Free People

1792

THE *TLOHONNIPTS* HAD LEARNED that a sea otter pelt brought $120 in Canton, China. That was a considerable fortune, the equivalent of around $6,000 today.[1] Sea otter fur is wonderfully thick and soft; it ripples silver and dark brown in any breeze. On the Northwest coast such pelts could be got for trade beads, iron files, rum, or guns. Some Chinook may have seen the tall white-sailed ships distantly, and it is likely they had heard that the whales-with-trees were sailing about. There could be no question of killing the invaders on sight, and thereby averting the tragedy that followed. The Chinook eagerly awaited their share of the fur trade.

Captain Robert Gray, a Boston merchant, is credited with discovering *Wimahl*. In the spring of 1792, after bombarding and destroying the Nootka village Nun-chah-nulth on Vancouver Island, he came south down the coast. At Grays Harbor a large canoe with twenty men came within half pistol shot. Gray fired a nine-pounder loaded with shrapnel and ten muskets of buckshot, dashing it to pieces and killing all aboard. Civilization was heading toward Big River.

On May 11th, 1792, Gray sailed the ship *Columbia Rediviva* in over the bar, and anchored off Chinook Point. Log keeper John Boit saw a beach, lined with natives, who ran along shore following the ship. Soon after about twenty canoes came off, and brought a good lot of furs and salmon. They appeared to view the ship with greatest astonishment and no doubt we were the first civilized men they ever saw.[2]

One of the things visitors mentioned about the Chinook was the alertness of their eyes. They seemed to view everything with astonishment, perhaps because their eyes remained bugged out a little as a result of nine months or a year on the cradleboard. They studied the look of ships, uniforms, and faces, and had excellent memories.

At least one Chinook remembered the first European ship to enter the river differently. Two decades later he told trader Robert Stuart:

> On the vessel's first appearance in the offing they were very much surprised and alarmed, but after her entering and anchoring in the river they were all seized with such consternation as to abandon their villages, leaving only a few old people who could not follow; some imagined the ship to be some overgrown monster come to devour them, while others supposed her to be a floating island inhabited by cannibals, sent by the great spirit to destroy them and ravage their country. However, a boat crew soon went ashore, who by their mild behavior, and distributing a few trinkets [established] a friendly intercourse that has continued to this day.[3]

Gray anchored off Qwatsamts village, where his sailors heard the name Chinoak. Polack was headman then. Boit logged "vast many canoes full of *Indians* from different parts of the river were constantly along side. The Indians very numerous and appeared very civil (not even offering to steal.)"

Thus, in a single log entry the name they would bear was introduced, and the Chinook were first categorized as *Indians*.

THEY DIDN'T LOOK much like *Indians*. Exploratory expedition scientist Charles Pickering wrote: "The personal appearance of the Chinook differed so much from that of the aboriginal tribes of the U.S. that it was difficult at first to recognize the affinity."[4] They were a short, thickset, brawny people, "full and lusty about the waist," according to maritime trader Charles Bishop.[5] The men averaged five-and-a-half-feet tall, 140 pounds, the women smaller in proportion. Their skin was relatively light; anthropologist Franz Boas compared them to European brunettes,[6] while Dr. Samuel Morton saw an Italian peasant coloring.[7] Some had reddish-brown hair, a color the Chinook particularly fancied.

Boit concluded, "The men at Columbia River are straight limb'd, fine looking fellows, and the women are very pretty."[8] Fur company executive George Simpson recalled, "Their looks on the whole are pleasing, being more fair and their features more resembling those of the whites than any other tribe I have ever seen."[9] Fur trader Alexander Ross called the women "well featured with something of a smile on the countenance, fair complexion, light hair and prominent eyes."[10]

Their faces were broad to round, but their cheekbones weren't particularly prominent. Their noses were low at the bridge and broad at the tip, with large nostrils. Their mouths were wide, sensual, and expressive, with full lips. Their eyebrows were wide, their earlobes small. Their slightly protruding eyes were small, dark brown, yellowish brown, or hazel and, again, very animated.[11] The men plucked out their scant beards and their body hair as well, but a few old men allowed a tuft of hair to grow upon their chins, whether as a privilege of age or the trace of an older style no one seems to have inquired.[12]

THEIR HEADS were artificially flattened. This deformation of the skull was the difference between a free person and a slave, and though it sounds disfiguring, most Europeans who saw flatheads didn't find it so. Simpson, a sophisticated world traveler, would describe it as

> not offensive to the eye, at least was not so to me at first sight and as none but the wretched slaves have round heads I began to fall into the Chinook way of thinking that they do not look so well (particularly the ladies) with round as with flat heads.[13]

Deformation of the skull must rank with Chinese foot-binding, European corset-tying, and American nose-reduction and breast-augmentation among extreme methods of improving human looks.

By the time Gray arrived, Comcomly had begun the series of marriages that would ally him with prominent families in several directions. His first wife, Kiasno, was Scapoose, from upriver in the Wapato Lowlands. She bore a son, who would be called Quasquas and later Cassacas. Comcomly had his son placed in a specially carved miniature canoe, swaddled among padding and laced down so he could hardly move. A pad of cedar-bark wool was placed on the baby's forehead and pressed down with a board hinged at the top of the cradle. As the infant's skull grew, the board shaped its growth, broadening it and making it narrower from front to back at the top.[14] His forehead receded, emphasizing his features. Quasquas' eyes may have bugged out but he felt little pain. He didn't see much either, for his eyes were shrouded by the board and the fringe at its end. He might have appeared dull-eyed and torpid, but felt discomfort only when his mother Kiasno loosened the board daily, to bathe and clean his body.

IF INTELLIGENCE, emotions, or other functions of the brain were adversely affected, no one reported it. Visitors thought the Chinook highly intelligent. Lewis and Clark found them "loquacious and inquisitive, with understanding by no means deficient in acuteness, and very retentive memories. To all our inquiries they answered with great intelligence, and the conversation rarely slackens."[15] Trader Wilson Price Hunt called them "the most intelligent Indians that I have met so far."[16] Simpson, the equivalent of today's multinational corporation executive, held them "without exception the most intelligent Indians and the most acute and finished bargain-makers I have ever fallen in with."[17] Townsend, an ornithologist and physician, went farther:

> The appearance produced by this unnatural operation is almost hideous, and one would suppose that the intellect would be materially affected by it. This, however, does not appear to be the case, as I have never seen (with a single exception, the Kayouse) a race of people who appeared more shrewd and intelligent.[18]

Philologist Horatio Hale rated them only "of moderate intelligence," and tried comparing them to the round-headed children of slaves to see if he couldn't detect some harm from head-flattening. He found none, except "the natural tameness and lack of quarrelsomeness of slaves as opposed to the natural pride and arrogance of slave owners."[19]

Humans are born exceedingly early in their development compared to other mammals. By swaddling and head-flattening their babies for nine months to a year, the Chinook provided the equivalent of another year in the womb, according to mythologist Joseph Campbell.[20] A cradleboard child hardly experienced the uncontrolled jerkings and helplessness of infancy. By the time he was released, Quasquas would have been physically mature enough to walk. It is roundheads (or other unswaddled babies) who experience that year of crawling and fumbling, which can hardly fail to color our adult consciousness.

FLATHEADS THOUGHT roundheads looked bumpy, like a dog or a rock. They called them "flea faced," and thought them mentally inferior.[21] Only the children of ne'er-do-wells, orphans, or slaves had round heads. Slaves were only rarely allowed to flatten their children's heads. Their progeny would be slaves in their turn.

How can it have begun? It must have had deep roots, perhaps from those ancient Penutian speakers of the Ice Age lakes. A lot of the peoples of America who artificially reshaped their heads spoke Penutian languages. Head reshaping was widespread in the Americas, with large head-flattening areas in the southeastern United States, and in British Columbia. The Maya of Central America, who may either have spoken an offspring of Penutian or been influenced by their neighbors (the Mixe-Zoque and Huave) who some scholars believe did, flattened their heads exactly as did the Chinook. Certainly anthropologist Ernest Hooton in 1940 speculated extravagantly when he suggested a marvelous migration:

> I am inclined to think that the ancestors of the classical Mayans were not very different from the white hybridized type which we call Armenoid—hook noses from Henry Field's Iranian Plateau race, round heads from the good old Alpines—and inspired with similar aesthetic ambitions to improve their head form. Eventually they picked up some Mongoloid features—hair, pigmentation, cheek bones, etc.[22]

Present scholars cannot permit themselves such speculations, but what a long march that envisioned, from the far edge of Asia to the Great Basin, then the Penutian diaspora, to British Columbia, Oregon, Washington, Idaho, and California, to southern Mexico, Central America, the Gulf Coast, and perhaps even the shores of

Naked Against the Rain

Lake Titicaca, where they likewise flattened heads.[23] Bishop noted:

> In side view it gives the head a most distorted appearance, resembling a human face carved out of a flat piece of plank, the thickness of the head from the back part of the eyebrow being often seen to be not more than half the breadth of the face, but in a front view it gives them a fine open countenance and preserves them to great age from wrinkles about the eyes.[24]

IT PROTECTED THEM from enslavement as well. We have followed the Chinook by their language, but that hardly mattered to them. It was the shape of a person's head that counted. The lower Columbia was the center of Chinook-style head-flattening, which extended three hundred miles south to north along the Pacific, from the Alsea to the Quinault. Beyond that, the Makah and the Klallam of the Strait of Juan de Fuca bound their skulls, but into other shapes, as did a number of groups farther north. The Salish-speakers to halfway up Puget Sound flattened their babies' heads, high-class Tualatin did so, Sahaptin-speakers beyond the mountains flattened heads, and, far up Big River on the Snake River, more than 325 miles from the sea, Lewis and Clark noted that the Walla Walla flattened the heads of their daughters.[25] Southeast three hundred miles, the Klamath and perhaps some Modoc flattened their baby's heads. (The "Flatheads" of Montana, however, did not.)

Beyond lived roundheads, who might be enslaved. But a flathead would purchase another flathead and return her to her home village.[26] A village where people flattened their babies' heads thus joined a widespread civility of at least 160,000 square miles, where people married each others' daughters instead of stealing them. It was a country where killing a roundhead was nothing much, but killing another flathead cost plenty.[27]

Were these the embryonic stirrings of a nationhood based on head shape rather than race, language, or culture? Flatheads spoke more than a dozen languages; lived in coast rainforest, temperate valley, and dry plateau; and varied widely in stature and shape; but treated each other as human beings.

FOR BEAUTY, it was hair the Chinook noticed. In a myth, a beautiful woman was described, as having "long, black, glossy hair, plump limbs and clear skin."[28] In the legend of the tyrant Tiapexwasxwas, it was recited:

> Then he would say to his favorite wife, Redhair, "Now loosen your braids. Walk about for me to see you, Redhair!" She loosened her hair and walked about. "Oh!" he said to her.[29]

Some villages wore their hair parted in the middle and braided in front of the ears; some left it free to the shoulders, or wound their tresses around their heads. People cut their hair in bangs, leaving earlocks at each side. Single and double braids were worn. The women plucked their eyebrows and oiled their hair with bear or sea mammal oil. They were fond of combing it with several styles of ornately carved combs. Long hair was much admired.

Chinook males went naked by preference most of the year.[30] When they did put something on, downriver it was an untailored mat shawl or fur robe, of muskrat or mountain beaver, sea or land otter, beaver, or bear. They made robes of rabbit and small bird pelts, cut into strips and twisted so fur or feathers showed on all sides, then woven into blankets. Against the rain they wore mats of cattail, tule, or grass. In Cold Moon they wrapped a fur around their torsos under their arms, like a vest. Ordinary robes covered only their backs and shoulders and fastened at the neck with a pin. Sometimes they draped a robe over one shoulder to leave the other arm free to work.

Naked Against the Rain

The women, however, wore a modesty garment. On the lower river this was a skirt of shredded cedar bark or silk grass, woven or twisted, which hung to the knees and looked something like a South Pacific grass skirt. Ross described the strands,

> flapping and twisting about with every motion of the body, giving them a waddle or duck gait. It does not screen nature from the prying eye; yet it is remarkably convenient on many occasions. In a calm the sails lie close to the mast, metaphorically speaking, but when the wind blows the bare poles are seen.[31]

Upriver in the Wapato Lowlands the modesty garment was a skin breechclout tied in front and behind to a waistband. Lewis and Clark thought the breechclouts drawn so tight as to be indecent. Only in the privacy of the woman's hut in back of the village could a woman be as naked as a man.

The women wove wide-brimmed conical hats that came to a flat or bulbous top, the general Northwest coast style. These they decorated with images of animals or geometric shapes.

The Chinook were canoe people, always in and out of the water, so they went barefoot year around, even in the occasional snow.[32] In the myths, men made long journeys wearing moccasins, but nobody ever saw the Chinook in footwear except far upriver, where they adopted the more protective clothing of their Sahaptin neighbors. Being naked has advantages in a temperate, rainy climate, for bare skin dries while garments remain wet and cold. Children were taught stoicism toward cold, leaving them free to go comfortably naked.

If their wardrobe was simple, their ornamentation was not. Lieutenant William Broughton of the British Navy declared that "in the decoration of their persons they surpass all the other tribes with paints of different colors, feathers, and ornaments."[33]

They painted their faces wholly or in bands of red, black, white, or yellow. The women wrapped three-inch bands of beads tightly around their ankles. Men (and women above the Cascades) bored holes in the septum between their nostrils and thrust pearly *haiqua* shells through, something like a white pencil moustache. (But the Nez Perce—pierced nose—did not.) Both men and women hung shells and beads from their ears, and some had lines, dots, or figures of animals or birds tattooed on their breasts, arms, or faces.[34] They loved wearing rings, and hanging carvings of animals and faces as pendants around their necks and wrists, or from gorgets. These were of stone, shell, hammered copper, tooth, bone, or wood. Many were excellently carved.[35]

Lest the Chinook sound too pretty to be real, we present fur trader Ross Cox's classic defamation. (The Chinook savored a good insult.)

> They were most uncouth-looking objects; and not strongly calculated to impress us with a favorable opinion of aboriginal beauty. Their eyes were black, piercing, and treacherous; their ears slit up and ornamented with strings of beads; the cartilage of their nostrils perforated and adorned with pieces of hyaquau placed horizontally; while their heads presented an incline plane from the crowns to the upper part of the nose, totally unlike our European rotundity of cranium; and their bodies besmeared with whale oil gave them an appearance horribly disgusting. Then the women—O ye Gods! With the same auricular, olfactory and craniological peculiarities, they exhibited loose hanging breasts, short dirty teeth, skin saturated with blubber, bandy legs, and a waddling gait.[36]

IN LATE OCTOBER, five months after Captain Gray had "discovered" and named the river, Lieutenant Broughton sailed His

Britannic Majesty's brig *Chatham* in over the bar, on orders from his commander, Captain George Vancouver, to reconnoiter the river Gray had told them about.[37] Broughton found the British merchant ship *Jenny*, Captain James Baker, anchored in what he named Baker Bay, the first indentation inside the mouth of the river on the north. Baker told Broughton that he had been in the river earlier, so it is possible he was the real "discoverer" of the Columbia, but he was under instruction from his owner, slave trader Sydenham Teast of Bristol, to speak nothing of what he saw. Baker sailed out, and Gray got credit for finding a river the Chinook had not yet lost.

Broughton explored the estuary, already deserted for the winter by the Shoalwater and Clatsop, then anchoring his brig, and manning its cutter and launch—neither much over twenty feet long —he headed up the river. It was late October, rainy in the estuary, but dry and temperate above. Fifty miles upriver, in the wide shallow above Wallace Island, he encountered his first Chinooks, when four Kathlamet canoes visited him. They sold him some fish and passed on. Around Mayger, Oregon, mile 58, nine more canoes of Kathlamet came to see him. They camped nearby and their mild behavior soon laid to rest his fears at their warlike appearance.

Aboard one of those canoes apparently was an elderly noble, headman of Neerchokioo, the farthest downriver Shahala village, where the Portland Airport is now. This man, who Broughton soon began to call the "Friendly Old Chief," became intensely interested in the strangely dressed, roundheaded floats-ashores. He accompanied them nearly a hundred miles, and performed several helpful services for them.[38]

A flotilla of twenty-three canoes met Broughton's two rowboats at Nayagogo, mile 75, where nautical battles were fought. Each of those canoes carried from three to a dozen men, and most if not all of them were longer than the British boats. The men wore elkskin armor and carried weapons, but when the friendly old chief told them of the peaceful conduct of the strangers they took off their armor and began to trade. None could be persuaded to part with their iron or copper clubs, perhaps product of Konapee's art.

A dozen miles farther, somewhere near Mahlnumax, twenty-five more canoes, manned by 150 men, confronted Broughton's party. Somewhat daunted by their numbers, the British pulled their boats to shore to dine, but declined to disembark. They scratched a line on the beach and forbade the Chinook to cross. Two nobles dared cross the line and they traded. The Chinook tried to speak to them, but the *tlohonnipts* could not understand. It would be interesting to know whether the river people were speaking the trade language to the strangers, but no words were written down by the sailors.

The friendly old chief tried to persuade them to visit his village as they passed, but they camped elsewhere. At the mouth of the Washougal River, mile 123, another fleet of ten boats came out to meet them.

NO ONE TRIED to stop the British. The Chinook treated the strangers as potential trading partners, not dangerous spirits or enslaveable roundheads. The openness and lack of fear with which the friendly old chief dealt with these strangers was singular, yet typical of the Chinook response on a number of occasions.

Broughton continued to the mouth of the Columbia Gorge, near mile 128, where sheer cliffs ahead convinced him that this was no Northwest Passage. He turned back. The elderly chief again invited them to his village. So had the headmen of Cooniac and Quathlapootle villages, but Broughton remained cautious. He named the stretch of river fronting the present Vancouver, Washington, "the Friendly Reach" in honor of the old chief. Charts still bear that name.

Back in the estuary, Broughton claimed all the land drained by Big River for the King of England. He may have offered some

Chinook a toast they would long remember. James Swan heard such a toast recalled in 1852 on Shoalwater Bay:

> Old Carcumcum has related to me the fact of her remembering the first time that any liquor was given to the Chinook. The *tyee* or chief of the vessel had gold dollar things, meaning epaulets, on his shoulders, and it was a man-of-war. They drank some rum out of a wine glass; how much she did not recollect; but she did recollect that they got drunk, and were so scared at the strange feeling that they ran into the woods and hid till they were sober. The rest, who did not get any rum, thought they had gone crazy or turned foolish.[39]

The river people had finally met the Europeans, and everything had gone smoothly. Thirty-eight years remained to them.

"Wishram Child." Photograph by Edward Curtis, courtesy of the University of Washington Library, Special Collections, NA 176

7

Skunk Cabbage
Holds the People's Breath

SPRING

BY FEBRUARY—"She is Growing Moon"[1] the Wishram called it—
they'd had their fill of drumming, dancing, and listening to the
myths, and of the long grey winter days. Someone was always going
down to the river to see if the smelt had come yet. The flavorful little *ihlhun* might run as early as January, or as late as April, and the
river people took them with nets or sharp-tined rakes. Cowlitz River
smelt were most desired, and the Kalama, Lewis, Sandy, and other
rivers had their runs. Herring and sardines also came to those rakes.

It became March, "Cottonwood Moon," or "Her (or small, or
the) Seventh Moon," as the Wishram called it. The trees began to
leaf out, dappling the somber evergreen hills above Big River. The
bodies of the people were covered with sores and their houses
smelled strongly. They were waiting for First Salmon to come and
change things.

THE MYTH OF SALMON told how Salmon spirit came up the river
with his numerous companions. The party came to a person who
said:

"At last my brother's son does arrive. If it had not been for me, your people would be dead. I held the people's breath."

"Who is that who is talking there?" Salmon asked.

"That is Skunk-Cabbage who is talking," his companions said.

"Oh, yes, they will eat him. Quick, let us go ashore."

Salmon landed. He gave elkskin armor, five elkskin armors were given to Skunk-Cabbage. Under his blanket was put a bone war club, beside his arm, and beside his other arm, another one. He was carried inland. He was put in the midst of willows.²

BREATH SHARED THE SAME WORD as soul in Chinook, as it did in Latin, Hebrew, and Arabic. The person claimed he had kept the people alive until Salmon arrived to feed them. Salmon rewarded Skunk Cabbage for his service to the people. The rewards were a description of the plant's club-like stamen and enfolding broad petals. Salmon places Skunk Cabbage in marshy ground where it will grow.

This dignification of Skunk Cabbage wasn't mere comic relief. As winter progressed, unhealed wounds and sores had troubled the Chinook more frequently, and by late winter even the wealthy had scabs and pus, which the river people found disgusting. But they knew plant remedies, the first of which to grow in the spring was skunk cabbage, followed by cow parsnip stems and horsetail sprouts. The fur traders would later adopt these remedies, realizing that something in those plants cured their scurvy.³ That something was vitamin C, of which the Chinook had been suffering an increasing deficiency since the last berries were picked. One of vitamin C's functions is helping wounds heal. The humble skunk cabbage contained the earliest available vitamin C in the springtime.⁴

As Salmon and his followers continued upriver, a seasonal litany of vegetables and creatures challenged Salmon, and he responded by rewarding them for their services. Small Arrowhead Root got two deerskin robes and small dentalia. Salmon announced that the people would give small dentalia to buy her. Rush Root got an elkskin shirt and feathered headdress. Large Arrowhead Root, the much prized *wapato*, was given three woodchuck blankets and long dentalia. Greens were rewarded and placed along the shore, and so on. The items and order in which the foods were listed differed from village to village, as did the people's diets. Some villages recalled grouse, quail, mudfish, chub, trout, eel, and sturgeon.

Once the salmon arrived, the people's troubles would be over. If they observed the taboos, First Salmon would come from his house at the bottom of the sea, leading countless *igunat*, their word for fish in general or Chinook salmon in particular. The species has also been call tyee, king, quinnat, or blackmouth salmon. *Igunat* offered their luscious pink flesh freely to the people. But should the fish be insulted or mistreated, they would cease to come. No man caught *igunat* or anything else unless they were willing to be caught. A man who boasted of how many he would catch, caught none, perhaps even died. A man who observed the taboos established a mutual regard between himself and the beings he fed upon.

FIVE KINDS OF SALMON swam up Big River, each in its season, each heading for ancestral spawning beds. The first run of *igunat* went up as early as February or March. These spring salmon ascended the Cowlitz, Sandy, and Willamette rivers. They leaped forty-one-foot Willamette Falls, surmountable only in the spring, when the Willamette's flow was high and the water below the falls was backed up by the flooding Columbia.

The Clackamas and Clowewalla who lived there fished with conical dip nets, ten feet deep and four or five feet wide at the mouth, with thirty-foot handles. They built wooden platforms out over the water, and netted fish as they fell back from leaping or rested in an eddy. The fish jumped fifteen feet, then swam up the rest of the way. One leap in ten succeeded. A man with a dip net could take twenty in an hour, averaging forty pounds or more each.[5]

Again the cry was heard, "They come, *igunat*," and someone landed the first one, which made him lucky all year, and the site where he caught it lucky too. He invited the people, who came to his home, where he performed the ritual.[6] Chinook ceremonies were not so complex that every man did not know them. They needed no priesthood to intercede for them with a distant, all-powerful *God*. The fisherman ritually cleaned and cooked the fish and made special distribution to old people and children; then everyone passed around the fish and took a piece. They disposed of the remains in a manner pleasing to Salmon.

IN HER EIGHTH MOON, April, Big River began to rise and some people took the boards off their winter houses and sank them in a nearby pond, or put them across two canoes and carried them to their fishing houses. Many simply left their winter plank houses standing. The winter village broke up, as families went off, some to one site, some to another. A group who wintered at Beacon Rock moved sixty-five miles to Willamette Falls each spring, while another band of the same winter village moved only two or three miles up the Columbia to the Cascades.[7] Chenewuth's band wintered on the Clackamas, and moved up to the Cascades of the Columbia for the summer.[8]

In the Columbia River Gorge there were fewer seine-net drifts. The Chinook fished from platforms with dipnets, or with harpoons equipped with Y-shaped foreshafts and points that detached, connected to the pole by three-foot lines.

To make a platform they chipped holes in the river bed at low water. When the water was right for fishing, several men held down the landward end of a log extending out over the water and a strong man walked out on it and dropped a support timber into the hole, then quickly lashed it to the log he stood on. Supported, cross-braced, and planked, it offered access above an eddy or falls.[9]

At the Long Narrows there were natural runnels through the paving-stone-like basalt rock, and when the water was right the Wishram made a dipnet to block a runnel exactly, and took such fish as they required. At the Cascades the Shahala made artificial runnels like that and did the same.[10]

Then the sky became alive with birds, which filled the lakes and marshes and sloughs and made the air raucous with their cries. Geese, swans, and ducks of a dozen varieties came north each spring. They rested among the Chinook, who took them with arrow, spear, or thin nets. A man might drift out under a pile of brush to pull the birds under by their legs.

WAS IT IN LATE MAY or early June that Comcomly's Chehalis wife Qwayaq bore him a second son? "Her Ninth Moon" the Wishram called May, and there is one tantalizing hint in addition to those numbers that suggest the Wasco and Wishram, at least, may have given birth to their babies all together in May. Pulitzer-Prize-winning novelist H. L. Davis, who grew up in The Dalles in the late nineteenth century, described the Indian women there as having their babies all at once.[11]

They had realized Qwayaq was pregnant from her loss of appetite and her morning sickness. Qwalwanxu,[12] an old woman known for her skill, was paid to come. She warmed her hands over the fire and rubbed Qwayaq's abdomen before breakfast each morning for a few months.

Qwayaq knew the taboos of pregnancy and childbirth. She must not sleep long. When she sat, none stood behind her or lay crosswise at her feet, lest the baby be born feet first. If she came to a creek she jumped it twice. She did not lie in the sun. She did not wear a necklace or bracelets, lest the umbilical cord wrap around the baby's arm or neck. She would not look at a corpse or any dead thing. She must not blow up a seal bladder. If she ate a trout the baby would faint as many as four times a day. Eating anything with a hole in it would cause the same hole in the baby. She must never stop or turn back in a doorway, for the baby would stop at the door of her womb, nor look at a dog with its eyes closed, lest the baby be born blind. She would not bathe overmuch, lest her bones become stiff. A tumpline around her body would cause the umbilical cord to entangle her baby.

Comcomly might not eat anything found, or singe a seal, shoot birds, or look at a corpse. Should he kill a raccoon the baby would die, while killing an otter meant a hard struggle against death.

WHEN IT WAS HER TIME they secluded Qwayaq in a corner of the house and called Qwalwanxu and a second midwife too, for Qwayaq was of the highest class. Her husband would gift them with long dentalia. They took out a floor board and dug a hole, into which they put hot stones. Then they wrapped a blanket around her and she squatted over the hole, steaming day and night, until her body softened.

When her labor commenced she held two upright posts, and chewed a stick or the corner of a blanket against the pain. She must not cry out, especially during the birth of her first baby. Comcomly watched as Qwalwanxu, the midwife, supported the squatting girl's rump and helped her press down again and again. She squatted—the natural position for childbirth—over fresh golden rush mats covered with *tupso*—finely shredded cedar bark—which caught their child.

The midwife cut the umbilical cord and tied it with elkskin. She bathed the infant in warm water and dried it with *tupso*, washed out its mouth and swaddled it in beaver and raccoon fur. The new mother was steamed until "the grandmother"—the afterbirth—

flowed out. They offered the grandmother beads and dentalia, lest she take the infant back, and turned her over if they wished to reverse the sex of the next baby.[13] Qwalwanxu said:

> The baby's home is the sun before being born. All children come from the daylight, that is their home. If their parents do not take good care of them, they think, "Well, I'd better go back." Then they get sick and die. Later, a child may take pity on its parents and decide to return. "Maybe my parents will be better to me now." Then the child is born again to the same mother, but is a different sex.[14]

For ten days the parents abstained from fresh food. Comcomly neither hunted nor fished, but could gather firewood. After five days Qwayaq was bathed with medicinal waters. For five more days she was secluded but she drank salmon-head soup to make her milk plentiful. Then she returned to normal life. And then, but not before, the cradleboard was carved, by an old person with Coyote spirit who was of the same sex as the baby and could understand the language of babies, as do dogs and coyotes.

ABOUT A MONTH LATER Comcomly invited the best people of the village to his house for the first of a series of celebrations that would establish the importance of the still-nameless child, not just in the eyes of the people of the village and of other villages, but in the mind of the child itself.

Qwalwanxu, who had Coyote power, listened to the baby's coos and cries and interpreted where it had come from and what its future held. They said that sometimes such a person could foresee how the infant would die. Can Qwalwanxu have foreseen this baby's end? Better not to.

They pierced each tiny ear twice and hung rings and ornaments from them. Comcomly distributed strings of dentalia to the people, and they feasted. But the child remained nameless. They called it after where it had been born, lest it die and the name be lost. The first year was a time of grave danger. Were they always so tentative, or was it only since the epidemics that they delayed?

The camas flowered in June, hyacinth-like flowers making the meadows blue as lakes, and the women took their digging sticks and went to work. Digging sticks were the symbol for female. The handle was horn or antler, ornamented and with a rectangular mortise cut through, into which she inserted a stick a foot or two long, curved for leverage. She pushed the stick in the ground, pried up a clod and took the bulbs beneath. A morning's hard work might yield two bushels of camas, about ninety pounds.[15] Sticks came and went but the handle was her lifelong tool and would be buried with her. In myths, when her stick broke it warned of trouble at home.

THE MOST IMPORTANT EVENT of a person's life occurred about a year after birth. When the boy was off the cradleboard, able to stand and walk, when the worst danger was past, Comcomly invited the people again. Three more holes were pierced in each ear. Not to have five holes in each ear was as laughable as to have a round forehead. Then they dressed the boy in finery and stood him between two others, amidst relatives and friends and people from far villages. The person on his left started the litany, the one on his right repeated it, and the guests responded "*Axi!*" with vigor.

"We want the mountains, rivers, creeks, bluffs, timber to know that this child is now called Quatqos."

"*Axi!*"

"We want to let the fish, birds, winds, snow, and rain, the sun, moon, and stars know that Quatqos has become alive again."

"*Axi!*"

Then anyone formerly acquainted with the previous Quatqos might come forward and ask whatever he or she wished. "I am glad to meet Quatqos again after so long," he would say. "I am glad this name has come to be spoken again; so I want Quatqos to give me a fathom of long dentalia."

"Yes," his parents said, "We want to give you that; he is going to be with us again." Thus they gave away many valuables and the guests would always remember Quatqos and spread his fame.[16]

The name was ancestral, handed down for generations in the child's lineage. No two living persons bore the same name. Names were archaic and untranslatable, and the most recent bearer was at least five years dead. Famous names were almost titles. Yet, though people wanted to be widely known, they never spoke their names to strangers. A shaman could steal a soul if he knew the name. To speak the name of a recently dead person called up the ghost and caused pain to the living. Some people changed their own names so as not to hear spoken a name the dead person had called them.

Again, at six or seven years, and sometimes later in life as well, a person might take a new name. This commemorated a life-changing experience, like an illness or an encounter with a spirit power. Quatqos would later be called Shalapau. Then, toward the end of his life, a father might hand his name, and position, on to his grown son. Comcomly would do that, and don another name. Upriver at the Cascades, a headman named Papke became the storyteller Menait, who helped preserve a lot of Chinook lore.[17]

The names weren't the family name; they ran in the family. Probably there were always bearers of such historic names as Coalpo, Chenamus, Shalapau, Taucum, Chinini, Cobaway, Twotillicum, Cassino, Stotkin, Slyboots, Tomaquin, Chenewuth, Tumalth, Tilki, Colawas, and Spedis along the river.

Quatqos nursed at Qwayaq's breast for two or three years, and might have continued for four or five. A Chinook mother would not deny a child her breast. He was taking soup and solid food as well. For fully six years he was not expected to understand anything. His grandparents, who raised him during those years, were not expected to teach him, punish him, or discipline him, only to guard and enjoy him.

In June, Coming in a Body Moon, the largest of the *igunat* came up, fish of eighty and ninety pounds, bound for spawning beds twelve hundred miles upriver. Those were the "June hogs" Columbia River fishermen remember and mourn to this day. Families with a good net-drift or platform were limited only by how many people they had to put the fish up on drying racks. Several families might own a fishing site and work it in shifts.

They sliced the fish open and laid them on structures of poles, protected by mats against the sun. A small fire of alder or maple beneath kept the air moving. When the flesh was dried hard they packed it away in baskets or buried it in the ground. A pinch filled the mouth with salmon flavor, a few bits made savory the soup.

When he was six, Quatqos passed into the age of reasonableness. Now he could speak clearly and was thought accountable for his actions. His training began. Each evening, fathers instructed their sons, mothers their daughters. Sometimes an older person was hired to come early in the morning to instruct a child in the traditions of the people.

Physical training began. Comcomly sent the boy to the top of the hill behind the village, then to ever-farther places. He was sent to an exact spot, to pile up rocks or to gather some plant found only there. An inspector went to check. At first the tasks were simple, but they increased in difficulty. The goal was not so much physical as spiritual strength; the getting of a spirit helper.

Stoicism was taught as well. Menait recalled a common experience. He fell asleep while listening to a myth, which he had been warned not to do. It was mid-winter.

An old man would say to me: "Go in bathing!" I would try to refuse, but in vain, so I just had to go. I was undressed entirely naked where they knew there was lots of ice and also it was pressed together tight. He would give me an ax for chopping up the ice. He would say to me: "You will chop right through it, you will dive under water, you will stick your head out, you will turn around, you will look to the rising sun, you will cry out, 'Wa!' you will shout."

He was to duck and rise and cry out to each of the cardinal directions and shout a fifth "Wa!" toward the sky. "Then enough; you will return home."

Now when I came home a fire was already burning. On the ends of my hair icicles were dangling. I was told, "Don't look at the fire; turn away from it, present your buttocks to the fire. It will blow at you and make you grow quickly." That is how I was done to in order not to be sick and in order to be strong, or, just so, in order to prepare one for a guardian spirit.[18]

SOON QUATQOS was accompanying his father at his regular tasks. Someone made a little bow and arrow for him. A girl was given a miniature root digger. Children learned by copying the parent. Though often the children of the village disappeared together after breakfast and did not return until supper time. They roamed the forest or played along the shore. Pioneer James Swan recalled:

Like all children they are fond of a swing. The boys were fond of making canoes either from flags, which were twisted so as to form a sort of boat, or from chips, on which they would start off on voyages down the creek. Sometimes a lad with more ingenuity than the rest would carve out a pretty model of a canoe from a cedar stick; and I have seen boys, with little canoes they had made, scarcely three feet long, fearlessly paddle about the water in those little cockles, which seemed ready at any moment to sink. Sometimes the boys would catch a lot of minnows, and then the girls would join them, and having made a little fire and a miniature rack for smoking fish, would imitate the manner of curing salmon, which, when done, were served up as a repast. The girls were very fond of making rag babies, dressing up clam-shells as children.[19]

The boys contested at swimming and staying under water. They shot at targets. Boys and girls alike ran foot races and played a ring-and-pin game. At the western edge of Nixluidix was a pair of slides worn three-quarters of an inch deep and smooth as glass down a leaning slab of basalt.[20]

Both boys and girls played a laughing game. A person from one side came across and was assailed with all manner of taunts, jokes, and insults. Keeping a straight face was the goal.[21] Lewis and Clark said the Chinook were "generally cheerful but never gay."[22] No one recalled seeing one laugh out loud. That game was why.

Comcomly may have threatened his son with *Atatahlia*, a hideous ogress who carried a big basket.[23] She came in night and fog to steal children and carried them home to eat. Ugly-faced *Atatahlia* had big eyes and ears. Her huge body was striped. There were also *Tsiatko*, giant monsters with eighteen-inch feet shaped like those of bears.[24] These furry, evil-smelling beasts gibbered and chattered like noisy owls. They lived in holes in the ground in the mountains, and came down to the river during fishing season where they went about at night stealing salmon, or children, and smothering babies.

Qwayaq evoked a legendary tribe when she reminded her son to eat his food. "The *Qtense* are going to eat up what has been killed for you," she told him.[25]

HIS GRANDMOTHER taught him about the Frogs, whose croak is pronounced *xwadet* in Kiksht:

> *Their mother sent them off to their uncle Lizard to tell him that the singing was ready to begin. She instructed them to call him Myth Age Lizard, but the little ones forgot. They called him just lizard, which made him angry and he would not sing. A month later she sent them again, and this time they did it right. He came and they all sang together:*
>> *"Now we are sitting on our xwadet*
>> *Now we are sitting on our xwadet, xwadet."*
> *Then Snake came. "Why you Snake!" cried the littlest Frog in a high voice, "You are pulling off my braids." Snake gobbled down the littlest Frog, and Myth Age Lizard came to lead them. Now they sang both night and day, for that was their month for singing.*[26]

THE GATHERING OF A GIRL'S first substantial pick of berries or dig of roots was cause for an important celebration. When she first filled the appropriate size basket by herself, her parents invited everyone and she gave away what she had gathered to the old people, and other gifts and food as well. She would not eat of her own first gatherings lest ill luck follow her. They celebrated various of her first gatherings, at one of which she was given her full size root-digger. Her father had carved it, or hired a noted carver to do so.

Boys celebrated first deer, elk, or bear but not first fish. Step by step, starting around seven or eight, parents taught their offspring that they loved them, food was to be shared, they were of good family and destined for lives full of success.

Called "flute player," this sixteen-inch-high stone statue is one of three that have been found. It has been suggested that it illustrates "The Story About Coyote." This privately held example was dug up near The Dalles.

8

What Coyote Did in This Land

MYTH AGE

ALL THINGS WENT UP THE RIVER. The Chinook moved upriver, the salmon ascended annually, the British sailed up the river, the smelt went up in thick schools. Likewise, Coyote went up the river. He did so every winter, wherever someone recited the many-tale epic of how Coyote made the world inhabitable and grew to maturity, while ascending Big River from the breakers at its mouth to the far shining mountains.

MYTH AGE COYOTE, the creative spirit and transformer of the world, was at the same time a greedy, selfish, lascivious Everyman. He had wonderful powers but he played all manner of tricks, many of them on himself. He would try anything, just to see what would happen. Coyote was dishonest, oversexed, forever ravenously hungry. He invented incest, suicide, and some of the meanest tricks imaginable, often for no apparent reason.

Yet the Chinook took him seriously indeed. Anthropologist Edward Sapir wrote of his informant Menait:

> Coyote he considers as worthy of the highest respect, despite the ridiculous and lascivious side of his character; and

with him he is strongly inclined to identify the Christ of the whites, for both he and Coyote lived many generations ago, and appeared in this world in order to better the lot of mankind.[1]

That lean-flanked one was the most human of the beings before the people came, the one without horn or tusk or claw. He made up the world as he went along. That was the Myth Age, a long while ago. In that world the creatures were still shaped like humans but on account of their predilections they were becoming the totemic animals they would be, developing and receiving their differences. "The people are coming soon," Coyote always reminded them. All this was preparation for the coming of the human beings.

FROM MEXICO to the northern Great Plains, from beyond the Rockies to the Pacific, the people told of Coyote. He had cousins far off too: Steppenwolf and Fox in Europe, Loki in Scandinavia, the spider Ananci in Africa, Monkey in China and India, Maui in Polynesia, Raven north along the coast, Crow in the Great Plains. Trickster is never the largest, strongest, bravest, or wisest of the actors. He is the most complicated, most like man.

Myth is the wrong word. "Myth" has come to mean ancient, romantic, but essentially untrue, stories. The Chinook word, *kani* or *kanum*, meant not just story narrative but nature, custom, and innate character.[2] These exactly recited tales were the scriptures of the Chinook. *Kanum* were their Bible, informing them where life came from and why things were as they were. Just as the language awaited only a grammarian, the holy book needed only a system of writing.

The people believed these stories were passed down exactly, and would criticize the reciter for mistaking a word. There was a lot of interaction, for the audience made a ritual sound—grunted "*Hugh*," or intoned "*Aaaa*," at regular places every few lines—with which they might respond to the tale. The teller shaped the story by his or her interpretation, as a play script is interpreted by the actors. The myths were poetic dramas, in an archaic language, with precise forms.[3] There were acts, scenes, stanzas, verses, and lines, marked by a stylized code of marker words.[4] The Chinook had a great assortment of stories in their repertoire, and new ones came to the village with wives or captives.

Myth people lived in houses but were foolish and incomplete. They lacked many basic skills. There were monsters all around; the world was uninhabitable. Rabbit was fierce and warlike, Skunk's farts killed, Blue Jay killed with his crest, tiny Wren attacked and killed Elk, Grizzly was a psychopath, rivers and mountains ate people. The earth itself ate people.

COYOTE IS THE WILD DOG we know so well now, having watched him spread to distant reaches of North America and far into Central America. Coyotes live near people successfully, while the other animals die out. But those are coyotes, while this is Coyote. Remember the little Frog Girls and do not confuse the animal with the actor. The Chinook word was *italapas* downriver, but far upriver they said *iskolya*, the Sahaptin word. Our word coyote is from *coyotl* in the Nahuatl tongue of Central Mexico.

The Chinook myths described him as lean-flanked, squint-eyed, and bandy-legged. Their neighbors the Klickitat said Coyote had the head of a man past middle age with grizzled hair, a coyote's skinny legs, and thin flanks.[5] He was an important actor all the way to the sea, where the Shoalwater told of him though they seldom saw coyotes. He was never a chief—Eagle or Salmon or Elk was chief —but Coyote was sometimes an older uncle of the chief.[6]

Sudden anger was the worst of his numerous flaws. Too often it affected adversely the destiny of the human beings who would come. Lust, gluttony, and stealing glory from others were Coyote's ways too. He never knew a good thing when he had it.

HIS EXCREMENT SISTERS, who lived in his belly, had most of the insights. He'd bring them out and ask what was going on. There'd be some banter. They called him bandy-legged or squint-eyed. They wouldn't tell him so he spat in his hand and threatened them with rain, which would dissolve them. They said that if they told him he would say that he had been thinking that himself. Then they told him what the taboo was or why something didn't happen when he wanted, and he said, "Indeed, I have been thinking that all along."

> His feces spoke thus to him and told him; always they were two, his younger sisters. And then the two jumped up into him; the one threw him down senseless, the other one jumped up into his belly quietly.[7]

It seems a humorous device to keep the story moving. He called them his Cayuse sisters sometimes, referring to a people far upriver. But perhaps it wasn't so simple-minded. It can be viewed as a graphic symbolization of that instant of insight that we call the intuitive leap, which artists, scientists, and other problem-solvers seek now, as people must always have done. Having pondered some problem night and day without success, we are squatting in another absorption, and the answer appears suddenly inside our head.[8] "I knew that all along," we say, at a new understanding or way of seeing, not a new fact.

PEOPLE TOLD of the mischievous song-dog all over the American West, but the river people may have been the only ones who strung together a coherent epic. This is not the same Coyote as the one who went upriver giving out the taboos. There wasn't just one Coyote, there were many, and some had names. There could even be more than one Coyote in camp at once.

This Coyote went up the Columbia performing larger deeds than rewarding Skunk Cabbage. This Coyote established the proper way to have sex, introduced salmon to the river, and defeated monster after monster. The Chinook and Sahaptin told an epic series of stories about him, many or all set in specific geographical locations. At a crucial point in this journey Coyote made a great discovery, and from that moment he was a mature Coyote, entirely dedicated to the welfare of others. In this growth to maturity, the Columbia River epic may be unique among Coyote stories. It is a ribald and heroic account, probably told with different arrangements of stories at each village. It has been almost entirely lost to the public since, though three versions, as well as a number of fragments, were collected and published by scholars.[9]

Fully told it is as pregnant of interpretation as Odysseus's peregrinations after the Trojan War, which it somewhat resembles. It is about the true nature of a man's life and a river's course, and some of the possibilities of human existence. What follows is mere outline of the Chinook epic, "What Coyote Did in This Land."

COYOTE THOUGHT: "Let me be on my way, going all over the land." Then he got ready, and off he went.

At the mouth of the great river, Atatahlia, a fearsome ogress, was tying people to their cradleboards and sending them drifting out into the raging surf with the command, "Go forever." After a while the board floated back with nothing but bones on it. Human life was not yet possible. On the shore, the people stood dumbly awaiting their fate.

Coyote came up. "I will try that, and soon I will return," he said. She tied him to the board and set him adrift, crying, "Go forever." But the people cried, "Come back again!"

After a while Coyote floated back, alive. Then Atatahlia was tied to the board and sent off, and when the board returned, only her bleached bones were on it. Now the people could grow up and populate the land. The people offered him a girl as wife, but Coyote replied, "No, I do not want a wife. I am to travel up the river."

Coyote came to a woman's house, where she lived with her numerous offspring. Coyote told her the people were dancing and the two of them must practice their dance steps before going to join them. They danced all in a row, the woman in the lead, Coyote at the rear. One after another Coyote wrung the little one's necks. When the woman started to turn, he called out, "Dance it right! You might mix up the children."

She was Myth Pheasant, teaching the little birds their strut. Coyote was wringing their necks. It was the dance of life he had invited her to, where people kill and eat other animals.

Finally one of the little ones managed to squeak, the woman turned, saw, and flew away, her children following. "When will you ever have a house?" Coyote scorned her. "You will be just Pheasant, you will only fly around."

Had he not killed so many, there would have been plenty of savory pheasants for the people.

Two sisters had all the salmon penned up in a lake. Coyote disguised himself as a baby and floated down to them where they were gathering driftwood by the river. "A boy is better than driftwood," the younger one observed, and persuaded the older one to let her take it home. Coyote pretended to sleep, and when they left he ate their food and stole their digging sticks. He broke the dam that penned the fish and the salmon poured out into Big River.

"You said, 'the child is good,'" the older sister said. "I myself thought, 'That is Coyote.' Now this day Coyote has treated us two badly. Now we have become poor."

Coyote said, "Now by what right, perchance, would you two keep the fish to yourselves?" He changed them into swallows, which will herald the returning salmon. "You two are birds and I shall tell you something. Soon now people will come into this land. Listen!" And the people could be heard, "du'lululu," like thunder rumbling afar.

Next he came to the house of another woman, her daughter just at puberty.

"I don't know what to do," the mother told Coyote, "her height remains the same, she doesn't grow."

"Long ago when I was only a young man I knew how to cure that," lean-flanked Coyote said.

He instructed the mother to send her girl down to the river next day, and finding a new thing growing there, to sit and wriggle and ride on it.

Next day he buried himself in the sand, and she rode and squirmed upon the new thing she found growing from the beach, but Coyote soon leaped up, crying "I am a man, and you supposed you would copulate on top of me?" He threw her down and copulated on top of her.

The girl ran crying to her mother complaining of this rape, but her mother, evidently looking at the girl's swelling belly, said "Oh, never mind, that old man caused you to grow."

Coyote encountered mischievous girls who stirred his lust from the far bank of the river, "Come make love with us, Coyote," they cried. He swam across, but now they were on the other bank. "Come make love with us." He swam again, but they had returned to the far shore. He transformed them into birds. Such girls would not make men dizzy with their teasing.

At Sketcutxat, Vancouver, Coyote encountered Wolves asleep around their campfire and pulled their noses and ears out long so people would beware of them. When they awoke they guessed who had done that, for everyone knew that Coyote was going around the land. They in their turn found Coyote asleep and pulled out his ears and nose to make him look like a coyote.

At Rooster Rock Coyote encountered a man with an enormously long penis wrapped around him like a rope. He was feeding it wood chips and bits of bark. Farther along the trail Coyote saw young unmarried girls bathing on the far side of the river. He went back and persuaded the man to trade penises with him. The man resisted. "Why no, I am accustomed to it," he told Coyote, but the squint-eyed one finally made him tired, and they exchanged. Coyote directed it underwater across to where the girls were swimming, and it penetrated the youngest one and held her fast. They cut it off where it entered her, and Coyote went back and exchanged with the man again. Coyote announced that such an enormously long penis would not occur any more, putting to rest certain masculine fears, and instead of feeding a penis wood chips, he directed that men find a woman instead.

 Next Coyote swam across and made himself look like an old man. The girl he had assaulted was sick. Her kin called on Raven to doctor her, but he failed. The villagers encountered Coyote lying there, looking old and wise, and he admitted that long ago he had known how to cure that. He fondled the privates of each of five girls sent to carry him to the village. At the sick girl's house he had the people put up a screen around her and invite the loudest birds to sing. Then he copulated with the girl again. Her screams were drowned out by the squawks and cackles. Flea finally spied him out, but Coyote eluded his pursuers and ran off up the river. The girl complained of this rape, but when her mother learned that the girl felt better she told her not to complain. "That old man did well to you."

*From the top of Skolups, Cape Horn, Coyote saw a man catch-
ing sturgeon by hand. Coyote descended and stole a fish.
When he discovered the theft, the man swung his finger like
a compass needle until it came to rest on Coyote. He came
ashore and Coyote saw that he had no mouth. Coyote cooked
the sturgeon, but the man only smelled the piece he gave him,
then threw it away.*

*Coyote took his flint knife and cut the man's face where he
thought a mouth ought to be, and a gust of bad breath came
out. They ate the sturgeon together and then the man took
him to his village, Nimicxaya near Beacon Rock, where Coyote cut everyone a mouth.*

The people there had large mouths and were big talkers ever after.

*Now Coyote encountered a man carrying wood between his
legs and turning somersaults that landed him on his head to
move along. He showed the fellow how to make a proper pack.
Then, learning that his wife was pregnant and unable to gather wood, he accompanied the man to his house. He found the
woman with a swollen finger, from which they expect a baby
to emerge.*

He had encountered people so primitive they didn't know how to
carry wood or make babies.

He pulled a thorn from her hand and squeezed out pus.

They had evidently heard that after something went in, it swelled
up and a baby came out.

*Coyote showed them the proper way by copulating with the
woman, but this time he demonstrated the act seriously and
declared the baby would be theirs.*

That was at Ninuhltidih, Hood River, where the people were said to
be shamelessly sexy, because Coyote taught them how.

In the next house he visited he asked an old woman for something to eat. She scraped slime and pus from her body and gave him a dish full. Coyote pretended to eat but threw most of it away and hid the rest in his quiver. Farther along he smelled something delicious. He ran about shouting "Wait for me, people, don't eat up all the food, I'm hungry!" After awhile he found that pus was savory sturgeon flesh. He ate it all, even chewing up his quiver and arrows, heedless of the future. Then he went back, disguised, to get some more, but she told him, "I don't know what I can give you. Coyote was here not long ago and I fed him my flesh, but he threw it all away." When Coyote perceived that she knew who he was and was teasing him he cursed her and continued on.

Had that squint-eyed fool been more appreciative, Sturgeon would have given freely of her flesh to the people, but now men must work hard to catch them.

He came to a big hollow tree that opened and closed in the wind. Convinced that it was opening and closing to his command, Coyote climbed inside and took a nap. When he awoke the tree wouldn't open. He shouted for help and a series of woodpeckers came to peck a hole for him to escape. As soon as he could reach through he tried to molest the pretty bird trying to help him. No other bird would come, so Coyote took himself apart. He threw his eyes out first, then all the other parts, but Buzzard nabbed his unguarded eyes. Coyote put himself back together again and substituted rose hips on long stems for eyes. With those he could see just a little bit.

When he groped his way to a house he fooled the woman who lived there into believing he could see a nit crawling on the sky. She couldn't see that. He talked her into trading eyes, and changed her into Snail. She would have weak eyes out on stems and would just crawl around; she would carry her home

Naked Against the Rain

on her back. "You will think you are getting somewhere," he told her, "but it will be the same place."

He envied Skunk his farts. He begged Skunk to trade anuses. "Oh, I am just in a dither about your anus. It is something that is so very nice," Coyote said. Finally he made Skunk tired and they traded. Coyote went off going "pupupupu," enjoying himself immensely. But when he stalked deer the deer heard him and bounded off, so Coyote went back and exchanged anuses again, foretelling Skunk's odorous future.

THE NEXT MYTH, called "The Story Concerning Coyote," is the single most important in the epic. Coyote performed an ignoble act, which the Chinook thought shameful, as do we, but they managed to find it humorous, and to connect it with something profound. By his misbehavior Coyote gained great wisdom and the listener was reminded of an important truth.[10]

It took place across from Mosier, Oregon, on the north side of the river at mile 175, a great geological conjunction where the farthest eastern rampart of the Cascade Mountains rises out of the earth in a great serpentine wall of layer-cake rock.

As he was going along he decided to stop and have a rest. Coyote piled up rocks over himself and swore everything to silence. Then he sucked his own penis.

In some versions he was forced to do this by a feather, which fell on his head, pushing it down.

"You have not done well by me," Coyote reproached the feather or whatever pushed him.

When he was finished he strolled down to the river. A canoe was passing and he hailed the people and asked them, "What is the news?"

"Yes," they told him, "Coyote was coming along and he covered himself with rocks. He sucked himself. That is the news that is traveling about."

Coyote rushed back up to find the rocks he'd covered himself with all shattered. Coyote hurried on, but everywhere he went the people were laughing about the shameless thing he had done.

This time he didn't require his Cayuse sisters.

"To be sure," Coyote announced, "even though it was I myself, the news did come out of there. Now the people are close at hand. Whatever they may do, if they should suppose that other persons will never find out such news, it will come out nevertheless."

Until that realization, Coyote had acted capriciously, sometimes helping and sometimes harming the future inhabitants. Having realized that truth would come out and everything be known, the Myth Age trickster came to maturity. After that classic shock of recognition, everything he did was bent toward the good of mankind. It was a transition worthy of the geological edge of a mountain range. *Idwotca,* "story," they called those rocks across from Mosier.

Now Coyote came to a little river and noticed a waterfall there. He enlarged the waterfall to make it better for netting fish, and created a flat place for the people's drying racks. He made a site to dig camas bulbs nearby. He created a good place to live.

At White Salmon River they were so afraid of the salmon in the stream that no one even dipped up water. He showed them how to dip water and made them fish spears. He taught them all about fishing and cooking and eating salmon. When they offered him wives he did not take them. He would not accept even money beads.

Naked Against the Rain

Next was the roasting pit of another Atatahlia and her husband Owl, where they cooked and ate people. Coyote tricked her into her own pit after convincing her to smear pitch all over her body. The people, who had been waiting to be roasted, held her down with forked sticks. When Owl returned, Coyote threw ashes on him and transformed him into a bird whose mournful hoot would be an omen of death. They offered Coyote a wife, and perhaps he tarried awhile there.

Next he encountered people wearing long poles across their shoulders to keep cracks in the earth from swallowing them. Coyote allowed himself to be swallowed and found himself in the darkness of the earth monster's belly. Around him he heard people groaning. Coyote made a fire and found the people lying about dead and dying. The monster called to him. "Ho, Coyote, I made a mistake about you. Get outside."

"Just how could I go outside?" Coyote said. "You swallowed me." Above he saw the monster's heart. Coyote took his flint knife and cut it off, and the earth-monster's dying convulsions threw all the people out. Coyote announced that the earth would no longer swallow people merely walking about. They offered Coyote two wives and he stayed a little while, but then he thought, "Oh, I have never sought women, I am merely traveling here and there."

He continued on, encountering people who told him a river monster was swallowing anyone who ventured on the water. Coyote went along taunting the water monster, "Swallow me, Itcixyan!" he cried. Finally the river spirit did so. Again, a dark empty place. "People," Coyote said, "build a fire and I'll stay all night." He lighted a fire and found people and canoes lying about. High above beat the monster's heart. Itcixyan realized his mistake and called, "Come out, Coyote, I didn't mean to swallow you." "How can I come out? There is no door."

What Coyote Did in This Land

Coyote built a ladder of canoes and cut the water spirit's heart with his flint knife. He had the people sitting ready in their canoes so when the heart fell free a great breath blew all the people out. Then Coyote announced that once in a while a person would drown, but the river would not kill everyone. They gave him ten wives and he stayed a while, but finally continued on.

He next encountered a monstrous mountain that sucked in birds and people. The mountain and Coyote had a breathing contest. Coyote won by tying himself to another mountain, and the sucking monster's belly burst.

THUS, IN A TRIO OF GREAT CONTESTS Coyote had made earth, water, and air safe for the people.

About there—seemingly associated with Nixluidix—were several outright anti-female stories. In one a female monster seduced men and then pushed them off a cliff. Coyote got on the inside and pushed her off. She had teeth in her vagina, which Coyote wore away with a series of the stone pestles used for salmon packing.[11] The story about *Tsagiglalal*, the woman chief he overthrew and placed on the rocks above to watch, was less virulently sexist, but still about the subjugation of the female.[12]

It must have depended on the village which of these stories were told. Coyote was undeniably sexist, but in their everyday life the Chinook were not so male-dominated as these Coyote stories suggest. It may be that they were related to some recent struggle over gender roles, perhaps related to the epidemics that swept over them.

Coyote next came to Skin, the first Sahaptin-speaking village above the Chinook. He named all those non-Chinook people up there Ilkaimamt and said they did not act right, had foolish ways, and all wanted to be chiefs at once. "It is not right that these people should be so proud," the bandy-legged one said. "I will humiliate them." He climbed up behind Skin and pissed on them, then stepped across the tops of thundering Celilo Falls and instructed the people of Celilo village how to behave.

No doubt the *Ilkaimamt* told that story differently.

FINALLY (in a Nez Perce segment of the epic):

Coyote reached The Sun, and wanted to ride across the sky with her. That was far toward sunrise, in Nez Perce country. He offered to be her slave. He would follow her about and work for nothing. She let him come with her across the sky and he saw everything. He saw how people were behaving: women eloping, things being stolen, people killing people. Coyote shouted "I see what you people are doing."

She let him come with her another day, and again he saw and shouted out. Then The Sun told him, "You are too mean. It would not be good that you should always tell on people. There would be trouble."

It is because of this that we do not find everything out. If Coyote had become The Sun, there would have been no secrets. Then he gave it up. There he stopped. He had arrived at the end.

"This is the Myth of Coyote," Menait concluded his recitation, "Thus-wise did the men of old in ancient times relate the tale. Today there are no longer such men of old."[13]

"*Kani,*
  Kani."

"The Myth,
  The true nature of things."

"Spedis, a Wishram." Photograph by Edward Curtis, courtesy of the University of Washington Library, Special Collections, NA 157.

9

The Chinook Invent a Language

1795

THE SHIPS OF THE FLOATS-ASHORES came more thickly. The schooner *Mexicana* under Juan Martinez y Zayas, a Spanish explorer, came into Big River in the summer of 1793.[1] Captain Adamson skippered the *Jenny* when it returned in 1793, 1794, and 1795. Captain Hugh Moore and his brig *Phoenix* from Bengal were there in 1795. More than forty American ships visited the coast between 1787 and 1807.[2] By 1795 the inquisitive, sharp-eyed Chinook had seen Europeans of the British, Spanish, American, and perhaps Russian tribes, Chinese carpenters and metalworkers, Africans and African-Americans, Filipinos, Hawaiians, other Polynesians, and perhaps Japanese.[3]

The Chinook had been fired upon by three different ships by 1795.[4] Some had been wounded, but none killed. The strangers merely sailed away, without offering blood payment. The Chinook learned to be careful of *tlohonnipts* until they were known for a time, or paid a second visit. Now they could tell the *Bahsten* from *Kin Chautch*. The *Bahsten* were from the village of Boston and others nearby, who called themselves Americans and had Eagle for their spirit. *Kin Chautch* were those who called George their king, and themselves British. A furry-headed Cougar was their spirit power.

So the Chinook quickly realized that the ship *Ruby* was *Kin Chautch*, when it came in over the bar in May 1795 and anchored behind rocky *Kais* (Cape Disappointment). The *Ruby*, 110-tons burden, with a crew of seventeen plus Captain Charles Bishop, was owned by the former slave trader Sydenham Teast of Bristol, England. Bishop was a capable mariner, skilled trader, and man of the world. His detailed account is not unduly colored by racism or the concept *Indian*.[5]

BISHOP FIRED A SUNSET GUN the 22nd of May from outside the river, then sailed in over the bar on Saturday the 23rd. The cannon had its desired effect, for the canoes came from every quarter, with many good furs in evidence. The people in the boats cannot have represented less than three or four villages, and probably included Shoalwater, Clatsop, Kathlamat, and perhaps Atsmitl, assembled for the spring fishing. All day the shipmen showed their wares: tea kettles, sheet copper, fine clothes and cloth, strings of beads, and other trade goods so much desired. They managed not a single trade.

The next day even more people came out in canoes. This time the flatheads demanded outrageous prices. The *Kin Chautch* bargained with all their might, but the price hardly wavered. Bishop, however, had decided to stay ten days, so he let the Chinook depart without buying a single fur. His discipline was noteworthy, but theirs was astonishing. They were of several villages and numerous rival families, dominated by no central authority. European traders would almost certainly have broken ranks.

Monday morning the Chinook paddled out and commenced selling. They knew exactly what Bishop would give, and he was gratified that their prices weren't too steep. They bought and sold for ten days, during which he took in 111 sea otter—the price in Canton having dropped, those were probably only worth a quarter of a million present-day dollars—plus fox, marten, lynx, beaver, deer, and elk skins. Bishop decided he might be back, so he sent a ship's boat out to a small island off shore and had his sailors plant potatoes, corn, beans, radishes, mustard, cress, celery, cabbage, and turnips.

BISHOP BECAME ACQUAINTED with some of the village nobles with whom he traded. He identified Taucum, a village headman, and his friend Chinini. Shelathwell and Comcomly were first and second headmen of another village. Bishop found Comcomly an endearing man, and they struck up a friendship. Taucum was evidently the premier headman of the village closest to the ship at that time, described as being on the Chinook River. Bishop was apparently unfamiliar with the name Columbia. Perhaps it was Wallakut village.

After ten days, the traders told Bishop frankly that they had sold him all the skins they had, but they would get more. They urged him to stay, but the *Ruby* lifted anchor June 5th, and on its second try made it safely to sea.

Bishop returned in mid-October to the best weather he'd seen on the coast, but braced against the rains and gales he'd heard were coming should he winter over. The Shoalwater Chinook came out to greet the ship with gifts of cranberries and smoke-dried salmon. Not for nothing did the Wasco call them *Idaqwim*, "They'll Give You Food." On the island, the potatoes were abundant and large, the radishes had gone to seed, and the other things had been eaten by birds.

Taucum had retired to his Shoalwater Bay winter house. He soon returned, with several of the village nobles, and trade resumed. Bishop was pleased to find that flogging a sailor who stole an arrow had a good effect on the Chinook, who stopped stealing small objects left lying around. He'd learned that they liked a gift now and then, and would return it with fish or berries. "Nor do they withhold their daughters," he noted, "some of whom are well featured young women."[6]

The Chinook identified the *Ruby*'s first mate as the father of a child by one of their women slaves. Williams, the mate, had been to the river with the *Jenny* in 1792. They would not bring the baby on board, for fear he would claim it.

TELEMMECKS PAID the bride price for Shelathwell's eldest daughter while Bishop was there. She was "one of the handsomest young women I have seen amongst them," Bishop wrote, and Telemmecks paid twenty slaves, twenty sea otter skins, a canoe, and twenty elk-skin battle dresses. Shelathwell's next daughter, Sitelmayoe, also beautiful, was also of marriageable age. Bishop asked the girl what her father would ask for her to accompany him on the ship, and was told to ask her father. Bishop did, and was told fifty sheets of copper and twenty fathoms of cloth and that first mate Williams stay with Shelathwell as pledge for her safety.[7]

Shelathwell and Comcomly built a house near where the ship was anchored, several miles from their home village, Qwatsamts.

> They are both very good friends to us, but the latter who is
> a little one-eyed man, has endeared himself to everyone on
> board. He often sleeps in my cabin and gives me many
> proofs of his disinterested kindness.[8]

In that passage, Comcomly at last comes into view. When and how he lost his eye will be discussed later. Bishop had a jacket and trousers made for Comcomly, to the Chinook noble's great delight. It may have been the first such suit of European clothes he got, but it was far from the last. Later, Comcomly visited the ship with a wife and little boy. That was probably his Scapoose wife Keasno and his oldest son, Quasquas, who might have been five. Comcomly was around twenty-five.

Bishop detected rivalry between Taucum and the other two. He thought they were all one tribe, and Taucum's village being closest

Naked Against the Rain

he seemed the head chief. Shelathwell and Comcomly came to visit or trade only when Taucum was absent.

Comcomly told Bishop a yarn about going up the river two or three hundred miles until they came to a strange village, where they landed and offered to trade trifling pieces of copper and iron for pelts. The villagers asked more. At their leader's signal the Chinooks all fired their muskets into the air. The villagers "never having heard or seen such a strange phenomena, threw off their skins and leather war dresses and flew into the woods." The Chinooks took the skins and leather war dresses and left the articles first offered. "For the quantity of goods we pay for one of these dresses they get sometimes twenty," Bishop admired, "but we suppose this mode cannot last long, as they will naturally be aware of a second visit of the kind."[9]

A YOUNG QUINAULT named Bocquoinue had come down accompanied by two slaves to marry a Chinook girl. He offered to sell two elkskin-armor battle dresses, which Bishop had realized were valuable trade items elsewhere along the coast. Bocquoinue told a story of some Englishmen being killed and eaten farther north, an incident that had occurred a few years before. Bishop, believing that Bocquoinue was one of the cannibals, had him seized and put in irons. Immediately all the wives of Comcomly and Shelathwell came running and tearfully clamored that it had happened a long time ago and the prisoner was just a little chief from somewhere else entirely, too young in any case, and he had come down to marry one of Shelathwell's daughters, so Bishop must free him! Which Bishop did, though he made Bocquoinue promise to return when the two chiefs got back from a trading expedition they'd undertaken. Bishop kept the two elkskin armors as bail.[10]

The captain visited the house of the absent Comcomly and Shelathwell, who had gone off on a trading expedition in one canoe with ten paddlers. Shelathwell's wife gave him a basket hat. The women told him the bad weather had been caused by his men. When the new moon had first become visible, the sailors had pointed at it, whereupon the Chinooks caught hold of their hands, saying it was *peshak*, bad; that they should offend the moon by pointing. This offense, they now told him, had been punished by the bad weather. The captain understood *peshak*, having heard it at Nootka Sound.[11]

WHEN BISHOP recorded that incident he provided a first toehold into a knotty question of Chinook history, a problem much argued since. Peshak was a Nootka word, and here were Chinook matrons speaking it, 350 miles to the south, only three years after first contact. They were using it not for some object made or sold by the Nootka, but for a concept as universal as "bad."

They were not, in all likelihood, speaking Chinook to Bishop at all. They were speaking a language simplified for trade purposes which, when fully developed, would contain words borrowed from more than a dozen languages. It came to be called the Chinook Jargon, Chinook Wawa, or the Oregon Trade Language.[12] The Clackamas called it *Chinugumt*, so that is probably something like its Chinook name.[13]

Trade languages have developed elsewhere. The Pidgin English of the South Pacific combines Polynesian, Chinese, and English. The Mobilian Trade Language of the Southeastern United States long predated the Europeans but died out soon after their arrival. A simplified Malaysian market language was adopted by Indonesia as a national language to unify numerous diverse islands after the Second World War, and a written literature has blossomed since.

The core of the Jargon consisted of Chinook words shorn of prefixes and suffixes, simplified to a very few verbs, with no tenses whatsoever. The scheme of the language was to name the object and then tell what to do with it: eat it, work with it, buy it. Adjectives modified this simplicity into an exceedingly versatile instrument. Fluency in Chinook Jargon required only about 250 words, none of which ever changed its sound.

THERE HAS BEEN CONSIDERABLE ARGUMENT about whether the Jargon predated the arrival of the Europeans.[14] Some have argued that only the Caucasians could have created a trade language. It was even suggested that the Hudson's Bay Company made it up. Since many of its nouns and all of its pronouns, numbers, adverbs, and prepositions were from Chinook, it can hardly have been a European invention. Europeans almost never learned Chinook. Philologist Horatio Hale noted:

> Notwithstanding the close intercourse which has been maintained with the Indians by traders and settlers for more than thirty years, only one instance is known of a white man having learned to speak the language with fluency. This man was a Canadian, who went to the country with Mr. Astor's first expedition, and has remained there ever since. In the course of a long illness, during which he was nursed by the natives, he chose to occupy himself in acquiring a knowledge of their tongue, and by so doing obtained no little celebrity among both foreigners and Indians.[15]

On the other hand, those who believe the Jargon included Nootka words before the arrival of the Europeans may be in error as well. They base the idea on a supposed brisk trade in slaves and *haiqua* between the Chinook and the Nootka on Vancouver Island. There is no evidence that such a direct trade existed, though individual parties seem to have traveled that distance occasionally. Most trade moved in shorter jumps. Further, no Chinook words were heard spoken in Nootka at first. The Jargon's range didn't stretch so far yet.

The trading ships brought in two dozen trade words from the Nootka language, which they had learned on Vancouver Island. Those words the Chinook quickly added to their already growing vocabulary of simplified Chinook and borrowed words, with which the coast Chinook tried to communicate with people who didn't speak their language. That would include Kathlamat, Multnomah, and Shahala Chinook, Quinault, Chehalis, Willapa, Tillamook, Clatskanie, Cowlitz, Tualatin, Kalapuya, and Molala. No other Nootka words were added after the original two dozen, but as the fur trade continued, many English words, and when the Canadians arrived, French words, entered the language too. Curiously, no Spanish words did.

IT WAS ALWAYS A DISH of local flavor, vocabulary and pronunciation differing from place to place and according to the native language of the speaker. Harsh gutturals were dropped by the coast people, French lost its nasal sound, English consonants were modified. "R" became "l," and the English "j" sound became "ch."

There wasn't just one word for an idea. Father might be said *papa* from the French, *oleman* (old man) from English, or *tillicum mama* (father person) from Chinook. Hale compared that with English, where we may say *dad*, from ancient British or Welsh; *father*, from Saxon; or *papa*, from French. Water was *chuck* from Nootka or *wata* from English. Fire was *olapitski* from Chinook or *paia* from English. One word might be popular one place, unused another. Over the years words superseded each other. *Tillicum mama* confused Europeans and disappeared. Along the Columbia, even *mamook*, "to do, make, or work," a major workhorse verb of the language, became obscene after a while, and was hardly used any more.

Mamook is a good example. By combining *mamook* with a noun, a verb-like idea was expressed. Prepare food was eat-make, ruin or spoil was bad-make. Fix was good-make. Go away was go-make. Teach was know-make. Delay was tomorrow-make. There would come to be literally hundreds of such combinations.

Meaning was created by stringing words together rather than changing them. This made the language easy to learn, for the sound of a word remained constant. Plural was shown by adding *hiyu*, many or much. A word took meaning from the words it was combined with. *Cole illahee*, cold country, meant winter. *Cole snass*, cold rain, meant snow. Many house meant a town, little man meant a boy. A word was what the speaker made it, verb, noun, adjective, or adverb depending on its use. The Jargon allowed great expressiveness with a minimum investment of memory.

The clustering of words into an idea had a surprisingly regular order, thought to resemble Kalapuya most, though Kalapuya contributed fewer than ten words.[16] Word order, on the other hand, was any order the speaker's native language would use, and rearranged sentences could still be understood.

There was not a hint of tense or mood. *Ahnkuttie* meant past, *alta* present, and *alki* future. Comparisons were expressed by stringing words. *Klosh* meant good, *elip klosh* meant better and *delate elip klosh* meant best. Adding *ahnkuttie* meant it used to be best. The opposite was *kimtah klosh*, not very good, and *delate kimtah klosh*, very worst. A remarkable number of ideas could be expressed. Examples of Jargon words borrowed from English include *shipman*, a sailor; *shipstick*, a mast; *slipstick*, a spar; *stickskin*, the bark of a tree; and *stickstone*, petrified wood.

How the Jargon was spoken told a lot too. Hale noted:

We frequently had occasion to observe the sudden change produced when a party of natives, who had been conversing in their own tongue, were joined by a foreigner, with whom it was necessary to speak in the Jargon. The coun-

tenances which had before been grave, stolid, and inex-
pressive, were instantly lighted up with animation; the low
monotonous tone became lively and modulated; every feature was active; the head, the arms, the whole body were in
motion, and every look and gesture became instinct with
meaning. One who knew merely the subject of the dis-
course might often have comprehended, from this source
alone, the general purport of the conversation.[17]

THE WORDS SPOKEN to Captain Bishop in 1795 at the mouth of the
Columbia were probably not the fully developed Jargon, but it
would become the language of trade all along the Northwest coast,
and was clearly based upon Chinook. It seems likely to have predated the coming of the fur traders.

It was the language Taucum spoke, when he brought Chinini to
visit and trade. Chinini had recently recovered from the mental distress that sometimes ambushed the river people, perhaps a Chinook
psychosis.[18] A person became melancholy and took to his bed,
pressing his forehead to the wall, like the cradleboard of old. He
ceased eating or talking. Chinini was afflicted for two months, during which he gave away all his wives, houses, canoes, skins, bows
and arrows, everything he possessed. Bishop was impressed that
those he had given them to returned them when he regained his
mental health.

Captain Bishop heard a good yarn about a war they claimed to
have made:

About six years ago the Chinook tribe united, and went with
100 large war canoes and nearly 100 smaller ones twenty
days travel up that river when they came to some great water
fall, up which they dragged their canoes into a lake, over
which they paddled ten days more and in the night came

unawares on a large tribe inhabiting the farther shore of this lake, the men were totally destroyed and the women and children made slaves and brought to Chinook in triumph.[19]

Trying to figure how far they were talking about, Bishop estimated correctly that they paddled about thirty miles a day upriver. He couldn't know to divide the distance by five. Five was the Chinook ritual number, the number of repetition it took to make a ceremony work, and therefore the one they were most likely to use in exaggerations. Eliminating the exaggeration gives four or five days to the Cascades, the portage, and two days farther up the Wahlala's "lake" at the head of the Cascades to the Tlakluit at the far end.[20] That is an accurate count, if Wishram was the objective. The largest Chinook battle fleet anyone ever counted numbered thirty-nine, so dividing the flotilla by five would probably be right too. This was one of several stories various persons heard of hostility between the Chinook of the coast and those of Wishram, all exaggerated in the storyteller's way.

Bishop recalled the Chinook girls as "fond of rings of brass round their wrists and fingers." The daughters of the wealthy nobles wore many copper ornaments and beads about their necks. "The women are very modest and reserved in their manners, and are kept in great subjection by the men, who sometimes beat them unmercifully, and are considered as much their property as their canoe."[21]

During three months Bishop bought about seven hundred large sea otter skins, worth over three million 1990s dollars. He also bought three kinds of fox, beaver, marten, and river otter, and whitened and doubled elkskin armor, which formed "a complete defense against spear or arrow, and was almost sufficient to resist a pistol ball."[22] He bought *wapato*, savory bulbs the size of pigeon eggs, unobtainable elsewhere on the Northwest Coast.

Bishop found the Chinook polite and considerate. When he was away from the ship they did not visit; he thought because they didn't want to cause alarm. He wrote that he never entered a house but he was fed, and his hosts were disappointed if he didn't eat heartily. They fed even the ship's dogs, and rendered every assistance and amusement to his people on shore and thus everyone had a good three months and were mutually pleased.

IN MID-JANUARY Comcomly was wrestling with one of the officers when the man hit him in the mouth. Comcomly complained of the offense to Captain Bishop, who laughed it off, saying that it was the English manner of play, and where nothing ill was meant, nothing ill was taken. The little one-eyed man left in apparent good humor, but when his wives came the next day to say that he was ill, and ask Bishop to come visit him, the captain declined to go, citing workload. "Comcomly had always discovered a very fickle disposition," Bishop recalled, "and I do not know what ill might have been intended had I gone."[23]

That evening, a musket ball whizzed over the ship. Alarmed, Bishop made ready and next day hauled out into the bay, to a more exposed anchorage beyond musket range. The day after, Comcomly came aboard. He admitted firing the ball, "at ducks," and did not intend it near the ship but it was very dark. They exchanged gifts. Bishop declared his intention to leave the river. The Chinook could not dissuade him. He had been planning to leave around January 20th from the beginning. Comcomly and Shelathwell went upriver for gifts.

Shelathwell brought three bushels of *wapato* as a parting gift. The ship's doctor had cured him of an ailment, and had once lent him an excellent greatcoat on his promise that he would return it within four days, which he did. Comcomly brought "fifteen woodcocks and several dishes of salmon trout." When Bishop asked about Bocquoinue, the Chinook told what sounds like another yarn, explaining that the poor fellow had been blown to pieces by gunpowder, set out to dry by the fire. Bishop paid Shelathwell for the two elkskin armors.

The Chinook crowded around, giving him gifts of fish and wapato, and followed the *Ruby* out over the bar, through waves halfway up its mast. It took fifteen minutes, in awful surf, and then they were at sea, headed for Hawaii. Bishop planted another garden before he left, but never returned to harvest it.

THE TRADING YEAR began in April and generally lasted through October, when the ships sailed off for the Sandwich Islands, to winter in tropical delight. In 1805 the Clatsop could name ten captains they thought might return within the year.[24]

The traders brought old muskets, powder, ball and shot, copper and brass kettles and pots, blankets, blue and scarlet cloth, plates, strips and sheets of copper and brass, wires, knives, beads, tobacco, fishhooks, buttons, coats, hats, trousers, and shirts.

The Chinook offered furs, elkskins, fish, berries and vegetables, baskets, hats, mats, and the favors of their young women. Syphilis and gonorrhea had come to them by then, but they did not crave alcohol.

When the Europeans learned that people would trade for dentalium shells and slaves, they bought and sold those. Some enslaved people directly. The Chinook recalled a *Bahsten* captain named Ayers who took a dozen Chinook men southward to slavery. Seven escaped in a ship's boat, and some were ransomed by the Tillamook, but only one ever reached home.[25]

Around 1801 smallpox again smote the people of the river, probably coming down the Columbia from the Plateau and beyond. Several hundred Clatsop died, four noble headmen among them. Four years later, the explorers Lewis and Clark saw whole deserted villages along the river and coast, legacy of that epidemic, and also at least one survivor of the epidemic of 1781-1782.[26]

Handle embellishment of a bone club found in the vicinity of The Dalles. Private collection.

10

A Tyrant Is Overthrown

TIAPEXWASXWAS WAS TEN FEET TALL *and his feet were three feet long. He could walk on water. His five-fireplace house was nicely fixed, with fish and animals carved on every side. He had a hundred wives, fifty on each side of the house. His hundred slaves lived in another house.*

Tiapexwasxwas never walked. His slaves carried him. Whenever he heard of a nice girl, he went and purchased her. When he did so, the return gift for the bride-price was invariably made in the blood of animals. No matter how much the bride's people gave him, he drank it all up. If they didn't give him enough they feared he might eat their daughter.

When a wife of his gave birth, he asked them, "What did she bear?" When they told him a male, he would say to his slaves, "Kill it!" The slaves would kill it. But if they said female, he told them "Take good care of the baby."

He heard them tell of a girl: "Oh goodness, a fine girl!" they said. "Her hair is right to the ground, it is yellow-brown." He told his slaves, "Take me tomorrow. I am going to buy her."

On the following day they laid him upon his canoe, and paddled him to her village. The villagers heard the news. "They are bringing Tiapexwasxwas to buy the girl." The next day he arrived and gave them her bride price. Her villagers said, "Where shall we find something that has lots of blood? That is the only thing they give as a return present to him. Blood."

So they sought everywhere, and finally, near the sea, they found a monster. They hit it, they burned it, they drained it through many holes and caught the blood in containers. They filled every container they had. "Oh never mind," they said of the rest.

He drank it. He drank up one container. He set it beside himself and drank another. He looked, and there was still much blood. He drank another. He thought, "I shall drink it all up."

No! He could not drink it up! He lay down. "Huu!" he said, "I am full now. Redhair has filled me up!" That was the way he called his wife from then on.

Another of his wives, Nadaiet, a Wasco, gave birth. The slaves and the wives had conspired together. "If it is a male, do not inform him. We shall say to him, 'A female.'" So then she gave birth, and he asked, "What is it?" "A female." "Very well." But she had borne a male child.

After five days Nadaiet bathed. She told her husband, "I am going home to visit. The baby will be bigger before I return." He gave his permission, and she returned home. She remained there.

Now she bathed him and her son got big. His feet were very long, like his father. She told him the story. "I came to hide you from your father. If they had informed him that you were a male, he would have killed you."

"Indeed!" said the son of Tiapexwasxwas.

The youth sought guardian spirits in the mountains. He returned after five nights of fasting. "Mother, the five Thunders and Lightnings have given me their strength."

"That is not enough," she told him.

He went again, and returned after five days. "I have the strength of five bands of Grizzly Bears."

"That is not enough."

A third time, and this time when he returned he had the spirits of five bands of Elk, but it was not enough.

Now she told him, "Do not seek power any longer on the mountains, but seek it by the water." He went to the water and got the power of five Whirlpools.

"That is not enough."

He went for the fifth time. He returned, he told her, "I have the power of five long-legged Water-Spiders. I have the power of five bands of Yellow Flies Running On The Water."

"That is enough," his mother told him.

Each evening Tiapexwasxwas had his slaves spread sand around his house and smooth it flat. In the morning he would say, "Look for footprints in the sand."

He would say to Redhair, "Now loosen your braids. Walk about for me to see you, Redhair." She would loose her hair and walk about before him.

"Oh!" said Tiapexwasxwas. Then he would say to his slaves, "Now then, take me yonder." They would carry him to the next in his nightly rotation of his wives. They would lay him down beside her.

His son thought, "Supposing I go see him?"

He came to his father's house and asked a slave, "Where will he be sleeping tonight?"

"Tonight he will sleep at Redhair's platform."

The son stayed there, and the next evening he went to where Redhair lay, and he lay beside her. She wondered that her husband had returned, but she accepted him. The youth arose next morning, and in the evening he came to her again.

"How long before he will get to you?" he said to Redhair.

"Dear, Oh dear, he was here shortly ago. It will not be until he has gone clear around his wives before he gets back to me."

After that he came to her each night, and in the morning went away. After a while he said to one of the slaves, "Show him my tracks tomorrow."

The slave informed Tiapexwasxwas. "Take me," he said, "I shall go see them." He put his foot in the footprint. It was somewhat larger than his own.

Then Tiapexwasxwas took to his bed and lay there for two days. Finally he rose. "Oh, I think that woman carried away a male child," he said.

He sent five slaves up the river. "Go see what she took when she went away long ago. The slaves reached the son's village. The son said to them, "Do not go back home. Remain here."

When they did not return the headman sent another five slaves. "You go too! Go see where they went to and did not return from." They went to his village, where they saw the other five. The son said to them, "Remain right here! Do not go back home!"

A third time the headman sent five slaves. This time the son said to one of them, "You go back. He will question you. Tell him that I have kept all the slaves."

Tiapexwasxwas questioned the returned slave. "Your son himself kept them at that place," the slave informed him.

"Really. That is just what I was thinking."

He said to his people, "We shall go tomorrow. We shall fight." They carried him to the shore, they laid him in his canoe. A flotilla of fifty canoes went up the river. "Now Tiapexwasxwas is on his way here," the people at the son's village said.

"Give me back the slaves," Tiapexwasxwas called out.

"Your son said no. He will not give them to you."

Then they warred. Tiapexwasxwas' people fled. Some went over to the son's side. Others did nothing. His son shot a canoe, and it burst. He shot another canoe and it too burst. The water was full of Tiapexwasxwas' people.

The father and son walked out on the water and fought hand to hand. As the old man's strength began to fail, he sank into the water. It would not hold him up any longer.

"Sure enough, you are my son!" said Tiapexwasxwas. "Now you may take everything; my name and all. I will not be like that any more now."

So then his son became Tiapexwasxwas the headman, and the old man had no such wives and no such slaves any more. He just walked about. Tiapexwasxwas the son took Redhair for his wife. He said to the other wives, "If you choose you may go back." Some of the women went back to his father.

After a while Redhair gave birth to two sons. By then the grandfather was old and infirm. He made toy arrows for his grandsons, and they played. The boys shot their grandfather, and after some time he became dead. And Tiapexwasxwas had many sons.[1]

THE LEGEND OF THE BLOODTHIRSTY TYRANT and his overthrow was told by the Chinook all up and down the river. Some said he had lived only a few generations before, and that his village was at Willamette Falls. Nadaiet, the mother of his son, was a Wasco, and Redhair may have been Kathlamet, Clatsop, or Shoalwater, for the monster they drained of blood sounds big as a whale. The name Tiapexwasxwas sounds like "Big-foot crane," or more likely heron, though no one translated it. The great blue heron, tall, raucous, wading birds with six-foot wingspans, are year-around residents along the Columbia, their wide triangular footprints on every beach, while cranes are seasonal visitors to a limited number of locations. In the United States in the nineteenth century, crane was the word used to describe what we now call the great blue heron.[2]

The story is called a legend because it told of what happened after the Myth Age, when the people had arrived and all the animals had taken their forms. The Chinook word for legend meant "to recall an account of."[3] Still, it is a well-worked story, a classic Oedipus myth of the overthrow of the father by his son, their big feet possibly symbolizing sexual potency. Did his thirst for blood represent the social and economic cost of such a tyrant?[4]

THE REALITY of Chinook political life was considerably different.[5] The nobles ran things. The nobles were the best people, with wide family connections, knowledge, skills, accumulated wealth, and inherited privileges. Inheritance was through both mother and father, but there were no family totems or powers to be inherited, only wealth, position, and rights to fishing and gathering sites.

Wealth was important, but the series of ceremonial announcements of childhood was more significant. With those ceremonies, the child of even a commoner grown wealthy could rise socially. The Chinook differentiated nobles from merely rich people, and rich from newly rich. There were people of good family who were neither rich nor noble, and wealthy persons with few noble connections, as well as nobles with little wealth.

Commoners were the dregs of Chinook society. They knew nothing, owned nothing, inherited no fishing sites, and had no wealth, trade, luck, or family help. Into that class sank bastards, outcasts, and orphans. They probably represented no more than ten percent of the population. Among them were the once-slaves, part-slaves, and half-slaves. No slave ancestor could be forgotten. And finally, the slaves themselves, who might number ten to twenty-five percent of the village.[6]

The nobles were few. The people between were most of the population, the "good" people, among whom there were people wealthier than the poorest nobles. Yet, in theory, any lousy boy with scabs and sores might rise, encounter a powerful spirit, make a fortunate trade, or, if the myths were true, miraculously impregnate a headman's daughter, and become so wealthy his sores would be seen to drip money beads.

The path was not usually so open. Like privileged people everywhere, the nobles kept their inferiors down, segregated their children from those of the commoners, and sometimes made the lower class people move off a little way to live in a separate village. Commoners were the ones who starved during hard winters. The headman had the right to seize whatever he wished from them, though he was supposed to make compensation. Some nobles had the right of seizure as well, but such seizures are said to have occurred only from misers who would not share food.

The Chinook ranked people not only by wealth and ancestry, but by how far upriver they lived. A Clatsop was thought better than a Kathlamet, who was socially more desirable than a Clackamas. The Tlakluit wanted to marry their daughters downriver among the Shahala or Multnomah. At the river's mouth, the direction of desirability turned sharply northward. A Shoalwater Chinook hoped to marry his daughter to a Chehalis, a Quinault, or even a Makah. Comcomly's Chehalis wife Qwayaq was more highly ranked than his Scapoose first wife Kiasno for that reason, though he is said to have liked his first wife better.[7]

CONTRARY TO THE LEGEND OF TIAPEXWASXWAS, the village headman, whom the *tlohonnipts* entitled chief, was not a true commander. Though the people might listen to his counsel, he had little outright power. He was expected to be strong, wise, gentle, courageous, loyal, resolute, generous, and responsible for the welfare of his people, but had only custom and persuasion to secure his will.

The position was hereditary. Usually his eldest son would succeed him, though another son or a relative might be chosen. The passing of power to his son by a living father, as in the Tiapexwasx-was legend, was regular. Lewis and Clark remarked on the young headmen, their fathers still alive.[8] Should the eldest son be a fool, or otherwise unacceptable, the other nobles would simply consult the youth's brother, or the former headman's brother. Or even another family. Selection was by consensus, not vote. Consensus was the rule in all such decisions. Protestant missionary Samuel Parker extolled Chinook politics:

> The chiefs have no power of levying taxes, and they are so much in the habit of contributing their own property for individual or public good that they are not generally wealthy. Their influence, however, is great; for they rarely express an opinion or desire which is not readily assented to and followed. Any unreasonable dissent is subdued by the common voice of the people. Probably there is no government upon earth where there is so much personal freedom and at the same time so little anarchy; so much subordination, peace, and friendship among the Indians.[9]

Ethnologist George Gibbs, an early and sympathetic visitor, called them "perfectly democratic, because in the absence of government or authority it cannot be otherwise."[10] This is anarchy in its classic form, a utopian absence of a ruler or of government, though the word has since mutated to mean disorder and the violent overthrow of governments.

A village headman needed wealth, political skills, and personal force. He dealt with strangers: exchanged gifts, offered food or lodging, and spoke with them. This gave him opportunities for profitable trade, but in lean times he was expected to feed his village. He judged cases of blood payment, which might include an occasional death penalty. That would have strained the network of family ties that governed the village. Persuasion was more respected than force, and mediation was a highly valued skill. A successful headman might be called upon to mediate between other villages.

Councils of village elders and nobles occurred, and older women attended. Downriver, such meetings were informal and unimportant, but upriver, they were held at night, with guards sometimes posted so no information could be carried out to a defendant, or to an enemy.[11] Again, consensus was the goal.

The headman was responsible for the actions of the young men of his village. He would make blood payment for a poor villager, either out of his own stores or by collecting from among the people. If the accused were a mere commoner, he might not intervene. When a whale washed ashore, the Shoalwater or Clatsop awaited the headman's arrival to divide the carcass fairly. When an elk hunter returned he took the meat to his headman, who gave him the hide and a share, then distributed the rest.

IN ADDITION TO THE HEADMAN, such shamans as the village possessed and the war chief, if there was one, had political power. Probably the village spokesmen had power as well.

The war chief was selected by the headman either for a single battle or a longer period. The headman did not go to war. He would have been too tempting a target. The war chief had powers that protected him from pain or death. He showed his power by inflicting hideous wounds on himself, which swiftly healed. This made him fearless. A sorcerer too could inflict pain or death, and so a wise headman took care not to offend a shaman.

The orator, or spokesman, was of upperclass birth, skilled in speaking, and knowledgeable in the special forms involved. Gibbs called some of them effective orators, "though in general their eloquence is of a very noisy and vociferous kind."[12] Orators assisted shamans in their ceremonials and the headman in formal speeches. They served as town criers, harangued the people, interpreted between groups, and spoke at important feasts. A spokesman was necessary when a headman spoke to commoners, whom he would not address directly. Women were also served by spokesmen.

The noble spoke in a normal voice; the spokesman repeated it loudly, in the appropriate language for the occasion, which might feature unusual words, traditional phrases, special intonations, and vocal qualifiers, and was sometimes in the ancient form of Chinook in which they recited the myths.[13] Would the spokesmen not have become their lawyers, in time?

In general, the Chinook society was individualistic but conservative, anarchistic in its lack of controls so anyone could always disagree and paddle away with his house planks, yet class-conscious and traditional enough so people upheld a hereditary leader. They criticized the *Ilkaimamt* upriver, among whom every man wanted to be chief at once.[14] (Though George Simpson commented that "every flathead who owns a slave considers himself a chief."[15])

COMCOMLY WAS NEITHER TYRANT nor distant patrician. According to fur trader David Thompson, he always addressed his people from a squatting position.[16] As the ships and years passed, his skills were honed and his power increased. His family also grew. He probably married Kiasno in the late 1780s when he was under twenty. She bore him Qwasqwas, later Chenamus, who visited Captain Bishop as a little boy. She next bore him Illchee, "Moon Girl," around 1797. Both children were fated to lives almost as interesting as their father.

Qwayaq, Comcomly's Chehalis wife, bore him Quatqos, later called Shalapau, his second son, much loved by the father. She also bore a daughter, Kahatlau. It is unclear who bore Raven, his second oldest daughter, but it must have been some time around 1808. He had a Shoalwater wife, who bore a daughter named Timmie, "Maiden," and a Willapa wife, who bore a daughter named Elowaka. Another daughter, Chowa, was mentioned, her mother unknown. His family was growing, as was his wealth.[17]

Carved bone figurine, probably Chinook, found in the vicinity of The Dalles. Courtesy of the Columbia Gorge Interpretive Center, Emory Strong Collection, Stevenson, Washington.

11

Clothmen Pass
1805 – 1806

THE TLAKLUIT seemed unsurprised when a party of about thirty mostly Euro-American males, one woman, and her infant, arrived from upriver late one October. They were led by two chiefs, wore cloth and buckskin, and paddled dugouts of the rudest sort. The Chinook showed sophistication in their dealings with these foreigners, whom they called *passissiuks*, "clothmen," later simplified to *passiuks* in the Jargon. The traders of Nixluidix greeted them like distant Sahaptin come to trade, rather than as potential enemies. The Wishram sauntered out to meet the strangers unarmed, in small groups and even singly. No instance better illustrates how unhindered by boundaries or fear of strangers the Chinook had become.[1]

The Wishram are rumored to have already seen French-Canadian trappers, come down from the mountains to trade during the great summer gatherings.[2] They had heard of the *tlohonnipts* who visited the people of Sealand, indeed used a variation of the word— *duxnipck*—themselves.[3] They realized that these cloth-clad braves were the same, and paraded their muskets, teapots, pans, and European clothing before the strangers, who were an exploratory expedition sent out by President Thomas Jefferson of the United States of America, a European-style nation-state which had established itself on the other shore of North America.

THE PAIR-NESS OF THE PARTY'S LEADERS was easy for the Chinook to understand. We-two, you-two, and they-two were as regular as me, you, or they in Chinook pronouns.

At the head of the Long Narrows, captains Meriwether Lewis and William Clark, leaders of the expedition, noted the first wooden houses they'd seen in two thousand miles, both occupied ones at Nixluidix and abandoned ones at Wakemap, and the next day saw their first coast-quality canoe.[4] Likewise, they noted that the language changed completely, as did the stature and looks of the people, their clothing, and their life-style.

Fishing was over for the year and *itkilak* stood piled in pyramidal mounds of thirteen baskets each on the black lava-rock pavement. Clark counted 107 baskets, and estimated ten thousand pounds of dried-and-pounded salmon. The Wishram storehouses were overflowing. The Tlakluit bargained hard for food or firewood, as was their custom, then invited the soldiers into their homes and offered appropriate hospitality.

"They call us *pah-shish'e-ooks* or cloth men," Clark wrote their approximation of the Kiksht word. One of the soldiers had a fiddle, the music of which delighted the Tlakluit. The people stayed late in the soldiers' camp, listening to this new thing and watching the soldiers dance. The next day, the clothmen carried their goods across the portage, and ran their five boats through the Long Narrows empty, narrowly avoiding disaster. They stopped for two days below the rapids on the Wasco side, as the word spread downriver that floats-ashores were coming.

The strangers purchased dogs and sometimes horses at every village they could, and butchered them on the beach before onlookers. Lewis later several times confessed in his journal,

> The dog now constitutes a considerable part of our subsistence, and with most of the party has become a favorite food. I prefer it to lean venison or elk, and it is far superior to horse in any state.[5]

At the Cascades of the Columbia the dog-eaters portaged their boats and baggage both, among Chinooks doing the same with *it-kilak* and other trade goods. The clothmen investigated the charnal houses of the dead. Below the rapids, they detected the effect of the ocean tides immediately, and hurried seaward.

THEY HAD ENTERED THE RAIN near Wind Mountain, river mile 150 just above the Cascades, and from then until their return up-river they seldom saw blue sky. During their journey to the sea they bought many dogs and visited or noted numerous Chinook villages. Canoes full of Chinooks came to visit them, offering trade, camping nearby, testing them with small thefts. The soldiers thought the river people "low in stature and ill-shaped."[6] Pinned down for many days by wind and waves on the north shore a dozen miles from the sea, cold, wet, and miserable, they were visited rather casually by curious Shoalwater, Kathlamet, and Clatsop.

> Five ill-made Indians left us and crossed the river (which is about five miles wide at this place) through the highest waves I ever saw a small vessel ride. These Indians are certainly the best canoe navigators I ever saw.
>
> They venture without concern in seas where other boats or seamen could not live an instant. They sit quietly and paddle, with no other movement, except when any large wave throws the boat on her side, and to the eye of the spectator she seems lost; the men to windward then steady her by throwing their bodies toward the upper side, and sinking their paddles deep into the wave appear to catch the water and force it under the boat, which the same stroke pushes on with great velocity.[7]

A few years later, fur trader Donald McKenzie would compare the Chinook to the *coureurs de bois*, French-Canadian canoemen of the fur trade: "I had imagined the Canadiens who accompanied me were the most expert canoemen in the world, but they are very inferior to these people, as they themselves acknowledge."[8]

THE EXPLORERS SAW most of the four or five styles of canoes paddled on Big River.[9] The Chinook bought and sold boats as we do cars, in addition to making their own. Finest of the designs was the Nootka style, a long flat hull with a finely curved cutwater and traditional beak-and-ears bow. The bottom was flat, without keel, and the sides angled up abruptly in what boatmen call hard chines. The stern was rounded and rose to a low post. The lack of a keel allowed the canoe to skid easily sideways under pressure of wind or current, instead of tipping. As for speed, a Nootka canoe easily defeated the champion longboat of the U.S. Navy in a nineteenth-century race.[10]

Many of the boats seen along Big River were head canoes, identified by their narrow, fin-like vertical cutwater at the bow and sometimes also the stern. This was a boat often seen on the Strait of Juan de Fuca and on Puget Sound, and may have been the ancient style of the region.[11] Many of the largest Chinook canoes were of head design, the bow and stern frequently mounted with tall sculptures of Coyote, Eagle, Bear, or man-like creatures. Fur trader Alexander Henry saw a Clatsop headman pass up the river one February in his new war canoe,

> about six fathoms long and wide in proportion, the stem [bow] rising perpendicular about six feet, on the top of which was a carved figure of some imaginary monster of their own rude imagination of uncouth sculpture, the head of a carnivorous animal with large ears erect, and arms (but no body) & legs clinging to the upper extremity of the stem, grinning most horribly, as it ploughed through the water. The large ears are painted green other parts red and black.

The stern also rises perpendicular about five feet in height and has no carved figure on it. On both sides of the stem and stern are broad strips of wood of the same piece as the stem and rising about four feet, and holes cut through them for the purpose of shooting arrows through.[12]

The imaginary monster was probably Coyote; his ears and grin reveal him. Eugene Duflot de Mofras, a French spy, saw more Coyote representations than other images on canoes along the Columbia.[13] Having an image both bow and stern may have been singularly Chinook. Lewis and Clark saw one such as they passed down the Friendly Reach, and named the island from behind which it appeared Image Canoe Island.[14] Other boats were decorated with fanciful paintings, white figures of fish, or a water monster with the head of a deer, the body of a snake, and feet near its head.

Women used ten- to fourteen-foot boats, two feet wide and nine inches or a foot deep, to gather *wapato*.[15] They carried the little craft under one arm, launched it into a marsh lake, and paddled out to fill it with bulbs. Next larger were sharp-ended three- and four-fathom boats, used to hunt seal in the estuary. It was probably one of those Lewis and Clark bemoaned the loss of, recalling that four men could carry it a mile without resting, yet it carried three men and twelve to fifteen hundred pounds of goods. Large boats ranged from five fathoms up. Lewis and Clark saw canoes of fifty feet and longer with pedestal ends and strange grotesque figures of men or animals, which they estimated could carry eight to ten thousand pounds of goods or twenty to thirty people.[16]

THE CHINOOK PADDLED squatting or kneeling along either side, a steersman (often a woman) elevated in the stern with a larger paddle. It took a day to travel down Shoalwater Bay from the northernmost Chinook village to the portage, part of another day to carry across, then about five days up Big River to the Cascades, a day to portage, and two more paddling to the Long Narrows.[17] Chinook *illahee* was thus about nine days from end to end. Pioneer James Swan observed that motivation affected the speed:

> When in the canoe all hands will paddle vehemently, the canoe seeming almost to fly. This speed will be kept up for a hundred rods [one-third mile], when they cease paddling and all begin to talk. Perhaps one has spied something which he has to describe while the rest listen; or another thinks of some funny anecdote or occurrence that transpired among the Indians they have been visiting, or they are passing some remarkable tree or cliff or stone, which has a legend attached to it, which the old folks never can pass without relating to the young, who all give the most respectful attention. When the tale is over, the steersman gives the word, "*Que-nuk, que-nuk wid-tuck*" (now, now hurry), when all again paddle away with a desperate energy for a few minutes, and then the same scene is enacted."[18]

If the visit were ceremonial, six or eight or twelve could paddle in perfect unison, slapping the sides of the boat with their paddles in time to one of the canoeing chants they loved to sing.

STILL PINNED DOWN by wind and waves in the estuary, the cloth warriors were visited by Comcomly and Shelathwell—Chil-lar-la-wil in Clark's orthography—and played out a little drama. One of the Chinook nobles had a two-pelt sea otter robe the captains thought the most beautiful they had seen. Nothing they offered would induce him to part with it, except Charbonneau's Shoshone slave/ wife Sacajawea's belt of blue chief-beads, the Chinook favorite. The captains finally offered the belt and the Chinook made the trade.[19]

By now another European import was spreading along the river.

Coming down, Lewis and Clark had seen two or three cases of gonorrhea, and about twice that many of syphilis, but at the mouth of the river they saw more. "Many of the Chinnooks appear to have venerious and pustelus disorders," Clark wrote, "One woman whome I saw at the creek appeared all over in scabs and ussers &c."[20]

Delashelwilt's wife repeatedly brought six or more girls to their camp to offer their favors. The captains thought them her daughters and nieces.[21] Whether any were slaves we cannot know, for the captains didn't mention slavery until months later when Kuskalaw, a Clatsop, offered to sell them a ten-year-old boy.[22] Clark, however, had his own slave, York, along on the journey. Apparently the clothmen thought skin color, not head shape, was the justification for enslavement.

The captains expressed frequent misgivings about the Chinook girls. "I think the most disgusting sight I have ever beheld is those dirty naked wenches," both men recorded,[23] exhibiting a curious bias, for they never wrote of a similar disgust at the naked men. Elsewhere they noted that the Chinook "appear to view sensuality as a necessary evil, and do not appear to abhor it in the unmarried state."[24] Even after crossing the continent with her, Clark still wrote of Sacajawea as "the squar-wife of our interpreter Shabono" in the journal entry describing trading her belt to Comcomly.[25] Lewis revealed some Chinooks' attitude when he recorded,

> Their conversation generally turns upon the subjects of trade, smoking, eating or their women. About the latter they speak without reserve in their presence, of their every part, and of the most formiliar connection. They do not hold the virtue of their women in high estimation, and will even prostitute their wives and daughters for a fishinghook or a strand of beads."[26]

And Clark agreed, "the Chin-nook womin are lude and carry on sport publickly."[27]

TEN YEARS after Bishop had visited, Taucum was still the most powerful headman of the Shoalwater. In addition to Comcomly and Shelathwell, Norcarte and the formerly mad Chinini were mentioned. The clothmen crossed Big River to form their winter village near the more abundant elk herds on the south bank. There they met the Clatsop headman, Coonia or Comowool, also called Coonia, and later Cobaway. Of this headman they wrote, "this we have found much the most friendly and decent savage that we have met with in this neighborhood."[28] They met also the Clatsops Kuskalaw, Stillasha, Shanoma, and Warholott.

Kuskalaw hosted Clark to a dinner party at his home.

> [He] spred down new mats for me to set on, gave me fish, berries, rutes, etc on small neet platteers of rushes to eate which was repeated, all the men of the other houses came and smoked with me. Those people appeared much neeter in their diat than Indians are comonly, and frequently wash theer faces and hands—in the eveng an old woman presented a bowl made of a light coloured horn a kind of surup made of dried berries which is common to this countrey which the natives call *shellwell.* This surup I though was pleasent, they gave me cockle shells to eate a kind of soup made of bread of the *shellwell* berries mixed with roots in which they presented in neet trenchers made of wood.[29]

When Clark was ready to sleep, Kuskalaw spread two new mats near the fire and sent his wife to bed as a sign it was time for all to retire.

The Shoalwater Chinook made such a bad first impression on the captains that they were for a time banned from the soldiers' camp. Some skillful Shoalwater had stolen guns from under the sleeping heads of the *passiuks* warriors. What daring! Henceforth, should Clatsop, Kathlamet, or Tillamook approach the clothmen's little fort they had to cry out "No Chinook!" to the soldiers. However, before they left the captains evidently realized that their first impression was exaggerated. The Americans, for their part, several times helped themselves to house boards from unoccupied houses and stole canoes, something a Chinook would never have thought to do.[30]

THE SOLDIERS made their fifty-foot-square fortress at a location called *Netul*, on a small tributary south of Big River. Instead of roofing it over sensibly they left twenty feet down the center opened to the rain, and closed the side compartments into little separate rooms. The chiefs lived on one side, the braves on the other. Roofed over, it would have been a medium-size Chinook house. They fenced the ends, and in that primitive structure they survived a winter that was dank even for the rain-caressed seacoast of Oregon. They recorded seven rain-free days from late October until late March.

Though adept at hunting, the clothmen apparently relied little on fishing. They were camped by a rich estuary and equipped with boats, but fishing is hardly mentioned in their journals. Fish were far from the favorite food of these beef and pork eaters. Indeed, throughout much of their nation, "fish eater" was a kind of insult in those times. They killed many elk but lacked skill at smoke-drying the meat, much of which rotted. Their buckskin rotted too. Their evident discomfort makes it clear how well the Chinook had mastered a difficult environment.[31]

THE CHINOOK evidently spoke to the soldiers in Chinook Jargon. The explorers heard many English and Nootka words among simplified Chinook ones. They thought they were writing down the Clatsop dialect of Chinook, but it was Jargon. One short sentence Clark heard was entirely of Nootka and English words: "*Cloch musket wake cumtex musket*," meaning "Good musket, not understand musket." The words derive from: *kloshe*, Nootka or an unidentified northern language, but not Chinook; *musket*, English; *wake*, Nootka; *kumtux*, Nootka, *musket*, English.[32] Further, Nicholas Biddle, whose earliest history of the expedition was from Clark's journal, with amplifications and explanations by George Shannon, one of the party, was informed by Shannon that Clatsop was a far easier language to learn than other Indian languages, which it assuredly was not. But the Jargon, by intention, was.[33]

How else but Jargon explain that Clark described the Tillamook Nehalem as speaking the same as the Clatsop-Chinook, and Lewis, a day or two later, recorded that the Kathlamet also spoke the same, though Kathlamet was a different Chinookan language? Later, as they returned up river, the captains described the Skillute at the mouth of the Cowlitz River, the Quathlapootle in the Wapato Lowlands, and the Cashooks of Willamette Falls as all speaking like those below.[34]

WAITING OUT THE WINTER, Lewis and Clark were visited by people from the lower river and coast. They saw the elder son of the shipwrecked mariner Jack Ramsay. Sergeant Patrick Gass described him as having "the reddest hair I ever saw, and fair skin much freckled."[35] Lewis and Clark described "dusky red hair" and thought he understood English better than the other Clatsops, even though he did not speak it. On his arm his father had tattooed his name, and he had refused to let the boy's head be flattened. Otherwise he was entirely Chinook.[36] They didn't notice his brother George, probably standing nearby, for he was dark-haired and had a flattened head. The two were young men by then.

Of the Clatsop the captains recorded,

The disposition of these people seems mild and inoffensive, and they have uniformly behaved to us with great friendship. They are addicted to begging and pilfering small articles . . . but do not rob wantonly nor in any large amount.[37]

Once, when the Clatsop took some elk left hanging by the soldiers, they sent a return gift of dogs. (The dogs managed to scamper off.)[38]

So well had Lieutenant William Broughton's toast inoculated the Chinook against alcohol that even after a dozen years of trading, the captains agreed, "these people do not appear to know the use of spirituous liquors, they have never once asked us for it."[39]

Lewis and Clark continued to appreciate

the wonderful dexterity with which they guide their canoes over the most boisterous seas, for though the waves were so high that before they were gone half a mile the canoe was several times out of sight, they proceeded with the greatest calmness and security.[40]

And noted that "the woodwork and sculpture of these people as well as their hats and their waterproof baskets evince an ingenuity by no means common among the aborigines of America."[41]

The explorers counted heads and houses and estimated a total of 17,740 Chinook along the rivers, sloughs, and bays.[42] That total doesn't include the Wasco or Washougal villages, which the explorers evidently missed, but does include twelve hundred persons called Clackstar and said to reside in twenty-eight houses on "a small river which discharges itself on the S.W. side of Wappato Island." Some scholars have argued that these are the Clatskanie. Some creeks but nothing like a river flow into Multnomah Channel. Scapoose Bay, fed by the creek of the same name, does. The Clatskanie, if they had a river village, ought to have been on the Clatskanie River, which enters the Columbia behind Wallace Island at river mile 50, thirty-seven miles below the lower end of Wapato (now Sauvie) Island. The Clatskanie were a hill people who hunted the Coast Range hills, like their Athabascan cousins the Kwaliokpa across Big River. Neither are listed by name in Clark's final "Estimate of Western Indians."[43]

There were sore throats among the Clatsop that winter. Some died. The soldiers thought it influenza. In January a whale went ashore south of Tillamook Head, and some Clatsops hiked over for a share of the oil and blubber, as did Clark and a party of *passiuks.* No ships wintered over in the river. It was warm until late January, then turned cold, and six inches of snow sat down, remaining an unusual ten days. The fleas finally died back a little. The soldiers, killing elk, found the foreshafts of Clatsop arrows in many.

SMELT RETURNED February 24th; elk shed their antlers the first week in March; by March 16th the Chinook were catching steelhead and waiting for *igunat.* The clothmen started back upriver on March 23rd, nearly a month too early to ascend with the salmon. They gifted the nobles with certificates of good conduct and medals. Many swans flew north on March 28th.

A Kathlamet village the captains labelled, "The dirtiest and stinkingest place I ever saw in any shape whatever, and the inhabitants partake of the [characteristic] of the village."[44] But they thought the inhabitants superior in wood carving. The Skiloot were in dispute with the Shoalwater, which had prevented them from visiting the clothmen's fort. They could go no farther than the head of the estuary, where they traded with the Wahkiacum and Clatsop. The Quathlapootle Lewis and Clark thought inferior at trade. They gave a medal to the headman, who handed it to his wife. The Mahlnumax were as good at haggling as the people at the mouth of the river. Lewis thought the people of the Wapato Lowlands "larger and better made than those of the coast."[45]

Opposite the upper mouth of the Willamette someone may

have pointed inland toward Vancouver Lake and told them that Konapee's son Soto lived there, beyond the lake. The captains thought it the name of a tribe, and wrote Shoto, not a very Chinookan-sounding word.[46] At Neerchakeoo, the lowermost Shahala village, Clark thought the people "sulky" when he tried to buy wapato, so he put the fear of *passiuks* into them by spinning the needle of his compass with a magnet, and throwing into their fire a substance that coughed and sputtered and changed the fire's color. Alarmed by this powerful conjuror, the villagers offered him baskets of *wapato* and begged him to make the noise and color cease, which it soon did. Since a house's fire had an individual spirit, their alarm can be imagined. The women and children hid in their beds or behind the men, who hung their heads in alarm. An aged blind spokesman orated with great vehemence against the clothmen, but no one did anything.[47]

Asked what happened to the much larger village abandoned behind their present house at Nechacokee, the most upriver Mahlnumax village, an old man, perhaps their headman,

> brought forward a woman who was badly marked with the smallpox and made signs that they all died with the disorder which marked her face, and which she was very near dying of when a girl. From the age of this woman this destructive disorder I judge must have been about 28 or 30 years past, about the same time the Clatsop informed us that this disorder raged in their towns and destroyed their nation.[48]

THE CAPTAINS heard a sudden change of language near the eastern edge of the lowlands, where no more than a dialect change of Kiksht ought to have been. "These people have a few words the same as those below, but the air of the language is entirely different, insomuch that it may be justly deemed a different language," Clark recorded, at that most downriver Shahala village.[49] Lewis took a vocabulary at the Cascades, and found the numbers the same as the Clatsop, but other words essentially different.[50] Jargon would be described so. This may have marked the eastern limit of those who spoke Chinook Jargon to strangers. There is no proof of this, but the extremity of the change implies that they were now hearing Kiksht, particularly if they had been hearing Jargon before, and their descriptions of the Clatsop, Nehalem, Kathlamet, Quathlapootle, and Cushooks below as speaking the same language, was certainly an error, for among those people were speakers of four, perhaps even five, different languages: Lower Chinook, Tillamook, Kathlamet, whatever the Lowland people spoke, and Kiksht.[51] And the inhabitants of the Cascades also spoke Kiksht.

THE WINTER UPRIVER had been a hard one, for as the soldiers approached the Columbia River Gorge numerous canoes came down, all of the occupants of which claimed to be starving. Two canoes passed back upriver, loaded with *wapato* and smelt. At the Cascades of the Columbia in mid-April snow stood close above the river, but the bottoms were greening up. However, Lewis learned that "the natives are not so much distressed for food as I was induced to believe."[52] Perhaps they were merely starving for savory smelt and *wapato*. Lewis and Clark labelled the Shahala unfriendly. The people of Wahlala village at the head of the Cascades were "the greatest thieves and scoundrels we have met with."[53] As the explorers portaged their goods up, "one of them had the insolence to cast stones down the bank at two of the men who happened to be a little detached from the party at the time."[54] That was the first of a series of skirmishes that would culminate in war eight years later.

A little later that day there was a dispute over a dog the soldiers had bought. A Shahala wanted to take the animal back. The cloth soldiers knew that this was regular Chinook practice, but refused, so someone stole Lewis's pet dog. A man who spoke "the Clatsop language"—perhaps a Jargon-speaker from downriver—informed them of the theft, and Lewis's dog was retrieved.[55] A Shahala was caught trying to pilfer an axe, and the soldiers closed their camp and went armed. Yet, the Shahala returned a canoe the soldiers had lost to the river.[56]

They learned that a ship's captain named Swippeton had visited the Shahala the previous winter from somewhere to the northwest, perhaps Puget Sound, with trade goods such as a pipe tomahawk and ship's biscuits.[57]

The Tlakluit awaited the coming of salmon. The captains thought the Wishram had profited by the harshness of the winter, for though piles of *itkilak* still stood about on both sides of the river, the people were better dressed than in autumn, wearing Plateau costume of moccasins, leggings, long robes, and shirts in the Nez Perce style. It may have been the weather. As the soldiers passed, the Wishram caught their first *igunat*. First Salmon ceremony was performed on April 19th in 1806, each child of the village passing and taking a piece.[58] The Wasco were out of their underground houses and living in mat summer houses at Winquatt, now the city of The Dalles. Camas were flowering.

The clothmen were weary and on their way home. They were low on trade goods and did not enjoy bargaining for horses, particularly with such masters as the Wishram. The Wishram, for their part, were accustomed to being treated with more respect.

Above, at the first Sahaptin village, a robe was stolen and the soldiers nearly burned Skin village. Lewis struck a native of Skin several times. Sergeant Gass called it the first violence of the expedition.[59] The cloth soldiers continued upriver. *Tsagiglalal* saw them go, as she had seen them come. The river people are said to have remembered Lewis and Clark as real chiefs.

A Wasco madonna, photographed by Benjamin Gifford in 1901. Courtesy of the Oregon Historical Society.

12

Salmon Come Thickly Upriver

SUMMER, 1809

SUPPOSE EVERYTHING was as it should have been that summer, all up and down *Wimahl*. From the Bar of the Columbia to the Long Narrows, fish came eagerly to nets. Many youths found spirit helpers. And Comcomly's daughter Illchee celebrated her first menstruation. The rain ceased early and the sky its blueness made.

June came, Advance in a Body Moon, when the *igunat* ascended in incredible thickness, and every drift and netting spot was full of men catching salmon. Then it became Rotting Moon, July, when the river people could not process the fish fast enough, and salmon lay about on the ground, and the stench of rotting flesh was thick across the land. When the giant *igunat* thinned out the *otsui-ha*[1] began to ascend, red-fleshed sockeye salmon weighing only a dozen pounds but the finest flavored salmon. Up small tributaries they swam, toward headwater lakes, and the people caught them with net and weir.

Eel-like lamprey—*isgakwal*—were inching their way up the rocks at Willamette Falls, climbing by their sucker mouths. They were another anadramous fish, slender, with a long fin and gills much different than other fish. They have neither upper or lower jaws, nor true teeth, and their skeletons are of cartilage instead of bone. The mouth of this animal is circular, adapted for sucking blood, and covered with horny spines, called "teeth." With this mouth they fasten onto larger fish, and grinding their way in, suck their prey empty. Pacific lamprey grow to thirty inches long on the Columbia. The Clowewalla pulled lampreys off the rocks or netted them at night by torchlight. They savored lamprey fresh-roasted or smoked.

Fur trader and historian John Dunn recalled summer:

> The women go a gypsying in the proper season to collect in the upper part of the country. This season is a time of hilarity; and the women bepaint their faces and persons with a sort of vermillion paint, partly to protect them from the sun and partly to present a gay and fantastic appearance.[2]

Each in its season came roots and bulbs to dig and eat, or to preserve against the winter. Each month had its flavors and its locations. Bracken fern roots were roasted in the ashes and peeled, a mealy, starch-rich food. Cattails roots they peeled and ate raw. They dug cow parsnip roots, and thistle roots, which were white and crisp when peeled raw, black and sugary when roasted. They ate them with oil, or made soup stock. Lupine roots tasted like sweet potato when roasted and pounded; pontentilla roots were a great favorite, they were like lily bulbs. They also ate wild carrots and onions of several sorts, and three or four kinds of camas as well. All these had their special recipe or use. They gathered near marshes, in high mountain meadows, prairies, and sandspits, and by lakes. The land was good, and that year everything came in its appointed time under a high blue dome with Thunder's wives standing up, the tall mounded clouds we call alto-cumulus.

The berries were a succession of delights. Nowhere are there more berries: salmonberries first in May, then strawberries, thimbleberries, blueberries, red huckleberries, blackberries, gooseberries,

Naked Against the Rain

currants, and blue huckleberries. In August salal berries ripened. Autumn berries were yet to come.

Whole different villages assembled during the summer. Each family had inherited rights and interests, which came from both sides of the family. If the mother was Klickitat, she and her daughters might go to pick huckleberries in the high meadows toward Mount Adams. If Tillamook, to gather wild strawberries on Nehalem Spit. Such long-term visits with kinfolk in other villages made the Chinook multicultural as well as multilingual.[3]

The women cut grasses, reeds, and strong flexible roots which they would be needing in their winter work of making baskets and mats. The raw materials they put aside in a correct manner so they would dry properly and season.

They lived in their mat houses, forty-foot-by-twelve-foot structures of poles and reed mats, smaller than the winter houses, but waterproof enough in the occasional rains of summer. Portable mat houses were another idea they had obtained through the Columbia Gorge. The other seacoast peoples lived in cedar plank houses year around. Only the Chinook, coast, river, and Gorge alike, summered in mat lodges. The *Ilkaimamt* of the Plateau lived in mat lodges year-around.

THE CHINOOK showed great foresight in their gathering, which was done not just to stave off hunger but to be ready to observe the sacred season of winter properly as well. Only a low-class person would disturb the round of dancing, singing, and story telling to seek food. Those of the highest classes made ready to feed their guests as well as themselves.[4]

Surplus food created wealth for the women, who traded baskets of roots, berries, and other foodstuffs as well as mats, baskets, and hats. The canoes full of roots and berries traveling up and down the river were women's trade, not men's, if they were actually trade. (A lot were probably exchanges with kinfolk.) Who owned the *itkilak*, product of his catching and her preserving, isn't known.

The women's food technology was far from simple. Camas bulbs, one of their staples, were first roasted for forty-eight hours in a ground oven, which produced a sweet black mush. This they pounded into a dough, shaped into large loaves, wrapped in grass, and steamed. They then broke each loaf up and refashioned the material into smaller cakes, which they dried under the sun. Camas cakes stayed sweet through the winter. They sliced them like English plum pudding.

They mashed, steamed, dried, ground, and roasted, made fruit leathers, soaked things in oil, rotted others, brined them, stored them in boxes, stored them in holes in the ground, hung them, smoked them, and performed other preparations.

Itkilak—dried and pounded salmon—took great effort. First they exposed igunat salmon to the sun until the skin slipped easily off, then stripped the meat from the bones and mashed it fine. They spread the rich pink flesh three or four inches deep on a mat for several days. It dried quickly in the parched air above Wind Mountain. They crumbled it again, and adding a little water, squeezed it through their hands until it was a homogeneous mass, which they spread out to dry again. Next they added steelhead oil and sometimes dried berries, and, having lined their special one-foot-by-two-foot baskets with dried and stretched salmon skins, they rammed the dried fish meal in as tight as they could with three-foot-long black basalt pestles, which came to be called salmon packers.[5]

They left such baskets of fish meal standing around in the open at The Dalles, with just a mat over them, or buried them in the ground. Even so, *itkilak* lasted several years. Ordinary smoke-drying preserved fish only for a season, one winter at most. They nibbled a little of the sawdust-like fish meal or used it for soup stock. It was powerfully nourishing.

It was also a triumph of pre-industrial technology that should not be underestimated. The equivalent food-preservation technique in Europe was pickled herring, invented in AD 1375 in Flanders. It lasted several years. It was the only meat that would, and remained the height of European food technology until 1809, when canning was invented. Pickled herring was a watershed event in European history, freeing at least the wealthiest class from the fear of famine. Given the sequence of Chinook movement upriver, it is possible that *itkilak* was known to them as early as pickled herring to Europe.

WITH THE EXCEPTION of their springtime vitamin C deficiency, the Chinook diet was excellent.[6] It was rich in protein and fat, light on carbohydrates, with adequate sugar, iron, phosphorus, calcium, and most of the vitamins, including A, B, B2, D, and E. Their bodies could compensate for the lack of carbohydrates by using the fat and protein. Salmon is far superior to beef as the basis for a diet, being rich in most of the above, plus potassium, iodine, and iron. Its flesh contains up to a thousand calories per pound and its rich oil is polyunsaturated and low in cholesterol.[7]

The Chinook were not without health problems, however. Many were blind. There may have been widespread trachoma, a highly contagious virus that attacks the soft lining of the eyelid. Smallpox blinds in a similar fashion. Strokes were not uncommon, and there were liver ailments and other gastrointestinal disorders, perhaps from eating spoiled food. They ate things that appeared rotten to Europeans. Infants who survived the first year had developed strong immunities to intestinal disorders.

Rheumatism, or osteo-arthritis, was probably common, and what was described as asthma, but sounds more like bronchitis, perhaps aggravated by the smoke in their houses. Dysentery or diarrhea were common as well, and diabetes may have been, as it often is in thickset people with low metabolic rates. The comas that often preceded their deaths may have been insulin comas, according to a contemporary physician.[8] Salmonella bacilli from spoiled food may have been prevalent, or viral hepatitis, or jaundice. Their teeth wore down to the gums at an early age. Some observers blamed this on the sand they ate with their fish and roots.[9]

Their concept of sanitation was, at the very least, different from our own.[10] They left fish remains lying around their houses, ate food without concern for cleanliness or spoilage, and emptied their bowels anywhere, often near the house. Garbage lay about and to European noses their villages stank. Fur trader Alexander Henry thought the Clatsop "uncommonly filthy about their houses," and wrote of the Clowewalla that "near the fire where they sit and sleep was tolerably clean and spread with mats, but elsewhere, and all around the house, were enormous piles of excrements."[11] Europeans were taken aback by the lack of shame the Chinook felt about bowel movements. According to Captain Bishop,

> It is no uncommon thing for them, while talking to another person, to squat down upon an occasion, which nature points out, even to some of the brute races, a retired spot for, and they, both men and women are to be met with in this situation close to the door of the house.[12]

Now they were lying on the belly of the land. It was Blackberry Patch Moon, or Huckleberry Patch Moon, almost too hot and dry, and there was a pause across the August land. The people had put away much against winter and the fish were not so thick in the river. They rested. The Clatsop and Shoalwater had clambakes on the beach, steaming the clams in grass on hot rocks.[13]

A Clackamas headman invited the people of his village to his house and they assembled around mid-day. The men went down to the river to sweat together in the rectangular, dirt-and-timber sweat houses the Clackamas built. They cooled themselves in the river, then ate the feast the women had been preparing. Afterward they sat around until sunset, telling the latest news, joking and chaffing each other. Several times during the summer the headman would invite them to spend an afternoon in this manner.[14]

MEANWHILE BOTH BOYS AND GIRLS were training to seek a *kawok*, a spirit helper. All noble youth, any commoner with gumption, even slaves and orphans, were encouraged to seek a *kawok*. It was said that about half of those who quested encountered a spirit, and that rank had nothing to do with success. Training had begun in childhood, and as puberty approached the rigor of the training increased, until finally each task was a full-scale quest; three to five days of fasting and intense exertion in a wild and lonely place. The youth was sent off to the top of a hill or to a certain beach, a cave, a pond, or an island. Sometimes he or she went to seek a specific spirit, but usually merely to a spiritual location, far from humans.

Carrying a slow-burning torch of cedar bark to kindle a fire, the seeker made a camp, tended the fire, swam back and forth many times, fasted, and stayed awake night and day. He or she engaged in exertions: running, diving, circling the fire. Soon the spirit-seeker was clean and free of odor, both inside and out, and light-headed as well.

The seeker was to advance vigorously, not to show fear or run, but to welcome an encounter. When he or she came to water the seeker dived five times. The spirit would not cross water. If frightened the seeker might lie down on the side nearest home. The spirit might look like an animal at first, then in the vision reveal itself in a person-like guise. The *kawok* would tell the neophyte what power he or she would have when grown.[15]

CULTEE'S GRANDFATHER was sent to seek *Ut-Onaqan*, a female spirit who had aided his ancestors. He already had three guardian spirits and was thinking of marrying. He was sent to a mountain top. On the second day, approaching the summit, he heard a howling and felt a chill. The howling increased; leaves fell from the trees; he grew afraid. He climbed a tree.

The sound approached; more leaves fell; he decided to go home instead. The monster pursued him. It gained ground. He thought of his guardian spirit Morning Star, and gained strength. But he tired again, and the spirit was close behind. He thought of his spirit Wolf, and spurted on. But again he grew tired and she gained.

He looked back and saw her. She had a row of pendant teats along her belly like a bitch, striking her legs as she ran.

He ran on until he came to a creek, which he forded.

He watched her come to the creek and saw that she was afraid. She blew on it as a deer does before it drinks, a nasal a . . . a . . . a. . . . She howled "Ua!" and he fainted.

Now in his vision he saw that she was a human being. She spoke to him. "I am the one whom your family and the people call Ut-Onaqan. I come from the top of that mountain. I like you. Look at me, person." He looked at her and saw that her body was full of arrows which had been shot at her. "You will be just as I am when you return home." He slept and awoke late the next day. He bathed and returned home.[16]

He had awakened the *kawok* from sleep. If the spirit liked the seeker it would serve the person for life. There might be other *kawok* of the same type, but each individual spirit was distinct. When the human died, the spirit mourned the loss, then went off somewhere and "sort of turned itself down." The spirit might wonder, "Who will wake me now?" At length, another person awoke that spirit again.[17]

A PERSON'S KAWOK—another word was *tahmanawis*[18]—might represent any of a variety of animals, birds, insects, or forces of nature. Any spirit might give health, wealth, and long life. Eagle, Deer, and Elk were usually hunting powers. Animals that ate human flesh such as Grizzly, Cougar, or Wolf were dangerous because the spirit might demand human flesh and the person be forced to satisfy the desire. Skunk, Grizzly, Cougar, and Thunder were extremely strong. Thunder was stronger than Grizzly, for Thunder burnt people while Grizzly only killed them. Sturgeon was a warrior's spirit, able to recover from wounds. Rocks and trees were warrior spirits too, for arrows could not hurt them. Mountain lizards, snakes, small insects, or birds helped people hide. Rattlesnake protected against snakebite. Perhaps one with rattlesnake power could send a rattler to bite his foe. Kingfisher was a fishing power, but stingy.

There was no taboo against killing the creature associated with one's guardian, but there were responsibilities. Someone with deer spirit might kill enough deer to supply the whole village, but not eat venison himself. On his deathbed he might eat a small piece and suddenly recover.

The Wasco recalled a story of a youth whose father goaded him into killing more game than he needed, though his Elk *kawok* had instructed him to kill only his present need. He slaughtered deer, bear, and four of five elk. The fifth one he pursued into a lake, where both sank to the bottom. He found himself among Elk, Deer, and Bear spirits. "Draw him in, draw him in," they chanted, and he was pulled close to the Elk. "Why did you disobey?" Elk asked. The spirit lectured him about why he should not have listened to his father, then withdrew its powers. "Cast him out, cast him out," the spirits sang, and he found himself on the shore of the lake. He returned home sick at heart and soon died.[19]

Spirits were not inherited, as they were farther north along the coast, nor were youths usually sent off to get a particular one, but it was more likely for a seeker to encounter the same spirit as a parent or teacher. That made the older person happy. Sometimes an old teacher sent his personal spirit ahead to await the seeker, and died soon after.

ATTRACTING A SPIRIT didn't by itself elevate the economic or social level of a person. Only the later collaboration between human and spirt gave wealth and powers. The seeker did not tell what had happened after returning from the quest, but took to his or her bed, sick, helpless, and frightened, and ate nothing for two or three days. A seeker who ate would have little if any power. Only years later when the spirit returned at a winter dance would the spirit become useful. The spirit was only a hope and a memory until then. If the spirit had given a song or a few words as clue, that would be the seeker's mantra, a lifelong meditation.

The spirit's identity remained a secret. People might guess, from what kinds of food he did not eat, or the words of her power song, but only at death would the spirit's name be revealed. It was a lifelong secret; indeed, whether a person had actually encountered a spirit was never known.

Individuals might continue to seek spirit helpers as long as they wished, and ambitious or spiritually oriented adults continued all their lives, particularly those seeking sorcerer's power.[20] Ordinarily, boys stopped seeking a *kawok* at marriage, and first menstruation marked the end of questing for most girls.

WAS IT DURING THAT PERFECT SUMMER that Comcomly's oldest daughter Illchee's arrival at puberty was celebrated? A boy's passage to manhood was not marked by ceremony, but the first five days of her first bleeding were the most important and frightening time of a Chinook woman's life. When it was discovered that she was menstruant, Illchee was immediately hidden behind partitions in a corner of the house. Shredded cedar bark was tied to her arms above the elbows and wrists, on her legs, and around her waist. She refrained from all food. She saw or spoke to no one. For five days she and those around her were in immense danger.

Upriver on this occasion the Wishram performed a five-day ceremony they called *waqhli*. At mid-afternoon the women assembled, their faces painted and ornamented with beads and feathers. They sang and danced for two hours. As night fell the men came to dance, carrying weapons and dressed in skins of bear and wolf. To the sounds of flint rattles and whistles fashioned of the thigh bone of the heron, those bear and wolf dancers entered the house with a wild rush and fearful yelling. They formed a line shoulder to shoulder, growling, roaring, clawing the air. They danced forward as far as they could go, then yelled in unison and retreated to the door in little jumps. Forward and back they danced for several hours. Then everyone but the menstruant girl enjoyed a feast.[21]

Downriver at Qwatsamts it was somewhat more sedate.[22] Moon Girl's mother Kiasno sent old men and women to invite the people of Qwatsamts and neighboring villages, but did not reveal the reason. When the guests arrived they were informed that it was to celebrate her menstruation. They sang and danced, then feasted and were gifted.

An old woman took care of Illchee, who was never seen. For four more days the old people came and sang and danced and feasted. The girl's power was extreme and dangerous; her eyes were particularly powerful. Both she and the people must be protected. On the fifth day the cedar bark was taken off her body and strings of dentalia tied in their place. A buckskin strap girt her waist, where it would remain a hundred days. Gifts of small value were distributed and the maiden came out, wearing a special headdress, perhaps a fillet of otter skin with beads, or with her hair done up and ornamented with shells and beads. The ceremony marked the beginning of her right to wear woman's ornaments.

But not the end of her observances. Now she might nibble a bit of the oldest dried salmon with a dab of grease. Gradually her parents let her eat more, but she got nothing fresh for those hundred days. She had a separate door to the house, and lived partitioned off, or in the women's house out back. She went to bathe daily in a creek far from the village. She must never pick berries, warm herself, or look at the sky. Each morning she scrubbed her body with rotten hemlock and boughs of cedar. Her face was painted red. She must never touch her own body or comb her hair. Her attendant did her hair in twin braids knotted behind her head. She decorated Illchee's hair with beads and gave her two sticks to scratch her scalp. Thus was she raised to be a princess, and indeed she was a princess.

Had she broken any taboo, misfortune would surely have followed. Shellfish would make her sick, huckleberries fall unripe if she ate one. If she went outdoors when the southwest wind was blowing, Thunderbird would storm. If she hung her cedar-bark towel on a spruce tree, it would wither. If she ate of a fish that was caught in a net, the net became unlucky. The same for a hook.

> She must rise earlier than the birds. If the birds should rise first she will not live long. If she does everything in the right way she will get old before she dies.[23]

THE KATHLAMET recalled a story of a girl who broke the taboos:

> The Gilaunalx hunted elk on Swalalaxost, Saddle Mountain, and their women gathered onion and rush roots on the prairie nearby. It was forbidden for a menstruant woman to go near the trail to the summit, up which they chased the elk, to drive them over the steep side of the mountain higher up. Sometimes they got sixty elk that way.
>
> Up there were two caves in the rock that were Thunderbird's town. There were bones of whales, of sea lions, and of

other kinds of sea animals. The girl who was just mature was told not to go to the prairie, but another girl told her that she had gone, and nothing had happened to her.

"Perhaps they only deceive you," the other girl said.

"Next time I shall go along when you go."

She went, her head covered with long dentalia, dentalia tied to her body. Now she disappeared. They searched for her.

"Maybe she went to the town of the Thunderbird," they said.

It became foggy. They searched for her near the rocks. They found her there, with all kinds of sea birds flying above.

"Come, we will go home," they said to her, but she did not look. They took her hand and pulled, but she did not move. Her face changed. Then her companions became frightened. They gave up and left her in the rocks there.

"Oh, that girl became crazy," they said. "She became a monster. We are all weak of fright." Then the people cried.

Next morning they went to find her but there were only feathers of sea birds lying there, piled that high. It became foggy, and they heard her singing shaman's songs in the rocks. When they came to the place she was, she sang shaman's songs. The people gave up and went home.

Therefore, it is forbidden to take girls who are just mature up Swalalaxost, because that girl was taken away. The Thunderbird took her.[24]

THE LITTLE GIRLS came to visit Illchee. She spoke to them as a woman, and gave them her old playthings, which were no longer proper for her. After the hundred days another elaborate celebration was held. Illchee sang and danced, attired in woman's finery. After that she could come and go as she pleased and was free to announce her interest in marriage and sing love songs in the presence of older women. She could insert the name of the man of her choice if she had one. But where would her increasingly wealthy father find a noble great enough to buy his firstborn daughter, his Moon Girl? She could hardly have guessed that her husband was already preparing to come to her from halfway around the world.

THE BEAUTIFUL SUMMER was coming to a close. Fall salmon were entering Big River, silverside or coho we call them, *oowun* to the Chinook, ten- to thirty-pound fish and fine eating. Calico or dog salmon came up, *utsiya*, ten- to twenty-pound fish, less fat than other salmon but easier to process because they didn't spoil so fast. Humpback salmon came too, *olaatsh*, of which both male and female turned dark red as they ascended and the males grew humped backs and hooked snouts.

Sturgeon, *inagwn*, came up again in late summer; half-ton giants with cartilage instead of bone. The Chinook never missed a chance to take sturgeon with hook, gig, or net when they came up from the deep river pools where those ancient fish grazed and drowsed.

In Shoalwater Bay they took flat bottom-fish in a novel way. Settler James Swan recalled,

> The turbot and flounders are caught while wading in the water by means of the feet. The Indian wades along slowly, and as soon as he feels a fish with his feet, he steps quickly on it and holds it firm till he can reach hold of it with his hand, when he gives it a jerk and away it flies far into the flats. They are easily taken by this method as their rough backs prevent them slipping from under the feet. The catching affords a deal of fun, as usually quite a number are engaged in the sport, and their splashing, slipping, screaming, and laughing make a lively time. These fish, like all the fish in the bay, are very fine and well flavored.[25]

But summer wasn't all hard food gathering like that. Mariner Peter Corney called the Chinook generally lazy and noted with scorn that "their young men lie basking in the sun on the sides of the river, for hours together."[26] It may be too extravagant to claim that the Chinook invented sunbathing, but they were doing it a century and more before the Europeans learned how.

If indeed the summer was splendid, as sometimes a summer is along Big River, then it was good that the Chinook should enjoy it. The year was 1809, and they had only a score of summers left.

Whylick Quiuck, a Shahala, also called Virginia Miller, with her Nootka-style canoe. Photograph by Edward Curtis, courtesy of the University of Washington Library, Special Collections, NA 178.

13

Blue Jay Knocks a Hole
In a Rotten Log

1810

BLUE JAY'S OLDER SISTER Ioi always used slang when telling him what to do. Her slang was vivid. She'd call a one-person canoe a "canoe for one leg," or long dentalia "widow shit." She wanted her brother to marry, so she'd have someone to help her dig roots, but not a young girl; "Marry a dead one," she told him. She meant old, but Blue Jay, who always took her slang literally, brought home the headman's recently deceased daughter.[1]

Blue Jay, the sharp-crested, raucous, Stellar's jay, played a psychopathic troublemaker in some Chinook stories, a brave but ruthless hero in others, but when he performed with his older sister he was pure buffoon.

I am wondering if you might knock a hole in a rotten log," Ioi said to him. "We lack any canoe." She packed lunch for him, and he went off into the forest to make a canoe. He went every day. Finally, he told her, "Go tell the village men to pull the new canoe out from the woods."

When the men got there to take the new canoe down to the river, they said, "What can be done about such a thing? How should we take along such a thing that is just rotten?"

They ate the lunch that Ioi had prepared, and then they went to work.

One of them said, "Just be slow and careful." They dragged the boat through the woods, but it broke to pieces. They went home.

Blue Jay told his older sister, "Those crazy ones you got for me! They just did every which way with it. They broke it to bits."

"No matter what you may suppose, it really was only rotten wood," the men told her. "We dragged it painstakingly and slowly, but it broke. It was just rotten wood."

"But it was you yourself who told me to hollow it out of a rotten log," Blue Jay told Ioi.[2]

CANOE CARVING was work for a man of special skills and spirit powers.[3] His tools were L-shaped adzes, wedges, ax or pounding stone, mallets, and abrasive stones for polishing. The best adze blades were nephrite from Alaska or jadeite from British Columbia. Those fine-grained stones took an edge almost as sharp as steel, but had to be resharpened after a dozen strokes.[4] The Chinook struck their long-handled L-shaped adzes toward themselves. Measurements were standardized in fathoms (arms outstretched), spans (a hand, fingers extended), and finger widths.

A large canoe required a tree ten feet through at the butt, six feet in diameter fifty feet above, and close enough to water to carry there after the canoe had been roughed out. *Icgan*, western red cedar, was the sole wood used. Indeed, *icgan* meant tree, as their word for the particular species *igunat* salmon also meant fish. Cedar grows most thickly near the coast, and intermittently, singly and in groves, to just beyond the Cascades of the Columbia. Big trees are fifteen feet in diameter and 250 feet tall. The wood is delightfully fragrant, free from resin, rot-resistant, and warp-free; it splits easy and straight, but is not notably strong.

The canoe maker found a drift log if he could, or selected a standing tree. In Her Leaves Moon, October, he bathed and fasted, consulted his spirit and girdled the tree around. He began to chip away, charring the wood with hot stones, until the tree fell where his spirit and his chopping directed. All winter he worked daily for a few hours and sometimes continued into the spring, with a helper or two if the boat was large. A medium-size canoe of five fathoms —thirty feet—might take three months,[5] but could be completed in six weeks or less.

The trunk was first cut and burned to the required length, and a little less than half was split away. The inside was charred and chipped out. That was the humor of making a canoe from a rotten log; a hollow log saved effort. The canoe was easier to make and suffered no loss of strength if the log was naturally hollow, and it is characteristic of western red cedar that a tree's center often rots away while the tree is still healthy and vigorous. There is often no way of telling from the standing tree.

The roughly hollowed log was rolled over and the canoe maker roughed-in the outside. In the spring the villagers carried it to water and towed it to the village to be completed. The inside was shaped to match the outside, the thickness gauged by placing a hand on each side.[6] A finished hull was three fingers thick at the bottom, two on the sides, and a single finger at the gunwales. Fur trader Robert Stuart praised their craftsmanship:

> If perfect symmetry, smoothness and proportion constitute beauty, [their canoes] surpass anything I ever beheld. I have seen some of them as transparent as oiled paper, thro' which you could trace every formation of the inside, and the natives of this river and its vicinity are the most expert paddlemen any of us had ever seen.[7]

The carver sweated and invoked his *kawok*, then propped the fully carved hull upright, and poured into it water tinctured with urine, which he heated with hot stones. He built little fires all around and continually wet the hull until the sides became soft and pliable. He began to bend them outward with thick sticks wedged between the gunwales. This gradually opened the sides to about thirty degrees off vertical, widening the hull six to twelve inches at the gunwales. He bent the gunwales even further, forming four-inch lips to turn the waves. Stretching was exceedingly touchy, requiring a profound understanding of the dynamics of the wood, lest the hull warp or become misshapen. Finally, permanent spreaders as thick as a canoeman's stout forearm were sewn in place just below the gunwales.

The bow and stern were now carved of separate pieces of wood and sewn in place. Spruce roots and cedar branchlets were the thread, tree resin gums made the joint waterproof. The outside of the hull was polished smooth with stones and painted black. The inside was finished with perfect rows of adze marks and painted red. Replaceable strips were pegged to the tops of the gunwales as protection, sometimes decorated with the bright joint-valves of sea snails, or sea mammal teeth.

The Chinook used five-foot paddles with T-shaped handles and a wide V- or U-shaped notch across the working end of the blades.[8] The notch works well for fending off logs or rocks, where a round or pointed blade would slip off, but why the Chinook notched them isn't known.

Such boats lasted ten or more years. The risk was of splitting. Cedar's advantage is also its weakness. Struck just so, on a rock or by an arrow, a boat might split from stem to stern, as the son of Tiapexwasxwas split the canoes of his foes. In addition, Chinook carvers sometimes made the sides too thin for practicality. Some boats could be seen flexing and distorting in rough water.

Canoes were central to the lives of the Chinook. The beach in front of a Chinook village was lined with boats. They covered them with mats and wet them frequently in hot weather. With canoes they caught their dinner, paid for their wives, and moved goods to sell. Sometimes they filled one with salmon eggs and challenged another village to an eating contest.

ALL THE PEOPLE of a village could go afloat at once, or they could move the village across the river and make a new village, as did the Kathlamet, in 1810. They had been living on the left bank four miles below Puget Island, where Lewis and Clark saw nine houses and estimated three hundred inhabitants. In 1810 they paddled across and joined the upper village of Wahkiacum, in a combined village near the present town of Cathlamet, river mile 35. There were seven houses in the new town, and their headman was Wakahohlk, who was a cousin of Stuliah, headman of Hlilusqahih, another Kathlamet village.[9] Had there been another pestilence to shrink two villages into one? Someone said they moved because of a fire. The four-hundred-year-old Scapoose house was abandoned around 1810 too.[10] Was there a connection?

OR HAD IT TO DO with the clothmen, who came that year and tried to make a fort at Oak Point? Aboard the ship *Albatross*, Boston registry, were Captain Nathan Winship, and a crew of twenty-four men.[11] They entered the river May 26th, 1810, took on a Chinook pilot, perhaps George Ramsay,[12] and worked their way fifty-four miles upriver, sounding as they went, until they came to the first clump of oak. There they selected a plot of low ground on the south bank, and immediately began building a two story blockhouse and planting a crop. These *Bahsten* had hogs, goats, and twenty-five Hawaiians.

The clothmen soon got up a quarrel with the Cooniac. They put several in irons on the supposition, that they were *Chee-he-lish*, who had some time previous cut off a schooner belonging to the Russian establishment of New Archangel, by the governor of which place he [Winship] was employed to secure any of the banditti who committed this horrid act.[13]

The Cooniac gathered to free their men, joined by the Shoalwater, who didn't want the villages upstream from themselves dealing directly with the European fur traders.

The year 1810 was the rainiest in more than a century.[14] The fort's walls were ten feet high by the time the Columbia rose to cover the floor, having already washed out the floats-ashores' garden. The Chinook crowded close, well armed and clearly unhappy. The Winship party tried to move to slightly higher ground a little downriver, but the Chinook fired shots, frightening the floats-ashores still more, and forced a landing party to retreat to the ship. Three chiefs came alongside, one of whom would have been Comcomly, by then headman of Qwatsamts. The trio were prevented from boarding, and harangued for their behavior by the *Bahsten*. The Chinook nobles replied that they were unafraid of the strangers, who should immediately move downriver. The *Albatross* sailed down, with the same native pilot who had guided it upriver, which satisfied the Chinook, who traded with the floats-ashores. Winship's assistant, William Gales, who wrote an account, explained, "The country was theirs."[15]

In Baker Bay, Winship had his sailors seize eight Shoalwater Chinooks and clap them in irons. This was intended to secure the release of some Russians said to have been enslaved by the Makah, and perhaps to punish the Chinook for their conduct at Oak Point. The captives begged their families to purchase the Russians. The Shoalwater denied they had any Russians themselves, but sent off canoes to try to ransom them. They did have some Aleuts they had purchased from the Russians, one of which they offered for twenty-five blankets and some tobacco.

The Shoalwater who had gone north returned to report that the Russians who hadn't died had already been freed. Comcomly said that the Quileute might still hold some of the Russians prisoner, but the Shoalwater couldn't deal with those people. He told Winship that some of the Russians had starved to death. Winship released four of the Shoalwater from irons. Four others were kept on board as hostages until the *Bahsten* left the river, which they did at last on July 19th.[16]

Though not a war-like people, the Chinook had faced down the clothmen.

THE RIVER PEOPLE had been reduced by repeated pestilences, but their strength and resolve were not diminished. Except when confronted by one of the new epidemics that swept their villages, their sorcerers and curers were reasonably successful.

They knew the difference between what a sorcerer and a curer—Ross said they called the latter *keelalles*[17]—could effect. For colds and fevers, broken bones and arthritis, their curers had herbs and poultices, splints, and other procedures.[18] They liked to raise blisters with coals or stinging nettles to relieve pains elsewhere, brewed various teas of roots and leaves for specific ailments, plastered sores and cuts with salves, scarified and sucked the blood from swellings, lanced infections, and cauterized wounds.

Most turned to fasting and bathing first, cold baths for rheumatism, sweats for colds and fevers, aches, and pains, or to help recover strength. The sweathouse was another import from the Plateau. The little domed structures had penetrated downriver to the Kathlamet, and even the people of Sealand would wrap themselves in blankets and lie by the fire. No one else along the coast practiced sweating.[19]

SORCERERS, once labelled witch doctors by Europeans, now more often called shaman, cured another sort of malady. The two terms aren't exactly equivalent, but they aren't very different either. Both made magic, both cured people; some individuals, more often called sorcerers, caused illness.

The maladies they cured included many that we might call psychosomatic. When an illness is not caused by some obvious external agent, is not congenital or hereditary, and does not occur in wild animals, it may come of struggles between the human mind and body.[20] Curing psychosomatic ailments depends as much on faith as on science. In this respect, the wholehearted drumming and singing of the patient's family and friends, and the dramatic performance put on by the shaman, all focused on the sufferer, compare favorably with our gleaming machines and all-knowing physicians in white coats. Psychosomatic illness is no less painful for having come from within, nor even less deadly, and many contemporary physicians believe that as much as half of mankind's ills stems from this mind-body malfunction.

WHEN THEIR DAUGHTER fell sick her parents sent a messenger with gifts and promises to the sorcerer. If the offer was sufficient, he (or she) returned with the messenger, carrying only perhaps some rattles, a headdress, and a spirit baton. Unlucky the child who crossed the shaman's path enroute, for it would fall ill.

He painted his face and took in hand his rattles and the people of the house sent the children away. He prepared himself with five deep puffs of his smoking mixture. Now the people were drumming with long poles against the roof, or on boxes, boards, or skins. Firelight danced on their broad faces. The patient lay in the center, near the fire.

Now the healer sang his power songs, summoning his *kawoks*. He studied the patient, but seldom touched or questioned her. The shaman might refuse the case if it appeared hopeless, or agree to try anyway for a certain fee. He described where and how the patient became sick, and named omens by which his success or failure could be predicted. Artist Paul Kane described what followed:

> Throwing off his blanket he commenced singing and gesticulating, in the most violent manner, whilst the others kept time by beating with little sticks on hollow wooden bowls and drums, singing continually. After exercising himself in this manner for about half an hour, until the perspiration ran in streams down his body, he darted suddenly on the young woman, catching hold of her side with his teeth and shaking her for a few minutes, as one dog does another in a fight, the patient seeming to suffer great agony.
>
> He then relinquished his hold and cried out he had got it, at the same time holding his hands to his mouth, after which he plunged them in water, and pretended to hold with great difficulty the disease which he had extracted, lest it might spring out and return to its victim. At length having obtained the mastery over it, turning himself round to me in an exalting manner, he held something up between the finger and thumb of each hand, which had the appearance of a piece of cartilage, whereupon one of the Indians sharpened his knife and divided it in two, leaving one end in each hand. One of the pieces he threw into the water and the other into the fire, accompanying the action with a diabolical noise which none but a medicine man can make.[21]

The object was a *yuhlma*—a wild spirit. Weak spirits the sorcerer might disperse by merely sweeping them off with his hands. He felt for the invisible *yuhlma* and tried to catch it. He rubbed one out between his hands and blew it away. Or swallowed it, adding it to his own power. But against powerful wild spirits or those sent by other sorcerers, he pressed both fists into the patient's stomach with all his weight, the patient groaning and struggling; then the shaman bent to suck a spot on the patient's abdomen or head.

Sucking out the attacking spirit was an essential part of Chinook sorcery. One name for a curing shaman was *gilaxaxana*, "one who sucks." Some other names used downriver were *laqewam*, "One having a shaman's song," or *gitakitelal*, "those who have the power of seeing." Upriver, they said *idiagewam*, "sorcerer," or *idiaxilalit*, "curer."[22]

"If I take this sickness out the patient is going to die [faint]," he warned them. He bent to suck. "Now!" he cried, and three or four strong men pulled him back by bands of deer hide against the power of the disease spirit. The patient "died," his assistant sprayed a mouthful of water to revive her, and the shaman spat the disease object into his hands.[23]

The sorcerer held the *yuhlma*. Five people took hold of him, by his legs, arms, and back. They tried to carry him to a box of water near the fire, but the spirit resisted. It escaped and the men fell down. When they got the conjurer to the water he put it in. The spirit got cold, it lost its power. They saw that it was made of the claws of a wolf, or of a bird. Sometimes it was the bone of a dead person, carved in the form of a man. It might be a glob of blood, a bit of bone or gristle, black, yellow, or white. Hairs tied around it told the shaman about the length and course of the illness. The shaman rubbed it in the water until it got soft and cooled.

It seems a little pathetic, viewed through our scientific eyes. *Wagwet*-bird shaman's curing song was:

> I wish my younger sister would move.
> I wish my younger sister would turn on her side.
> I wish my younger sister would sit up.[24]

Fur trader Gabriel Franchère concluded, "thus these tricksters impose upon simple and credulous children of nature. It often happens that a sick person who might have been saved by a bleeding or a simple purge is carried off by sudden death."[25] His suggested cures remind us of how far Western medicine has come since 1810.

IT WAS DEATH, not pain, the Chinook feared. For so sensual a people, they were remarkably stoic, going barefoot in the snow without concern[26] and sleeping in the rain under a single blanket.[27] But death they were not very sure about. They used the same word for death as for all forms of unconsciousness but sleep. They had a lot of stories about people who were dead for several days, then awoke and told of what they had seen in the world beyond.

Cultee's grandfather wanted to marry a Cooniac girl, but they tried to give him another girl he did not like. Then sickness came, the people dying after three or four days. Cultee's grandfather fell ill. He died.

> Then he went to the country of the ghosts. He reached the trail. He saw two people carrying a stick. When he came near, he saw that they were the posts of a house. Then he came to a person who dragged his intestines on the ground. When he came near he saw that it was a mat of rushes. The road was full of the tracks of people. Now he came to a large creek. He looked across and saw a large town. He heard people making canoes. Then a person came up to him. He recognized one of his mother's relatives who had been dead long ago.
>
> He said, "Did you come at last; They are waiting for you. The news of your arrival has come already. They will buy for you the girl whom you like. She and her mother have come across." Then that person left him.
>
> The grass at that place was three fingers wide and was more than a man's height. It was moved by the wind and

sounded like bells. He heard it ringing all the time. The grass told the people on the other side what was going to happen. Now he saw that woman and he thought, "I do not like her. She looks just like her mother. Her face is sore all the time." He saw her in that manner.

Then another person came to him. He recognized his uncle. They all came up the river. His uncle spoke: "Let us go to catch seals." His uncle took a line. He gave him something that looked just like soap. "Eat that," he said.

He ate it, but he did not like it. Then he turned his head toward the land and spit out what was given to him. His uncle who was looking toward the water said: "What does he want to eat? He refuses what I gave him."

Then he thought: "I just came here and they scold me already. I will return." Then the sun shone on his right side. He did not walk. He just turned round and then fell in a swoon. Now he recovered. He heard people crying.[28]

Wishram who died saw another land from a distance, the inhabitants of which appeared happy. The ghosts did not speak to them, but they vaguely heard voices, saying, "This person is not good enough to remain here. Go back and learn to be a better man." The dead person felt a force pushing him away; he whirled about and at that moment was alive again.[29] In another case, a man died but revived when his family argued about the disposition of his goods. He arose, gave things as he wished, then lay down and died again.[30]

The land of the ghosts was across a river or on an island. The ghosts remained there five years, or until the flesh and bones had disappeared.[31] At night they could return to the village. They were dangerous because of their fondness for the company of the living, whom they would try to entice to join them. In the land of the ghosts it was always spring or summer, the fields were green and flowers bloomed, berries ripened, water flowed. They danced each night in a ten-fathom house.[32]

BLUE JAY VISITED *memaloose illahee*, the land of the dead:

Ghosts came and bought Blue Jay's sister Ioi. They took her home with them. After a year Blue Jay went to search for her. He asked various birds where ghosts went, but the birds did not know. He asked an old Wedge, who offered to take him there if he was paid. Blue Jay paid, and was carried to the land of the ghosts. He arrived near a large town. He found his elder sister. "Are you dead, Blue Jay?" she asked him. "No," he told her, "Wedge brought me."

All that house was full of bones. A skull and bones lay near his sister. "This is your brother-in-law," Ioi told him. "Ana!" thought Blue Jay, "that Ioi is lying all the time."

After dark that ten-fathom house was full of people. Blue Jay hung around. Now Ioi sent him off to fish with a dip net. She told him not to speak, to keep quiet. He went with a boy, out on the river were other people, some of them were singing. Blue Jay joined in. Instantly there was silence. He looked at the boy in the stern of his canoe, he saw only bones. Then Blue Jay became quiet, and when he looked again there was that boy again. When Blue Jay spoke in a low voice, the boy replied, but when he spoke loudly there was only a skeleton.

They fished, and Blue Jay caught two branches. He threw them back. He caught a net-full of leaves, and threw those back too. The boy seemed to be gathering leaves, he put them in the canoe. Blue Jay caught more branches. He saved a couple for the fire. Then he returned home. But they had caught nothing. The boy brought up a mat full of trout, he told Ioi that Blue Jay had thrown away all that he caught. Ioi told

Blue Jay that those were their food, the leaves were trout, the branches fall salmon. He told her of the branches he had saved. She went out and brought back two salmon. Where had she gotten them? She told him they were the branches. "Ioi is always lying," Blue Jay thought.

On the beach in front of the village all the canoes were moss grown and full of holes. Blue Jay commented upon it. Ioi told him to be quiet. "They are not people but ghosts," she told him.

Again they fished all night. Blue Jay teased the boy, he shouted and the boy was nothing but a pile of bones. They caught leaves and branches. Blue Jay shouted at people in the other canoes, and they became nothing but bones.

Ioi told him that a whale had washed ashore. Blue Jay ran to the beach, but the whale was only a log with thick bark. He found the people peeling off the bark. He shouted at them and made them skeletons. He kicked their skulls around. He peeled off pieces of the log and carried them home, and behold, they were blubber.

He would change a child's skull with an adult's skull. Then the big head pulled the child down, the man's head felt light. Blue Jay exchanged legs too, old and large and men and women, interchanged. The ghosts began to dislike him. They told him to go home. Ioi tried to stop him from playing pranks. He threw Ioi's husband's skull, he broke her husband's neck, but a man cured him.

Blue Jay set out for the land of the living, but did not follow his sister's instructions about carrying water to put out fires he would encounter. He died in a prairie fire.

"Kukukukukukukuku, Ioi," Blue Jay said. "Ah," she said, "he is dead." Ioi came to fetch him. Her canoe looked pretty, he told her so. "You said it was moss-grown before," she told him,

"Now you are dead, you see things differently."

*The people were there, gambling with beaver teeth, play-
ing at disks, singing and dancing. Blue Jay met her husband,
he was a handsome chief. "Ioi is always telling lies," Blue Jay
thought. He could not believe he was really dead. She tried to
show him. She pointed out the canoes he had thought mossy,
the former bones he had kicked. Blue Jay shouted at the people, but they did not change, they only laughed at him now.
Then Blue Jay became quiet. He stood near the dancers. After
five nights he entered their house. His sister opened the door,
she saw him dancing there, dancing on his head with his legs
upward. Then Ioi turned back and cried. Now he had really
died, he had died a second time.*[33]

THE GHOSTS FED THEMSELVES by dipping a feather in a stone bowl
of oil and brushing it across their lips. After five years the souls
crossed another body of water. The Chinook did not know where
they went. They could no longer return. There was no reason to fear
them. They seem not to have believed in reincarnation except of
dead babies, which went back to baby-land but might return again.

Perhaps diabetic insulin comas shaped their confusion about
death, and their tales of returnings. Death loomed large in the Chinook consciousness, and not just since the epidemics.[34] For some
centuries their art had exhibited ribs and backbones, stylized skeletons. Wherever they traveled, the canoes of the dead stood about on
cliffs and islands, reminding them of the departed. The ghosts
wanted the living to come join them. Since the coming of the first
pestilence, more and more people had followed the ghosts.

As babies they lay in a cradleboard shaped like a canoe. In death
they took their final rest in a canoe propped high on stout posts, its
prow downriver. That was the final outcome, when Blue Jay
knocked a hole in a rotten log.

Basalt owl carving, found on Sauvie Island. Courtesy of the Oregon Histori-cal Society.

14

The *Bahsten* Make a Fort

1811 – 1812

THE COLUMBIA BAR was a fearsome thing, five miles from bank to bank, two to three miles of raging, frothing surf, not infrequently blocking the entire entrance to the river. The Chinook could master the bar, but seldom did. When the elements were in opposition, for example a strongly ebbing ocean tide augmenting the river's flood, opposed by a southwest storm wind, the waves steepened incredibly and crashed in cannonade, unbroken from shore to shore.

In early April 1811, the ship *Tonquin*, New York registry, arrived off this watery battleground at just such an inauspicious combination of tide and wind. Captain Jonathan Thorn was undeterred. He sent his chief mate and four oarsmen in one of the ship's boats, to sound a channel. Only one of the oarsmen was experienced at rowing. The boat was carried away and the five never seen again.

When the bar calmed two days later another of the *Tonquin's* boats was dispatched, but could find no entry. Several Chinooks on the beach by the rocky cape tried to beckon them to the north channel, but the boat retreated to the ship. A third attempt to sound the channel found four-fathom depths, but barely managed to claw its way back to the *Tonquin*. The fourth attempt, again with only one experienced sailor, led the ship into the breakers, but the boat was carried away and three of its five-man crew drowned. Struggling in the relentless surf the ship struck bottom repeatedly. At nightfall Thorn had to drop anchor on the roaring, crashing bar. Finally, late that night, wind and tide came around and they sailed in to safe anchorage behind Cape Disappointment.

THE SHOALWATER CHINOOK greeted the strangers as always, with fish and berries, but the Pacific Fur Company, as these floats-ashores called themselves, had no immediate interest in trade. They had been sent by John Jacob Astor, a New York fur merchant and capitalist, to build a trading post.

A few days later, two of the partners, Duncan McDougall and David Stuart, scouted the south shore of the river in a boat manned by six men. The Astorians, as they would come to be called, returned by way of Chinook Point, where they were hosted by their new friend Comcomly. They slept over in his house. When they prepared to set out for their ship the next day, he counselled them not to, for the wind was wrong and eight-mile-wide Baker Bay was shallow and open to the wind. The now-paramount headman of Qwatsamts may have noticed that these particular *Bahsten* were inept small-boat handlers compared to the practiced sailors of the other ships.

They launched anyway, but a mile or two from shore took a wave and capsized. McDougall couldn't swim, and all of them would have been in mortal peril had not Comcomly been close behind. He fished them from the waves, dried them off by a fire on shore, then took them back to his house where they were pinned down by a three-day blow.

In addition to saving the eight men trying to get back to the *Tonquin*, the Chinook had saved the oarsmen of another boat that had set out from the *Tonquin* to rescue them and overturned as well. Yet in a similar overturned boat and rescue the same week, Alexander Ross recorded that the Astorians suspected the "sordid rascals had upset us willfully in order to claim the merit of having saved us, and therewith a double recompense for their trips."[1]

During that prolonged visit McDougall, headman of the Astorians, met Illchee, Comcomly's oldest daughter, probably around sixteen at the time. McDougall would later be described as having an "irritable, peevish temper," and as being "choleric" and "an active, irritable, fuming, vainglorious little man and elevated in his own opinion," who had great plans but few achievements.[2] Illchee was a true princess in the most modern sense of the word, the product of her father's by then pre-eminent wealth and power.

THE ASTORIANS decided to make their fort at Awakat,[3] river mile 14 on the south bank. They unloaded some of their goods and thirty-three men there, and the *Tonquin*, with twenty-seven sailors and traders, turned back to sea and headed north to seek furs.

At the mouth of the Columbia, or at Grays Harbor, or near the mouth of the Hoh River, Thorn encountered a native, ostensibly fishing from a boat, who claimed to know pilotage and the languages where they were heading. This may have been George Ramsay, called Lamsay, the Indian-looking younger son of Jack Ramsay, who is mentioned by several sources, or it may have been a Quinault named Joseachal, as Duncan McDougall recorded. Whichever it was, it may well have been his intention to offer his services as a pilot and interpreter for the *Tonquin*. Thorn brought him aboard.[4]

Astoria, America's most ambitious venture on the farthest shore, sprouted directly across Big River from Comcomly's Qwatsamts. Within that frontier fort would occur a literary flowering that provides many insights into the Chinook, though often highly slanted ones. Astorian Alexander Ross, who published his recollections (including the description of Duncan McDougall above) in 1847, was described by Hudson's Bay Company executive George Simpson as, "A self sufficient, empty headed man . . . whose reports are so full of bombast and marvelous nonsense that it is impossible to get any information that can be depended on from him."[5] (Simpson was astute, but catty, and many of his thumbnail biographies read like that.) Ross Cox, who published his reminiscences in 1832, can almost be counted upon to misunderstand everything. Franchère, first published in 1854, was more sympathetic, while Alexander Henry, who arrived somewhat later, wrote a journal, originally published in 1897, which though more meticulous, shows a bias against the Chinook in general and Comcomly in particular.[6]

Still, facts crept in. The journals from that outpost, some of which Washington Irving used to write his bestseller *Astoria*, and the several other journals of the participants published since, provide an overlapping set of rippled windows into the first few years of the settlement at the mouth of the Columbia, and of what the Astorians saw of the Chinook, still living in their own houses, fishing their accustomed drifts, sunbathing naked beside their river.

THE ASTORIANS who remained were short on trade goods, most of which were aboard the *Tonquin*. They set to work building their houses and putting together a small sailboat, the *Dolly*, which they had brought knocked down.

The Chinook traded with the newcomers for food and furs. At first the river people were fearful of selling the Astorians fresh salmon, lest they cut it across the backbone and the salmon cease coming to the river. They brought baked salmon to sell, already butchered, and demanded the flesh be eaten by sundown. The clothmen finally convinced them just to bring the fish.[7] The Astorians cut the salmon any which way, but there seemed to be just as many salmon as ever in the river. The taboo was evidently unclear on how soon the salmon would cease coming.

In order to keep the price of pelts reasonably high, the Chinook spread the word that these new *tlohonnipts* were dangerous monsters, cannibals with whom only the Shoalwater and Clatsop dared negotiate.[8] Meanwhile, they confided to the Astorians that the natives of the region were brute savages who harbored only malice toward all clothmen. Thus, the Chinook were able to buy furs and to sell furs, and a steady, well-regulated trade was maintained.[9]

In July the Astorians began to comprehend the Chinook strategy. They estimated the Chinook were taking a hundred percent markup to collect, transport, and warehouse the pelts.[10] The *Bahsten* were furious. They had come halfway around the world to gull innocent savages and found the Chinook instead. A few months later, at a trading post far inland on the Okanogan River, Ross gloated that he had bought 1,550 beaver pelts, worth 2,250 pounds sterling in Canton, for trade goods that had cost 35 pounds sterling, a markup of 6,429 percent.[11]

Henry commented in his journal,

> They are a hard people to deal with who must be allowed their own way—that is to say, if we cannot agree on price, the only way is to wait until they cool off, and show no anxiety to trade until they propose it themselves . . . but we are determined to have our own way. . . .[12]

THE ASTORIANS decided to introduce themselves to the savages farther away and invite them to the fort. To guide them they enlisted a headman named Coalpo.[13] In July, Coalpo led them up Big River as far as the Cascades, introducing them at various Wahkiacum, Kathlamet, Kalama, Multnomah, Quathlapootle, and Shahala villages. At the Cascades, Coalpo said that he feared to continue upriver, the people above being his enemies. In August Coalpo guided a party north up the coast as far as the Quinault. The Quinault had piles of furs they said they had intended to sell to the Chinook, but promised to come to Astoria. The other Chinook knew all that transpired from their cousin Coalpo. The Quinault may have visited Astoria, but their trade did not turn around. Quinault furs and those from up Big River continued to flow to the Astorians by way of the Chinook, who continued to take their wholesaler's markup for more than a decade.

In the Columbia Gorge, a few miles below the Cascades, the Astorians had encountered the descendant of Konapee, one of the early floats-ashores. Clerk Alfred Seton recalled,

> We passed the cabin of old blind Soto, a solitary fisherman, who calls himself a white man: his story is—and his albigineous look seems to confirm it—that he is the son of a Spaniard; a ship of that nation, in long-by days, had been wrecked at the mouth of the river; a number of its crew reached in safety the shore; the Clatsops, who inhabit Point Adams, massacred them all except four, one of whom, whose son old Soto is, settled in the country; the others, wearied with an Indian life, went into the interior, with the expectation of finding their way to some settlement of their countrymen; but no tradition of their fate has reached the present race.[14]

Soto may have been the man who lived along Lake River when Lewis and Clark passed upriver in 1806 and named a group Shoto. He told them his father had left when he was quite young.

In August, when many people came to the estuary to trade and fish for sturgeon and salmon, the Astorians grew fearful.[15] Their fort still lacked palisades and their cannons were unmounted. They suspected the attack the Chinook had warned them of, and noticing that Comcomly was conspicuous by his absence, feared the worst. They sent word for the little one-eyed chief to visit them, but he did not come. They sent word again. A third time they sent not just word but gifts, and he appeared. "Dissembling our opinion of his conduct," they received him eagerly. Comcomly reassured them of their safety, and trade began, for which he and his two sons, now called Shalapau and Chenamus, got suits of European clothes.

The word "Indian" continually came between the Astorians and reality. When the Clatskanie of the Nehalem Hills killed three Astorians, they ascribed the murder to "Indians," not differentiating between the Chinook, who lived in villages of cedar-plank houses, and Athabascan hill tribesmen, who roamed the forest.

On August 6th Coalpo informed the Astorians that the *Tonquin* had been blown up, after a murderous struggle between the crew and natives on Vancouver Island. Only Lamsay (or Joseachal) survived, for he had been treated as a fellow native by the Vancouver Island people. He had jumped into a canoe full of women when hostilities began, and been covered and protected by the women. He was enslaved for a time, then ransomed and returned. It was his story of Thorn's insolence and the ensuing treacherous and explosive revenge that passed into history. The last surviving Astorian had touched a match to the ship's powder magazine, after waiting for the natives to board the apparently deserted ship.[16]

AS AUTUMN APPROACHED, the Astorians found themselves few—their numbers had dwindled from the sixty-eight who left New York to thirty still living—and far from home, with only the little *Dolly* for transport, and hardly any goods to trade until the next ship arrived the following spring, if it arrived. An overland party, expected to join them, hadn't.

Driven by fear of "Indians" and emboldened by the dread of smallpox the natives so often confessed, McDougall seized upon a desperate deception. Assembling the nobles of several villages, he displayed a small bottle and told them that it contained the smallpox spirit, which he would let loose should any offense whatsoever be committed against his people. Horror-struck, they begged him not to uncork the bottle. They professed their friendship to the *Bahsten*, and argued that it would be unjust of McDougall to destroy them for something done by other people several days' paddle away. McDougall finally put the bottle away. He was known forever after among the Chinook as the Smallpox Chief.[17]

At the Cascades that summer, David Thompson of the rival North West Company, returning upriver from a reconnaissance of Astoria and the lower river, was asked by a Shahala,

> Is it true that the white men have brought with them the smallpox to destroy us, and also two men of enormous size, who are on their way to us, overturning the ground, and burying all the villages and lodges underneath it; is it true that we are all soon to die?[18]

AT THE UPPER END of the Long Narrows portage, Thompson's party encountered a group of

> men from thirty to fifty years of age . . . from near the sea [meaning Chinooks] each armed with a double dagger, a bow, and three quivers of arrows, they formed three rows on the slope above. The arrows were all poisoned, as we later learned; each man had one arrow to the bow and three more in the hand that held the bow. The notch of the arrow was in the bow string, but not drawn. I directed my men, who formed a line of three feet from each other, to direct a steady aim at the most respectable men, and not vary their aim. My orders were, as soon as they drew the arrow to fire on them, but not before; in this anxious posture we stood opposed to each other for fully 15 minutes (it seemed a long half hour), when the upper rank began to break up, and in a few minutes the whole of them retired, to our great satisfaction; for

a single shower of arrows would have laid us all dead.

We hardly knew what to make of these people; they appear a mixture of kindness and treachery; willingly rendering every service required, and performing well what they undertook, but demanding exorbitant prices for their services, and dagger in hand ready to enforce their demands. Fortunately they were content with tobacco of a cheap quality. Still, there were some few kind men among them, and more than one man came close to us with his dagger, and in a mild voice warned us of our danger and to be courageous. Their determination was to kill and plunder us, but they were equally determined that not one of them should be killed in so doing; there was no chief among them, each man appeared to be his own leader; whatever conduct in canoes they may have as warriors . . . on the land they were bungling blockheads.[19]

FORT ASTORIA would eventually grow to two hundred yards square with fifteen-foot palisades. After resupply ships began to arrive regularly they built bastions on the southwest and northeast corners armed with four- and six-pound cannons.[20] They expelled all the Chinooks and closed the gates at night, though sometimes when the night was stormy they let favored nobles sleep inside.

In the spring of 1812 a party of clothmen began to straggle downriver to the fort. This was Wilson Price Hunt's overland party, sent by Astor to support the sea party.[21] They had met such disasters crossing the mountains that two of them had gone mad. The Chinook were surprised that those who had come in ships should know those who came overland, and that those who arrived overland should return home by ship.[22]

In March of 1812 a party of seventeen Astorians encountered trouble ascending the Long Narrows past Wishram. They were pestered and annoyed, and there was considerable pilfering, including the theft of knives, handkerchiefs, a tin box of dispatches on its way to New York, and two rifles. One Astorian's head was bloodied with a club. In response, the clothmen shot and killed two Tlakluit men.[23]

Three months later an upriver-bound party of sixty men in two barges and ten canoes were victims of a canoe upset at the Cascades. When the Shahala salvaged their goods but returned only half there was a scuffle and arrows were shot at or near the Astorians. They hesitated nervously for a few days below the Long Narrows, then portaged safely up past Nixluidix, and camped beyond on the south bank.

Made brave by their successful portage, three Astorians decided to reclaim the rifles stolen three months before. Donald McKenzie, a gentleman; Alfred Seton, a clerk; and Joe LaPierre, the cook, paddled across to Nixluidix, and seeing no one about, ascended a winding path among rocks and crags a hundred yards to the town. Not even a dog barked. A boy of twelve or fourteen appeared and directed them to a house somewhat larger than the others. They crawled through a door two feet wide and three high. No sooner had they entered than they heard a rush of feet from outside, where before there had been no one.

They found themselves in a room twenty-five feet by twenty feet, at the far end of which was a bright fire, and beyond it a sixty-year-old chief. Around them, three deep, sat the nobles of Wishram, wrapped in robes with only their faces visible, squatted around three sides of the room. The Tlakluit stared at the ground, apparently not interested. The headman gestured for the clothmen to sit on the vacant side. There was silence.

The *bourgeois*, McKenzie, ordered the other two to keep their eyes on the chief, and if he signaled his fellow Indians, to shoot him and make for the door. The clothmen filled and offered a pipe, but it was refused. Now McKenzie spoke, telling them

that the white man had come into their country for the purpose of trade, bringing them blankets, axes, knives, etc, to exchange for their peltries; that their desire was to live in peace and friendship with their red bretheren; that though they possessed arms, which in their hands resembled thunder and lightening, in others they were useless; that the chief might know this, from having one of the white men's guns, which was valueless to him; that he had brought over from his camp two blankets, an axe, some beads and tobacco, to exchange with the chief for the white man's gun, which he would show if the chief was willing to do so; that the white men's nation, though few here, were as numerous as the sands on the shore; that they were, when unprovoked, as gentle as the deer that roamed in their woods; but when angry, as dangerous as the rattlesnake that glides among the rocks.

A long silence followed, stretching out for minutes. Now and then the chief glared at them. At length he arose, and started speaking in a low tone, "but warming as he progressed, until he wound himself to a paroxysm of violent rage." Seton interpreted his harangue as conveying

that his ears had drunk what the my-ai-whoot (the white chief) had said; but that it was spoken with the serpent's tongue; that the *passiuks* had already been many moons in the country, and where could one of his tribe point to a blanket, an axe, beads or tobacco, they had given them; that his country had no furs, therefore the white men passed his people as dogs; that the blankets the white chief had with him, as well as the young chief's gun and the white man's slaves ought to be left with him, as a comfort for the death of his brothers, whom a few moons since the white men had killed; that his eyes had not yet done weeping for their death; and that the white chief had now come to deprive him of his only consolation in his calamity; that the white chief was a brother of the white men who had killed his brothers; for his young men had that day seen the pale-faced coward who lost his gun.

The headman paused, and McKenzie took advantage of it. The three rose, their guns trained on the chief. They clicked the locks, and "advanced" to the door. It was near sunset as they came out, hurried down the path, and paddled across to their camp. No one followed. They slept safely and continued on the next day.[24]

ALL THIS *Tsagiglalal* saw from her rock above the town. The Wish-ram killed by the clothmen were placed near her. There seemed to be a pattern. The Chinook talked, pestered, argued, pilfered, and tried to negotiate. The clothmen passed by without giving gifts or even talking. They established no relationship. Though both the Cascades and the Long Narrows were classic passes, where toll or portage fees would have been charged anywhere on Earth, these newcomers wished to pass through without a word.[25]

The Astorians were evidently not very good at gauging the person they were dealing with. Alexander Ross, when they first passed the Cascades in July 1811, had been detailed to guard duty, but decided to help carry. He grabbed a bundle of tobacco, but was worn out by the first hill. He signalled a Shahala that he would give him all the buttons on his coat if the Indian would carry it. At first the Indian refused, but after Ross went over the transaction again, the man grabbed the tobacco and took off, with Ross right behind him. Near the end of the four-mile portage the Shahala threw the

Naked Against the Rain

tobacco down a two-hundred-foot cliff. Ross had to go get it, amid the general laughter of about fifty other Shahala. After all Ross's labors bringing it back up, the Indian demanded payment, and the Astorians decided they had better give him Ross's buttons.[26]

If opposed, the clothmen often replied with gunfire. Having killed, they demanded restitution of their goods. They evidently had no respect for the value of human life. In 1813, farther upriver, Nor'wester John Clarke hanged a Nez Perce accused of pilfering his personal silver wine goblet.[27]

Kalliah, called Indian Mary, a Shahala. She has also been called Mary Stoo-quin. Photographer unknown. Courtesy of the Oregon Historical Society.

15

Coyote Visits
The Spring of Abundance

AUTUMN

Now ACORN MOON was standing up, and soon Her Leaves Moon when the leaves fall. The autumn sky was dappled blue and white, with a few refreshing showers. The people burned the prairies in the Wapato Lowlands so the camas would grow more thickly. The hills were spotted yellow with big leaf maple and alder, and red with vine maple among the dark evergreens.

More fruit ripened: bearberry, mealy and mild; tart Oregon grape; cranberries in the bogs north of the river; and sour crab apple. Shotberry ended the berrying.

Fur-bearers were fat and those who had a hunter's spirit took pride in bringing home meat. Deer and elk hunting loomed large in the Chinook mythology, as it does in our own, but with hardly more relationship to real need, for fishing was how they got their living. They were neither very good at, nor very interested in, hunting animals, according to some of the floats-ashores.[1]

They hunted whitetail and blacktail deer and thousand-pound Roosevelt elk. Men stalked singly or in a group with a leader, driving their prey toward a pit, a bowman, or a cliff, such as the one-hundred-foot wall called Elk Cliff, above the Willamette River at

Dunthorpe. Lone stalkers disguised themselves with the head of a deer or elk. They stalked black bear, and in the winter smoked them out of their dens. Upriver, they hunted mule deer and elk, and mountain sheep on the high cliffs of the Columbia Gorge.

Beaver they took at night with a harpoon, and rabbits in nets across rabbit trails. Muskrat, woodrat, raccoon, porcupine, mink, squirrels of several sorts, and mountain beaver they hunted, both for food and pelts. They used only the skins of wolf, coyote, grizzly, badger, skunk, and rock squirrel.

In autumn the air became loud with migratory birds again. The Chinook had names for all the kinds of ducks and geese that came their way: redheads, scaup, canvasback, ringnecked, harlequin, and butterball ducks; mallard, pintail, baldpate, wood duck, and blue and green teal; Canada, cackling, and snow goose; crane, great blue heron, white swans, and black brants.

Upland too they hunted: grouse, pheasant, and snipe, with a brush whip. They ate the eggs of every bird except gull. But not the flesh of eagle, condor, crow, owl, hawk, blackbird, heron, fishhawk, kingfisher, cormorant, raven, or gull. Insects, turtles, snakes, or frogs they considered disgusting food.

In October the women harvested *wapato* in the marshes from the Cowlitz to the Washougal, where the bulbs of the arrowhead plant, named for its graceful leaf, were abundant. The acorn- to walnut-sized bulbs were scattered in deep mud, connected to the tall plant by fragile tubes that broke easily. A woman combed with toes or fingers through the muck, sometimes in water to her chest. If she was lucky she might find and steal a muskrat's store.

In addition to burning the prairies, they weeded the death camas out of their camas beds, for the deadly white-flowering kind can only be told from the edible blue-flowering ones when in flower. Otherwise, with the exception of nicotiana (which we call tobacco), they practiced no agriculture.

THEY SMOKED A MIXTURE of leaves, including bearberry, two varieties of nicotiana, and combinations of the leaves of manzanita, dogwood, madrona, salal, or the bark of red willow. Lieutenant Charles Wilkes judged one mixture mild but pleasant.[2] Tobacco came to be called *kinootl, kinoos, kimoolth,* or *bacca,* in the Jargon.[3] The Chinook planted one or both of the nicotiana, growing it from seeds. Botanist David Douglas discovered a tobacco plantation:

> Although I made diligent search for it, it never came under my notice until now. They do not cultivate it near their camps or lodges lest it should be taken for use before maturity. An open place in the woods is chosen, where there is dead wood, which they burn and sow the seed in the ashes.[4]

The Wishram claimed that four or five puffs of their smoke was sufficient. More than that might render a person unconscious for up to half an hour. Douglas said of Comcomly's brother Thaamux, "he smoked greedily, seized the pipe and inhaled any particles of the smoke in the lungs, so that he would regularly five or six times a day fall down in a state of stupefaction."[5]

Sorcerers and headmen always smoked. A shaman might take five ritual puffs before beginning a cure. Smoke strengthened and made lively his or her spirit. When the Clackamas saw a girl smoking they said, "It is not for nothing, probably some spirit power told her: Smoke!" But if they suspected someone of just smoking without a spirit's command, they said the smoke would stay in and choke him, he would become sick and enfeebled.[6]

The headman offered smoke at council, passing the pipe around the circle. A man might smoke a pipe in the evening. They inhaled deeply and held the smoke in. Several visitors observed that in addition to inhaling, they swallowed the smoke. Lewis and Clark wrote, "I have no doubt the smoke of the tobacco in this manner becomes much more intoxicating and that they do posses themselves of all its virtues in their fullest extent."[7] They used two types of pipes, one L-shaped with three-inch arms and a long wooden stem, the other like a cigar holder, smoked by turning the head back and holding the pipe upright. Men carried such pipes on cords around their necks. Many were finely crafted of blue-green or black steatite and other materials, and carved so thin the coal glowed through the stone.[8]

THE WASCO told a curious story about tobacco:

> *An Arrow Point Maker cut his finger and liked the taste of the blood so much that he ate his whole body, down to just bones, only his heart and some flesh below his shoulders where he couldn't reach it remained. He went to the village and ate all the people there. His wife fled, running on the tops of the grass so he could not follow, carrying her baby. She sought asylum at the house of an old man who made arrows with which he shot tobacco. His daughter made little tobacco bags.*
>
> *The wind howled around their house. She begged the man to hide her. Then the skeleton came, the blasts of wind rattled its bones. It stamped around the fire, destroying the old man's arrows, until the tobacco-hunter snatched a long arrow point and thrust it into the skeleton's heart. It fell and was only a pile of bones. The wind died, and they threw the bones outside.*
>
> *When his quiver was full the old man went out, returning later with tobacco. The man and his daughter lived on smoke. Neither ate anything. They smoked what he brought home until it was gone and then he went out to search for the tobacco people again. They grew on the hills above the house. He shot them and they fell down.*
>
> *Now, when the woman's son was old enough, he secretly followed the old man out to hunt, and shot them as the old*

man did. Five bunches of tobacco fell. The old man was over-
joyed, and called the boy his son-in-law. His daughter mar-
ried the boy, who hunted tobacco for all of them, filling the
house with tobacco. He and his mother resurrected their vil-
lage and all the people arose again. At last his mother grew old
and weak. She announced, "My daughter and I will go south,
and we will give authority to women to smoke. When a
woman smokes, she will be a medicine-woman." The son an-
nounced, "I will be a guardian spirit to help people. Those
whom I help will be good hunters."[9]

SOME PEOPLE SUPPOSE the Chinook to have been "less advanced"
because they did not farm, keep herds, or build of stone. They did-
n't need to. Their cultivation of tobacco shows they knew how to
farm. Weeding and burning the camas beds was minimum farming. As with the status difference between piling stones, which remain, or building with wood, which disappears, it depends on who
is doing the classifying, and whether for comfort or for longevity of
structure. Old wooden houses are fine to live in; stone perhaps less
comfortable.

The Chinook were as well fed as any people on the continent,
and probably among the best fed on earth. They were the belly people of the Wishpoosh Myth, a Sahaptin tale of how the world and
its peoples were created.

Wishpoosh was a beaver monster with eyes like fire, huge
claws, and outrage in his heart. Coyote went up to battle
Wishpoosh with a spear, which he plunged in the monster's
side. They battled down the Kittitas Valley, then down the
Yakima Valley, the rivers forming increasingly large lakes be-
hind them. As they struggled and tumbled they cut the chan-
nel for the rivers. They battled down the Columbia. Coyote's

struggles made the channel wider as Wishpoosh dragged him on. The monster tore through the high Cascades, forming the Columbia Gorge. Where Coyote pulled rocks and trees from the shore, waterfalls sprouted.

At the mouth of Big River Coyote almost drowned in the waves. Wishpoosh was still strong, he gorged on salmon, seized whales and ate them. He threatened to kill everything. Coyote rested, then consulted his sisters who lived in his stomach.

The Sahaptin-speakers who told this story had the curious notion that it was three talking huckleberries who lived in his stomach.

The huckleberries instructed him to change himself into a fir-tree branch and the Beaver monster swallowed him. Coyote changed back to Coyote and cut Wishpoosh's heart.

Coyote and Muskrat dragged the dead monster up on the beach and Coyote began butchering it. He announced that from Wishpoosh's body he would create the races of people to live along Big River.

First, from the belly of the monster he made the Chinook, "for all the people knew that they were gluttons." He declared that they would be short and thick and have weak legs, that they would trade. From the legs he made the Klickitat, swift of foot; from the arms the Cayuse, good with war clubs; from the ribs the Yakima, protectors of the poor; from the head, the Nez Perce, men of brains and great talkers. Coyote gathered the blood and offals and threw them far eastward to become the Snake, Paiute, and Shoshone of the desert.[10]

To remain the belly people the Chinook worked diligently. Now the last fish had gone up the river to spawn and the birds had passed southward. The sky loomed gray on gray and the black rains of November fell. It was Traveling in Canoes Moon; Frost Moon was coming, or Snowy Mountains in the Morning Moon. The Chinook had retired to their cedar-plank houses, they worked at drying, preserving, and packing; at mat and basket making; at mending nets and carving canoes and houseposts.

They gathered acorns and hazel nuts to store in underground caches, dug on hillsides where the rain would run off, or under the floorboards. They made a snack the Europeans later called Chinook olives.[11] They dug a hole for their acorns near the door of the house, and emptied the urine trough into it each morning. The urine leeched through the acorns, removing the bitter tannin and imparting a flavor of which they were very fond. After four or five months steeping they ate them as snacks. The Wishram steeped acorns in natural potholes by the river, in a kind of blue mud flavored with the aromatic seeds of a plant resembling wild mustard.

Urine had no connotation of unclean to the Chinook. They used it as shampoo, and no doubt associated its odor with cleanliness, as we do lemon or pine. As shampoo, urine leaves the hair clean, soft, manageable, and slightly bleached. When rinsed out, it leaves no scent. Likewise, it was added to the water when steaming canoes, and used in tanning hides.

They had all sorts of good things to eat in their storage holes. Raccoon's grandmother had paper salmon, dried summer salmon, dried and pounded salmon, smoke-dried salmon, salmon backs, dried camas, blackberries, dewberries, and acorns in her storage holes before her greedy grandson ate them all up.[12]

Herring eggs they got by placing cedar boughs in water. At Sealand they collected cockles, mussels, three or four kinds of clams, oysters, and crabs. There were crawfish up every creek. Seals swam up Big River as far as Chinook was spoken, sea lions to Willamette Falls and the Cascades. In addition to the five kinds of salmon and the sturgeon, lamprey, and smelt, there were trout, chub, mullet, and bream.

THE WATERS OF ABUNDANCE! The Clackamas told about that in a story in which old man Coyote was traveling about with Thunder Boy. That miraculously wise youth sent Coyote to sit by a spring, and say to it:

"Give me food to eat!"

"Do not look at the spring," Thunder Boy told Coyote, "Turn the other way. Close your eyes."

Coyote did as he was instructed except he kept looking at the spring. It sounded "lish," the sound of girlish laughter. He saw nothing. Again he said, "Give me food to eat." He turned the other way, shut his eyes for a moment, then turned and looked. A little pan floated in the water, with a few huckleberries, bits of mashed dried fish and fish fat, a few other things. He thought, "I shall throw them into my mouth in a single swallow." He poured it all in his mouth, but when he looked the plate had as much on it again. He poured it into his mouth. He looked. Still food. He ate it. More food. He thought, "Now I am getting full. I shall take some of this for Thunder Boy too."

When he offered it to Thunder Boy, he said he was not hungry and told Coyote to put it in his quiver for later. "Now take back their pan," the youth instructed.

"I shall take a look at their hands," Coyote thought, "I shall take hold of them. I shall pull her out of there."

He said to the pool, "I have brought back your platter here." Again the sound of girlish giggling. "Where do the girls live?" he thought, "I wish I could see them!"

He placed the platter in the water. "Here is your platter." Again, the spring sounded girlish laughter. Coyote put it into the water again, he turned and looked, no pan whatever. Coyote thought, "I wonder where the hand came out from?"[13]

THE CHINOOK were fortunate Coyote hadn't ruined that resource too, as he ruined so many others. Nature was mysteriously, inexhaustibly profuse. The land and water fed them. They did not look too closely to see the hands.

The women had many recipes, particularly for soups and stews, in which their larders of fresh and dried roots and bulbs, meats, berries, and fish could be combined. Their diet sounds less monotonous than that of ordinary Europeans of the time. Their names for the types and cuts of fish were comparable with our own for steaks, chops, and roasts.

Botanist David Douglas was fed by Cockqua, a Chinook noble, who brought a sturgeon ten feet long and three feet thick, weighing in Douglas's estimation four or five hundred pounds, and asked which part he should cook for him. Douglas "gave the preference to my host," which Cockqua took as a great compliment, and served Douglas "the most comfortable meal I had had for a considerable time before, from the spine and head of the fish."[14] The spine and head of salmon were likewise esteemed. Salmon-head soup, rich, nourishing, and flavorful, strengthened invalids and nursing mothers.

They pit-roasted, steamed, boiled, and broiled food. To boil they filled a wooden box, stone bowl, or watertight basket with water and added rocks hot from the fire, having rinsed them of ash. They added more hot rocks as needed, using wooden tongs. Their soup stock was from leftover cooking liquid, bones, and blood. Clams, oysters, and crabs were steamed on a grill of sticks over boiling water. Broiling was on sticks beside the fire, often with containers to catch the fat.

They ate twice or three times a day, but had between-meal snacks as well. Slaves served them, around the fire. First, water and towels of shredded bark were passed for the diners to wash themselves. Drinking water was passed too, for none might drink during the meal. They placed food on clean mats or shallow platters of wood. Their most elaborate serving dishes had names and were painted and inlaid with shells.

Menus varied according to what was available. While they harvested, they gorged, so every month had its flavors. They liked to have both fresh and preserved foods at each meal. The menu might include fruit syrup, roots, meat or fish, berries, and soup or stew. They liked contrasting flavors and textures. One taste treat was alternate mouthfuls of dried salmon eggs and peeled thimbleberry shoots. Dried bracken fern roots alternated with herring or smelt eggs was another. They brewed herbal teas of leaves and flowers. They required no salt.

The Chinook ate with their fingers and with spoons. Washwater and towels were passed several times during a meal. A proper person ate and drank delicately, the mouth never open wide enough to show the teeth. Bowls of fish or sea-mammal oil sat about, serving as their cream and salad dressing, dip and flavoring. They dipped berries, roots, and meats alike in oil. Whale oil commanded a high price, seal or sea lion oil was prized for both food and paint. They sometimes drank oil straight, "like milk," according to Alexander Henry.[15] After the meal and a final hand-washing a person might drink water, but to do so during the meal meant one had overeaten.

The Chinook loved to eat and they ate well. Their myths are full of tales of food. Characters withhold it, steal it, complain about it, refuse to share it, or have too much and wish up a glutton monster with disastrous results.

They competed at eating. Kaalas recalled an eating contest the Sealand Chinook fomented with the Clatsop.

Immediately after the evening meal a canoe was brought in, two large rocks were placed in the bottom, and then it was half filled with salmon eggs. Thereupon the visitors were invited to start eating. The Clatsop did their best, but could only reduce the quantity sufficiently to expose the tops of the rocks. The hosts then began and ate until the eggs were almost gone, a much larger quantity than their opponents had consumed. Then they chided the Clatsop for their small appetites.

This angered a visiting shaman. He retorted that they could hardly be expected to show their appetites just after a large meal. Furthermore, he threatened to "poison" the eggs and split the canoe wide open. At this his friends rushed to him and begged him not to start any trouble. He was finally dissuaded and left the dance house. Then the hosts ate the remaining eggs and the young men lifted the canoe high over their heads while exclaiming over the victory.[16]

They were the belly people all right.

THEY WERE MEN AND WOMEN as well, combatants, as everywhere, in the battle of the sexes. There are signs of some kind of shift in the relationship of Chinook men and women just before the Europeans arrived. There may have been a struggle, in which the men were either putting, or trying to keep, the women in a subservient position. Coyote said there would be no more women chiefs, but when Comcomly's mother's father had no male heir, for a while she was headperson of proud Qwatsamts.[17] There were rumors of other women leaders.[18] Perhaps these were anomalies, caused by the epidemics and their low birth rate, so that no male heir was available.

Chinook women carried heavy loads and paddled canoes, often steering them. They paddled with the men into battle. Shamans and curers were of both sexes. Many occupations that elsewhere were solely female were performed by both sexes. When there was a guest, the husband did the cooking. That was his prerogative, not his duty.[19]

Men wove the big seine nets, sewed more often than the women, and made things of wood, bone, horn, and stone. Men hunted, fished, and warred. Women gathered roots and berries, prepared and preserved food, cooked, manufactured things of reed, rush, bark, or grass, and paddled to war. He gathered firewood, she packed it home. He dropped the deer by the door; she carried it inside. Her art forms were more geometrical, his more figurative.

Lewis and Clark commented:

> Notwithstanding the survile manner in which they treat their women they pay much more rispect to their judgment and opinions in many rispects than most indian nations; their women are permitted to speak freely before them, and sometimes appear to command with a tone of authority; they generally consult them in their traffic and act in conformity to their opinions.[20]

Their goods were separate. Whatever she made or earned belonged to her, except her sexual services, if her husband offered them. Lewis wrote of their prostituting their wives and daughters for trinkets.[21] If her husband died, his blood relations and the older children inherited such things as weren't left on his burial canoe. If the widow did not stay to marry his brother, she took the younger children and her own possessions and returned home. She had no further share in the village she had married into.

Divorce was supposedly at the discretion of the husband, but a woman might leave her husband and return to her parents. There was no ceremony of divorce, nor was the bride price returned. Adultery and incompatibility were mentioned as reasons. If her husband sent her home to her parents, they might offer him gifts to take her back. If he did so, it was believed that she would be a better wife thereafter, for her parents had invested so much in her.[22]

Adultery by a wife was punishable by divorce, disfigurement, or even death. The Shoalwater cut off an adulterous woman's ears or the end of her nose;[23] the Wishram whipped her.[24] They might bind her hand and foot and lay her close to the fire until she confessed. The offended husband could kill his wife's lover if he had an unquestionable case, though he had to make blood payment to the man's kin. But a wealthy adulterer could buy his way out. He paid her husband or father-in-law. The husband must be satisfied, or violence would ensue. Not a few battles were fought to satisfy such jealous rages. Though, as we'll see later, the battles were more operatic than bloody, with casualty figures ranging from none to two at the most.

Even the suspicion of adultery was punishable in some cases. A Wishram man who met an unrelated woman on the trail stepped off, sometimes as far as ten feet, to avoid touching her. It was not unheard of for a poor man to try to gain wealth by causing some rich man unwittingly to touch his wife or daughter, then demanding payment for the affront. An unmarried man did not offer food or drink to a married woman.[25]

Women traded as well, and perhaps as often, as men did, and drove as hard a bargain. George Simpson noted approvingly that men sent their wives to their home villages with outfits of trade goods. All the Europeans reported the women came to sell them food, baskets, hats, mats, and other craft objects.

Not that life was a gambol. Astorian Gabriel Franchère thought the women burdened with the hardest labor,[26] and Peter Corney called them complete drudges, though cheerful.[27] Captain Charles Bishop observed them in great subjection by the men, who sometimes beat them unmercifully.[28]

The men had control. The girls had more numerous ceremonies in girlhood, but spirit questing continued longer for boys. The women wore modesty garments. Whether bark skirt or breechclout, these coverings indicated something valuable, owned, protected.

Women were, at least during their child-bearing and -rearing years, expected to be passive, submissive, and soft-spoken. Men ought to be active, dominant, and outspoken. The superior wife expressed herself by encouraging her husband and raising her sons well. She helped her children get spirit powers. Bad women deserted their children, rejected or tricked their suitors, or aided others' adulterous affairs.[29]

Unfaithfulness was uncommon. Even the Astorians came to admit that. Those who said that husbands sold their wives as prostitutes often misunderstood a genuine lack of sexual inhibitions. But when a Fort Astoria clerk tried to renew his acquaintance with a woman who had been his lover before she married, he was coldly repulsed.[30] Adultery was the cause of bloody strife, and none claimed that it was frequent.

After menopause women shed their docility. Stories about Grizzly Woman, named for an animal the Chinook truly feared, were probably expressions of fear and resentment of women past their child-bearing years. In numerous stories Grizzly Woman savages whole villages, enslaves men, kills the people.[31]

In a sense there were two villages: that of the men and their families, in their long rectangular houses in front, and that of the women, in their smaller houses out back. The men were all Chinooks, most of them born in that village. The women were almost all from somewhere else, and many spoke other languages. In a winter village at Willamette Falls, Henry noted women wearing cedar bark skirts, leather skirts, and breechclouts as modesty garments in the same village, an indication of the far-flung origins of the women.[32] However docile they behaved beyond, one wonders what they spoke of in those women's houses out back.

A noble's wife was served by slaves, fed like an aristocrat, and housed in comfort. Yearly she became more arrogant and opinionated, if that was her bent, and when the children were grown her husband no longer had strict control of her. She might become powerful and domineering. In the Grizzly Woman myths she was vain, narcissistic, jealous, sadistic, stupid, and psychotic. She murdered people. She was the headman's wife.[33]

Almost any wife was at least materially better off for living in a village of the Chinook, for they were wealthier than their neighbors. The division of labor was not much different from our own, and the roles weren't rigid. When the fish were running, the men did not disdain to lend a hand at cleaning them. If his wife was sick, a man packed home the firewood, and if he was out alone and hungry, he dug up roots to feed himself. It did not endanger his masculinity to do woman's work.[34]

Whatever their situation, the Chinook wives seem to have borne it with equanimity, for as Astorian Alexander Ross noted, "The females are excessively fond of singing."[35]

"Wishram Girl." Photograph by Edward Curtis, courtesy of the University of Washington Library, Special Collections, NA 211.

16

The Gossip of Two Cultures
1812 – 1814

COMCOMLY MUST HAVE BEEN in his early forties when fur trader David Thompson described him as "a strong, well-made man, his hair short, of dark brown color, and naked except a short kilt around his waist to the middle of the thigh."[1] He was certainly the richest Chinook, and the most skillful at dealing with the floats-ashores.

He visited the Astorians' fort with one of his wives, whom Thompson recalled as "a handsome woman, rosy cheeks and large hazel eyes, and being well dressed with ornaments of beads and shells, had a fine appearance, both were in the prime of life. She had a fine boy of about nine months old, in their kind of cradle."[2] That was probably the woman Astorian Alexander Henry called *La Blanche*, French for pale or white.[3] Which of his wives she was is unclear, as is the name bestowed on Comcomly's third son.

Comcomly's family continued to prosper. Chenamus, his eldest son, was around twenty and Illchee was of marriageable age. Evidently, Astorian Duncan McDougall had been much attracted to the girl, or perhaps to forming an alliance with her father,[4] for he sent two clerks to offer ten each guns, blankets, and fathoms of beads for her hand in marriage, with five more of each to follow within the year.[5] Comcomly, who had himself made alliances by marriage with Scapoose, Chehalis, Willapa, and Shoalwater by then, accepted McDougall's offer.

Though the shipmen had found Chinook girls free with their sexual favors, they were unlikely to have encountered such highborn daughters as Illchee. Upper-class girls of marriageable age were closely watched. It was difficult for a man to meet or speak to one. Illicit relations were rare at those social levels. A noble girl caught in premarital sex was worth a lesser bride price, for her parents were judged careless. It was just the ordinary people and slaves who held sexual activity "no disgrace if unaccompanied by childbirth, which they take great care to prevent. This commences at a very early age, perhaps ten or twelve years."[6] George Simpson understood it well when he wrote,

> Chastity is not looked upon as a virtue except in regard to ladies of the very first rank when the parents are desirous that they should be allied to great men, in which case they are closely watched indeed, are never allowed to cross the door except after dark and then attended by slaves.[7]

He noted however that such vigilance did not always keep the young ladies from their dalliances.

In offering a bride price of fifteen each guns, blankets, and fathoms of beads, McDougall was not over-generous. The Quinault Telemmecks had sixteen years before bought Shelathwell's eldest daughter for twenty each slaves, sea otter skins, and leather war dresses, plus a canoe.[8] A young nobleman's extended family started collecting a bride price as soon as the boy reached marriageable age. Earlier still they had begun to consider which family to ally themselves with. They sought a hard-working girl who would be a good wife as well as a good family connection. Sometimes they consulted the youth himself. Love was not unknown among the Chinook.

A girl selected, messengers were dispatched to her parents with initial gifts and an enumeration of those that would follow if the offer was accepted. If their offer was refused, the first gifts were returned. The suitor family might make a larger offer.

If accepted, preparations began immediately for the wedding. The full bride price having been assembled, the groom's family set out for the girl's village. They camped nearby until her family was ready to receive them, then landed from canoes on the beach in front of her father's house.[9]

A spokesman advanced and announced each gift and who had given it. The bride's father's spokesman called out which of his relatives was to receive it. Now women of the bride's family brought out baskets and bags tied with strings of long dentalia and called out the names of the recipients.

The bride's family spread a tanned skin and the bride was carried out on the back of a woman, wearing her finest garments and ornaments. She sat on the skin and her new mother-in-law and another woman took off her garments and ornaments, which they distributed among their party, and then dressed her in new robes, combs, and beads, which her family removed and kept in turn.

Now the groom was carried forth on a man's back and placed beside his bride, and his clothing and ornaments were likewise taken and replaced. An old woman danced around the couple, singing and throwing feathers into the air. The girl's family tore apart strings of dentalia and scattered them on the girl's hair; the groom's relatives pretended to "louse" her of these—picking them like lice from her hair—and then scattered more *haiqua* over the groom's head for her people to louse.

The couple was then covered with a blanket and danced around, which completed the ceremony. The groom carried his bride into the house on his back. They would remain secluded in their bed for some days. The two had not spoken, perhaps had never met before. Their first memories of each other would be of extended love-making.

Outside, the families feasted, sang, and danced for two or three days, and the groom's party carried off the decorated platters, carved horn spoons, and other utensils. After a few weeks the couple was carried to the groom's village, and the undressing and replacing ceremony was repeated: clothes, ornaments, lousing, and food, and the visitors carried off the utensils.

UNLESS THERE WAS a great difference in the relative wealth of the two families the return gifts were worth nearly as much as the bride price. The Chinook reckoned eight of ten blankets were returned, four of five strings of dentalia. Thus, the real bride price was a fifth as large as the public display. After a year, or upon the birth of the first baby, another series of visits was initiated, with food, festivities, and gifts, which were sometimes of more value than the original bride price.

Such lavish displays were for wealthy nobles. Ordinary people exchanged a few gifts. A poor youth might try to get a wife for himself. If his offer was refused he could hide in the woods and carry her off. He would not dare to rape or otherwise harm her, however. Her family fetched her back, but if she returned to him twice he was accepted. He gave her family what valuables he could and her relatives attended the wedding.

The Chinook said they bought their wives, but really they were establishing the social status of the couple. Nothing was actually sold. They didn't speak of the loss of a young woman's services, or sell their interest in her welfare. Her husband might mistreat her, as some husbands will, but could not kill or dispose of her. The husband wanted the bride price high, for that made the woman's value high, and their value as a couple likewise. Unions not sanctioned by at least some bride price were not thought legitimate or permanent. The offspring were "something picked up."[10]

WHENEVER A CHINOOK FAMILY COULD, they married with someone from a distant village.[11] They took pride in marrying with different groups, the nobles marrying with families in a circle of villages up to a hundred miles around. The couple generally lived in the husband's father's house, but if the husband was poor, or his father-in-law lacked a male heir, they might live with the bride's family. Lack of a male heir was the case with Comcomly's Shoalwater grandfather, and may have been why Comcomly was brought up at Qwatsamts rather than at his father's Quinault village. The manner in which the Chinook passed on names suggests Comcomly's maternal grandfather was the previous Comcomly. The grandfather's name was never recorded.

Sometimes the alliance was entered into so early that infants of two years were married.[12] Children remained with their parents until they were at least six years old, at which time a girl might go to live at the boy's house, though they probably remained apart until the ordinary age for marriage. Sometimes a man bought a little girl, who did not come to live with him until puberty. Or a grown woman was purchased as bride for a baby boy. Pioneer James Swan observed that it was common for a Shoalwater boy to marry an older woman, or for an older man to take a girl as his wife, for they said two young people would be too foolish to know how to behave, while an older person could teach the younger.[13]

Should a woman's husband die, she might be claimed by his brother. Remarriage to brothers or sisters was so deeply rooted that the Chinook word for paternal uncle was the same as for stepfather, and likewise the word for maternal aunt also meant stepmother.[14] That saved confusion when a parent died. If another man married her, he paid the bride price to her husband's family, rather than to her parents.

A man might have as many wives as he could afford, but few had more than one. Taucum had ten, Comcomly only four. The first wife, or the one from the best family, occupied a more prominent place in front of visitors and was treated with more deference. The wives all lived in the same house, each tending her own fire and cooking for herself and her children. Visitors described "connubial felicity" and "perfect harmony."

No one would expect Chinook and *Bahsten* marriage customs to coincide, but the wedding of Illchee and Duncan McDougall, a little more than two years after they first met, shines a queer light on the customs of the *tlohonnipts*. The wedding was celebrated on July 20th, 1813, when Comcomly, with his family and entourage, crossed from Qwatsamts to Fort Astoria.[15] Washington Irving preserved the Astorians' memories:

> That worthy sachem landed in princely state, arrayed in a bright blue blanket and red breech clout, with an extra quantity of paint and feathers, attended by a train of half-naked warriors and nobles. A horse was in waiting to receive the princess, who was mounted behind one of the clerks, and thus conveyed, coy but compliant, to the fortress. Here she was received with devout, though decent joy, by her expecting bridegroom.
>
> Her bridal adornments, it is true, at first caused some little dismay, having painted and anointed herself for the occasion according to the Chinook toilet; by dint, however of copious ablutions, she was freed from all adventitious tint and fragrance, and entered into the nuptial state, the cleanest princess that had ever been known, of the somewhat unctuous tribe of the Chinooks.[16]

Irving did not mention the gift of beaver and otter pelts with which Comcomly is said to have carpeted the path from the beach to the fort gate, a distance of perhaps a hundred yards.[17] That was a kingly return gift indeed but a misdirected one, for the taboos of John Jacob Astor forbade any individual ownership of furs. His gift belonged to the Company.

Ablution meant washing with water in Irving's time, when no white person did so very often. In the year 1800 there was not a single bathing establishment in London. People hardly bothered to wash their hands, let alone their feet or other body parts. The Chinook, by contrast, bathed communally once and often twice daily, the women separate from the men.[18]

ANOTHER BATHING INCIDENT illustrates the viewpoint of the Europeans, or at least of diarist Alexander Henry:

> This afternoon I had an opportunity of observing the total want of modesty or even decency in the women on this coast. I was walking on the wharf, where several women were washing themselves, as is their daily custom, in the small ponds left on the beach at low water. They were perfectly naked, and my presence did not affect their operations in the least. The disgusting creatures were perfectly composed and seemed not to notice me. Although they stood naked in different postures, yet so close did they keep their thighs together that nothing could be seen. The operation over, they used their cedar coverings as towels, and after drying themselves, tied them around their waists and walked away.[19]

The clothmen soon demanded that the Chinook wear trousers when at the fort, though there were as yet no clothwomen to be offended.[20]

ILLCHEE WENT TO LIVE with the *passiuks* at Astoria, and her father made good use of the connection, for he was a frequent visitor. He sat in on their councils and took an active interest in their affairs. Irving charged,

> He was particularly frequent in his visits to the blacksmith's shop, tasking the labors of the artificer in iron for every kind of weapon and implement suitable to the savage state, insomuch that the necessary business of the factory was often postponed to attend to his requisitions.[21]

Henry put it more crudely, labelling Comcomly a "mean, niggardly fellow,"[22] and "a troublesome beggar."[23] Nine months later Henry revealed his ignorance when he sniffed disdainfully,

> Mr. McDougall this afternoon completed the payment for his new wife to Comcomly, whose daughter she was; he gave five new guns and five blankets 2½ wide, which makes 15 guns and 15 blankets, besides a great deal of other property, as the total cost of this precious lady. This Comcomly is a mercenary brute, destitute of decency.[24]

Illchee proved not just some little Indian wife, but The Princess she was now called. Henry delighted in recording gossip of The Princess's domestic life:

> Battle between Mrs. McDougall and Ignace's woman [Ignace was an Iroquois who had come west with the Astorians] regarding the latter's children, who were playing with some trifling thing, when the former lady, who is haughty and imperious, took the playthings from them and set them bawling; the consequence was a slap from the mother. Royalty was offended, and a dreadful row ensued.[25]

The next day:

> Mr. McDougall revenged the insult offered to his lady yesterday, slapping and kicking Ignace's boy, which I conceive was very improper, for what business had she to go into Ignace's woman's tent to interfere with the children?[26]

And a few days after:

> I understood today that Mrs. McDougall's woman was yesterday forced by her brothers to go to the village; they actually dragged her aboard the canoe.[27]

COMCOMLY WAS VISITING McDougall, who was showing him a "blunderbuss," when the weapon discharged so close to the Qwatsamts headman that he ran out in alarm. A guard misinterpreted what was occurring and fired a shot at Comcomly, which fortunately missed. Weapons appeared in every hand, and a fight was only narrowly avoided.[28]

The "Indians" simply refused to play their roles correctly. Henry recalled an incident:

> Comcomly and his suite came over. I had a misunderstanding at dinner with the troublesome old fellow, who would not accept a piece of goose; he said it was not fit for a Chinook dog, and went off in a pet. When he came back I gave him a whole goose, and made him a speech on the proprieties. He ate his goose, drank his wine and porter, and seemed to care little about us. The Americans have spoiled this Indian by allowing him too many liberties aboard their ships.[29]

AS ELSEWHERE, European fur traders tended to prefer hunters to fishermen, nomads to more settled people. They liked those with many furs they would sell cheap better than those with negotiating skills who sold dear.[30] The attitude of the traders was well expressed by Ross Cox, when he recalled of the Chinook,

> The good qualities of these Indians are few; their vices many. Industry, patience, sobriety and ingenuity comprise the former; while in the latter may be classed thieving, lying, incontinence, gambling, and cruelty. They are perfect hypocrites. Each tribe accuses the other of "envy, hatred, malice, and all uncharitableness." Even the natives of the same village, while they feign an outward appearance of friendship, indulge in a certain propensity called backbiting.[31]

James Swan later decided that Cox "does not appear to have devoted much time to the investigation but treats it in rather a flippant style."[32]

DAVID THOMPSON recalled,

> Every man is armed with what we called the double dagger; It is composed of two blades, each of six to eight inches in length, and about a full inch in width, each blade sharp pointed with two sharp edges; each blade is fixed in a handle of wood, in a right line with each other, the handle being between both blades; it is a most formidable weapon, and cannot without great danger be wrested from the holder; several of them took a pleasure with a whet stone sharpening each edge to flourish their daggers close to our faces.[33]

Thompson commented on Comcomly's courage, describing how he went out in a canoe with three slaves to meet a war party of a dozen large canoes, and talked them out of battle.[34]

Comcomly's oldest son, Chenamus, told the Nor'westers he'd had a quarrel with his father in consequence of the old man's having injured his musket; he boasted of having given his father a severe beating. The clothmen still hadn't learned to like Chenamus much, preferring his younger brother, Shalapau.

The floats-ashores had taken to calling Comcomly's progeny by fanciful names: Chenamus was "Prince of Wales," Shalapau the "Duke of York," Raven was "Princess Sunday," Kahatlau was "Princess Margaret" and McDougall's wife Illchee reigned as "The Princess." Shalapau was thought to be Comcomly's favorite and heir. He was fluent in English, and could read and write. His father must have spoken English pretty well by then too, though no one mentioned this. Lamsay was learning both English and French.[35]

IN 1813, faced with the war between Britain and America, expecting the imminent arrival of a British ship of war, and perturbed at Astor's failure to supply them with adequate trade goods, the gentlemen of Astor's Pacific Fur Company dissolved their organization. They then sold their furs and goods to a handful of North West Company men, visitors from upriver who had been starving on the beach in front of Fort Astoria while waiting for a ship, for a promise of thirty cents on the dollar.[36]

"The Americans," John McDonald of the North West Company told Astorian Alexander Ross, "have been very enterprising." "We are called Americans," Ross replied, "but there were very few Americans among us—we were all Scotchmen like yourselves."[37]

A month later, the British sloop of war HMS *Racoon* crossed the bar and anchored in Baker Bay. Comcomly hurried across to Astoria in his big canoe propelled by eight slaves, who paddled in perfect unison. He told McDougall, "*Kin Chautch*'s ships are coming to carry you all off as slaves. We are not afraid of *Kin Chautch*'s people. I have got eight hundred warriors and will not allow them to enslave you. The Americans are our friends and allies."[38]

McDougall did his best to soothe his father-in-law. He promised that the British would not harm his people, and gave Comcomly another suit of clothes. He forbade him going aboard the *Racoon*. Then McDougall hurried across the estuary to greet his British masters. Ross sneered,

> As soon as McDougall had left the *Racoon*, his royal father-in-law with a squad of followers repaired to the ship to pay homage to the British Captain. Then the crafty old chief traduced the Americans and extolled the British, expressing his joy that he had lived long enough to see once more a great ship of his brother King George enter the river. Then, with a grin of contempt, he remarked, "The Americans have no ships to compare to King George's ships." Saying this, he laid a fine sea otter skin at Captain Black's feet and prepared to leave the ship.[39]

Captain Black gave him a flag, lace coat, cocked hat, sword, and bumper of wine, and next day, Comcomly visited Astoria in full British uniform, with Union Jack flying.

Irving heard that after that Comcomly

> no longer prided himself upon his white son-in-law, but, whenever he was asked about it, shook his head and replied that his daughter had made a mistake, and, instead of getting a great warrior for a husband, had married a squaw.[40]

On December 12th, 1813, Astoria became Fort George, and those of the *Bahsten* who didn't decide to return east became *Kin Chautch*, under a new headman, John McDonald, called *Bras Croche* for his crooked arm. "Comcomly soon got into his sleeve," Ross related, "and before the former was twenty-four hours in office, the latter had a new chief's suit on."[41]

SOME OF THE FLOATS-ASHORES tried to piece together an idea of the Chinook cosmology, and botched it badly. Gabriel Franchère, perhaps the most sympathetic of the Astorians, heard that *Etalapass* created mankind, but like flesh statues, inoperative. A second diety, *Ecannum*, less powerful but more benign, took a sharp stone and opened their mouths and eyes and gave motion to their hands and feet. He then taught the use of canoes, nets, etc, and obstructed the river, so the salmon could be caught.[42]

It would be forty years before George Gibbs began to make some sense of that. Gibbs heard that the world was originally inhabited by different beings, some of which became extinct, while others became the animals and birds. They possessed spirit power, which they employed for good or evil, but pre-existed Coyote's changing the world, which Gibbs described thus:

> One of these, who in no way appears to have differed from the rest, except in his vocation, gave the world its present form, fitting it for the habitation of man. On the appearance of the human race, another beneficent being destroyed the giants and demons . . . or converted them into animals, taught mankind the arts of life and gave him fire.[43]

Both of those were Coyote. The earlier beings, "the Kannum or Ecannum of the Chinook," were the Myth People. Gibbs complained that Franchère's translator had "fallen into error in supposing Ecannum to be a representation of Lucifer and associating this idea with the oriental devil worship." Gibbs concluded that Coyote, though immortal, was not the creator of the former inhabitants, but that they existed of themselves.[44]

THE CHINOOK bested the Nor'westers at trade as they had the Astorians. In the spring of 1814 they sold them two hundred fathoms of smelt, which turned out to be very poor eating. When the clothmen complained, the Chinook trader expressed surprise that the *Kin Chautch* didn't know smelt only taste good every other year (a palpable lie). The Nor'westers had to throw a hundred fathoms away.[45] They, no more than the Astorians, could make fat profits off the Chinook-speakers.

In April the following year, when a strange ship entered the river, McDougall sent Lamsay, now "the Chinook messenger," to identify it.[46] It proved to be the long awaited North West Company supply ship *Isaac Todd*, aboard which was the first clothwoman the Chinook had ever seen, barmaid Jane Barnes, of Portsmouth, England, along as mistress to Donald McTavish. Her yellow hair and blue eyes turned many a head, not the least among them that of Chenamus. He offered to make her his head wife over the other four, to pay her relatives a hundred sea otter skins, and to free her forever from carrying wood, drawing water, or digging roots. She might sit at her ease all day wearing her own clothes, and smoke as many pipes of tobacco as she thought proper. She refused, but moved ashore into Alexander Henry's room. It is unclear whether they were lovers, and she left the river not long after. At Fort George they heard she'd found her place as mistress to a wealthy *Kin Chautch* in Canton, China.[47] In fact, Captain Robson, who'd carried her to China, resigned his captainship, and took her as his wife back to England. Further, they returned to visit Fort George a few years later aboard another ship of his captaincy.[48]

SOBRIETY BEING A VIRTUE of the Chinook,[49] the clothmen plied them with drink. The North West Company offered a bottle of rum for every ten skins. Yet, the Chinook continued to resist. On one occasion, the gentlemen at Fort George got Chenamus drunk, and sent him reeling home. His father sped across the river to remonstrate with the traders for this behavior, demanding that in future they withhold strong drink from any Chinook.[50]

Naked Against the Rain

Trader Ross Cox contributed,

> All the Indians on the Columbia entertain a strong aversion
> to ardent spirits, which they regard as poison. They allege
> that slaves only drink to excess; and that drunkenness is de-
> grading to free men.[51]

Yet, among the gifts with which the Nor'westers curried the favor of
such headmen as Comcomly, Daichouion, Ashualax, Coniah,
Coalpo, and the rest, were always bottles of rum.[52]

ALEXANDER HENRY NOTED a marked increase of venereal disease
in 1814. The local women were much afflicted with it, and two of his
men could not walk.

> When the Americans first landed here in 1810 there was but
> little of it among the natives; but it was soon communicat-
> ed to them by the whites, who brought it not only from
> New York but also from the Sandwich Islands. Lewis and
> Clark had mentioned two or three cases of gonorrhoea and
> twice that of syphilis on the whole river less than ten years
> before.[53]

Henry sketched a grisly scene:

> Mr. Franchère went to desire Coalpo's family to come and
> remove and bury the body of their deceased slave girl, lest
> the hogs should devour it. They did so, but in a barbarous
> manner, by dragging it perfectly naked down to the water,
> tying a cord around the neck, and towing it along the beach
> for some distance: they then squeezed the body into a hole,
> pushed it down with a paddle, and covered it over with
> stones and dirt. The poor girl had died in a horrible con-
> dition in the last stages of venereal disease, discolored and

swollen and not the least care was ever taken to conceal the parts from bystanders.[54]

More permanent liaisons with the Chinook women proliferated. Donald McTavish, who'd brought Jane Barnes, took up with the Chinook former mistress of Astorian Benjamin Clapp.[55] Henry commented that McTavish dressed his *tête platte*, "flat head," in fine black broadcloth, twenty-three shillings sterling a yard, and gifted her mother as well.[56] Henry recorded, "Mr. A. Bethune, Mr. Wm. Henry and old Joseph Cartier took each of them a Chinook woman with the approbation of Mr. D. McTavish."[57] Clapp apparently took up with another Chinook woman, while French-Canadians Perreault and Masson each took a wife, by leave. Clerk William Wallace Mathews married Kilakota (or Kshiah or Kelaksta—stories vary), said to mean "little songbird," daughter of Coboway, the premier Clatsop headman.[58]

The clothmen found the Chinook women good and faithful wives.[59] The babies, however, were the victims of a terrible conflict between the customs of the two cultures. George Simpson heard,

> A most inhumane practice existed here after Fort George was established, of the children of the whites by the native women being murdered by the mothers; this arose from the circumstance of the fathers insisting that the heads should not be flattened and the mother preferring to sacrifice her child to having it ranked as a slave.[60]

Two cultures had come together and engaged each other, and so far it was going pretty well. The Europeans had killed only two of the Chinook, even though they were convinced that their trading partners were cheating them by making a profit on their investments. Some on the one side were making attempts at inter-

Naked Against the Rain

personal relations with some on the other side. Their meetings were not so one-sided that there was a victor and a victim.

The Astorians, now called Nor'westers, were far more dependent on the Chinook than they would have liked to admit. Now that a white woman had at last been seen, and much appreciated by the sound of Chenamus's generous offer, there could be no doubt that these *tlohonnipts* were indeed human beings, and though they didn't flatten their heads, they could not be confused with slaves. As for the Chinooks, they seemed well prepared to join the European way of life, and prosper in it.

George Allen Charley, son of Matote, called "Lighthouse Charley." The head-dress isn't Chinook. Photographer unknown. Courtesy of the Pacific County Historical Society.

17

The *Kin Chautch* Make a War
1814

CHINOOK JUSTICE was based on blood payment.[1] A person's worth could be computed, and an injury or death reimbursed. On account of this concept, in lieu of courts to solve intractable disputes, the Chinook occasionally had to fight their fellow flatheads in sanely moderate, somewhat comic-opera, generally maritime battles.

MURDER WAS THE MAJOR OFFENSE, whether from jealousy about a woman or in reprisal for an earlier killing. The Chinook idea about natural death was hazy. Paul Kane heard,

> It is the prevailing opinion of the chiefs that they and their sons are too important to die in a natural way, and wherever the event takes place they attribute it to the malevolent influence of some other person, whom they fix upon, often in the most unaccountable manner, frequently selecting those the most near and dear to themselves and the deceased. The person selected is sacrificed without hesitation.[2]

So, on various occasions, persons tried to kill a dead boy's mother, a girl who would not marry a youth who later died, a headman the deceased had taken a meal with some months before, or a neighboring shaman who had failed in a cure.

When a killing had occurred, a council of village nobles was assembled to decide whether the murder was justified. Upriver, such councils were of prime importance; downriver they were less so.[3] Public knowledge played the role of evidence. An eyewitness might be afraid to speak for fear of revenge, but word got around. Having good cause or the death's accidental nature might absolve the defendant, but confession was of no importance.

The price was computed in slaves, canoes, long dentalia, or other property. It represented the standing in the community of the dead person, the anger his family felt, and perhaps support for his children. Five or six noble families might have to go together to pay for the murder of a noble. When a middle-class person had been killed the blood payment was much less, and the killer would not be condemned to death. A commoner who had killed an upper-class person was merely rubbed out by the noble's kinsmen. Between two commoners, no one interfered.

"The sun was high when I killed him," a Chinook murderer told Dr. William F. Tolmie. "It was not done in the dark. I have paid the price of his blood, and what more could I do?"[4]

If the victim was a shaman known to practice witchcraft the villagers took that as the cause, and it was thought justified. If someone paid a shaman to send a spirit in attack, the fault lay with the person who had paid. A shaman was too dangerous to tamper with. He set his own price for a murdered kin, as did a war chief. A war chief might take immediate personal revenge. More often there were months of negotiations, offers made and rejected, and bargaining continued up to the last moment.

MEANWHILE, the murderer, whether justified or not, had fled the village to fast and purify himself alone.[5] An old man with powers worked him over for five days: blackened his face and made him rings of cedar bark to wear. He walked about blowing a bone whistle or chanting, day and night. After five days his face was painted red. He continued a month, and then hung his wrappings and water bucket on a cedar tree, which withered.

If the murderer must die, the killing was done by what the Wishram called an *idiahipshulit*, "he kills in secret," with his long double-edged, sword-shaped weapon, formerly of whale bone or wood, later of metal. He struck a heavy blow, crushing the skull.[6]

Otherwise negotiations continued. The disputants called in the chief of a neutral village to mediate. Such grievances accumulated and festered all winter: murders unpaid for, witchcraft, insults and injuries, the death of a headman, the abduction (willing or not) of a young wife, and in one case the broken arm and knife wounds a headman's son sustained while killing his sister's ravisher.[7]

IF THE DISPUTE could not be settled, in the spring between fish runs, the opposing villages set a time for the Chehalis to come down to fight the Shoalwater or some Tillamook to paddle up to rage at the village of Kathlamet. Thus Cowlitz had opportunities to shoot at Scapoose, or the Shahala to do battle with the Mahlnumax, all according to the Chinook rules of warfare between flatheads.

War was not something the Chinook gloried in. The Kathlamet told a story of two young men from Seamysty village, at the mouth of the Cowlitz River. They were hunting seal at night in a fog when a flotilla of warriors passed and invited them to join. One youth declined, but the other went along. The war party traveled upriver into Mahlnumax country and went ashore to fight.

When one of them was hit, they carried him into the canoe and laid him down there. The people fought a long time. Then one of them said, "Quick, let us go home, that human being has been hit." Then the man thought, "Oh, I went with the ghosts." They brought him home, where he told his friends, "I was told I was shot, but I did not feel pain anywhere." When daylight came he fell down dead, blood gushing from his mouth and dark, berry-like objects from his anus. His friend who did not go, did not die.[8]

WAR WAS GOING WITH THE GHOSTS. The people were generally peaceful along *Wimahl*. But when a dispute could not be resolved, they looked to their weapons and their canoes. What better place to show off a new six-fathom boat than in battle at Nayagogo, "Where There are Blows," the wide place in Big River where the Lewis, Lake, and lower Willamette join it. Or where the Cowlitz joins Big River, or in Baker Bay off Qwatsamts, or above Wallace Island? Places where the water was wide and the current not too strong. It was probably not by accident that when Lieutenant William Broughton first ascended the river he encountered Chinook flotillas at canoe battle sites.

Each side assembled its boats. A force of forty canoes and three hundred men was seen,[9] another of thirty to forty boats with two hundred and fifty warriors, another of twenty-eight boats with three to a dozen men in each, and others of ten and thirty canoes.[10] The visitors either lodged with their enemies or camped down the beach. If the hostility was great, they spent the night before the battle whooping and shouting, defying each other with cries, taunts, and sarcastic remarks.[11] They also danced and chanted to excite themselves, and painted themselves black, red, and yellow.[12] Seers predicted the outcome of the battle and interpreted the visions of the dancers.

"THE CHINOOK INDIAN armed cap-a-pie is a most unsightly and hideous being," wrote Alexander Ross.[13] Defensive armor was more highly developed than offensive weaponry. The elkskin cassocks, two layers of hardened hide, whitened and painted, covered them from neck to ankles and would stop an arrow, or a pistol ball at a dozen yards.[14] The Chinook also had armor of parallel wooden slats bound together horizontally over the fighter's chest and torso. They wore helmets of elk hide, basketry, or wood, covered with fur and feather decorations, and carried hardened elk hide shields eighteen inches across and brightly painted.

Their weapons were bow, knife, lance, and club. Their two-part arrows had a twenty-inch main shaft of cedar with a five-inch fore-shaft of yew or hardwood, pointed with stone. Their stone arrow-heads were exceptionally fine, expertly flaked of opal, chalcedony, chert, petrified wood, jasper, agate, quartzite, obsidian, or basalt. The upper Chinook participated in one of the greatest arrow-point manufacturing districts in the world, and passed both techniques and stones downriver.[15] The people to the north and south along the sea coast lacked stone points, making do with bone, shell, or fire-hardened wood. The Chinook all used stone points.

Their lances they never threw but jabbed at an enemy. They had once thrown spears, using throwing sticks—called *atlatls* by scholars—that extended a man's arm and increased his power. The arrow-launching bow arrived at the Columbia between 500 and 100 BC and superseded the atlatl after hundreds of years of dual use.[16]

ARMED AND ARMORED, the combatants sent their old women and children to safety, or to an observation area, like the basalt ledge at Nayagogo[17] or merely the beach at Qwatsamts. Some of the women paddled. Now they boarded their canoes to make war.

The two flotillas approached each other, shouting taunts and jibes. They canted the canoes away from the enemy so the fighters were protected by the high side, and the paddlers propelled the boat on the low side. Sometimes they raised boards with loopholes above the gunwales, or decked the front ten feet of the canoe for bowmen to stand on, behind protective boards.

Then it was volley and fire, but starting at a good safe distance and sometimes not getting very much closer. In a battle Alexander Henry saw at Nayagogo, Cassino, the premier headman of the Wapato Lowlands,

> opened fire at long range, without intending to kill anybody, for fear of rendering the enemy desperate, as in that case they might rush in and fight at close quarters; and he was aware that unless blood were spilled he had no danger to apprehend from them.[18]

Sometimes they successfully concluded the battle without anyone getting hurt, after an exchange of gifts to satisfy the participants. In serious battles, one, or even two persons might be injured before the bloodbath ceased. Cultee described the outside limit:

> When people of both parties have been killed they stop. After some time the two parties exchange presents and make peace. When a feud has not yet been settled they married a woman to a man of the other town and they make peace.[19]

Franchère likewise noted that "as soon as one or two people are killed, the battle ceases. If it is the people of the village attacked who are worsted, the other do not retire without receiving presents."[20]

Certainly the Chinook showed a high regard for the value of a human life. They minimized their losses but still satisfied the need to rage and maim felt everywhere by cheated lovers, mourning kinfolk, and powerful young athletes.

IT WAS SAID that Comcomly's father Komkomis and allies from Ilwaco and Wahkiacum once fought a battle against the Mahlnumax over rights to dig shellfish.[21] It may have been at that "Battle of

Wappalooche" that Comcomly lost his eye. A headman never went to battle, for he would be too tempting a target, but his son might. If the battle occurred around 1790, Comcomly would have been nineteen or twenty, a most warlike age. There is no evidence whatsoever, but it would solve a couple of problems, and it makes a better story. When Captain Bishop first met Comcomly in 1795 he was around twenty-five years old. He had already lost an eye and gained a Scapoose wife, Keasno, from the Wapato Lowlands.

As scion, Comcomly would have been the prime target in a battle, but it was his way to take a leading role. His eye put out, the warring parties might well have settled the dispute by marrying a daughter of the Scapoose to him. That is a plausible explanation for why his first wife Keasno was Scapoose. Comcomly was of the finest families. His father was Quinault. His first wife should have been selected for maximum prestige, a Chehalis, Quinault, or even Makah.[22] Indeed, his second wife Qwayaq was Chehalis, and she always took precedence over his Scapoose first wife, though Comcomly is said to have liked Keasno better, as her son Shalapau took precedence over the upriver woman's son, Chenamus, though Chenamus was senior.

Comcomly's first wife would never have been Scapoose unless there was some special reason, as might have been the case in the aftermath of battle where he had been wounded. It was not as a side effect of smallpox, for though smallpox blinded, it did not remove the eye, and he is always described as "one-eyed," not "blind in one eye." No evidence about how he lost his eye has come down to us, however, so this is pure speculation.

THOSE CAREFUL NAUTICAL BATTLES were how the river people solved disputes with other flatheads. But beyond the human beings were the roundheads, and those the Chinook fought more savagely, to be sure. Their most dangerous neighbors were the Quileute to the north and the Northern Paiute to the southeast.

The Quileute, who lived on a couple of small rivers north of the Quinault, were at odds with most of their neighbors. It has been suggested that they are a remnant of the original inhabitants of the Olympic Peninsula, driven into a last enclave by more recent invaders. The Quileute raided for slaves north and south. The Clatsop, 120 miles south of them, recalled one such raid.

A Clatsop youth returning home from a spirit quest encountered Quileute on the beach, preparing to attack. He dodged their arrows and ran to warn the village, but they thought he was merely lightheaded from fasting. They ignored his warnings. The boy and his grandfather fled inland. The Quileute attacked at dawn. They killed some visiting Tillamooks who were sleeping outside, and captured many young boys, then retreated to their canoes.

The Clatsop followed, causing many casualties among the raiders. They pursued them out to sea. As the Clatsop gained on the Quileute boats the Quileute began clubbing the boys and throwing them overboard. Some sank, but others swam to safety. Retreating homeward the Quileute stopped to beg food of the Quinault. Their hosts discovered that the men in the canoes were propped up corpses, only three or four of the raiders remained alive in each canoe. At Clatsop, the body of the Quileute chief was disemboweled, beheaded, and scalped. His head was stuck up on a pole.[23]

A Chinook village challenged unfamiliar canoes that passed without stopping. Should the strangers be friendly visitors of peaceful intent they might continue, but others were attacked, pillaged, and enslaved. That, theoretically, was what the roundheaded fur traders risked when they passed without recognizing challenges.

UPRIVER, the Wishram and Wasco had longstanding grievances against the Northern Paiute. Tamlaitk, of Namnit village at the mouth of the White Salmon River, told how the Shoshone, as the

Chinook called the inlanders, used to lie in wait in the hills south of Big River and kill parties of women digging roots. Once, when the Shoshone were more persistent than usual, a party of six hundred men, Chinook from Wasco and Nixluidix, Sahaptin from Wayam and Skin, set out to attack them.

Ascending the Deschutes River by night they heard what sounded like the howls of coyotes, but turned out to be the Shoshone's scalp dance. The river people surrounded them and attacked at dawn. Tamlaitk claimed they killed five hundred of the inlanders. Even allowing for the usual five-fold exaggeration, this still suggests great bloodshed. Returning, the river people encountered unprotected camps of Shoshone women and children along the Warm Springs River. They captured forty and killed the rest. Back at Wasco they held a dance. Anyone whose wife or child had been killed or captured could brain one of the captives with a club.[24]

"WE DREAMT that we all became covered with blood," Menait recalled of another battle. "And then in the morning our chief said: 'Now I shall tell you people what I dreamt. Now this day we shall die. I have seen the Paiutes. If we are to see them, it will rain.'"

"Now I shall tell you what I, for my part, dreamt," said another. "A grizzly bear ran away from us, toward the setting sun. And then we caught only the grizzly bear's son."[25]

When fighting upriver the Chinook wore Sahaptin clothes, used Sahaptin weapons, and fought in Sahaptin ways. David Thompson heard of old women sent out to catch rattlesnakes and pull their fangs and poison sacks. An arrow was dipped half an inch into the poison, which dried to a dark brown varnish. Even a scratch was said to be fatal.[26]

Scholars have suggested that the Paiute had been pushing northward for a long time.[27] One theory had the original home of those Uto-Aztecan-speakers near Death Valley in southeastern California, and their expansion beginning around AD 1200. They may have pushed the Molala over the Cascades to the western foothills. The Great Basin was a harsh, hungry place. Any people might want to reach the salmon-rich river. Evidently, the Sahaptin and Chinook didn't want them to. Another theory had the Shoshone living on the river until the Sahaptin drove them away.[28]

THE ASTORIANS had seen some comic-opera nautical battles but not those bloodier conflicts with roundheads. That colored their view and helped promote the struggle that followed. Robert Stuart, after witnessing and describing a Chinook nautical battle, concluded "Their military power is an undisciplined rabble, unfit to contend with one-fifth their number of whites."[29]

There had been a history of theft and confrontation at the Cascades and the Long Narrows since Lewis and Clark passed upriver and were threatened at both places.[30] It would seem the clothmen would have modified their practices, but they did not.

Alexander Ross called the Long Narrows "that noted resort of plunderers, where few can pass without paying a heavy tax."[31] It was a lie. The *passiuks* had never done more than share smoke, and seldom that. In 1812 the Wishram tried to make the strangers understand in every way they could, inspecting the Astorians' bales and boxes and pointing out that the Tlakluits' forebearance merited a reward and they could not understand why people who had so much were not more liberal.[32]

Had the Wishram been Swiss tollgate keepers instead, would the Scottish gentlemen have been so niggardly?[33] The *passiuks* had little or no trade for the Shahala, White Salmon, Wasco, or Wishram. Once in a while they hired a few men to carry their canoes and goods over the portage. More often they didn't even stop to smoke, and offered no gifts at all. The people of the Rocky Mountains got guns for their pelts. The people of the Gorge were suffering a loss of status and power. Lewis and Clark concluded it was their numbers that allowed them passage, but it was their guns that got them past the proud Shahala and Tlakluit without tribute. The clothmen's passages had been armed ones from the start.

Ross had a glimmering when he recalled,

> Had they the moment the Indians threatened tribute, instead of paddling up in the middle of the stream, stopped and made for shore, held out the hand of friendship, and smoked a pipe or two of tobacco with them there would have been an end to it. This was the tribute the natives expected but the whites set the Indians at defiance by trying to pass them in the middle of the stream.[34]

Henry understood the situation: "They well know it is only by having fire arms they can be upon a footing with their enemies. Plunder seems to be the main object of these people and not blood."[35] Indeed, in March the *tlohonnipts* heard that the Nez Perce had attacked the Wishram, not previously their enemies. Refugees told how a vast number of Nez Perce and their allies fell on the Tlakluit in winter, killing many, burning women and children in their houses, and carrying off others as slaves, while the survivors fled in panic.[36]

IN LATE DECEMBER 1813, a large party of Nor'westers coming downriver cannonaded the Shahala woods with their three-pound cannon, in response to "the whooping and yelling of the savages, who kept prowling in the woods round us" at night, and to some children's unpointed arrows shot into their camp. A man named Plessis was wounded in the ear.[37]

Hardly more than a week later, in January 1814, a party of only seventeen North West Company traders, in two canoes heavy with seventeen packs each of trade goods, started up the south bank portage around the Cascades. They had missed the cannonading party in a fog, and did not stop to speak with the Shahala, nor check their arms, nor post strong guards. When the Nor'westers were widely dispersed along the rugged four-mile portage, some Shahala men brandishing lances and bows began to trifle with the goods near where Alexander Stewart stood. He pointed his weapon at one and several times pulled the trigger, as though to kill him, but the weapon misfired. The Chinook's bows did not. Stewart took two or three quick arrows, one deep in his shoulder, one shallow in his side and lung.[38] A "half-breed" named Finley rushed up and shot one of the Shahala dead. Both sides fell back, but another Shahala was gunned down. The clothmen abandoned their baggage and retreated to their boats. They sped off downriver with the wounded Stewart aboard.[39] The Shahala likewise fled, not even disturbing the abandoned goods until the following day. A wounded Nor'wester hunter called J. B. Sakanakee, a Nepisangue Indian from the east, watched them from the woods, then slipped away and started a painful, solitary retreat to Fort George.[40]

THAT CONFRONTATION was the last straw. The *Kin Chautch* determined to go up and teach the Shahala a lesson.[41]

First they consulted such headmen as they knew among the Clatsop, Shoalwater, Wahkiacum, and Cooniac. They succeeded in recruiting Coalpo, who brought along his wife, "a high born lady of some consequence." They sent for Comcomly, but perhaps their emissary was of too low a rank,[42] or perhaps the one-eyed chief knew better than to involve himself, for he did not.

Coalpo was variously labelled a Shoalwater, a Clatsop, a Wahkiacum, and even a "Chickelos chief from Classet to the northward of the river on the sea coast."[43] He had established a village a little down the beach from Fort George. The Astorians agreed that he was intelligent and an inveterate enemy of the upriver Chinook (meaning the Wishram, for he had introduced the Astorians to the people at the Cascades). He claimed to have gone up and burnt the Upper Chinook houses not long before. Yet, George Simpson, who saw them ten years later, observed,

> [Coalpo] is nobody, as his lady rules the roost; she is very proud of her ancestry; she is the best news monger in the parish and through her I know more of the scandal, secrets, and politics both of the out and inside the fort than from any other source; she is much attached to the whites and has repeatedly saved the establishment from being cut off by giving timely notice of the treacherous plans of the Indians.[44]

The attackers armed themselves with "beside the ordinary arms and accoutrements, two great guns, six swivels, cutlasses, hand grenades, hand cuffs," and provisions for ten days.[45] Commanded by their war chief, John McTavish, eighty-five Nor'westers under "ten sails"[46] started upriver on January 20th, accompanied by Coalpo and wife in a canoe paddled by eight slaves. They camped the first night behind Puget Island, mile 42, and made the lower mouth of the Willamette, mile 87, the second. There they enlisted Cassino, the most powerful headman of the Wapato Lowlands.[47] The third night saw the implacable armada at the mouth of the Columbia Gorge, mile 120.

Meanwhile, Coalpo's wife "gave us much useful information . . . regarding their customs in adjusting any misunderstanding between hostile nations, such as giving a slave or making some other payment for anyone killed."[48] She was evidently trying to explain blood payment, and that killing a man was a graver offense than pilfering objects to the Chinook.

> [Cassino] informed us that the principal instigator of that affair was a chief called Canook of the *Cathlathlaly* village

on the north. This fellow, it seems, on seeing our party of two canoes only passing up river, formed a plan to pillage them. He assembled the warriors of the two villages below and made a long speech, telling them that we never traded anything of consequence with them, but took our property further up, to their enemies, the Nez Perce, and that there was a favorable opportunity to better themselves. They agreed, and all went armed up to the *Cathlayackty* village, where the harangue was repeated. That village also joined. Then they all came down to meet our people at the portage on the south with Canook as their war chief. Another village, situated a few miles above the portage on the north, was invited to join, which they soon did. Early in the affair a chief of the latter village, and one belonging to the *Cathlayackty* village were both killed.[49]

The next day the fur traders passed Soto's house. He was now living near Nimicxaya village below the eight-hundred-foot crag called Beacon Rock, the village where Coyote cut the people's mouths. Not far above, just below the lowest rapid, on the north bank, they saw men hidden on a hill, behind trees and rocks. They watched a canoe of six armed men singing battle songs run the swift, steep, lower rapids and land. On the beach, an old woman sang her song of mourning and danced. That was Canook's village, perhaps Kamigwaixat, "Upper Road," which Henry called Cathlathlaly (the people of Thlaly). Cassino went to speak to the enemy, while thirty armed Shahala "looked suspicious, their bows bent and arrows nocked. Canook came to the water's edge, with the eye of a hawk, watching our every movement."

The cloth warriors camped on Strawberry Island opposite the village. The next day, their ten-day provisions running low after five days, they bought fifteen or sixteen dogs from their foe.[50] They spent a rainy afternoon butchering meat on the beach, then crossed the river and ascended to inspect the site of the attack. Cassino went off to visit relatives, and returned with one gun, two shirts, and a few teakettles.

After buying more than twenty dogs and a horse from the Shahala, Franchère recalled,

> Since we had now provided ourselves with enough food for several days, we informed the Indians why we had come and told them that we were determined to kill them and burn their villages if they did not bring back to us, in two days, what they had stolen on the seventh.[51]

The clothmen ascended to the village at the head of the rapids on the north bank, Wahlala, "Their Lake," which Henry called Cathlayackty, (the people of Yackty). They found another old woman mourning on the beach. Camped on an island, they watched several canoes of armed men cross. Cassino returned again, with five guns, some kettles, and a few trinkets. They must have discussed attacking Wahlala, for Henry complained, "This filthy village is well situated for defense, on rising ground with a pond behind and on one side."[52] They bought another horse to eat instead. Before the shot that killed it, twenty armed Shahala had been in sight. The shot brought thirty more, well deployed for a fight. Canook was among them, but the fur traders could not seize him.

Coalpo's wife at this point claimed Cassino had tried to bribe her with two fathoms of red stroud blanket and other gifts. She didn't say what he wanted for so small a price, only that she had refused. The expedition returned to the campsite near the scene of battle. The next day they advanced back down to Strawberry Island. Now two old women sang, cried, and danced on the beach opposite. Henry complained, "These Old Hogs annoyed us very much."[53]

It was then that the Nor'westers scored their major triumph. They captured an unarmed Shahala who had come to their camp as guest of Cassino, and held him for ransom opposite Canook's village.[54] The poor fellow's two wives brought a few more stolen weapons, and "during a long conference between them and the prisoner both parties appeared much affected, sobbing and crying."

For four more days the clothmen camped there. The captive's wives brought a few more goods. The wives had to sell a slave to Canook to buy beads to give them back to the clothmen. Canook labelled the *passiuks* a bad lot to kill two Shahala, then want their property back. He said he would give them no more, and told his people that they were only men, arrows could kill them.

Out of food and hope, the punitive expedition retreated downriver. They set their captive free at Soto's village and fled.

Ross lamented, "This warlike expedition was turned into ridicule by the Cathleyacheyachs, and had a very bad effect on the Indians in general."[55] Coalpo's wife told all who would listen that their peaceful behavior was more due to timidity than humanity. She said they ought to have slaughtered all the Shahala.[56]

THE CLOTHMEN lost an unknown number of guns. Two were stolen from their camp while they negotiated,[57] and fifty were listed in the shipment. Both Henry and Franchère claimed they got all fifty back.[58] Listed as lost were 183 of 200 axes, 460 of 475 pounds of tobacco, 2,988 of 3,536 gun flints, 152 pounds of shot, 134½ out of 140 pounds of powder, most of 93 copper and 101 brass kettles, 6 dozen daggers, 6 gross of awls, 328½ dozen metal buttons, 40 blankets, 62 looking-glass plates, 17 gross of thimbles, and great quantities of other trinkets, utensils, and food.[59] Not to mention face.

The Shahala must have finished the sacred season of winter in real style. Certainly the *passiuks* had proved that it was not only the Chinook who fought comic-opera wars along the Columbia River.

The war of 1814 even elicited a flash of respect for the Chinook from Alexander Ross, an unlikely admirer. He wrote that the Indians had "taught the strutting and plumed bullies of the north that, although they were North-Westers, the lads of the Cascades did not respect their feathers."[60] The Nor'westers, who did indeed wear feathers on their hats, and the Astorians who had been enlisted by them, apparently weren't getting along perfectly.

YET, IT WAS AS THOUGH the Nor'westers had won. The Shahala never again contested the passage of a fur trade party.[61] Within two years Donald McKenzie had changed the relationship between fur traders and Indians completely. Late in 1816, winter caught a forty-man party he commanded at the Cascades, headed upriver with sixty ninety-pound packs of trade goods. Instead of being pillaged, that brave fool who had dared the Wishram headman's house to re-cover two rifles simply moved in with his friend, the Shahala head-man Shylawiffs, scattering his men and baled goods around the vil-lage. Six months later the whole five thousand pounds of goods re-mained intact and the clothmen and Shahala had become well ac-customed to each other.[62]

McKenzie was greeted with rejoicing whenever he visited the village afterward. Ross recalled an old headman telling McKenzie his pleasure that the trader always stopped to smoke and took the village children by the hand. Several times the headman mentioned tobacco, but just as many times the friendly gesture toward their children.[63]

The year after, McKenzie instituted a procedure of passing dis-patches upriver with the Indians instead of with large armed par-ties of Europeans. Letters sent that way moved as swiftly and as safe-ly, at far less cost.[64]

Though, at the Long Narrows, the resistance continued longer. In 1817 Ross recorded a powerful confrontation there, though with-out harm to either side,[65] and as late as 1829, Simpson described a confrontation barely averted at that easternmost edge of Chinook *illahee*.[66]

A Chinook spirit image, carved on an antler adze handle. Courtesy of the Peabody Museum, Harvard University.

18

Comcomly Buys Secrets

1818

PETRAN, A SHOALWATER WOMAN, heard that Comcomly purchased a slave from one of the northern groups, perhaps the Stikine
of British Columbia, specifically to learn the rituals and forms of a
secret society.[1] It seems more likely that the secret society reached
the Chinook from the Quinault, who had two, but Petran's account
may indicate how recently this dark, powerful knowledge had come
to the river people.

Whether by slavery or trade, the Chinook did learn of the secret
societies.[2] There was one at centuries-old Neahkeluk, the main Clatsop town, and one across at proud Qwatsamts. Perhaps they had a
society at Awaxamin, "Sunnyside" on the Naselle River off Shoalwater Bay. No one learned whether the Kathlamet or Mahlnumax
had secret societies, but the Wishram and Wasco did not,[3] and there
is no mention of one among the Clackamas.

Only upper-class men or women could become members of secret societies, and only those with appropriate spirits. Black Bear
spirit was strongest, then Cougar or Skunk. Those spirits gave the
ability to inflict and endure self-torture, then miraculously recover.
If a boy encountered such a spirit during the quest, he returned
home and informed his teacher, but no one else. He slept for three
days, after which a feast was held to announce his acquisition of a

spirit helper. Years of training followed. The youth was instructed in the rituals and songs of the society. Meanwhile, his family accumulated goods for the ceremony of initiation and to gift the teacher.

When the teacher thought it time a rehearsal initiation was held, to test the youth's powers. If the test was unsuccessful, he must train and fast until another try was more favorable. When he succeeded, the initiation was much the same as for any guardian spirit. After three days of segregation and fasting the initiate danced, accompanied by attendants dressed in the skins of animals, with masks depicting the character or spirit being dramatized. They imitated the creature in their dance. Masks, much used north up the coast, were infrequent among the Chinook, though the Tlakluit carved representations of *Atatahlia* to frighten their children.

The initiate's dance depicted his spirit. Next, he demonstrated his resistance to pain. He walked through the fire, or leaped and danced across, or stood in the coals. He might slash his arms and body, then perform an instant self-cure. John Dunn saw a Clatsop performance:

> In times of pretended inspiration and communion with the great spirit they seize a fleshy part of the body, about the stomach and ribs, in one hand, and plunge a dagger right through the fold, without drawing blood. I have seen some of them thus gashed all over the front of the body.[4]

After performing, the initiate dashed out and plunged into the river or bay, then returned to his partitioned-off chamber until the next night. The fourth and fifth nights were much like any spirit dance, ending in a great feast, but without distribution of gifts. Afterward the initiate wandered in the woods or along the beach alone for a few days or as much as a month. When he returned he was a full member. That gave no particular benefits; only his accomplishments and acquired wealth did that.

Fewer women joined than men. Initiations were held in winter, and since there were few members, usually a single person was initiated. During other secret society performances the experiences of the people of olden times were dramatized in pantomime and song, in which the audience joined.

Other performances had other purposes. Petran recalled:

An enmity existed between two members of the society. A gathering was arranged wherein one was expected to prove his superiority over the other and thus end the friction. One of the pair was a man, the other a woman. The former had been quite generally suspected of witchcraft. He possessed "knife power"and caused others to become wounded. The woman's power, which permitted her to find lost or hidden objects, was phrased as hunting power and symbolized by a bow and arrow. She had not yet been a victim of the man's witchcraft, but clairvoyant powers enabled her to divine his intentions.

At the ceremony he hid his knife, with the point directed toward her, while she was in the inner room. She then danced out with bow and arrow in hand in imitation of a hunter. She began to search for objects in the room, all the while singing that her bow and arrows were much further reaching in their power than his knife. An intentionally hidden object being more difficult to find than one accidentally lost, she first recovered various articles of the latter nature. But soon the knife was brought to light and thrust into a board of the wall.

The woman then shot at it with her bow and arrows, hitting it time after time without an exception. She next retired to the inner room while the knife was again hidden, this time in the sand by the fire. The woman reappeared wearing a blindfold. Without removing it she turned toward the fire and shot the knife out of the sand. Again it was hidden, during her absence, and this time she lay flat on the floor while shooting, but hit the knife nevertheless. Under such disgrace, the man gave up entirely and lost his power, as usually happened when one was publicly humiliated.[5]

IF COMCOMLY did buy a slave with knowledge of the secret society, the slave might have been a woman, for grown men weren't enslaved, only boys before puberty. Women might be reduced to slavery at any age. Yet, it is hard to imagine a woman strong enough to endure a secret society initiation becoming docile enough to be a slave. Perhaps some secret society member traded knowledge for freedom.

Slavery was an area-wide practice, but not on the scale the Chinooks practiced it. Among nearby flatheads and on Puget Sound perhaps ten percent of the population were in bondage, but in the wealthy Chinook villages twenty-five percent were. Coalpo's village was more than forty-five percent slave in the early 1820s.[6] How large the trade was before the floats-ashores arrived is problematical, but clearly it increased as the fur trade did. A wealthy headman owned ten or more slaves; even a commoner might have a slave or two. They were good investments, being portable and self-propelled, and retained their sales potential for years. Old family slaves stayed; newer ones were bought cheap and sold high. While not defending the abominable practice of slavery, it should be recalled that Athens in its golden age was fifty percent slave, and in 1775 America, black slaves constituted about one-fifth of the population.

The Chinook didn't generally raid for slaves themselves, though sometimes an adventurous upper-class man might gather his friends and go seek out roundheaded Paiute or southern Kalapuya girls berrying too far from home. Other groups raided regularly and brought their captives to the Chinook. Among flatheads, the

Tillamook, Klamath, and Klickitat raided south, the Cowlitz north. Up the coast, the Quileute, Makah, Kwakiutl, and Nootka were slavers.

A Shasta-Molala slave, stolen four hundred miles south of Big River, recalled:

> I was then a boy of about four years, while my brother was about six. I well remember the day the [Klickitat] charged on us at a river where we were living. It was about noon of a summer day when I and my brother by the river heard the Columbia people give their war cry on the opposite bank. Immediately my father was hit in the eye by a Columbia River arrow. The enemy crossed to the side we were on. Our people scattered, fighting all the time. My brother and I hid between some boulders. The last I saw of my mother was when she ran by our hiding place with my father following with his eye out. I and my brother were found right away. We were taken to Sketcutxat [Vancouver]. I was kept by one family while my brother stayed with another. After a long while I was given to a Wishram family with whom I remained. We were so well cared for that my brother and I never had an idea of running away after we were grown boys. We both forgot our own language.[7]

IN ADDITION to being abducted, people could become slaves by failing to pay their debts or could gamble away their freedom. Someone too poor to pay a blood price might be enslaved instead of killed. The Chinook didn't allow orphaned children, or the offspring of Chinooks too poor to keep them, to be sold, as did some people or tribes.

Chinook slaves were purchased as much for prestige as for usefulness. It has been suggested that like whale hunting farther north, slaves may have cost more than they returned. Slaves, *haiqua*, and decorative objects signified prestige, hardly related to buying and selling fish and roots.[8]

It was the Columbia River Gorge, again, that facilitated the slave trade and made the Chinook rich. The way to tame a captive was to move the girl or boy so far from home that return became unthinkable. The Gorge allowed that in both directions, changing the world itself from variations on green to shades of tan and buff, or vice-versa. The captives came from every direction. At the Long Narrows slave traders dealt in southern flesh: Paiute, Shasta, Pit River, Rogue River, and Umpqua, but never Salish, Sahaptin, or Klamath.[9] At *Wimahl*'s mouth the Shoalwater brokered northerners: Quilleute, Klallam, Makah, Nootka, Puyallup, Skagit, and Nisqually, as well as Kalapuya.[10] Slaves from the Willamette Valley and from the coast to the south were sold into bondage through the Clatsop. At Willamette Falls the Clackamas bought and sold the children of the Willamette Valley and of the Umpqua and Rogue valleys farther south.

ONE THING favoring the idea that Comcomly bought a knowledgeable slave is that the enslaved were often of the upper class at home. There was both profit and honor in enslaving a noble.

However high his or her birth, once a person had been enslaved all status was lost. Even if the slave escaped and returned home, the people there were generally slave-owners too, and former enslavement could never be forgotten.[11] Nor could a woman rise to freedom through marriage. The Chinook claimed they did not even use slaves as concubines.

Opinion varied about the plight of the enslaved.[12] True, the owner could work a slave long and hard, beat him, throw ashes in his face, taunt, ignore, or murder him. George Simpson thought Chinook slaves lead a life of misery, indeed I conceive a Columbia River slave to be the most unfortunate wretch in existence; the proprietors exercise the most absolute authority over them even to life and death.[13]

He was correct; yet, the daily life of a slave was not altogether dreadful. Slaves usually lived in the same house, ate from the same pot, and did the same work as their owners. A girl might become the lifelong companion of a girl her own age, or the household drudge of a lady of good family. Males paddled the owner's canoe, gathered wood, helped pull nets. Slaves had the same considerable leisure as their masters. A slave might go into a neighbor's house, sit down, and engage in conversation with the people there.[14] A slave's opinion might be respected, and a slave's ridicule was deeply felt. (When the Astorians got Chenamus drunk, Comcomly's prime complaint was that the slaves had laughed at his son.)[15]

An ambitious slave might be put in charge of other slaves. He might buy his freedom, though he would have to pay two or three times the price of an ordinary slave to buy himself. Slaves were encouraged to seek a spirit helper like anyone else, and it was said that success came as often to the slave as to the free. A slave who obtained a powerful spirit—a gambling power, or a shaman's spirit— would have a chance at freedom. Everything a slave earned belonged to his master, but finally his earnings would be too much for the owner to accept.

A slave could marry. There would be no exchange of gifts. Usually it would be with a slave of the same household, but sometimes an owner might buy a mate for a favorite slave. The children of slaves had round foreheads and would be slaves in turn. Unless, as is said to sometimes have happened, a family adopted a baby and let its head be flattened.

Love between a free person and a slave was unthinkable, so naturally it sometimes happened. The Kathlamet told of the son of a headman who loved a slave. He was so humiliated by the constant scolding of his parents that he went off and became a lake spirit, after diving many times, perhaps to drown himself.[16] The Clackamas remembered an upper-class man who fell in love with a slave girl. She stole her master's valuables and they fled into the mountains, but a shaman with tracking power told the people where to find her. They sent two slaves to kill the slave girl and bring back the valuables, but did nothing to the upper-class man. But among the Shoalwater, it is said, an upper-class man who married a slave was degraded to the status of slave, and their offspring were enslaved.[17]

They often sent slaves off on such independent errands as the above. Why would the slave return? Evidently some captives accepted their fates. Should one try to escape, the Wishram burnt his feet or cut them with a knife, the Shoalwater cut off his ears.[18] If a slave was unhappy the Chinook sold him onward.

At death the slave's true plight was revealed. To avoid having to purify the house, the people carried a dying slave out and stuffed him in a hollow tree in the forest to die. Or tied some stones to her and tossed her in the river. That way no one had to touch a corpse. Only a slave would touch the corpse of a slave.

Worse. When a prosperous noble died, a slave or two was killed to paddle for him and to serve him in the afterlife. Someone smashed the slave's skull and they buried him under the burial-canoe support post. Likewise, a girl's lifelong slave companion, or a noble woman's favorite. Sometimes the slave was tied alive to the corpse, face to face, and placed in the burial canoe or vault. After three or four days the family might send another slave to put the poor demented captive out of his or her misery.[19]

As for the spirit society, it was merely the peak of Chinook magic. They had other secrets as well, for example spirit batons, cedar or maple sticks two or more feet long and several inches wide, carved to represent the owner's guardian spirit, usually in full figure with separate legs and arms and the head in proportion.[20] The stick was painted and inlaid with shells, and hung with feathers, claws, teeth, deer hoof rattles, and cedar bark. These power-objects the conjurors called *utsaxo*, and referred to as the spirit power itself.

The conjuror sang his or her song many times, then placed his power baton in the hands of a person who lacked a spirit helper. Presently that person began to be jumped around by the baton. The conjuror sang faster and the stick moved more strongly. The person couldn't stop it or let go. Even persons who disbelieved in spirits were unable to stop the baton from moving.[21] The sensation described resembled an electric current, the muscles in tonic spasm. The stick danced the person until he fell over in a rigid fit, and still the stick moved, until the conjuror loosened the subject's hands by blowing on them, or soaking them in warm water.

Shamans used the power-stick to help find lost objects or people. A conjuror gave her stick to someone and began to sing. The stick shook, and drew the holder along. The audience followed, singing. The stick led them to water. "Put me in a canoe, quickly, he has drowned!" the seer cried. A canoe was brought; the conjuror followed the baton and found the body in the water.[22]

The stick was carved, by its owner or by someone paid, to match the owner's memory of the spirit. Like other Chinook spiritual practices, batons referred only to direct contact between the individual and the spirit. Power could not be inherited, purchased, or family owned.

Equally powerful as spirit images were carved and painted boards called *ikimoqdih* which stood around the house.[23] These were a style more ancient than the batons, and continued in use after the batons appeared.[24] An owner talked to his board. He "bawled it out" if results weren't forthcoming.[25] A man might press himself against his *ikimoqdih* in time of trouble, and at once his difficulties vanished.[26] In council, the pipe was presented to the spirit board.[27] The space in front of one was dangerous. A child who strayed there became ill.[28]

Yet, Gabriel Franchère recalled, "They have some small sculptured figures, but seem not to value them greatly, and offered them in exchange for trifles."[29] Peter Corney noted, "The houses are decorated with rude carved images, which they call clamas, or gods, but they do not seem to pay any kind of homage or attention to them."[30] Not even the missionaries accused the Chinook of idolatry.[31] They left the board beside its owner in death, or lost it in the forest.[32]

THE CHINOOK believed a human being had two souls.[33] One was like a fog or breath. A man's was eight to ten inches in diameter, a woman's somewhat smaller. Their word for soul and breath were the same, as the Latin word *anima* meant current of air, wind, breath, or the vital life-force. The other soul was a baby-like manikin a few inches high, which could leave the body and travel about while the person still lived. Should the little manikin cross a certain river, however, the breath left the body and death followed. The manikin might be lured away by ghosts (who always desired human company), or a shaman might steal it, or it might merely wander too far. When a person was badly frightened and later became listless and quiet, the seers knew his soul had gone wandering.

Sometimes the seers went to seek a lost soul.[34] As many as three or four seers circled, dancing and singing, roaming the corners of the house, seeking the patient's manikin soul. They wandered aimlessly, seeking the trail, speaking to the soul, urging it to return. Those seers could see a soul better than other shamans could. They conferred and announced their findings. They sat in a file, as though in a canoe, entranced for hours.

Naked Against the Rain

Now one of them gave his assistant his spirit baton and manipulated him into a trance. The baton moved, it began to lead. The seers entered a trance by vigorous chanting, and set off to follow the spirit. Hour after hour they sat entranced, the people drumming and chanting around them. They traveled all night, sometimes two or three nights, their bodies still in the house. When they neared the land of the ghosts the ground was sandy; the footprints of the souls could easily be seen. The seers reached the river of death, that stream that flows through so many cultures' ideas of death. Canoes awaited the souls for paddling to the world beyond. Once across, none returned. The seers did not dare pursue them.

If they found the soul on this side of the river, the seers encircled it and the strongest clasped it in his hands. He felt a pulsing or beating. If a person was to die, his soul felt heavy. If he would recover, it was light. The seers restored it to the patient's body at dawn, by rubbing it back into his or her head.

But if the soul had taken the left-hand path, or eaten anything the ghosts offered, entered a house, or crossed the river, it could not be retrieved. If it drank water it shrank and the patient died. And anyone the seers recognized in the land of the dead was also in mortal peril. It might be a soul that had strayed but not been missed yet. It must be retrieved and replaced. A canoe seen there would soon be broken.

The seers might distract the ghosts by creating a deer and sending it bounding away. The ghosts would pursue it and forget the soul. Likewise, the dead might send false clues. Once a group of seers followed what they thought was a herd of elk, whose eyes shone in the dark, but it turned out to be a single snail.

Should an evil shaman find someone asleep, he stole her soul and hid it near a corpse, or in a thorny place, beneath a house or in rotten wood. The victim fell ill. Her relations paid a seer to seek her soul. But if the shaman's spirit had already begun to gnaw on her soul before they found it, she died.

Shamans and seers had frightful powers. They learned by apprenticeship. Some experienced shaman might note a youth's potential at his spirit initiation, and take him as an assistant. For five years he accompanied the teacher on cases and learned the secrets of the trade. He sought more spirit helpers. At length he was ready to perform alone. He had neither earned anything nor paid anything during the apprenticeship. It was thought an honor to teach and to learn.[35]

The would-be shaman felt his powers. He tested himself.

He sent disease to the bark of a tree. The bark bursts at once and falls down. Then he thinks: "Indeed, I have the powers of a shaman." When an eagle sits on top of a spruce tree, the shaman sends disease against him. He falls down at once, his mouth full of blood. Then the candidate thinks: "Indeed, I have the power of a shaman."[36]

At the initiation he sang his songs and gave away everything he owned. Holding back meant he had no faith in his spirit's power to provide for him. The teacher took the student on his back and danced to make him strong. The initiate became stiff and unconscious. Assistants laid him on a platform and the shaman blew over him. He arose and sang. He tried his new powers.

He called out "Who is sick?" Someone came forward and lay down. He sucked the spot, he sang and the others danced and sang. He sucked out the sickness and held it in his hand. He swallowed it to feed his spirit.[37]

The other shamans tested him by trying to hit him with a disease spirit. If they could not hit him they said, "Behold! He is really a shaman." But if he was only bragging they hit him and he died at once.[38]

UPRIVER, there were *idiakewam*, who could bewitch, and *idiaxilalit*, who could cure such bewitchment.[39] The Clackamas called a curing shaman *itgagiwamax* or *idyaxilalit*.[40] Downriver, *gitakikelal* could see souls, curing shaman were called *tlqewam*.[41] Women shamans were as powerful, though not as numerous, as men. Shamans charged what the market would bear if the patient recovered, but were expected to host winter dances and distribute lavish gifts.

The three or four shamans of an average village had professional ethics, including an unwillingness to reveal the name of a shaman who attacked a patient.[42] They were secretive about each other's knowledge and behavior. Two or three shamans often split a fee. They were a special interest group within village and region. They earned many valuables and became important. Becoming a shaman was a ladder up which ordinary people or even those of the lower class could climb.

THE CHINOOK recognized four kinds of disease: wild *yuhlma*, disease spirits that floated about and were attracted by failure to observe the taboos; *yuhlma* sent by shaman on their own or for pay; soul loss, when the smaller of the individual's dual souls wandered off; and natural or accidental illnesses, treated by another sort of medicine.

Yuhlma were like arrow points. They hit the body and lodged within. A Clackamas shaman said,

This sickness is right here, just like a little fish or a small salmon. I have tried to catch it, but it slips by my fingers. It goes by and high up, it is swimming and wriggling around.[43]

An eighty-five-year-old Wishram shaman revealed,

This doctoring is true. I have been curing for more than 60 years and have met all kinds of diseases. Some diseases are bad. When a person is bewitched he will surely die unless the shaman has a much stronger spirit than that killing the patient. When a person dies of witchcraft, the body cracks in many places, although they may appear before he expires. Such cracks are not deep, perhaps only an eighth of an inch, just enough to let the blood run freely. The body turns various colors, especially red and blue stripes, lengthwise of the body. This shows that he was bewitched by a strong shaman. A shaman who undertakes to take such a spirit out of the sick person must have a stronger spirit himself. If not, even though he draws it out, it will kill the shaman and both will die. In five days the shaman is dead. Some important bone of his body breaks, a leg or his spine. This happens not from an accident but while he is lying sick abed. So curing is very dangerous and a shaman must be treated well.[44]

IT WAS A DANGEROUS WORLD. Bewitching was not uncommon.

When the wife of a man is taken away, he secretly pays the shaman, who sends disease, sometimes to the man, sometimes the woman. Or a woman gives many dentalia to the shaman to send disease against the murderer of her elder brother. Sometimes she marries the shaman, she gives herself secretly in payment, and then sends her husband to kill her enemy. Thus were many feuds created, the shamans battled back and forth, death came to both parties.[45]

Should a *yuhlma* sent by a shaman be destroyed, the shaman might die. A bewitched person about to die might speak in the voice of the shaman who had bewitched him. "I'm so-and-so," he cried, "You can't put me down. I'm sorry for you, but it's your own fault. I'll win the fight."[46] In response to this knowledge of who had bewitched their kinsman, the victim's relatives revenged themselves unless blood payment was made.

Children were kept away from a conjuror, lest their souls be taken, or his vengeance strike. In particular they were not to run behind his back, which would frighten and disturb his spirit, and cause him harm. Something dropped or a loud report would do the same.

Another kind of seer prophesied the future. The seer Tsaax once spoke to the Atsmitl of Shoalwater Bay: "I feel sorry for the oysters; I feel sorry for the people. All the oysters will die. A great storm will come, all the oysters will be killed." That winter a hard freeze at lowest tide killed almost every oyster in the bay. They were scarce for thirty years thereafter.[47]

But the power of the shaman was not unlimited. Should the villagers ask him to sing for good weather, he might say, "When the sun stands there and there it will clear up." More likely he would admit, "It is too difficult for me, probably it will not clear up. I can not do it."[48]

MCDOUGALL AND ILLCHEE evidently didn't work out as husband and wife. A later visitor heard that on one occasion The Princess scorned her husband for his ways:

> You profess to be a great chief; but I see you hard at work every day, behind the counter and at the desk, and your time is so fully employed that you have scarcely time to eat your food, or to enjoy the society of your wife a moment. See there [pointing at a pig in its wallow], that is the true chief; he has no labor to perform, like a slave; when hungry, his food is served up, he fills himself, he then lies down in

the soft mud, under the influence of the warming rays of the sun, sleeps and takes his comfort.[49]

McDougall sailed off to California in 1814, spent a year in Hawaii without his bride, and visited China before he returned, after an absence of twenty months.[50] When he departed for a new post in April 1817 she did not accompany him; whether by her wish or his no one recorded. Duncan McDougall "died a miserable death at Bas de la Riviere, Winnipeg, later that same year."[51] Perhaps he still carried his smallpox vial with him. Moon Girl, around twenty, was a childless widow. She returned to her father's house across the wide estuary.

McDougall had set a precedent. Cartier discharged his woman for having a venereal disease. Benjamin Clapp deserted his Chinook wife. William Wallace Mathews deserted Cobaway's daughter Kilakota and their baby, Ellen.[52] Yet, some of the clothmen learned to be good husbands.[53]

In 1818, THE CLATSKANIE again struck, killing five of the clothmen. By now the Nor'Westers knew enough not to revenge themselves on the Chinook. That year too it was learned that Fort George might revert to the Americans. The *Kin Chautch* had to give it back to the *Bahsten* according to the settlement of the War of 1812.

Comcomly tried to change his name and elevated his second son to leadership. Several fur traders noted that he called himself Madsue (or Madsaw), meaning "Thunder."[54] The traders continued to call him Comcomly. Shalapau, formerly Quatqos, called Duke of York by the *passiuks*, was the one elevated to headman. In passing over his oldest son, Chenamus, once Quasquas, now the Prince of Wales, Comcomly was said to be acknowledging the prestige of Shalapau's north-coast mother. He may have been expressing his personal politics as well. The younger son had mastered reading and writing. The traders praised him as their friend, but viewed Chenamus as bloodthirsty, cruel, tyrannical, and ill-disposed toward the whites.

Even Cassino, the pre-eminent Wapato Lowlands headman, was Comcomly's son-in-law. Though we have no account of the wedding, later events suggest that some time between 1818 and 1820 Illchee married Cassino, and thereafter bore him a son.[55]

Probably Comcomly thought he could retire. He was around fifty, and his name could hardly grow larger. Perhaps he wanted to "just walk around." That would never happen.

"Sees-Use, Columbia River Tribe." **Photograph by Major Leeander Moor-house, *courtesy of the Oregon Historical Society.***

19

Where Conjurors Assemble

WINTER

Now it was Winter House Moon, cold and wet. Cold Moon loomed ahead, when for ten days or so the Walla Walla Wind Brothers might triumph, bringing with them brilliant blue skies and biting cold. Snow might sit down for a few days, under that bitter east wind, or freezing rain blow down the Columbia River Gorge.

"Now we are lying in the middle of the backbone of the land," the Clackamas told each other. "We shall be going the opposite way now, we are going toward summer."[1]

They didn't hunt or fish or gather food during two winter months—roughly December and January—not even take steelhead, which were in the rivers then. Everyone went home to the winter cedar-plank house, the patrilinear family village. Even the girls who traded their pleasures to the fur traders returned home for the sacred season, when they danced and sang their spirit songs and recited the ancient myths.[2]

The supernatural spirit returned one winter, many years after the seeker's youthful wilderness encounter with the *kawok*.[3] The person fell ill, and a shaman diagnosed the malady as caused by a spirit. She or he must sing the guardian spirit's song or suffer and die. If she did not know the song, putting off the spirit would only make her sicker. The people were invited to dance and sing for five nights.

The people assembled. They entered in a single file behind the shaman and two drummers carrying ten- to fourteen-foot poles three inches thick, painted and decorated as the initiate had directed. They came in dancing and singing, beating time on circular hand drums, circled the fire five times, and at a signal from the patient, all sat down. Even those without spirit helpers attended, and the slaves sat around the edges.

They slung the decorated poles horizontally from the rafters and the drummer pounded them against boards set up for the purpose. Other drummers beat with sticks on planks, boxes, and skin drums. They wrapped their hands in shredded cedar bark and drummed three days without sleep, fasting all the while. They drummed themselves into a trance; they drummed until exhausted. They were well paid by the father of the initiate.

AFTER FEEDING THE FIRE a bit of dried salmon and other tidbits— the fire danced too and must be fed—they began to sing their guardian spirit songs. They were trying to find one like the initiate's, of the same spirit or of similar sound. When the initiate heard the right one she grew warm and fell unconscious. Then they coaxed her song out of her. The *kawok*'s words were vague after all those years, and she could not recall the song. There were people called "one who catches on to the song" who needed only a faint mumble to interpret it. Whoever's song made her feel better stayed near her the rest of the dance and helped.

Should no one sing a song that relieved the patient her family sent out to farther and farther villages. If no one was found with an evocative song, the patient lapsed into unconsciousness and died. But usually the patient sang. Immediately the guests learned the new song and joined in. It would be dangerous to sing it alone at first.

Downriver, among the Shoalwater, the shaman announced the kind and quality of the spirit and how she had obtained it. But up at the head of the Long Narrows that was strictly forbidden. A Wishram or Wasco's guardian wasn't named until he or she lay dying. Then he might divulge it.

NOW THE SINGING AND DANCING became general, though still centered around the initiate, who remained in bed and continued to fast. She sang first each night, her hair hanging loose over her face, and then in turn each person who had a power song sang it, and the people joined in. The singers grasped an upright pole and flung their bodies about. The initiate gave each singer a few gifts, feathers or articles she was wearing. She didn't have to make gifts, but if she didn't people would think her cheap and her power second rate.

A person's dance might imitate a spirit. A bird would wave her arms and spread her fingers, crying like the species. People also wore symbols of the creature, feathers, fur, or skin, a necklace of vertebrae, claws, or teeth of the animal. Their associates might guess which spirit even though they were never told.

Visitors from another village came. They waited outside the door so as not to interrupt the singing. At a break, they beat loudly on the door and entered shouting. Their headman sang several of his songs, taking perhaps twenty minutes, then one by one the visitors sang.

They sang all night, with pauses to eat. Individuals came and went. Some sang while others slept or ate in a separate house. As the hours and days rolled by, the fervor and excitement increased. The dancing only stopped to comply with the initiate's requests. Her spirit helper might demand a robe of such and such fur, or one of the blankets of feathers twisted into strips, or to have her face or body painted, or her hair cut some special way. If she requested something they had to get from outside, everyone went out and entered again in single file, singing. If she requested food, everyone ate that food. If water, everyone drank. She might ask for some kind of meat, chew a piece, consider it for a moment, then throw it in the fire to feed her spirit. But ordinary eating, or laughing, in the dance house was forbidden.

More and more people arrived. The fifth night the house was crowded and their fervor nearing a climax. People fell unconscious, mysterious events occurred, their spirits possessed them utterly. Singing and dancing for days on end, the repetition became their intoxicant, as psychedelic as a substance.

THE NEXT MORNING there was a final feast and gifts for those who had come to help the initiate. She named the foods to be served. A shaman directed them to some particular spot where the food was found readily available. They sang her song one final time and the patient arose at last, confirmed in her relationship. The people might linger a day or two, "cooling back down" and enjoying their good feelings with each other.

From then on, the initiate sang her song at any season, if sick or in need of help, and each winter at the dances. But woe to a person whose spirit returned for the first time at any other season. There would be grave difficulties. It was not permissible to gather and sing like that in any but the sacred season of winter.

Even if no one fell sick with the return of a spirit, the Chinook held five-day dances throughout the sacred season. They traveled in canoes from village to village. Sometimes a rich man built a special dance house for the occasion. They sang and danced and conjurors demonstrated their powers, as when, in myth, Skunk hosted the people.

The chieftainess sang her conjurer's song, she made a house and invited all the people. Blue Jay led the chorus.

The maggots danced, "We make the rotten meat move," was their song. Blue Jay joined right in with them, they gave him a mountain goat blanket. His wife would not put it on, and Blue Jay observed that rightly it was better not to wear beautiful garments where conjurors assembled.

The geese sang their song, "we pull out the seagrass, it drifts away." They gave Blue Jay a goose skin blanket.

Elk danced, "We hiss on bluffs, we make Zzzzz on bluffs," they sang. A blanket of the skin of a young elk for Blue Jay, but his wife would not wear it.

Wolves danced, "We carry deer fawns in our mouths; we have our faces blackened." They gave a wolf blanket to Blue Jay.

Skunk, the chieftainess, sang alone. "Blue Jay's and my ancestors used to keep company," she sang.

Grizzly sang too. He sang too long, he danced too long. A person outside complained. Grizzly said he'd tear him up and eat him. The one outside said he had a braid on one side of his head only, he could kill a man before noon. Grizzly went out, he said, "Behold, the arrows are growling."

Gray Crane danced, Coyote was her husband. He sang his shaman's song, "Do not look back, younger sister, because you cause our children to make mistakes." While she danced he bit one of the children, he tore off its neck.

Rabbit sang, "Step aside, step aside, post, heha, heha. I will shoot you." He spanned his bow and Blue Jay told the post to step aside. Blue Jay got a rabbit skin blanket, but his wife would not put it on.

Skunk the chieftainess continued to sing her song. Blue Jay asked Robin to go out. He said she would kill the whale quickly. Five times Blue Jay asked his older brother Robin to go out.

Then Blue Jay shouted, "Skunk is a farter, she will make sick those whom she invited to dance." Then Skunk farted, and the whale fell dead. Blue Jay was blown away. He stuck in a knothole. The people cut up the whale. Blue Jay called to Robin to get him out of the knothole. When the blubber was all cut, Robin went up and took him out. Then Blue Jay got only meat of the whale.[4]

PERHAPS THE WHALE referred to was one a sorcerer attracted at Sealand, where a strong man might sing his spirit song and attract a whale to the beach. That brought great prestige, and winter was the right time, for the forty-ton gray whales were migrating south along the coast. Cultee recalled,

A person who has a supernatural helper of the sea sings to bring a whale. No woman who has her regular menses enters, no young person, else a person might see the singing who has cohabited the preceding night. Only old people, boys and young girls, help sing. For five days he sings. Then a youth is sent and told to look seaward. Five times he is sent; then, indeed, he finds a whale adrift. The singer is covered with down. He places a pole upright on the beach and says: "Here a whale will drift ashore," and indeed, it drifts ashore there after he has sung five days.[5]

Don't think the Chinook were helpless prisoners of those taboos. They could manipulate them in their favor. They sent a youth who had made love the night before out beyond the whale, which drove it inshore rather than away.

Bewitched and beached, a gray whale was a windfall. A small one yielded three hundred gallons of oil, plus meat and bones. The Shoalwater awaited their headman, who divided it in span- and hand-width strips, and distributed them among the people. Two spans and one hand (nearly two feet) was worth a thirty-five-shell fathom of dentalia in one account, a cut of merely two spans (eighteen inches) a groundhog blanket.[6] The Clatsop tied straps of kelp to claim a cut without waiting for their headman. Newcomers cut where there were no straps, latecomers took the bottom of the whale. Should a man cut where another had strapped there would be trouble.

THINGS GOT WILD when conjurors assembled. Those were the *tahmahnawis* men, the strong ones. *Tahmahnawis* meant the spirit power posessed by an individual, as well as the magic performed by the conjurors, ghost, spirit, or anything supernatural.[7] When a person heard them sing his song he "became like fire inside." He might call on someone to cut his flesh, then eat of it or drink his own blood. It was his spirit having him do that. After a winter of dances he had rows of scars up each arm. Or her spirit might demand bird or animal blood. Some bird spirits were like that. People danced as close to the fire as they could stand. A strong man took another on his back, and leaped through the fire. One with warrior spirit pulled out a thick roll of skin and sliced off the end. The wound healed swiftly. His torso was covered with such scars. People held red-hot stones in their hands, swallowed snakes, took fire into their mouths.

Cultee's grandfather once lured a sea lion to the dance house with his conjuror's song. He told the people, "Where may that old man come from? Perhaps he will come from Nehelem to see the dance, perhaps he will come from Clatsop to see the dance." No one knew what he meant. Early in the morning, when everyone slept, an old woman awoke and saw someone in the door. She thought they were being attacked, she awakened the people. When they lit their torches it became visible in the doorway, its face large as the moon. The people said, "Oh, a monster has come to our house," but

Cultee's grandfather said, "Is it a monster? It is that old man who comes to see the dance. He has come to give you food." It was a sea lion, which they killed.[8]

Spirit songs were sparse, evocative sketches of the spirit or of an event.[9] Rabbit sang, "I am standing and sneaking around, I stand on my haunches in the underbrush." Owl shaman's song was "This is how my little bill goes—it is noisy. My legs are covered with feathers, my eyes are yellow-green." A girl with the spirit of grease sang, "While going beside the lake, a fish flapped ashore right there, a fatty one, a fatty one." An elk hunter sang, "If the orphan boy remembers what is told of olden times, if the orphan boy remembers what is told of olden times, he shall excel all others." A boy abandoned by his entire village sang, "*Atse! Atse!* My feathered cloak waves freely over me!"

They sang the song again and again, changing word order, syllable stress, and length of vowels and otherwise altering it as the spirit taught them at the moment. Throughout their lives they meditated that enigmatic song. It was in their thought and behind their thought, as his Zen *koan* fills the mind of the monk.

MYTHS WERE ALSO SPECIFIC to winter. Mere legends of older times might be recalled in any season, but the myths were sacred, recited only in the dark months of the sacred season. Myths revealed the origin of things. Some things came about because a changer made it so directly. Coyote was often the changer. But he was also sometimes an announcer, who foretold how the world would be in the future. Changers were few, but announcers were many and need not be important or sympathetic characters.

Grizzly Woman announced the future usefulness of trees in one myth. She had killed the woman she picked berries with and tried to kill the woman's children, but Blue Heron flipped her into the river, where she floated down into a log jam. Crow pecked at her crotch and made her bleed. That was the origin of menstruation. Grizzly Woman smeared the blood on her face and wandered about asking the trees, "Hey, how do I look to you?" One tree replied, "Ugh, whenever will blood be used to paint a face?" and she announced, "Smoke producer! Our people are getting pretty near now. Should they burn you, you will merely sizzle and go out. They will toss you out of the fire." Another tree responded, "Why, indeed, your appearance is something very good," to which Grizzly Woman replied, "Oh, isn't that nice, younger sister! You will be good to burn, your bark, your limbs, and you yourself will be good to burn." She went through all the trees that way, announcing their burning, carving, basket making, and other potential uses.[10]

UPPER-CLASS MEN AND WOMEN of mature age recited the myths, and were always paid something for doing so, if only a handful of roots. They recited the exact words, in a stately, archaic Chinook, dancing, singing, and acting out the story. Everyone but young children had heard the story before. Older people were as familiar with the words as the recitalist. No deviation would go unchallenged. Interpretation was possible, however, in other aspects of the telling. By inflection, intonation, timing, and body language the story's meaning could be greatly changed, even reversed.

Altogether, about 125 Chinook myths were recorded properly and exactly.[11] There are some other bits and pieces, explanations of geographic features, etc., but many aren't trustworthy, having been written down by untrained settlers. Anthropologist Melville Jacobs estimated that we have properly recorded versions of what would have been about five percent of a Chinook village's repertoire.[12] These stories were inherited from many sources and differ widely in style and character. Some were peopled by totemic animals, but others have named or unnamed characters and no animals at all. Some were told across the continent. Anthropologist Franz Boas traced a Chinook flood myth, in which Muskrat dove down and brought up mud to end the flood, eastward two thousand miles to the Algonquin and Sioux.[13] Stories moved down the Columbia with trade, came with wives from afar, even from slaves. Myths were portable and lasted a long time. Some span the globe. Their origins are shrouded in mystery.

The same myth might mean something entirely different, either to another people, or to the same people at a different time. A new myth was restyled to fit the local way of telling, and translated into the older Chinook, full of special words and phrases. Quotes from those scriptures were their storehouse of allusions and cast of character types, coloring their daily lives as literature, film, and television color ours.

THE RECITALIST SPOKE in a voice of low timbre and enunciated even more carefully than usual. He took all the parts and spoke "with relish and assurance in a style recognized by his family as formal, contrasting with ordinary talk."[14] It was a dramatic performance, not a literary one. Reading even contemporary play scripts is difficult. We can hardly imagine the richness from the bare myths, copied down laboriously word for word. The poetic form of the Chinook myths has only recently been rediscovered by Dell Hymes.[15]

As in other scriptures, the myths were fleshed out by commentary. Whole books are written about biblical stories a few lines long. The meaning of Chinook myths was likewise discussed, interpreted, and explained, and taught to the young, but a moral was only latent in the story, and may have changed a lot over the centuries. Bare as skeletons, pared to the essentials and nothing more, myths survived. A discussion of how a girl ought to react to an offer of marriage would be illustrated by quotes from "She Fooled Him with Her Dog."[16] A father taught his son the importance of keeping one's temper by recalling how, in "Badger and Coyote were Neighbors," Coyote attacked a bug and the people died forever instead of reincarnating each spring like the leaves.[17]

Listeners weren't passive. The audience responded aloud at regular poetic intervals. The Clackamas responded, "*Aaaa*" while the Shoalwater grunted, "*Hugh*." These responses added another level of meaning and emotion, and may have informed the reciter how his listeners felt about his interpretation.

The myths were terse, understated, yet in some cases monotonously repetitive to our ears. There were no descriptions of landscapes. A journey through the waterfall-laced peaks of the Columbia Gorge would be no more than "he started, he went along, he got there." Descriptions of the characters were likewise missing. If the character was totemic, its description was known and resembled the animal. Trout Girl had a rather sharp mouth and was good looking. Sturgeon was big, his body light in color. Everyone knew what Cougar, Coyote, and Blue Heron looked like.

FIVE WAS the Chinook ritual number. In a myth, the oldest of five brothers went off on a mission, made an error, and was killed. One by one his younger brothers followed, each performing the same incorrect act—for example, breaking a meadowlark's leg and continuing on—and suffering the same fate, being killed and hung in the smoke hole. Finally the fifth and youngest brother stopped to splint the bird's leg, and was rewarded with the knowledge necessary for success in the mission.

Four times the Chinook shaman performed a ritual and the fifth time it worked. The Hebrew ritual number was seven, as when the walls of Jericho fell; Christianity emphasizes three. A secular equivalent is the joke punchline, which occurs on the third repetition among Euro-Americans. For the Chinook, a story where the magic worked on the fourth repetition, as it did for many other groups of the region, seemed premature and lacking in tension. A Hebrew ritual of seven repetitions would seem overlong, as their five seems boring to us, our triggers set for quicker firing.

Five meant many, ten very many. Their largest myths segment into five acts, as ours tend toward three. Their poetic phrasing segments into sets of threes, interlocked into fives. For the reciter of myths, five repetitions gave rich opportunities for color and interpretation, and there were slight variations in each repetition.

They had myths of all lengths, from a fragment of a single scene to great three-generation epics. Those of the middle length are compactly dramatic. Like drama elsewhere, the stories were divided into acts and scenes, with humorous interludes to break the tension and sometimes an epilogue to tell what happened later. Transitions are mostly absent. A period of years is bridged by a single inflected word, *ana*—so then—and variations.

THEIR MYTHS were the stuff of dreams. The Darkness Woman kept darkness in her box; the animals invaded the sky up a ladder of arrows; babies grew to manhood in a stanza; heroes leaped mountains in a bound; water restored sight; oil brought a person back to life; a feather bled to warn of disaster; her heart was hidden in a woman's hat, or her little finger.

Among those plot devices were profound insights into human psychology. Hearing the stories year after year, meditating their twists, many of the people came to understand their deeper meanings. Some meanings weren't so deep: hiding a mother's life in her basket hat was a symbol of womanly conscience. Hiding a woman's heart or life force in her little finger is deeply symbolic even if a Freudian-style interpretation of little finger as clitoris is not intended.[18] We can't even guess what some devices meant.

One shouldn't assume that symbolism was not implied, or that the audience didn't understand the symbols. A telling anecdote was

Naked Against the Rain

reported by anthropologist Elizabeth Jacobs about her Nehelem-Tillamook respondent, who was unlikely to have been more sophisticated than a similar Chinook. Jacobs had copied down a tale about Wild Woman, the Tillamooks' earthy female protagonist. In the story Wild Woman became angry at something apparently innocuous her husband, High Class Crane, told their children to say to her,

> *"I looked down the river," Crane instructed the little children to repeat, "and there was a small canoe down there, and there was a person paddling. He does not sit up straight, that one who paddles, he is kind of stooped over. And that canoe is not perfect, it is somewhat lopsided, that canoe! After a while I looked up in the sky, and oh, that sky was all clouds, and I saw a bunch of grass growing up on that sky."*

Jacobs asked her informant, "Why was Wild Woman angry?"

"Oh, that old woman was only pretending to be mad," the recitalist replied,

> She was just excited [sexually]. That story was a description of her genitals. The canoe was her vagina and the one paddling was her clitoris. The grass on the sky, that meant her [pubic] hair and her belly. Oh, she did not like it when he said the canoe was lopsided. That was making fun of her, a little.

Jacobs found the explanation astoundingly Freudian.[19]

THE STYLIZATION of Chinook stories began with the first sentence, which resembled a newspaper lead paragraph, usually telling who, what, and where. "Badger and Coyote lived there," one began. "There was a chief of a town, his relatives lived in five towns," began another. "People were living there. They were continually smoke-drying salmon and various things. There was a widow."

The ending was likewise a formula: "*Kani, kani.*" The Myth, the true nature of things. Sometimes Cultee added, "Tomorrow good weather."[20] Menait said "Thus did the tale take place."[21] Wasusqani sometimes concluded "Hurry! Summertime is coming, grouse are hooting, story, story."[22]

OLD AGE, the ending of life, resembles winter. Among the Chinook it brought respect and freedom from duties and taboos. A woman was released from the rules that had bound her during child-bearing years. Old people were the repositories of the wisdom of the people. Knowledge changed slowly enough for memories to be of great value. Old people recited the myths and were teachers. A woman past menopause commanded respect.

Death was not far behind. Though the average lifespan was around thirty or thirty-five years, some individuals lived as long as we do now. But the curer came oftener and sang longer, the grandmother grew weak and had no teeth to chew her food, went blind, became a problem to her relatives. A person who could not travel at the appropriate season was a considerable burden. Most families took care of their elders nonetheless, but sometimes they carried an old person to a hill, off the trail at a distance from the village, or to some other deserted spot, left food and water and a covering of skins, and went away. First they asked if it was all right to do so, and were assured that it was.[23] No wealthy or noble person would be put away in that manner, however.

SUICIDE TOOK ITS TOLL. Fur trapper Peter Skene Ogden thought the people of the Columbia River, particularly women, killed themselves "under some momentary impulse of desperate excitement."[24] Paul Kane compared them to salmon battering themselves to death against the falls. He thought "suicide prevailed more among the Indians of Columbia River than any other portion of the continent which I have visited." Kane attributed such deaths mostly to gambling losses.[25] Thwarted love was mentioned too, and in the legends people do away with themselves out of shame or sorrow.

Coyote taught them how. In "Badger and Coyote were Neighbors" Coyote suffered the death of all five of his children:

> Now Coyote tried in vain to drown himself.
>> He did not die.
> Then he built a fire,
>> he made a big fire,
>>> he leaped into it there.
>> He did not burn.
>>> He did not die.
> He took a rope,
>> he tied it,
>>> he tied it on his throat,
>> he pulled himself up,
>>> once more he did not die.
> He took a knife,
>> he cut his throat,
>>> he did not die.
>> He did every sort of thing
>>> that he intended for killing himself.
> Now he quit,
>> he merely wept all day.[26]

WHEN DEATH APPROACHED, a person upriver would at last reveal the identity of his guardian spirit. He called for some article connected with the spirit—deer meat, or a wolf's backbone set on a pole, or five elkskins. Then he told how he got his power, and perhaps recited omens he had learned then. A Wasco with Elk spirit said that if he was going to recover it would rain and hail, but if it did not he would die. One with Deer spirit might eat a few bits of venison after all those years of never tasting deer flesh, and swiftly recover.[27]

Death came eventually. It would have been less permanent and less frightening had Coyote not, like the Greek Orpheus, bungled the job of bringing dead people back from the land of the ghosts.

AFTER HIS FIVE CHILDREN were killed and he failed at suicide, Coyote made a pack basket, and in the spring went and gathered their bones. He laid them tenderly among ferns in the basket. Then he started for home, proceeding very slowly and gently. By the third day the children were beginning to talk.

> "You are lying on me," he heard, "Move a little."
>
> He went more slowly still. Now an insect ran across his path. She sniffed the air and said, "Coyote is carrying dead people along." He paid no heed, though she ran across repeatedly. Finally he laid the basket down with utmost care and went after her with a stick. When he lifted the basket again they were chatting, they were saying "Move around slowly and carefully, we are making our father tired."
>
> He proceeded so carefully that when he camped he could still see his previous night's campfire.
>
> By the fifth day they were laughing. He went painstakingly. That insect ran back and forth in front of his feet, insulting him. He forgot. He loosened his pack and let it drop.
>
> "Ohohoh," his children sounded. He chased the insect, he returned, he lifted the packbasket again. He did not hear them talking. When at last he uncovered the packbasket again they were dead. Just bones. He buried them, and he wept.

Coyote said, "Indeed, I myself did like that. The people are close by now. Had I brought my children back, then the people would have been like that. After the leaves they would have come back to life. Such persons would be revived on the fifth day of ritual."[28]

FOR TWO MONTHS they recited stories and sang for their spirits and danced, in the sacred time of winter. No European mentioned witnessing their winter dances in the year 1820, but they occurred nonetheless. By then some Chinooks understood the concept of numbering years, but one wonders whether even their most prescient seers could guess they had only a decade left to enjoy their rain-gladdened riverside Eden.

Though inscribed "Chinook Indian, Columbia River," this is probably a portrait of Cassino, the most prominent headman of the Wapato Lowlands when he was painted by Paul Kane at Fort Vancouver around 1847. Courtesy Stark Museum of Art, Orange, Texas.

20

Fort Vancouver Rules

1825

BEYOND THE ROCKY MOUNTAINS, the two great corporate fur traders of North America had long struggled for supremacy. Their weapons were words, laws, knives, and guns. In 1821 the companies merged, the North West Company joining the Hudson's Bay Company, under the latter name. What might have been a mere corporate merger turned out to be most important and unsettling to the Chinook.

Strangers who come to live at the mouth of Big River often find it cool, damp, and depressingly overcast. Those who remain must become content with the mild grayness. The Astorians disliked the climate from the start, and the Nor'westers in their turn agreed.[1] They longed for sunshine to grow crops. Their ships rotted in the dank salt air. They grew suspicious and darkly morbid under the looming clouds. Upriver somewhere, they believed, must be a land of sunshine and tillable prairies. Like the salmon, smelt, and sturgeon, like Coyote and the Chinook themselves, the floats-ashores were headed upriver.

The joint occupancy declared in 1818 between the United States and Great Britain left the Canadian border in doubt. At the time the Hudson's Bay Company took over Fort George, it was widely believed that the Columbia River would be selected as that border, so the Company gentlemen had good reason to remove to the north bank of *Wimahl*. Indeed, the Americans might arrive at any moment and reclaim the remains of their fort.

Dr. John McLoughlin, the incoming superintendent, and Alexander Kennedy, the previous superintendent, surveyed up the Columbia. The idea had always been to move to somewhere around the mouth of the Willamette, but now they looked only at the north bank. The most suitable site they found was Skatcutxat, "Mud Turtles,"[2] ninety river miles above Fort George and five above the upper mouth of the Willamette. It had a firm, gently sloping bank, and opened on broad benches suitable for farming behind. They would build their fort there and name it after Captain George Vancouver, as a reminder that he had surveyed the coast and sent Lieutenant Broughton up the Columbia to a dozen miles beyond their proposed fort in 1792.

COMCOMLY UNDERSTOOD the effect of the move from the start. Company executive George Simpson, who had come out to oversee the integration of the region into the Hudson's Bay Company and stayed for the move, recalled that when they learned the trading post would be moved, "The poor Indians appeared in great distress at being deserted by us, and my old friend his majesty Comcomly actually shed tears when I shook hands with him at the water side."[3]

The pattern of Chinook trade, long established and vigorously maintained, was shattered by the move. Formerly, at natural or human borders, a state of animosity was maintained so goods had to be traded across from village to village. The Shoalwater maintained a quarrel between themselves and the Skiloot, but let the Wahkiacum and Kathlamet come down and trade. The Shahala portage at the Cascades represented such a border, unless the traders were kin. The Clackamas kept the Yamhill-Kalapuya away from the falls, though the Mahlnumax encouraged the Tualatin-

Kalapuya to walk across the Tualatin Mountains to trade. The Dalles area was such a border and trans-shipment point. Perhaps there was such a border between the Kathlamet and the Mahlnumax, as portrayed in the Kathlamet story of going to war with the ghosts.[4] Animosity made for good trade.

In 1825 the Hudson's Bay Company moved upriver to Fort Vancouver, leaving a small outpost at Fort George (including Lamsay to pilot their ships).[5] Even that soon dwindled, and the fort disappeared, though Lamsay remained. Cassino, most prominent headman in the Wapato Lowlands, soon began blockading traffic on Big River. His people challenged Chinook or Kathlamet canoes, in order to prevent them from selling their furs directly to the Company at its new fort.[6]

Simpson, a consummate businessman, understood the situation well when he wrote of the coast Chinook,

> They are however keen traders and through their hands nearly the whole of our furs pass, indeed so tenacious are they of this monopoly that their jealousy would carry them to the length of pillaging and even murdering strangers who come to the establishment if we did not protect them.[7]

Simpson dissuaded Cassino from his blockade, and Big River became for the first time open, which increased the Company's profit and cost the Clatsop and Shoalwater a large part of their thirty-year monopoly.

They did not give up easily. Comcomly's son Chenamus spread a rumor among the Chehalis that a Company trapping and trading party led by John Work was coming to attack them. Work managed to reassure the Chehalis, and by offering higher prices than the Chinook, cut out the middleman, always a desirable goal for a commodity buyer.[8]

Fort Vancouver, intended to govern a quarter of North America, was to be large and grand. They misjudged the shoreline, and built too far from the water, but after a couple of years moved down closer to the river and built again. High palisades enclosed a broad area which would eventually become thick with houses, barracks, warehouses, workshops, and an Indian store. During the day a steady stream of visitors came to buy or barter. It was exceedingly polyglot, people from many continents and islands, and its main language was Chinook Jargon.

By 1825 *Chinugumt*, the Chinook Jargon, had swollen to include many European words.[9] The initial Nootka words remained, but no new ones had been added. Philologist Horatio Hale made the first complete and accurate dictionary in 1841. He counted 111 Chinook words, 41 English, 34 French, and 18 Nootka words, a number of Chehalis ones, and 10 or less each from Nisqually, Yakima, Wasco-Wishram, Kalapuya, Cree, and Chippewa. Hawaiian, though the Kanakas (as they called themselves) had been on the river for over a decade, contributed not a single word. Hale's list totalled about 250 words.[10]

French words were employed for body parts. Usually the French gender prefix *la* or *le* remained at the front of the word, for example *laboose*, or later *lapush*, the mouth; *latate*, the head, brain, sense, or intellect; or *lemooto*, sheep. Serious English concerns were expressed in such ideas as *tomalla* (tomorrow), *waum*, *dly*, *nem*, and *law*. English also provided the words for man, sun, moon, and stick. Considering the guttural complexity of the original Chinook language, it is surprising how many Chinook-based words did last.

Chinugumt was a living, growing language at Fort Vancouver, where speakers of French, English, Chinook, Kathlamet, Kiksht, several Salish languages, several Sahaptin ones, Cree, Chippewa, Kalapuya, Hawaiian, and other tongues met and traded and lived together, in the "Kanaka Village" that grew outside the palisades. The Jargon was no one's native language, but was the central means of communication between the common people. French-Canadian husbands spoke to their Cree or Kalapuya wives in Jargon, Hawaiians addressed Cowlitz in Jargon, and Celts traded with Indians in Jargon. There must have been children for whom it was nearly a mother tongue.

There were stories, perhaps floated by the Company, that the Jargon was created by the Hudson's Bay Company and spread purposely via the French-Canadian canoemen. The Chinook core of the language gives the lie to that, but pioneer Gilbert M. Sproat expressed it better when he wrote, "Such an achievement as the invention of a language is beyond the capabilities even of a Chief Factor."[11] The strong and durable Chinook core seems to indicate not just the language's place of birth, but its pre-European origin.

WORD FORMATION CONTINUED. Many were onomatopoeic, which came of the Chinook language, though the early lexicographers were unaware of that and often listed such words separately. Jargon words like *tin-tin* for a bell or the striking of a clock, *tsik-tsik* for wagon or wheel, from the sound of a wooden axle, were regular Chinook word formations.[12] Combinations of different sources such as *tummwata* for waterfall, combining the Chinook *tumm*, from the sound, with the English *wata*, were frequent. In a three-language combination, *lum-pe-chuck*, "rum and water," *lum* was from English *rum*, *pe* from the French *puis*, (beside, next, afterward, or then) and *chuck* from the Nootka for *wata*.

Opitsa meant knife, *opitsa yahla siks*—knife his friend—meant fork. An original word in Jargon was *pelton*, crazy or foolish, from Archibald "Judge" Pelton, a free trader picked up by Wilson Price Hunt's overland party of 1812, who went mad in the mountains and was brought to Astoria.

ONE OF THE LAST GREAT EVENTS at Fort George was the wedding of another of Comcomly's daughters, Raven, called Princess Sunday, to Company clerk Archibald McDonald, in 1823.[13] Five months later she bore a son, called Toole by the Chinook, Ranald McDonald by the *Kin Chautch*. Toole was later told that during the marriage ceremony, "A distance of about 300 yards was a path of golden sheen, of richest furs, viz. of prime beaver, otter (sea and land), nothing less! not even seal fur, then of no account in the fur trade."[14] The family story was that Comcomly gave those furs to the groom, and again the Company took the furs, no Company employee being allowed to own furs. Ranald McDonald would later complain that those furs should have come to him, as sole heir.

"My father married the youngest daughter, then still in her teens, of 'King Com-comly,'" he recalled, "the father and the maid nothing loathe. Her personal name in Chinook signified Raven, probably from the color of her hair, for black in complexion she was not, but like her sister (Mrs. McDougall) was rather of Egyptian brown."[15] (The editors noted that the Chinook word for raven was *koalexoa*,[16] but whether that was really her name is unknown. Raven in Jargon was *KaKa*, or caw caw.)[17]

His mother died "a few days after my birth." The boy was raised for the first few years by Comcomly's sister Carcumcum,[18] and called Toll-Toll by his grandfather. Toole thought that meant boy.

RAVEN'S UNTIMELY DEATH was one of many. In the two years preceding September 1825, Comcomly lost eight members of his family,[19] including Raven; his second oldest son and heir Shalapau, formerly Quatqos; and a younger son whose nickname may have been "the Duke of Clarence."[20] (The latter was probably the babe-in-arms one of his wives had carried when he visited the Astorians in 1814.) Comcomly was around fifty-five by that time. He killed a slave, or slaves, to bury beneath his sons' canoes. A neighboring headman noted for his curing skills had tried to save the sons but failed. Chenamus had him murdered. To further revenge himself, Comcomly established a new *memaloose* so near the offender's village on Point Ellice, river mile 10, that the village had to move. Dr. John Scouler saw that *memaloose*:

> The canoes had a curious and melancholy appearance; they were covered with lace coats, silks and beads and every article which the deceased possessed. Comcomly's sons had their fowling pieces by their side and a loaded pistol in each hand. Occasionally the old man visits the grave of his sons and exposes their bodies to see that all the ornaments remain about them, and if necessary to put new blankets and mats around them. One of the canoes contained the remains of Shalapau, the favorite son and intended heir of Comcomly. This young man, had he lived, might have raised his countrymen far above their present condition. The Indians never talk of him without shedding tears, and as proof of his zeal to acquire knowledge it needs only be mentioned that he had made some proficiency in reading and writing and could talk English fluently."[21]

Comcomly, having earlier conferred his authority, and possibly his name, on Shalapau, and renamed himself Madsue, must have suffered great pain. It is hard to tell how much authority the old man had really given to his son. He remained active.

Across the river Cobaway (sometimes called Comowool, Coone, or Coniah), pre-eminent chief of the Clatsop, also died in 1824. Lewis and Clark called him the kindest of the Chinook they met. He was said to have had twenty wives, and to have once owned Konapee (though it was more likely his grandfather or great-grandfather who owned the ironworker). Yet Cobaway died without a male heir. The apparent low fertility of the Chinook, coupled with the scourges of epidemic pestilences, were undoing them.

No one is sure what killed them in 1824 but such mysterious "mortalities" were also occuring to the north along the coast, and far inland on the Plateau.[22] It cannot have been smallpox, for the Chinook knew both its name and horror. They would have told the clothmen. Influenza might have been the killer, or measles, or some disease not marked by recognizable symptoms. It might have been several coincidental diseases.

JUST BEFORE THEY MOVED, the clothmen made a census, the *Fort George Report of 1824*. It listed people as slave or free, male or female. Counting all categories there were 130 Clatsops, 720 Shoalwater, 190 persons in Coalpo's village near Fort George, 335 Kathlamet, 775 Mahlnumax, and 250 Shahala. No count was made of those above the Cascades, the Clackamas, or those at the falls, and whole villages were unlisted. The total was only 2,400, less than a quarter of the 10,190 Lewis and Clark counted along the same waterways a generation before. The Chinook villages averaged twenty-four percent slaves, and Coalpo's village down the beach from Fort George was forty-seven percent slaves, but Comcomly's village had a hundred male slaves, twice as many as Coalpo's.[23] Slaves were by then the number one item of commerce all along the coast, much stimulated by the maritime fur trade. The Hudson's Bay Company "encouraged" the freeing of slaves, but let their employees own them if they wished. The American spy William Slacum may have been biased when he charged in his report that slaves actually constituted a source of free labor for Company operations.[24]

The wealth of the Chinook increased. To the fur traders it appeared the wealth of a select few but probably the Chinook custom of sharing provided a strong trickle-down effect. The Europeans liked to trade with chiefs, so chiefs appeared. After Astoria was built the wealth of the chiefs increased greatly. Displays of wealth by the few successful headmen burgeoned. Power and wealth became important for their own sake rather than for the good of the people.

The nobles eagerly married their daughters to the Europeans. Cobaway married three daughters to the clothmen, Comcomly four. He didn't just marry them to the floats-ashores either, but far and wide. Comcomly had a Shoalwater son-in-law, who married Elowaka, a daughter by his Willapa wife. He was father-in-law to his upriver rival Cassino, Illchee's second husband.

The Chinook were spreading their area of contact by then. It was said that Comcomly visited the Makah, at the tip of the Olympic Peninsula. Some said he visited Nootka, and the Nootka headman, Maquinna, came south to visit the Chinook. Only the Quileute and their cousins the Hoh along the Olympic coast to the north were not friends and marriage partners of the Chinook. Lamsay fathered a son, evidently by a Makah noblewoman, called Yellow Cum and destined to be a tribal leader.[25]

Despite his personal tragedies, "his one-eyed majesty" Comcomly was still "the principal personage" along the river in 1825, according to George Simpson.[26] That well-traveled executive ranked Coalpo next, though his wife ruled the roost and prided herself on her ancestry, and Sachla third. Sachla, not previously mentioned and not identified as to village, had recently married his daughter to superintendent Alexander Kennedy. Lady Coalpo was so threatened by this that she was

> quite outrageous and indignant and pressed hard that I should take her daughter (a buxom damsel of 18 or 20 who has never yet seen daylight) even for the few weeks I have to remain here, with a dowry of 100 beaver, in order to re-establish and confirm her rank.[27]

That was a real change from Chinook customs: the bride's family providing a dowry, in a status marriage not meant to be lived out. Certainly any marriage between nobles brought increased status, but this was husband buying. The Tualatin headman Kamac is said to have married a woman from among Cassino's people, by which he "made his name good."[28] But in a status marriage, the wedding itself becomes the important event; consummation may not be required.

IT WAS THAT SAME KAMAC whom Cassino hired to kill a shaman.[29] Cassino, though unranked by Simpson, soon began to loom larger as geography improved his position. Simpson thought him the most intelligent Indian he had met.[30] It is open to question whether that meant that he always favored the whites against his own people in order to enhance his wealth and power. He seems often to have done so, and resorted frequently to violence to stay on top.

Astorian Gabriel Franchère first wrote Cassino's name as Keasseno.[31] It would appear as Cassanov, Kyeassino, Carsino, or Kiersinno.[32] Perhaps Kiasno was closest to the true sound,[33] but Cassino was most often written. He might have been born around 1790. Franchère described him as a young man in 1811, and located him as headman of the Kalama village, which was probably an error. Alexander Ross knew him as headman at Wacomap, near the mouth of Multnomah Channel, while others located his village at Nayagogo, Clacksta, or Clannaminnamun, all located near Wacomap.[34] He accompanied the 1814 war party to the Cascades and acted as a mediator. They said he was tall for a Chinook, with a large frame and a broad face wreathed in a pleasant smile.[35] They said he could read character and make friends. Alexander Henry thought him brave and avaricious, with many enemies.

When the Hudson's Bay Company moved up to Fort Vancouver, Cassino moved his village to Wakanasisi, "Butterball Ducks" (butterball or bufflehead were common in the marshes and lakes behind in fall and winter). It was located five miles below the fort, opposite the upper mouth of the Willamette, between Vancouver Lake and the river. Thereafter Cassino was much seen at Fort Vancouver. He was supposed to be able to muster a thousand warriors, and at the height of his power had ten wives and eighteen slaves but only four children.[36]

Artist Paul Kane recalled:

Casenov is a man of more than ordinary talent for an Indian, and has maintained an influence over his tribe chiefly by means of the superstitious dread in which they hold him. This influence was wielded with unflinching severity toward them, although he has ever proved himself the firm friend of the white man. Casenov for many years in the early period of his life kept a hired assassin to remove any obnoxious individual against whom he entertained personal enmity. This bravo, whose occupation was no secret, went by the name of Casenov's skoocom or evil genius. He finally fell in love with one of Casenov's wives, who eloped with him; Casenov vowed vengeance, but the pair for a long time eluded his search until one day he met her in a canoe near the mouth of the Cowlitz river and shot her on the spot. After this he lived in such continual dread of the lover's vengeance that for nearly a year he never ventured to sleep but in the midst of a body guard of 40 armed warriors, until at last he succeeded in tracing him out, and had him assassinated by the man who succeeded him in his old office.[37]

DR. JOHN MCLOUGHLIN, a white-haired giant, succeeded Mr. Kennedy as headman at Fort Vancouver, and there was now a firm hand in charge. Simpson reported the Shahala

more peaceable and quiet than I ever saw an equal number on the other side of the mountains; it was not so many years

ago as on this very spot they attempted to pillage a brigade
... but since that time they have given little trouble.[38]

Even separated by almost a hundred miles of river, Comcomly
never lost his access to the fort, or his importance to the Company's
operations. Though Lamsay probably did the routine pilotage,
Comcomly didn't miss a chance for a show. When the annual Hudson's Bay Company supply ship—the arrival of which was the
biggest event of the year—approached the bar, Comcomly spotted
it from his lookout above Chinook Point. His canoe was launched
by his team of slaves—he'd started with six paddlers and worked up
through eight, then twelve, to twenty by this time—and he went to
meet the ship in military uniform. The ship lifted canoe and paddlers aboard and the old man piloted them in across the bar and up
the 106 miles of shifting sandbars and channels to Fort Vancouver.
Edward Ermatinger described him "marching into Vancouver with
all his naked aides and followers, rigged out in a British General's
uniform ... minus the pantaloons."[39]

BLUDGEONED BY WAVES of death, their idyllic anarchy degenerat-
ing, the Chinook had finally begun to guzzle alcohol. Botanist
David Douglas wrote in 1824, "They will make any sacrifice to ob-
tain it,"[40] and McLoughlin noted them "much addicted to liquor"
in 1827.[41] Simpson heard they had begun to drink around 1822.[42]
The Company forbid the use of alcohol in trade. It wouldn't sell to
the Chinook lest they drink up the value of their furs and be unable
to barter for more.[43] The Chinook got alcohol from such maritime
fur traders as called at the mouth of Big River, but those were few,
if any.

IN 1826 THE CLOTHMEN began to plow and plant crops near their
new fort. More alarming to the Chinook, the floats-ashores persist-

ed in robbing the canoes of the dead, not just of valuables but of bones as well. Dr. John Scouler stole three flattened skulls, was seen, fled to his ship, and dared not disembark again.[44] Kane stole a skull at the Cascades.[45] Townsend stole a girl's corpse, and had to give it back to her brother, who cried bitterly as he carried her off to her resting place.[46] Dr. Townsend persisted, and successfully stole several skulls on a later occasion.[47]

Yet the living, Simpson recalled, were "wonderfully healthy, being rarely afflicted by any other than imported diseases."[48] Among the latter he included venereal ones "so prevalent that nine whites out of ten who have been resident at Fort George have undergone a course of mercury."[49] Apparently theft and promiscuity were not just Chinook vices.

Back in the winter houses, unseen by the clothmen, the infected babies were dying, the old people were dying, the young scions were withering. The shamans were blamed and assassinated.

At least Chinook women who had married clothmen no longer killed their babies rather than let them grow up with the bulging natural foreheads their husbands demanded. Simpson found the practice of flattening the heads of mixed-marriage offspring much abated.[50] The roundheads had won.

Truly, the basket ogress *Atatahlia* had returned to kill the people, and human life was again becoming impossible. This time there was no Coyote to battle her. The Chinook endured.

Tsinistum, called Jennie Michel and said to have been the last of the Clatsop living on Clatsop Plain. Photographer unknown. Courtesy of the Oregon Historical Society.

21

Now They Were Sitting
On Their Frog's Croak

SPRING, 1829

OF ALL THINGS, the Chinook treasured Big River most. "That's all the Chinook wanted anytime was the river," a Wasco said.[1] The river had made them prosperous, and had sophisticated them to new ways. The river fed them and made them important. Their culture was rich and multiple, and they were a people unbound, because *Wimahl* flowed past them. Water spirits were the most powerful.[2]

Down from the dry highlands the river brought them the personal spirit quest, mountain goat robes, mat summer houses, bitterroot, kous, Coyote myths, elkskin armor, dried and pounded salmon, chipped stone points, and ideas of personal merit and equality. Up from the lush seacoast came canoes, slavery, rod and slat armor, accumulated wealth, woodworking skills, ideas of noble birth, strings of long dentalia, ground stone implements, dried clams, spirit batons, and high-ridged cedar-plank homes.

Fashion and ideas swept both directions. The Clackamas and Wishram cut their hair in bangs; the Clatsop cut slaves' hair that way. Women as well as men pierced their noses with *haiqua* at the Cascades and above, but only men did so below. The women wore cedar bark skirts below Sauvie Island, leather breechclouts above.

Every village had its own mix of styles. Upriver Chinook mourned in whiteface, downriver in blackface. Canoe burial below, charnel houses above. Rock art downriver to Nayagogo. Wooden houses upriver to the Long Narrows. Sweat houses downriver to the Kathlamet. Head-flattening upriver clear to the Walla Walla. A shifting panorama of ideas and ways, alive with change, and the cosmopolitan Chinook selected among them.

THEY LOVED TO TALK AND TRADE and be visited by friends. James Swan described a visit:

> They were expecting friends they had not seen for a long time. As the time approached, they would be careful to collect as much food as they could, to give their friends a kind of reception, and someone or other was kept constantly on watch for the expected canoe. The weather, the wind, the state of the tide, all were discussed, as to the probable effect each would have to hasten or retard the coming of their friends.
>
> At length a canoe is seen in the distance. Can it be they? No, it is not like their sail; but perhaps they have got another. Yes, it must be; it is they. All now is glee, and the canoe comes up the creek, and nears the shore.
>
> Instead of rushing into each other's arms with congratulations and embraces, not a soul advances to greet them. All have gone into the lodge, and each one, at his accustomed place, appears as calm and is pursuing his avocations as if they never dreamed of any one approaching them. The party in the canoe then comes ashore, leaving all their traveling equipage in charge of a slave or two, apparently for the purpose of first ascertaining if their visit is welcome.
>
> They all then enter the lodge, and seat themselves

around the fire and near the door. No one takes the slightest notice of them, nor is a word spoken. I have thus seen them sit for ten minutes. At last a few guttural words from the visitors are answered by a grunt from the others. Other clucking sounds are then heard, and gradually they begin to talk, but not much. Food is now set before them, and, while they eat, they begin to grow social, and at length they throw off all restraint and gabble like so many geese.[3]

As for what they talked of, George Gibbs observed:

Their conversation is exceedingly lewd. The most indecent subjects are discussed or jested upon. When two canoes meet they exchange the news and chaff each other.[4]

THOUGH THE END WAS SO NEAR that their seers had begun to sense it, life went on as before. Illchee, deserted and then widowed by Duncan McDougall, later married to Cassino, may have been a few years over thirty and visiting Qwatsamts when her nephew Toole recalled:

a handsome woman; of proud queenly mien: reminding me of Egypt's Cleopatra, as pictured to us. I distinctly remember her, living in widowhood with her parents. Though my aunt, she was no friend of mine; seeming ever to have some pique against me, which, however, I did not regard, as I did not then understand our relationship. She was childless—if I mistake not—while, I believe, I was not only the baby favorite, but the heir presumptive of the old King according to Chinook and general Indian law. Some old people of the Columbia, after the old man's death, used to call me, or speak of me, as Com-comly, or shortly, Comly MacDonald: but why, I never enquired, nor knew, nor cared to know.[5]

Born in 1824, Toole can hardly have remembered her a widow or visiting living in her parent's house much before 1829, and as we shall see, such a condition would have been impossible after 1830. Certainly his disclaimer shows doubt. We can only guess that he was too young to understand the situation, or that the family still cherished memories of their alliance with the Astoria headman, McDougall.

Around then the wife of the headman of the village nearest Cape Disappointment, probably Comcomly's daughter Elwaka, killed two female slaves to accompany her daughter to the land of the dead, or as the Reverend Samuel Parker heard, "to row her canoe to the far off, happy regions of the south." Parker described her as "a woman of more than common talents and respectability."[6]

BAHSTEN SHIPS had begun to appear on Big River again, and contested at fur buying with the Hudson's Bay Company. This can hardly have displeased the Chinook. In June of 1827 Captain John O. Dominis brought the ship *Owhyhee*, Boston registry,[7] in over the bar and anchored off what had been Fort George. The fort had been abandoned in 1825, trashed, and partly burned.[8] Dominis collected timber for spars and masts and traded a little for furs, but departed after a few weeks.

He returned in the spring of 1829 and for more than a year pestered the Company gentlemen mightily.[9] Dominis sailed the *Owhyhee* up the Columbia to the mouth of the Willamette and to Vancouver, anchoring here and there, trying to buy pelts. Captain D. W. Thompson soon arrived commanding the ship *Convoy*, same owners, to join Dominis on the river. They sent ship's boats to Willamette Falls and sailed to the Cascades. The Americans gave three blankets for two beaver skins, the Company only one blanket for five skins. The *Bahsten* asked six beaver for a gun, the *Kin Chautch* required eighteen. Chenamus bought a gun from

Dominis in August.[10]

The Hudson's Bay gentlemen reassured each other that the *Owhyhee* and *Convoy* were only coasters, they could be driven off. They erected a tent at the site of Fort George and then a house, and began buying at the mouth of the river again, after a lapse of several years. They slashed their price for a gun from eighteen beaver to three, for a blanket from five skins to one, and rates on other goods in proportion. Even after the *Owhyhee* and the *Convoy* left the river, the Company men still hurried from village to village buying furs, so the natives wouldn't have any to sell to the next *Bahsten* trader.

The Company had opened a trading post at The Dalles, but in 1829 closed it. The Wasco were so outraged they sent a war party to Fort Vancouver. Dr. John McLoughlin had Cassino assemble a flotilla of thirty canoes from Wakanasisi and the other Wapato Lowland villages. According to historian Samuel A. Clarke, the Wasco were so impressed with the fort, particularly with a bagpiper in a kilt, that they retreated without bloodshed.[11]

THE *CONVOY* WAS RETURNING to the river in August 1829 when its crew witnessed a tragedy that led to an atrocity. The annual Company supply ship *William and Ann*, back for a fifth visit, started in across the Columbia Bar right behind the *Convoy*, evidently without a pilot in a worsening bar, and ran aground. Thompson, who'd made it safely into Bakers Bay, looked back to see the other ship founder. He sent a boat to try to save the crew, but his men lacked the strength to claw their way across the steepening waves of the bar. During the night, the *William and Ann* broke up, with the loss of all hands. A bonanza of trade goods washed ashore, some salvaged by the Clatsop.[12]

By the time word of the tragedy reached Fort Vancouver, the story included the grisly, baseless rumor that the Clatsop had massacred the survivors.

The *Kin Chautch* knew better, or should have. During thirty-seven years of intercourse, nineteen of them at shore trading posts, not a single European had ever been killed by one of the Chinook-speakers. The Clatskanie had killed, some Tillamook had killed poor mad Pelton, and the Quileute had murdered fur traders, but no Chinook had murdered a single one of the floats-ashores, at least none that left any trace in history. For all the clothmen's alarms and excursions—and they had several times accused the Chinook of being bloodthirsty—the worst attack chargeable to any Chinook were the three arrows Alexander Stewart took in 1814 at the Cascades, after he tried several times to shoot someone. And Stewart survived.

It was not that the Chinook could not shoot straight. Peter Corney confirmed that:

> One day some of our people were practicing the bow on board; they stood aft, and endeavored to strike a small looking-glass placed on the bow of the vessel, but none of them could succeed. An Indian, who was standing by, laughed most heartily at them, and taking up his bow, stood on the stern, and shooting, broke the glass in pieces, at a distance of 95 feet, the mark being about three inches square.[13]

Unfortunately, the Klallam, who lived three hundred miles north on the Strait of Juan de Fuca, and bound their heads round into a sugarloaf, had the previous year been accused of killing five Hudson's Bay Company men. Various Chinooks had offered to show their loyalty by serving as mercenaries against the Klallam, but McLoughlin turned them down for fear it would cause dislocations in his fur supply. Still, the Klallam had put the *passiuks* in a punitive mood. They sent chief factor William Connolly ahead to investigate what had happened to the *William and Ann* and to try to recover the goods. A fifty-five-member war party soon followed.

By now they were commanded by men of firmness and authority. Though the goods were fully insured, and the international-al laws of marine salvage made the flotsam of a sunken ship the property of the finder, exactly as the Clatsop argued, the Company warriors sailed down to demand that the Clatsop return their goods, among them ball gowns ordered from London by some of the gentlemen's wives.

The Clatsop headman Kateyahun, who had succeeded Cobaway after his death five years earlier, refused. Worse, he returned two rather insulting items—"an old brush and a swap"—and said they would return no more. The clothmen prepared to land. The Clat-sop ordered them away from their town. The floats-ashores opened fire with a cannon. They landed and burned down the Clatsop's an-cient village with all their possessions inside. They killed Kateyahun, whom they charged with "skulking about." Still thirsting after blood, the war party crossed Big River and killed two Shoalwater, also charged with "skulking about." Dr. McLoughlin's account noted they killed them for their "aggressive impudence, rather than . . . murder." McLoughlin knew there had been no murder.[14]

Had he not he would soon have learned from Captain Thomp-son of the *Convoy* that there had been only death by drowning. Sev-eral boat-loads of goods had been retrieved by Company men be-fore the war party arrived, according to Dominis.[15] The war party demanded the Clatsop deliver up goods, not murderers. Had they really thought there had been killing they would have acted differ-ently. You may suppose that the Company indemnified Kateyahun's heirs for his murder while skulking around his own village, or the villagers for the destruction of their centuries-old homes. If so, the meticulous Dr. McLoughlin neglected to record it.

The clothmen had disliked the impudent Chinook from the start. The Chinook bargained too well and did not need European goods badly enough. They enjoyed some of these goods, but re-mained independent of European ways. George Simpson suggest-ed that it would be beneficial to switch them to wearing British woolens.[16] Beneficial to whom? They liked going naked, why struggle into damp cloth trousers? They liked fish and roots, why addict themselves to pig or cow meat and wheat bread? They were not hungry enough yet. They did not have to buy clothes or tools or guns in order to live. They made their living with their nets, which they knew perfectly well how to manufacture. More often than not it was the Europeans who were dependent upon them, for food or advice or assistance. Only as their numbers shrank and their world crumbled had they begun to become addicted to alcohol. Only then did the Chinook begin to fall into dependency.

THE CHINOOK POPULATION was much reduced, but still substantial. At their height, before the first epidemic, the Chinook may well have numbered more than thirty thousand. By comparison, there were about four thousand Cheyenne, and most of the other famous Plains tribes were of similar sizes. The League of the Iroquois numbered eleven to fourteen thousand in the seventeenth century[17] and the north and central Nootka were perhaps six thousand.[18]

The earliest Chinook census was by Lewis and Clark, in 1806.[19] The captains' total of entirely Chinook villages came to 17,540, if their Clackstar are included as Chinook. The explorers left out the Washougal and the Wasco. They estimated 200 Clatsop, 400 Shoalwater, 200 Wahkiacum, 300 Kathlamet, 2,500 Skilloot and Cooniac, 250 Kalama, 900 Quathlapootle, 1,200 Clackstar (doubtfully Clatskanie), 2,530 Multnomah, 460 Shoto, 1,800 Clackamas, 850 at Willamette Falls, 2,800 Shahala, 800 White Salmon and Hood River, 1,400 Chilluckittequaw, and 1,000 Wishram. Those numbers were related to which time of year the explorers passed and counted, fall or spring. Much of it was hearsay and guesswork.

Anthropologist James Mooney extrapolated from Lewis and Clark's *Journals* to estimate the Chinook population in 1780, before the first epidemic, and came up with 21,700.[20] That was conservative, given that the explorers saw villages totally abandoned and others reduced to half their former size up and down the river, and in consideration of the Chinook's low birthrate. It is possible there were twice as many Chinook before the smallpox epidemics of 1781-1782 and 1801, though recent research suggests aboriginal populations may have rebounded more quickly than previously thought.[21]

Jedidiah Morse, working from lists compiled by Astorians Ramsey Crooks and Robert Stuart, estimated there were 14,900 Chinook in 1820,[22] but the 1824 Fort George census estimated only about a third that many, which suggests the die-back in those five years was terrible indeed.[23] Yet Simpson still thought,

> The population on the banks of the Columbia river is much greater than in any other part of North America that I have visited, as from the upper lake to the coast it may be said that the shores are actually lined with lodges.[24]

The highest estimates anyone on the scene made of each group were: Clatsop, 1,300; Shoalwater, 1,700; Wahkiacum, 400; Kathlamet, 600; Skilloot, 2,500; Kalama, 200; Multnomah, 2,530; Quathlapootle, 1,100; Shoto, 460; Clackamas, 1,800; Clowewalla and Charcowah, 850; Shahala, 2,800; Hood River and White Salmon, 2,200; Wishram, 1,250; and Wasco, 900.[25] Those figures total around 20,000 even after the two earliest epidemics, and a farthest outside possibility of close to 40,000 before the first epidemic.

BY 1829 THERE WERE fewer of them. But, life is full of risk, as the Chinook well knew, for they played at games of chance with avid delight.[26] (They played no strategy games, like chess or checkers, though bargaining was certainly a strategy game to them.)

They gambled at any time of year, and a game could go on for days and weeks. To the Chinook, such contests were not between the human players, but their spirit helpers. It was not how you played but whether you won that mattered. A victory gained by cheating was no less sweet. They would stake anything, strip themselves of their blankets, even sell themselves part by part for terms of years. Or until the next winning streak allowed them to pay off their debts.

A WASCO MYTH told of Eagle, a Klamath, who came to the river to gamble:

At first he won all the games. He gambled with Crow, Hawk, Raven and many other people. Toward the end, luck turned against him. Crab was called on to take part in the game. After that Eagle lost everything that he had won and all that he had brought with him. He gambled off his buckskin dress, his moccasins, arrows, everything. Then he bet one arm, lost; lost the other arm; bet one leg, lost; bet the other leg, lost. He lost one whole side of his body, one eye, one ear, all of one half of himself. Then he played and lost the other half of his body. His life was now in the hands of those with whom he gambled.

The victors cut off his head and hung it in the smoke hole.[27]

CANADIAN ARTIST PAUL KANE recalled,

They play with much equanimity, and I never saw any ill feeling evinced by the loser against his successful opponent. They will cheat if they can, and pride themselves on its success; if detected, no unpleasant consequence follows, the offending party being merely laughed at and allowed to amend his play.[28]

They played several kinds of hand games, generally in teams. The strongest gamblers of the village represented it against the gamblers of another. They played *itlukum*, with sets of four carved bones or antlers, or *lahull*, with ten disks like poker chips, which they divided in two packages to delude their opponents. The women played *omnitook*, a game with four beaver teeth, in winter and spring, and another game with four long bones hidden beneath a basket in summer or autumn.

Seated opposite, in rows ten feet apart, they drummed and sang their gambler's spirit songs, and the crowd behind made their bets, as the tension grew. Their singing Kane found "peculiarly sweet and wild, possessing a harmony I never heard before or since amongst Indians."[29] Finally the opposing leader made a guess, signalling merely left or right with his hand, and the hands or packages were opened to show whether his spirit had overcome his opponent's spirit. Ten sticks in the ground kept the tally of the gamblers' shifting fortunes.

They played games of physical skill as well, for example a field hockey game in village teams, with three-foot sticks and a carved yew root for a ball, which they called *wakalkal*. The woman played a version called *watlaktlak*, with two nine-inch batons of hardwood joined by a thong, which they threw toward the goal with four-foot sticks. *Alkolloch* consisted of throwing spears at rolling rings only three inches in diameter. Another game was rolling checker-like disks at a hole protected by pins. They shot with bow and arrow, ran foot races, and swam competitively. They were nearly amphibious, as George Simpson admired, "The [Chinook] male and female are excellent swimmers; they even surpass our Sandwich Islanders and remain under water a longer time."[30]

Settler Thomas Nelson Strong revealed,

Among themselves or with their intimate friends they are not at all reserved, but joked and told stories with the utmost freedom. There are few more joyful or animated sights than a camp or party in good luck: The little children and the dogs; a mingled, whooping, joyful mass, eating, sleeping and playing all day long. Even the little baby with its tightly bound head and body strapped to a board hung up against a tree, looked around with his little beady eyes in contented amusement, and unless frightened, never cried.[31]

They visited, feasted, and gambled. They lolled in the sun when the sky was not making its badness. They had no priests or politicians, and owed no larger allegiance than to their village. It seemed so normal. Probably life would continue like that forever.

"*Xwadet, xwadet*," sang the frogs, in their time for singing.[32]

EVEN THIRTY YEARS LATER, James Swan, who lived among the surviving Chinook and Chehalis on Shoalwater Bay, arguing against the underlying idea of a treaty between the American government and the Chinook "tribe," wrote of the people he knew:

> one great difficulty is, that an Indian is essentially different from a white man in all his habits, customs, feelings and desires. They like to have the white men come among them and cultivate lands, and they like to trade with the whites for their commodities, but farther than this they do not want. They neither wish to adopt the white man's style of living, or his language, or religion.[33]

SO TOO THE VILLAGE DOGS: small spotted curs, black, white, brown, and brindle, with long heads and pointed noses, small eyes, erect pointed ears, and short smooth hair, longer at the tail. They resembled more than a little the coyotes, with whom they had been interbreeding for thousands of years. George Gibbs recalled the dogs clearly:

Quarrelsome and cowardly, inveterate thieves, suspicious and inquisitive, they are constantly engaging in fighting amongst themselves or in prowling about the lodge for food.[34]

It sounds a bit like Coyote himself. Even in the most classic myth, the dogs were already domesticated, as though the Chinook remembered them walking beside their ancestors across from Asia to the New World. Although they sold dogs to others for food, the Chinook didn't eat dog, not even in myths and legends of starvation or ceremonials.

"The approach of a stranger was heralded by short sharp yelps, succeeded by a general scamper," according to Gibbs.

But a stranger was coming the dogs would not herald. The Chinook had one more round of the seasons and one last river to cross.

"On The Beach—Chinook." Photograph by Edward Curtis, courtesy of the University of Washington Library, Special Collections, NA 225.

22

Tales of Hunger, Fears of Dying

LATE WINTER, 1830

FOR TWO DARK MONTHS the Chinook had danced and sung and demonstrated their powers, attaining a natural high and hearing again the myths of ancient times. Finally, in Shoulder Moon, they began to sing for the warm Chinook wind. They wanted the smelt to come to them. They wanted to sing the salmon up the river. They wanted spring to come.

Even amidst plenty they frightened each other with stories of starvation. Up in the Columbia Gorge, the people at Ninuhltidih — Hood River — recalled enduring a terrible winter when it snowed for seven months without stopping. The snow buried the tallest trees out of sight and the people lived under the snow. Downriver at the Cascades, the Shahala were catching salmon. There was no snow whatsoever upriver at the Long Narrows. It snowed only at Dog River. The people under the snow did not know it was summer everywhere else.

A little bird came with a strawberry in its bill to an air hole they had made up out of the snow. They asked what it was that had brought such a storm, and it was discovered that one of the girls in their village had struck a bird. It was proved against the girl, and they offered her parents a great price for her. The parents would not sell her for a long time. At last the people bought her, and putting her on the ice as it floated down the river, pushed the ice into the middle of the stream. In that way they got rid of the snow. A few days later a Chinook wind came bringing heat. The snow melted away at once and things began to grow.

The girl floated on, day and night, down the river. Five years she floated. At the end of that time she came back to the place where she had been put on the ice. When she returned, there was but a small bit of ice under her, just enough to hold her bones up. For she was almost gone, only skin and bones remained. They took her into the village. She died. She was no longer accustomed to the smell of people and died from the odor of them. After a time she came to life, but it was a year before she could eat much.

Every summer after that she was nearly frozen to death, and went all bundled up; but in winter she was too warm, she would take off all her clothes and go naked.[1]

IN A CLACKAMAS ACCOUNT of such an extended winter, the people ate up all their food:

Their headman summoned the men to come and sweat, and they walked across the snow by placing boards on top. He offered them the remaining food. He started taking the houseboards to burn. "What were they going to eat upon another day?"

The headman sat thinking about what he could do for his people when a little bird came. He threw a stick, the bird dropped the red thing in its beak, it was indeed a strawberry. He realized it must be summer elsewhere. The headman took a pair of boards and advanced across the snow, placing one in

Naked Against the Rain

front of the other. The snow grew thinner and then disap-
peared, the sun came out. He went to the strawberry fields and
began to eat. He did not become full. He turned, and saw that
the strawberries were going right through him. He plugged his
anus with grass and ate more. Now he got full. He filled his
moccasins, his hat, everything he wore, with strawberries.

Then he realized he should go to Willamette Falls. There
he gathered eels that were climbing the rocks by their sucker
mouths. He threaded eels on hazel sprouts, only stopping
when he realized that he might become exhausted. He carried
eels and strawberries back across the snow, board by board.

Again he burned the planks of his house. He told his wife
not to roast the eels, just throw them on the fire so they would
cook faster. They fed the first ones to their children. Then they
shared the food with the starving people of their village. She
warned them to cook them quickly, but some roasted them as
they always had, and died while they were waiting. That night
the snow melted; by dawn there was absolutely no snow, just
foam on the ground.[2]

DEATH COMES AT LAST to all living things, though the Chinook
were not so sure that applied to headmen. They kept the body three
to five days in the house, during which friends and relatives left gifts
with the departed and hung things around the corpse and stuffed
its mouth with dentalia. A chief's dead daughter was dressed in her
finest; each hair of her head was threaded through a bead. A well-
born youth was tied with fish bones, shells and beads were scattered
over his dressed and painted body.

They had a kind of shaman, called *iyahihhlihlih* in Kiksht, who
could receive communications from the spirits.[3] These proto-mor-
ticians were well paid for undertaking the dangers and ritual pu-
rifications associated with touching a corpse. The morticians were

among the most highly developed specialists of the Chinook, though, like spokesmen, canoemakers, slaves, and headmen, they fished, too, if ever they were ritually clean enough to do so.

The corpse lay on a plank, an *iyahihhlihlih* at his head and another at his feet. The people sang and danced at the other end of the house. Visitors came to lament, speaking in whispers, from morning until dark. Slaves offered water and shredded bark to wash their tear-stained faces. Even the slaves mourned. Relatives cut their hair and changed their names, with appropriate public announcements, sometimes for only a year, sometimes permanently. They ceased speaking such words as reminded them of the deceased.

All night the shaman sat by the body. Toward morning the ghosts began to make demands. The shaman struck the shadows around the body with sprigs of wild rose to quiet them. "We are having trouble," he told the mourners. "This dead person is asking for something. Wait until I get through. I am going to sing."[4] He sang his spirit song. The ghosts might carry off another person if the shaman's spirit were not strong enough. All night he struggled, striking at the shadowy places. All day the mourners danced, moving slowly forward in a single file. After a few days the body could be moved.

WHEN IT WAS TIME to take the body to the *memaloose illahee*, the land of the dead, the Chinook removed a board from the side of the house so the ghost would not be able to find its way back in. If the deceased were their headman they might tear down the house and rebuilt it elsewhere. If he had been a great headman they burned it down. Any house was emptied for a while and then purified with burning branches. They carried the body to the river and placed it in a canoe, at full length or folded face down with knees to chest. The Chinook position to ward off spirit attack was similar, crouched on knees and elbows holding one's ears.[5]

Naked Against the Rain

The people of Sealand and the lower river up to the Shahala placed their dead in canoes or boxes raised five feet or more above the ground by posts and cross-beams or in a tree.[6] The body was wrapped in mats and skins and covered with finery, its mouth, eyes, and nose filled with money beads. They left no food, but placed familiar objects around, and painted the posts with his guardian spirit image. A brave man's battle headdress was placed on a pole stuck in the ground. A shaman's rattle hung from the stern. Taboos protected the valuables. A person who robbed the dead soon fell ill and died.

The canoe was holed, to kill it, and its bow pointed downriver. The canoe was not holed to prevent robbery; a hole could be patched and the boat paddled away. All the objects left were killed with holes so they could accompany the deceased to the land of the ghosts. Over the canoe they might place another boat, turned upside-down, for protection. Even a third canoe might enclose the two, all covered with mats and tied with ropes. Less wealthy corpses they put in wooden boxes and placed in a tree.

EACH VILLAGE had its *memaloose illahee*. Rank on rank they stood, on Point Adams, along Shoalwater Bay, near Altoona on the Columbia, along Elokoman and Steamboat sloughs, on islands in Kathlamet Bay, on Mount Coffin and Coffin Rock, and upriver on Warrior Rock at the foot of Sauvie Island. Up the Washougal River was a *memaloose*, but some of the canoes were on the ground there. Above that, they put their dead in wooden charnel houses. A famous group of those stood beside the portage at the Cascades. Above that there were several on islands.

All those were prominent places, though not ordinarily right next to a village, as Comcomly had placed one near the neighboring village in his grief. A person could hardly travel by canoe without encountering *memalooses* and being reminded of mysterious death. Death frightened the Chinook. They were not sure what it meant, or why it happened, and now it came in waves. The people died and mourning seemed permanent.

Archaeologist William Duncan Strong made a strong case for what he called a "Ghost Cult" among the river people. Much of his evidence was the ribs and backbone motif that was central to Chinook carved art in wood, bone, antler, and stone. In addition, Strong pointed to two Ghost Dance movements of later years, and numerous stories of persons returning from the land of the dead. He concluded from the antiquity of some of the carvings that the epidemics had intensified, rather than caused, this Chinook preoccupation with death.[7]

The Shahala charnel houses were eight feet square with gabled roofs, in which they piled the bodies up like cordwood, three or four feet high. The one halfway up the Cascades portage on the north bank had eight or ten such buildings, where the people of the Cascades had placed their dead for centuries, perhaps ever since they moved up to the rapids seven or eight hundred years before. The houses were decorated with pictures of spirit helpers on the walls, and baskets, bows, arrows, digging sticks, clothing, *haiqua*, trinkets, and spirit boards as well as broken canoes were heaped about.[8]

The Wishram had once put their dead in vaults at the head of Colawesh Bottom, and below the rimrock where the three-foot-wide face of *Tsagiglalal* could watch them. Later, as times grew bad, families quarreled and began stealing valuables from each other's charnal houses. Some said they put salmon bones into each other's dead, thus ruining the fish run.[9] The Tlakluit burned the sheds and began to place their dead on an island, where they could be observed from shore.

Naked Against the Rain

DR. JOHN SCOULER inspected Mount Coffin, a few miles below the mouth of the Cowlitz River, where the Skilloot put up their dead:

All the canoes of the dead are placed along the steep sides of the rock near the river, and none of them were placed toward the summit. The canoes are not raised from the ground, as is the custom in many places. The canoes are covered by boards fixed firmly by cords and pressed down by large stones. On many of these canoes were placed carved wooden dishes such as they used to steam their sturgeon in. On lifting one of the boards I disturbed a serpent who had taken up his abode in the canoe, which contained a complete skeleton. In this canoe I saw many of the ornaments of the deceased, which consisted of beads, hyaquass, and . . . trinkets. The steepness of the rock prevents the canoes from accumulating, as they roll into the river when they begin to decay and are carried out to the ocean. The canoes are in some instances ornamented with feathers and boards painted with rude resemblances of the human figure. This method of burying the dead is very affecting. The solitude of the place and the assemblage of so many objects with which we are not accustomed to associate serious ideas, deposited as mementos to the dead, can not but form an interesting contrast and give rise to some of the most serious reflections.[10]

THE CLACKAMAS, at least in recent times, practiced ground burial. In one grisly instance, a man summoned his dead brother's slave and said to him:

"You have been very good to your master, waiting on him all the time. He thought of you as his own son, fed you the same food he ate, and you also thought warmly of him and treated him as a father. Now you can see he is gone forever and never again will be seen. You have no one to attend to at home, so you may go with him. Now get down in the hole and cover yourself with part of your master's clothes; be there beside him."

He was then lowered into the grave and buried alive.[11]

After the body was put up the dead person's family mourned for five or ten days, morning and evening, at some spot away from the house or near the body. A Shoalwater lamented:

Oh our mother; why did you go and leave us so sad?
We can scarcely see for the water that falls from our eyes.
Many years you lived with us and taught us with words
   of wisdom.
You were not poor; neither are we poor;
You were not weak; your heart and limbs were strong.
You should have lived with us many years,
And told us more of the deeds of ancient times.[12]

WHEN A BABY DIED the Wishram took the trimmings off the cradleboard and burned them. Then they exposed the board and the baby's toys and dishes and things it had been fond of to the sun, up among the rimrocks behind the town. As the sun bleached the board, memories of the baby faded and the pain of the parents as well. A dead adult's cradleboard, saved all those years, was likewise purified at death.[13]

When a headman's child died the father went to visit a nearby headman, who gave him three slaves, canoes, strings of long dentalia, and other valuable gifts. These he distributed among his people, keeping only two slaves. Should the neighboring headman refuse there would be war. Thus they consoled each other for their grief.[14]

Naked Against the Rain

After a year the body was gathered and rewrapped. A father came and cleaned the corpse of his child, and rearranged the things. He might do that annually for five years. A son cared for his father's canoe.

A WIDOW REMAINED behind a screen in the house for five times five days, and went out only at night. Her husband's relatives cut off her hair and she wailed night and morning. She bathed and rubbed her body with sweet-smelling herbs, wore her oldest garments, and did not laugh or make light of the dead.

One Clackamas widow did what was forbidden: she went about all day, carrying her daughter on her back. She heard a voice: "Where are you going, widow?" She saw her husband protruding to the waist from the ground. She replied, "Oh, begone! You stink!" She returned home and told the people about it and the following morning they found her dead.[15]

A widow mourned for one year and then her husband's relatives said, "Now be glad, your brother-in-law will marry you."[16] Then she put on new clothes. But if she had a young child they told her to be glad sooner, and she was. A widower went off and mourned on a hilltop for five days, fasting and consulting his spirit, and then avoided fresh meat or fish for a month.

When the child of Myth Age Bear died she mourned him, crawling about.

She found herself beneath salmonberry vines, heavy with fruit. The berries dropped upon her, tempting her to break her mourning fast.

    Keep away!
      Salmonberries!
    Just dead is my child,
      Salmonberries!

But they continued to fall on her until finally she took hold of the vine, she bent it down and started to eat them.[17]

Thus did nature at last cure the mourner's grief.

WHEN THE WIDOW'S MOURNING was completed she might announce it publicly. Lieutenant Wilkes saw a large, buxom woman with seven attendants, finely dressed. A crowd gathered.

Every half hour they would arrange themselves in a row, and the widow at their head, affecting a modest downcast look, would commence a chaunt, informing the bystanders that her period of mourning was out, that she had forgotten her deceased husband, given her grief to the winds, and was now ready to espouse another. This chaunt was accompanied by a small movement of the feet and body, which, with the guttural song and consequent excitement of such an exhibition, caused the fair ones to wax so warm that the perspiration rolled down their painted cheeks; this, with the crimson flush, all tended to add brilliancy to their dark eyes, as they were now and then cast around upon the multitude who seemed all admiration.[18]

LATE WINTER was a time of dying. They wanted spring to come. They sang their spirit-power songs.

Now also Crow sang. In truth they were all singing, they were thinking, "Now it will become warm." Truly, they were calling the West Wind, trying to make warm weather, for they were feeling cold. Everybody was singing, and now Crow sang. Now the wind was blowing, it rained and the West Wind blew. And then Crow went out and took her fish bag and found fish. The

Naked Against the Rain

wind was blowing hard, and the fish were forced clear up on shore. Then Crow caught a big salmon and ate it.[19]

If Crow, the least of them, the dirty old woman living at the far end of the village, caught a big salmon, could spring be far?

SHOULDER MOON was over, when the people pressed so close to the fire that they had to turn their faces over their shoulders. When the leafy trees were at their barest and the evergreens their darkest, the sky rolled endlessly gray on gray, and everyone watched for the smelt. Those *ihlhun*, shimmering little silver and dark gray fish, were delicious fresh or dried, the oil much sought after. A million-bodied school fish, a silver squirming mass, the smelt always entered the Cowlitz, and sometimes the Kalama, Lewis, Sandy, and Washougal rivers, and Tanner Creek in the Columbia Gorge just below the Cascades.

The Skilloot and Cooniac caught them near home. The Clatsop and Tillamook paddled up to join them. The Mahlnumax and Shahala had their smelt rakes ready, ten feet long and two inches thick, studded on one or both sides with rows of sharp bone teeth, which impaled the fish. They could fill a canoe in a few hours. They also used long-handled conical nets in the smaller tributaries.

The Chinook strung smelt side by side and draped them among the smoky rafters to dry, then traded them by the fathom. Or, if they wanted the oil, they piled the fish out back of the house to rot for a little while, then boiled and pressed them, skimming off the oil into bladders.

THE SMELT stimulated everything. The sturgeon rose out of their deep pools to feed on the smelt, and sea lions swam upriver after them. The Chinook took sturgeon and sea lion as well. Sturgeon, called *inagwn*, sometimes weighed over a thousand pounds, and grew thirteen feet long. The Chinook relished their flesh more than salmon. They probed the pools with hooks or harpoons, or used purse seines, elongated bags hung by poles between two canoes and baited with feathers or something white. When the sturgeon was within, they closed the mouth of the bag by means of ropes. Sometimes they hung many hooks baited with mullet off a strong line set across a stream. Once caught, they might stake a live sturgeon in the river to keep it fresh. Getting such behemoths in the canoe was difficult, but they knew a trick of pulling the fish's head into the boat and then twisting so the body rolled in. A man could haul in a sturgeon several times his own weight that way.[20]

In February when the river was full of sea lions, twenty Kathlamet canoes would gather at the head of the estuary at ebb tide. They placed their fastest boats at the ends of a wide crescent of canoes and at lowest water started downriver. The flotilla surrounded the sea lions, which dived. When they surfaced, the hunters beat on their canoes and shouted. The sea lions dived again, and rose, and were frightened again. Short of breath, the great tawny mammals shambled up on the grassy sandbars of the estuary, where the people followed and killed them easily. When one was shot the other sea lions gathered around and all were killed, ten or twenty at a time, and the meat was distributed among the villages.[21]

Or two men went out in a smaller boat, three or four fathoms long, and harpooned a sea lion. The beast swam downriver. A quarter of a mile of line ran "*xulelelelele*" across the bow and the boat flew through the water. They cried out, half in fear, and sturgeon fishermen came to their assistance, tying a second and third canoe to the rope. When the sea lion finally tired they hauled it ashore.[22]

THEN THE SMELT continued upriver and spawned and the river became quiet again, though Big River was never without some fish. Last year's salmon was rotting now, and the game animals were still lean and watery of flesh, but the women went out and dug newly sprouted skunk cabbage, cut cow parsnip stems and early horsetail sprouts, and the people's skin began to heal and grow clear again.

Then Long Days Moon was standing up. The wind shifted and the marshy lowlands warmed. Snow melted from the mountains. Buds swelled. The sky showed an occasional patch of blue. People were always going over to the river to see what was happening. They strained their ears to hear the cry come up from below, "*Igunat! Igunat* are coming." They had survived another winter after all.

Owl petroglyph, on a boulder at Skamania Landing, Washington. Drawing by the author, from a photograph.

23

Cole Sik, Waum Sik

AUGUST, 1830

Wasusgani recalled that their seers had warned the people. They said, "The ague is on its way here. Dear, oh dear! Now another thing!"[1]

BIG RIVER'S ANNUAL SPRING FRESHET crested late in 1830. The Hudson's Bay Company farmers couldn't plow the lower garden along the river until the 11th of July.[2] The Company ships came and went: *Ganymede, Cadboro,* and *Vancouver* were engaged in the coast trade. The American ship *Convoy* returned to the river in February, sailed up to the Cascades and almost to Willamette Falls seeking furs.[3] In May, the new Company supply ship *Isabella* went aground coming into the river on the same sand that had claimed the *William and Ann.* The *Isabella* broke up, but there was no loss of life and much of the cargo was saved.[4] In June, the Company ship *Eagle* arrived for the first time.

The American ship *Owhyhee* had been trying one and another place along the river all winter long. Captain John Dominis spoke with John McLoughlin, who offered to sell him lumber. Dominis wanted furs.[5] He spent the early summer of 1830 just below Naya-gogo, putting up salt salmon in rum hogsheads and trying to beat the Company at pelt buying. Sometime during July Dominis is said to have realized that the Chinook were selling their best pelts to the Company, their culls to him. Later visitors heard that in his fury he uncorked a medicine vial, letting loose the spirit within as reprisal.[6] He then departed the river, headed for Hawaii. The *Kin Chautch* had made trade unprofitable for yet another *Bahsten* merchant.

The vial of disease story sounds like an echo of Duncan Mc-Dougall's smallpox vial at Astoria.[7] It was still being told in 1841.[8] Some Hudson's Bay Company men believed it was the plowing of the earth at Fort Vancouver that loosed the vengeance of *God* or the horde of spirits, that now smote almost every person in the Wapato Lowlands, and many beyond.[9]

"IN THE MONTH OF AUGUST," missionaries Daniel Lee and Joseph Frost wrote, "at the time of harvest, the intermittent fever began to shake its burning, freezing subjects."[10] David Douglas put the onset around July 26th.[11]

Wasusgani recalled what happened to the Clackamas.

Soon then some person got the ague. He lay with his back to the fire, he only got colder. They threw covers over him, but the ague got worse. His whole body shook. Now he got feverish, he got thirsty for water. They gave it to him, he drank it. Then he died.

Their village was a large one, but they all got the ague. In each and every house so many of the people were ill now. They would go to the river, they would go drink water, they would go back home, and directly as they were proceeding they would drop right there, they would die.

There was one woman who went toward the river. She died. Her little son was crawling about there. People who were going along in a canoe at that place, they said, "Looks

like a person or something is moving around. Let us go see."
They went, close by they saw a child crawling about. He had
crawled to her, he was suckling her.[12]

John Kirk Townsend heard of it from a Company gentleman:

Near what had formerly been a thickly populated village he
counted no less than 16 dead men and women, lying unburied and festering in the sun in front of their habitation.
Within the houses all were sick; not one escaped the conta-
gion; upwards of a hundred individuals, men, women, and
children, were writhing in agony on the floors of the houses, with no one to render them any assistance. Some were
in their dying struggle, and clenching with the convulsive
grasp of death their disease-worn companions, shrieked
and howled in the last sharp agony.[13]

THEY WOULD CALL IT *cole sik, waum sik* in the Chinook Jargon,
"intermittent fever" or "ague and fever" in English, or sometimes
merely "the ague," which meant chills. They knew no more exact
name in 1830, only the symptoms, which were alternating teeth-
chattering chills and sweat-drenching fevers. It struck Chinook and
clothmen alike.

Such a horror had never come to *Wimahl* before.[14] The Chinook knew nothing of the fearsome spirits that were assailing them;
their curers had no remedy. That was a great misfortune, for one
was apparently available, known to at least one *passiuks* medicine
man, though he would not arrive until the worst was over.

"THEY DIED OF THIS DISEASE in such numbers that their bodies
lay unburied on the river banks, and many were to be met with
floating down the stream," Paul Kane stated.[15]

"Villages which had afforded from one to two hundred effective warriors are totally gone; not a soul remains," David Douglas wrote to a friend. "The houses are empty and flocks of famished dogs are howling about, while the dead bodies lie strewn in every direction on the sands of the river."[16]

McLoughlin estimated seventy-five percent of the Chinook living between salt water and the Cascades died; a stretch of 145 miles.[17] In 1830, already wasted by two or more sieges of smallpox, and possibly one of measles, by syphilis, gonorrhea, and no telling what other European pestilences, by the lowest estimate three to five thousand still survived there.[18] A great majority of those died during the first three weeks of August, 1830.[19] In the Wapato Lowlands the dieback was easily ninety percent.

AT THE NEAREST VILLAGE to Fort Vancouver Peter Skene Ogden and party, faced with innumerable corpses, piled the bodies high and torched what had in July been a sixty-family village, and burned the forest around. Hearing cries, they saved one old man, apparently the sole survivor. He died the next day. Wakanasisi, a few miles farther and of a similar size, was likewise deserted.[20] Someone said McLoughlin ordered Michel LaFramboise, on his way to the Willamette after beaver, "to rescue the few wretches that were left," and burn the villages of Sauvie Island.[21]

Comcomly was dead, and most of his people with him. They claimed that a thousand died there, slave and noble alike, writhing on the mat-covered floorboards of proud Qwatsamts and the other river villages.[22] The old man was sixty or sixty-five years of age. He had seen many things through his one remaining eye. Some of his family and followers did survive. Whatever was killing them didn't seem to like salt water, or perhaps it was because summer was cooler there.

The Clatsop villages contained a small remnant of their former population. The surviving Wahkiacum, Kathlamet, Skilloot, Cooniac, and Cowlitz gathered in a single small village near the present Cathlamet. Quathlapootle, Mahlnumax, and Wacomap had utterly vanished, the Nakwaiih, Shoto, and Washougal were gone, Deer Island was depopulated, and Kalama was obliterated. The Clackamas and Shahala were hard hit, though some survived. Only the White Salmon, Hood River, Wishram, and Wasco, all those above the Cascades, were mostly spared the shuddering chills and killing sweats, though the ague is said to have killed some people as far upriver as The Dalles.[23]

THE EUROPEANS SUFFERED from ague and fever as well. On September 25th the sick list at Fort Vancouver comprised seventy-five of the fort's eighty-five men, not counting their women, children, and slaves. Dr. McLoughlin reported:

> The intermittent fever is making a dreadful havoc among the natives of this place and one-half of our own people are laid up. Frightened at the mortality amongst them, the Indians came in numbers to camp alongside of us, giving as reason that if they died they knew we would bury them. Most reluctantly on our part we were obliged to drive them away.[24]

It was in October that McLoughlin estimated three-quarters of the Chinook between salt water and the Cascades were dead. His estimate was conservative. The *passiuks'* sick list was down to fifty-two men. By November the suffering had ceased. Only one white man had died, in November, probably of complications.[25]

To whom could the survivors turn? Who would put up the dead properly, burn down or move the long cedar-plank houses, rebuild them? How could they speak when every word reminded them of their relations? Why had they survived while all the others had died? Their minds became addled. They took to speaking other languages. Many wished only death. They had been left behind by everyone, like the mean boy in the myth who was abandoned by the whole village.[26]

Not abandoned for long. In September of the following year McLoughlin again recorded, "The fever and ague is raging with as great violence as last year. A few days ago we had sixty-eight on the sick list. Indians report that the mortality among the Indians of the Willamette Valley has been great."[27] He specified, "the mortality has been very great among the Indians from Oak Point to the Dalles." Again, in the summer of 1832, the pestilence raged.[28] Not until 1833 could McLoughlin report fewer cases.[29] In 1835 Townsend recorded that from Cape Disappointment to the Cascades, "probably there does not now exist one, where five years ago there were a hundred Indians."[30] It was a classic dieback. Even the Black Death, Europe's worst epidemic in historic times, killed only half the population. Townsend saw "an occasional miserable wigwam with a few wretched half-starved occupants."[31]

The dying did not stop at the Columbia River. In 1832 John Work led a Company beaver-trapping party south to Klamath and Pyramid lakes, then down the Feather River into the Central Valley of California.[32] His party certainly carried the disease, for as David Douglas recorded, among the Europeans at Fort Vancouver "only three individuals out of 140 altogether escaped it."[33] Intermittent fever broke out along the Feather River in 1832. By 1833 it was epidemic throughout the Sacramento and San Joaquin valleys, as deadly there as along the Columbia. It has been estimated that twenty thousand Miwok, Maidu, Yokuts, Wintun, and Costanoan died in the Central Valley of California, and there were fearsome diebacks among the Paiute of Pyramid Lake in western Nevada and the Klamath of south central Oregon.[34]

THE DISEASE STRUCK MAINLY NEAR WATER. McLoughlin thought it must be caused by marsh miasma. Peter Skene Ogden attributed it to "foul exhalations from low and humid situations."[35] It has since been diagnosed, by one or another authority, as scarlet fever, cholera, measles, whooping cough, influenza, dysentery, typhus, or malaria.[36]

Scarlet fever was well known and would have been diagnosed by the two physicians—Meredith Gairdner and William F. Tolmie—then at Fort Vancouver. Dr. Tolmie arrived in 1833 fresh from a cholera epidemic in Glasgow, but did not think it cholera.[37] Measles was well known; whooping cough has other symptoms. So does influenza, though flu as well as dysentery may have accompanied the killer disease. Typhus, a very real suspect, has symptoms similar to the August pestilence, but its usual season is spring, it is less deadly to the young, and it causes a characteristic rose-colored rash, which no one noted.

Quinine is diagnostic between malaria and typhus, curing the former without affecting the latter. The Hudson's Bay men had—and used—quinine. Dr. Townsend encountered an Indian girl with the ague being treated by a shaman. He dismissed the native curer and administered "an active cathartic, followed by sulphate of quinine, which checked the disease, and in two days the patient was perfectly restored."

Townsend treated two other children before his quinine gave out. He then substituted an extract of dogwood bark, "to each of the children about a scruple of the extract per day. The second day they escaped the paroxysm, and on the third were entirely well." Back East the Indians used dogwood or aspen bark against the ague, and Townsend expressed surprise the Chinook did not know of it.[38] That was in 1836, too late to save the Chinook of the Wapato Lowlands. Those barks, it must be noted, suppress the symptoms but do not cure malaria.

That quinine cured the ague was common knowledge. A decade later at Fort Vancouver Company gentlemen told Paul Kane that they had "supplied the Indians liberally with quinine and other medicines, but their good effects were almost entirely counteracted by their mode of living and their obstinacy in persisting in their own peculiar mode of treatment."[39] That sounded better than admitting they drove the Indians away from the fort. They had, in any case, too little quinine the first year to share much. They probably at least offered quinine to Cassino, Illchee, and their son, all of whom survived, perhaps in the fort, not at doomed Wakanasisi. Perhaps those were the Indians liberally supplied with quinine.

IT IS ALMOST CERTAINLY MALARIA the Chinook died of: that feverish malady of the fetid tropics, since recognized as the most important of all infectious diseases. Ague and fever was the name commonly used in nineteenth-century America to describe the disease that would for a while be called miasma and finally malaria. Its cause was unknown until 1897. Though it is most frequent in the tropics, malaria does strike more northerly regions. Further, when a virulent strain attacks people totally lacking in acquired immunity, it can kill a high proportion, as it did in Russia in 1922, when six million died.[40]

Malaria would continue in small numbers in western Oregon for the next century.[41] Outbreaks were common in Portland and the Willamette Valley until around 1930, when the Anopheles mosquito

—malaria's only means of transmission—was sufficiently reduced by public health measures to eliminate transmission.[42]

Plasmodium—the parasitic protozoa that causes malaria—has a complicated life cycle, requiring both the Anopheles mosquito and a human host. Its nonsexual reproductive cycle happens in humans and its sexual reproductive cycle in that one particular kind of mosquito. Along the lower Columbia, Anopheles has a breeding season of only three or four months in the warmest year, but the mosquito is equal to the task of filling its niche, producing five generations in ten weeks.[43]

ONE QUESTION REMAINS: Which came most recently to the Columbia, the Anopheles mosquito or the malaria plasmodium?

Lewis and Clark noted a mosquito-like creature in addition to the ordinary mosquito when they passed through in 1805–1806.[44] Can that have been Anopheles? Anopheles in general are twice the size of the more common Culex mosquito and have an entirely different posture, standing on their heads while drinking blood.

If the mosquito was not already in the region, it could have come in a ship's water cask containing mosquito larvae, introduced to the Columbia when the cask was emptied for fresh water. In the years following 1830 the gentlemen of the Hudson's Bay Company liked to blame the ague and fever on Captain Dominis of the *Owhyhee*. Dominis' vial probably didn't contain mosquito larvae though, and he probably wasn't guilty of bringing mosquito larvae in ship's water. The *Owhyhee*'s two stops coming out were Juan Fernandez Island, off Chile, which isn't listed in the literature of malaria, and Hawaii, which has never suffered human malaria.[45]

The *Owhyhee* could, however, have introduced plasmodium, in the blood of a crew member, when it returned in October 1829. The rumor that the ague first appeared in 1829 was first mentioned some years later, but there is no authentic documentation. The lateness of the ship's arrival could explain that. McLoughlin specified 1830 as the first time the disease raged.[46] But the plasmodium-carrier could as easily have been aboard the ill-fated *Isabella*, which arrived May 2nd, or the *Eagle*, which came in June 10th, both for the first time.[47]

The onset of the disease was so sudden, and the devastation so widespread and complete, that the mosquito seems likely to have been present already. Two species of Anopheles mosquito are presently indigenous to the lower Columbia: *freeborni*, the most numerous, found all over Oregon, and *punctipennis*, found only west of the Cascades.[48] The latter is therefore the probable culprit, though the dying didn't entirely stop where the climate changed, around the Cascades.

Given that Anopheles were already present, the plasmodium spread with great rapidity thanks to Anopheles' breeding rate. This frantic reproduction was also why, in this century, Anopheles so quickly adapted to DDT, defeating the World Health Organization's nearly successful effort to eradicate the insect and thereby obliterate plasmodium and eliminate the disease.

The female Anopheles mosquito lives through the winter to lay her eggs in clear, partially sunlit water, not stagnant pools as the Culex mosquito does. The offspring hatch in July and later, which fits the late July outbreak. Flooding meant little, the eggs being laid near springs, nor did the winter have to be mild, as some authorities have supposed.[49] The Columbia froze from bank to bank at Fort Vancouver during January 1832,[50] an extremely severe winter for the Wapato Lowlands, yet ague and fever returned a third time that summer.[51] Clearly there were already Anopheles in California, for Work's party could not have carried mosquitoes with them overland.

As for the survivors, almost everyone they knew was dead, noble and slave, feared conjuror and lowly boy with running sores, all dead. Their language became painful, if not impossible, to speak, so they stopped speaking it. The Shoalwater took to speaking Chehalis, the Clatsop spoke Jargon or Tillamook. Their culture came unsewed, untied, unplugged, and unglued. The survivors wandered off, demented by the incomprehensible tragedy that had overwhelmed them. Even stone-faced *Tsagiglalal* must have wept.

On April 3rd, 1835, Nathaniel Wyeth recorded of Sauvie Island,

A mortality has carried off to a man its inhabitants and there is nothing to attest that they ever existed, except their decaying houses, their graves, and their unburied bones, of which there are heaps. [52]

They were gone, simply gone, and lucky to be so. What Chinook, immersed in relationships, would choose to live when everyone he knew was gone? They may have shrieked and howled in their dying agony, but the dead were fortunate.[53]

The survivors knew that they were doomed. Nothing could protect them. They knew no reason to expect tomorrow to dawn, or themselves to be alive to see it. They did not seem to care very much.[54] They built only little houses.[55]

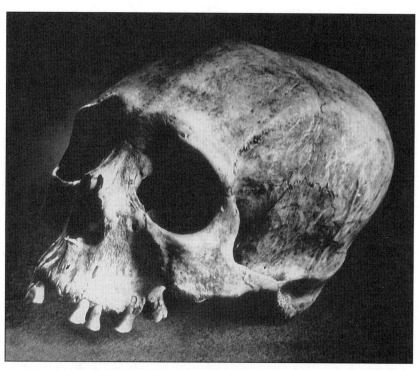

Comcomly's skull, when it was on display at the Clatsop County Historical Museum. Photographer unknown. Courtesy of the Oregon Historical Society.

24

Comcomly's Skull

AFTERWARD

"Little there but darkness and blackness and desolation," wrote Hall J. Kelley of the mouth of the Columbia in 1834. "Heard but little more than the sighs and cries of misery in the perishing remnants of the Clatsop and Chinook tribes, and the roar and rage of mighty waters."[1]

PROPERLY, THE STORY ENDS with Comcomly's death, but the far ends of the net need knotting off. This is where Coyote gets tired.

After Comcomly's sweating, shivering agony ceased and his two souls passed across that farther river, the survivors put his remains in a canoe up on posts. Unaccountably, they did so across the river behind the site of old Fort Astoria, rather than at Point Ellice. One post was carved with an elk-like image, perhaps one of Comcomly's spirit helpers. The other, a comb-shaped image, may have represented *Madsue*, Thunder, his later name.[2] The body lay there for a year or two, and then, fearing the grave-robbing propensity of the *tlohonnipts*,[3] his relatives carried his remains off into the woods and buried them in the earth.

Not far enough into the forest or deep enough in the ground. In 1834, Hudson's Bay Company physician Meredith Gairdner dug up the corpse and cut off its head. "I will endeavor to procure you the whole skeleton," Gairdner wrote a friend. "The mummy-like state of preservation which dead bodies of the Indians attain is curious. I assure you no small resurrectionary labour was necessary to get at Comcomly's." Gairdner shipped the head to England and left Fort Vancouver. He died in Hawaii the following year. Perhaps the taboo against robbing graves had power after all.[4]

Comcomly's head went to the Haslar Museum of the Royal Naval Hospital near Portsmouth, England. Someone noted on Gairdner's letter,

> Comcomly was one-eyed. His head reached England in the dried state mentioned by Dr. Gairdner, but with the features greatly distorted and pressed to one side. The moisture commenced to become very offensive in about five to six months, notwithstanding a liberal application of corrosive sublimate; it was macerated and the brain removed. 11 June 1838.[5]

Chenamus ruled in his father's place. The Europeans disliked him. Now he had buried most of his relatives. In 1814 he had four wives. When he died in 1845 he left no known descendant.[6] His sole remaining wife, Aillapust, a Willapa whom the settlers called Queen Sally, outlived him by fifteen years.[7]

ONLY TOOLE, called Ranald by his father's people, traveled as far as the old man's skull. He studied three years at the Fort Vancouver school, and then, in 1834, his father Archibald McDonald sent the eleven-year-old son of Comcomly's daughter Raven east to school at Red River, Manitoba. A Japanese boat with three surviving sailors had drifted ashore north of the Columbia in 1833.[8] They were ransomed by the Company and brought to Vancouver not long before Ranald left for school. They must have deeply impressed the boy. In

1839, already working in a bank in St. Thomas, Ontario, the idea that his ancestral Chinook were of Japanese descent preoccupied young Ranald.

At twenty-one he quit his job at the bank and set off for Japan, well aware that Nippon was closed to foreigners. He worked his way down the Mississippi, then around to New York, where he shipped before the mast for the Orient. Off Hokkaido, he talked the captain into putting him adrift in a small boat, which he purchased. He landed and was seized and imprisoned in Nagasaki, where he was well treated but interrogated at length. He conducted English classes for fourteen Japanese, including the principal interpreter when Commodore Perry opened Japan to foreigners in 1854. Japan expelled McDonald in April 1849. He returned to America the long way and ended his days near Spokane, Washington, in 1894.[9]

Illchee's adventures weren't finished either. After Duncan McDougall's death she had married Cassino and borne him a son. When exactly remains a mystery. George Simpson stated that it happened before 1824, Paul Kane that it was shortly after McDougall deserted her, and thus 1818 or thereafter. No observer recorded the marriage, or the birth of the child, but Cassino, Illchee, a youth described as their son, and two slaves survived the pestilences of August. The son died in February 1836, after a protracted illness thought to have been consumption (tuberculosis). Cassino broke with Chinook tradition by having him buried in the ground at Fort Vancouver. He had the coffin built extra large to contain the goods the youth would need in the land beyond.

Cassino then tried to kill his wife, The Princess, so she could accompany their son to *memaloose illahee*. He told the *passiuks* that the greater the sacrifice, the more propitiated the departed spirit. Evidently Illchee did not agree. She fled, and appeared the next morning at the gate of Fort Vancouver, claiming sanctuary. Several days later her surviving relatives came upriver after her and carried her to safety.[10] She must have been around forty years of age. We know no more about her almost-too-interesting life.

CASSINO KILLED A GIRL named Waskema instead. Waskema was described as pretty and accomplished, with exceedingly beautiful hair. Cassino's son was said to have sought her in marriage and been refused. That implies that he was in his teens at least, and Illchee and Cassino probably married in 1820 or earlier. Cassino sent two slaves to where Waskema was making moccasins. They hid until she embarked alone in her canoe, then rushed out and shot her twice in the chest. They threw her body in the river and broke the canoe. Her brother Tapeo complained of the murder but to no avail.[11]

Though his army of "a thousand warriors"[12] was gone, Cassino remained in Dr. McLoughlin's good graces. Fort Vancouver needed an Indian *chief* to maintain authority over the few survivors and such new Indians as trickled into the empty land. In 1841 Lieutenant Charles Wilkes, commander of a U.S. Navy exploratory expedition, recorded of Cassino,

> He now stands alone, his land, tribe, and property all departed, and he left a dependant on the bounty of the Company. Cassenove is about 50 years of age, and a noble and intelligent looking Indian. At the fort he is always welcome, and is furnished a plate at meal time at the side table. I saw him quietly enter the apartment, wrapped in his blanket, and take his seat at the lonely board. He scarce seemed to attract the notice of any one, but ate his meal in silence, and retired. He has always been a great friend of the whites, and during the time of his prosperity was ever ready to search out and bring to punishment all those who committed depredations on strangers.[13]

Naked Against the Rain

They would maintain him at considerable sacrifice. Soon after, Cassino had a slave shoot a man accused of robbing a burial canoe. Though the shooting took place inside Fort Vancouver, and Cassino stood nearby watching, he was merely reprimanded.[14] Dr. John McLoughlin's favorite walking stick had an ivory head carved in the likeness of Cassino as a young man.[15] The clothmen claimed he ruled all the land between the Cowlitz and the Cascades, but that was one big *memaloose illahee*. Some Klickitat had come down to live where fourteen-house Quathlapootle had stood, and other Klickitat moved into the all-but-empty Willamette Valley. The ponds and shores of Sauvie Island were utterly deserted, silent except when the steamboat *Beaver* chugged past in 1836.

Cassino found more wives. One, Waslameth, remained with him when he died, at Vancouver, on December 10th, 1848. The *Oregon City Free Press* eulogized him as the last leader of the Chinook and a great friend of the Europeans.[16] The latter, certainly, was correct.

SUCH SURVIVORS AS REMAINED were scattered, stunned, their spirits broken. Tuberculosis came to them. The cool damp climate and crowded winter houses spread it quickly. They coughed and spat, bled from the lungs, burned, sweated, lost weight, grew weak, and died. In 1840 women and children began arriving across the Oregon Trail, and with them came children's diseases for the first time. Chicken pox in 1840, then scarlet fever and whooping cough. In 1844 dysentery spread up from the mouth of the Columbia, as did typhoid, brought from Hawaii. In 1845 typhus came with Steven H. L. Meek's party across the southern branch of the Oregon Trail. In 1846 cholera came across the Oregon Trail. In 1847 measles came to kill them, brought up from California by a Cayuse and Walla Walla hunting and trading party and swiftly disseminated all over the Northwest.[17] Victims went to sweat and the measles came out all over them, even on their eyes. Those victims whom the curers poured cold water on died, those that just lay down under blankets recovered. Mount St. Helens belched fire and smoke intermittently from 1842 through 1846. Ash rained on the river. When Canadian artist Paul Kane painted it he put in naked Chinooks standing and sitting in two canoes, awed at the volcano's red glare.

THE MISSIONARIES began to arrive by ship in 1834. Their pilot was Indian George. The same Lamsay who may have survived the *Tonquin* massacre had likewise been spared by deadly August. He had become identifiable now though; some time around 1830 he had lost his right eye in a battle with a hair seal. From then on, he was described as "one-eyed" Lamsay. He, and sometimes his brother Jack Ramsay, were mentioned as river pilots in the accounts of missionaries, spies, and explorers alike for the next dozen years.[18] Having been young men when Lewis and Clark saw red-haired Jack, they must have been in their fifties in 1841 when Lieutenant Wilkes described how they lay down to sleep in a driving rain, merely covered with a blanket, and awoke refreshed next morning to pilot his ship again. Jack had at least one daughter, who married a Scottish fur trader, and George had a son called Yellow Cum who was the most powerful headman of the people at Cape Flattery in 1846.[19] These were no doubt "half-breeds" to the whites, as was Toole to his father Archibald.[20] That was a concept the Chinook would have had difficulty comprehending. Wasn't anyone who could afford to marry someone from afar, creating half-breeds?

The missionaries set up their houses of worship. Before that, the Chinook had seen Christianity only in the behavior of the sailors and traders. These newer floats-ashores wanted to interest the survivors in their "sky chief," *saghalie tyee* in the Jargon. The Reverend Samuel Parker found the Shoalwater and Clatsop not much interested in learning about Christianity.[21] They would listen courteously, but expected to be listened to in turn. Particularly difficult

Naked Against the Rain

to "instruct" were the nobles. The converts were mostly slaves or the lower sort of commoners.

A French priest, Father Lionnet, "resided at Chenook for several years," Swan observed,

> devoting his time to the conversion of the Indians, but with indifferent success, the whole known fruits of his labors consisting in the various names he had baptized them with. This fact he afterward acknowledged in a letter written by him, on his return to France, to the postmaster of Chenook.[22]

The Clackamas don't seem to have taken the missionaries very seriously either. Wasusgani recalled,

> When the person-who-continually-prayed came to this place he told them, "You should pray all the time, the chief above will see you. But if you do not believe it, then you will have tails, like the various animals that run about in the forest." Now, my husband's mother would say, "Dear, oh dear! Probably it would be something different when we play woman's shinny. We would whip each other with our tails."[23]

Cassino told his people at Vancouver, "Follow the priests if you like; as for me, I have been too wicked, I am not able to change; I shall die as I am."[24]

More succinctly still, when asked to take an oath before the Pacific County grand jury in 1853, the Shoalwater Chinook Yancumux "stated that he neither knew or cared anything about the white man's God, though he had heard the priests tell about it."[25]

SOME CHINOOKS turned to alcohol for inspiration. Wasusgani recalled that men got drunk and began singing their spirit-power songs. The other people would join them, but the drunken one would fall asleep. The next day they told him he must not do that.

Power songs were sung in winter. To protect him they were supposed to do the whole five nights of dancing and singing and gifting. Alcohol was a short cut to the intoxication of the sacred season.[26]

In the 1850s, James Swan, who lived three years among them and loved them, wrote of the Atsmitl of Shoalwater Bay, "For the most part they are a miserable, whiskey-drinking set of vagabonds . . . the race of the Chinooks is nearly run."[27] Yet he noted, "I have never known of an instance, during their wildest drunken freaks of fury or rage, where one of their own children was hurt or badly treated, although at such times they are very apt to treat their slaves with barbarity."[28]

George Gibbs, likewise a sympathetic observer, wrote,

> The case of the Chinooks and Cowlitz Indians in particular seems desperate. They are all intemperate and can get liquor whenever they choose. The speedy extinction of the race seems rather to be hoped for than regretted, and they look forward to it themselves with a sort of indifference.[29]

Even in the Columbia River Gorge, where the villages had suffered less from the terrible dieback of the 1830s, alcohol killed them. Edward Curtis heard of it from Tamlaitk:

> In the youth of Tamlaitk, who was born in 1825, the houses of the Indians, placed close together, extended from Hood River to Indian Creek, and many families, not finding room on the level now occupied by the town of Hood River built their homes on the bench above. On the northern side of the Columbia the whole flat at the mouth of White Salmon River was filled with houses. Whiskey began to be sold on the northern side, and canoes full of drunken Indians returning home would capsize, the helpless natives sinking like stones. Whole families were thus wiped out in a moment.[30]

Their focus on spiritual intoxication, their low metabolism, and their unfamiliarity with the drug alcohol made them vulnerable. Not only to alcohol. Samuel Parker commented that even if a Wishram was "suffering from hunger and nakedness, his first request is for tobacco."[31]

THE REVEREND JOHN FROST noted that infanticide was much practiced by the Clatsop. The women told him they had become poor, and if they allowed many babies to live they would not be able to provide for their husbands. He estimated that only two of ten or twelve babies born since November were alive in February.[32]

There were dark tales of premature burial as well. Cobaway's daughter Celiast tried to stop a band of Clatsop from burying a man not yet dead. They were afraid that the salmon would not enter Neahcoxie Creek if the corpse remained above ground. They were not allowed to kill him, so they would just bury him. Celiast couldn't stop them.[33] In June the following year a male slave was likewise buried alive.

Not even the dogs were spared. Though the clothmen had stopped eating them, they were still killing them. The surviving Kathlamet and Cowlitz lived on Alockman Slough near the fledgling settler town of Cathlamet. The settlers were trying to raise sheep. They complained that the cougars and the Chinook dogs were eating their sheep. Thomas Nelson Strong recalled that when the river people would not kill their pets,

The white men formed an impromptu protective association and shot the dogs whenever they could catch them until the dogs learned the trick of running into the lodges whenever they saw a white man around with a gun. This protected them for some time, until the sheep were nearly gone, when something had to be done, and then one of the white men with a rifle in hand for emergencies and a colt's revolver in the other for dogs, boldly went into the lodges and shot the dogs there. It was risky work. The inside of the lodge was all smoke and confusion, and the children and the Indians hid the dogs in the beds, but canine curiosity was too strong and every now and then a dog would stick his head out and bark. Crack would go the revolvers, half a dozen more dogs would break out simultaneously, and it would be bow-wow, crack, crack, until the revolver was empty. In this way the dog pest was kept down and the sheep were given some chance for their lives.[34]

The Chinook dared not protect even their own homes. Their tenure along the rivers was done. A priest observed, "In former times the houses were high and solidly built, but after the fever had ravaged, people expected to die any day; and that is why, these poor natives say, they no longer take the trouble to build." Behind some rude huts beside the Clackamas River he saw "traces of long lines of lodges which used to cover the terrain; the longest behind measured 157 steps in length. Such was the village of Tlakemas before 1830."[35]

IN THE EARLY 1840S wagon trains began trundling across the Oregon Trail. The Clackamas became well acquainted with the pioneers. Wasusgani recalled,

> Now it was close to the time when the myth people arrived. The very first ones who came were tall myth people. They came in their wagons, oxen pulled them. They lived there [Oregon City]. They traded pans, buckets, various dippers they gave me. I gave them various smoke-dried things. I do not know how long a time after, and then a great many myth people came.

They gave me various things. Whatever they gave, skirts, some sort of waist, they would examine us, they would laugh at us. They gave me quilts. I saw them there, I learned there. I saw how they cut calico. I cut it that way. I sewed and made quilts. I do it like that today.

They gave us new pans, and these we used for looking [as mirrors]. We laughed and laughed when we looked at ourselves. One old man named Kamisdiqnq had one new pan, he looked at it all day long, he lay down holding his pan, he would not let go of it. He would sit holding his pan. Wherever he laid it he would cover it so no one would take it.

They gave me a hoop skirt. I put it on, I showed it to the people, they laughed at me. They said to me, "Let us see you walk about." I walked about, they laughed at my skirt.

We baked potatoes in ashes and they popped. We said, "Oh dear, these potatoes are a different kind of thing." We laughed at them. Some people would not eat those potatoes, but there were others who ate them forthwith.

One Boston woman showed me how to make wheat bread. I showed it to them the very first time that I made it. We laughed at my wheat bread. I learned all sorts of things from that Boston woman there. Her name was Barclay, a good Boston woman. That is why I made various things to be my own foods, the very things that the myth people ate."[36]

The Wishram remained consistent; the struggle between the sexes continued unabated. Joseph Drayton, an artist with the Wilkes expedition, traveled upriver and noted, "Their women seemed to be of more consequence than is usual among savages, and some of them even took command over the men."[37] Evidently the women were holding their own.

IN 1850 JOSEPH LANE estimated fewer than 700 Chinook.[38] In 1851 Anson Dart counted 80 Clatsop, 142 Shoalwater, and 36 slaves in five bands (including as one the Kathlamet-Cowlitz village), 13 Chinook at Willamette Falls and 88 up the Clackamas, 120 at the Cascades, and 482 Wasco and Wishram. His total was 985.[39]

In 1853 smallpox struck Shoalwater Bay, wiping out most of those who remained.[40] At Wishram, which had still attracted 1,500 visitors in 1841,[41] the same epidemic killed 250 Tlakluit and frightened off their former visitors, who never returned.[42] Thus withered the centuries-old trade mart.

Wasusgani spoke of a white doctor at the hospital in Oregon City who the Clackamas believed poisoned them. When a person was taken to the hospital they shaved off his hair and gave him medicine with water and he soon died. One of the orderlies who was Indian or part Indian warned a patient, "Be on your guard!" and instructed him to spit the medicine out and not drink the water. The doctor told him, "Drink the medicine now!" but he refused to swallow it. He spat it in a handkerchief the orderly gave him. Where the medicine touched his mouth he was burned. His relatives took him home. The white medicine man fled that very night and was never seen again. "He must have come to live there just to kill the people," Wasusgani said. "The myth people just fixed up the disease for us. They wanted this country of ours."[43]

The plug from the Darkness Woman's box had become lost forever. At Willamette Falls in June, 1840, the Reverend Gustavus Hines found

> about 150 of the most filthy and degraded looking beings in human shape that our eyes ever beheld. Surely, we thought, it will take the labor of years to elevate these Indians from the depth of their pollution into a civilized and Christian people."[44]

GEORGE GIBBS, a scholarly, sympathetic man, argued for the creation of reservations. The Chinook, he wrote,

> live almost altogether among the whites, or in their immediate neighborhood, taking and selling salmon and doing occasional work, and for the rest letting out their women as prostitutes. They would not long remain away from their old haunts, and probably the assignment of a few acres of ground for their villages and cemeteries, and the right of fishing at customary points, would effect all that could be done . . . each tribe in one village at some place not yet occupied, and constituting a reserve. This, except during the salmon season, might remove them somewhat farther from temptation.[45]

In 1851 Anson Dart treatied with the people of the coast at Tansey Point. The Shoalwater refused to talk until Washington Hall was removed. Hall had arrived in 1849 and laid claim to the ground upon which once-proud Qwatsamts stood, at Chinook Point. He renamed it Chinookville, stole a woman slave, sold whiskey to whoever would buy, built a house, and fenced off the creek that provided the village's fresh water.[46] Dart agreed that Hall must go. He wrote a treaty giving the Chinook their own land as a reservation during their lifetimes. Not one of the thirteen treaties Dart executed was ever ratified by Congress. Hall stayed another four years, was elected County Commissioner by the floats-ashores, and had the Pacific County seat moved to Chinookville. The Hudson's Bay Company paid Hall for land to build a trading post there.

In 1855 Governor Stevens of Washington Territory tried to write a treaty but little came of it. The Shoalwater got some timber rights on the Quinault reservation and a few went to live in a tiny reservation at Tokeland on the north shore of Willapa Bay. Others of the Atsmitl, both Chinook and Salish, settled on a point of land called Bay Center in Willapa Bay.

In 1856 the Yakima led other Plateau and Puget Sound peoples in revolt, hoping to drive the floats-ashores away. Few if any Chinooks joined them. A force of Yakima and Klickitat attacked the Army blockhouse and the houses of about a hundred settlers at the strategic Cascades portage, by then served by steamboats both above and below and spanned by a primitive railway. The attackers killed seventeen settlers and soldiers and wounded ten more. When reinforcements arrived by steamboat, the Yakima and Klickitat melted into the forested mountains.

The soldiers found a huddled band of resolutely neutral Shahala who had sat out the war on an island. The soldiers knew they had not fought, but their war chief, Colonel George Wright, tried all the men anyway. He proved to his satisfaction that they had fought because their gun barrels were dirty with burnt powder. He hanged nine of eleven for having dirty barrels. Interpreter L. W. Coe quoted the Shahala headman Chenewuth as offering ten horses, two women, and a little something for every *tyee* if they spared his life. When they put the rope around his neck he gave a terrific "war whoop." His last words, in Jargon, were "*Wake nike quash copa memaloose!*" (I am not afraid of death!) The rope didn't work so they had to shoot him.[47]

Upriver the Wishram weren't even implicated in the uprising, but the soldiers got someone's permission to confiscate their horses and level their ancient, historic town Nixluidix, promising to repay them later. After sixty-five years they sent a man around to ascertain the damages. He found the amount difficult to determine. No payment has yet been made.[48]

Now began the Chinook diaspora. The Tlakluit were sent north to join the Yakima and Klickitat on the Yakima reservation. They live among the Sahaptin. The Wasco went south to the Warm Springs reservation where they live among the Tenino, Tygh, and other Sahaptin-speakers and their old adversaries, the Northern Paiute. The Shahala were split between the Yakima and the Warm Springs reservations. The Shoalwater stayed on the bay mostly, except in salmon season.

The Clackamas were slated for removal too. Wasusgani was warned by her Boston woman and hurried home. Her husband, Watcheeno, had already broken up their canoe. They tied up everything they could and the next day the soldiers took them above the falls and by flatboat up the Willamette and the little Yamhill River to Dayton. They gave them beef and pork, sugar, grease, potatoes, flour, and other foods. "Some of the old people would not eat it. They just cried, and the days following that they were still crying." Wasusgani was proud that she knew how to eat beef and pork. Her Boston woman had taught her everything.[49]

The soldiers named some men to be chiefs. People of many languages lived in tents at Dayton for quite a while, while the appointed chiefs were taken around to look at the country. At Grand Ronde, a valley in the Coast Range west of Salem, the men saw camas, wild celery, familiar things to eat. They were tired. They chose that place. The Umpqua, Shasta, Takelma, the Tualatin, Yamhill, and other Kalapuya, the Yonkalla, and the Clackamas came to live there.

> Now they brought soldiers, they took care of us. Wherever we went, they gave us a paper. They stood on each side of the road, they held guns. Some people ran away, they went back to where their home village was. Such person got no land.[50]

The Clatsop were supposed to go off to a reservation, but some who wanted to live in the old ways hid themselves seventy miles south of Big River, at the mouth of tiny Salmon River beside bold Cascade Head. They lived on cedar and salmon until 1875, when the clothmen made them go live with the others at one or another of the rapidly shrinking reservations: Alsea, Grand Ronde, and Siletz.[51] Some Clatsop merely remained on Clatsop Plain. Tsinistum, called Jenny Michel by the settlers, was said to be the last of those.

The Chinook were never a clannish people. They greeted anyone who came in peace to trade or marry. Class was important to them, but geography, politics, or language weren't. Anthropologist David French called them "a people unbound," who could merge easily and lose their identities.[52] That might have been a good model to learn from now.

EVERYTHING HAD TO CHANGE, even the landscape. Mount Coffin, the memaloose on the north bank just below the Cowlitz River, had been there forever. All the Europeans described the big rock festooned with canoes. Everyone guessed a different height, from 80 to 710 feet. It was probably around 300 feet tall.

Lieutenant Wilkes, leader of the United States Exploring Expedition of 1841, spent a day making astronomical observations from the top of Mount Coffin. He noted, "The canoes used by the Indians as coffins are seen upon it in every direction in all stages of decay." Later that day his boat crew "carelessly omitted to extinguish the fire they had used for cooking their dinner, and as we were pulling off to the brig, I regretted to see that the fire had spread and was enveloping the whole area of the mount."[53]

It burned all night. Wilkes "took the earliest opportunity of explaining to the Indians who were in the neighborhood that the fire was accidental, and, after receiving a few small presents, they appeared satisfied that it was so." Paul Kane heard there were two to three hundred canoes on Mount Coffin when it burned, and the Indians he talked to expressed "much indignation at the violation of a place which was held so sacred by them, and would no doubt have sought revenge had they felt themselves strong enough to do so."[54]

A decade later Mayes Stone acquired Mount Coffin as part of

his donation land claim. In 1863 Stone sold it to D. W. Bush, who sold it to Star Sand and Gravel in 1906. Star Sand and Gravel quarried most of the basalt knob away, then sold the stump to Weyerhaeuser Company in 1954. The timber giant gnawed it off to grade level and erected buildings where it had been. A spot on river charts is still labelled Mount Coffin, but the mountain itself is gone as though it never existed. It is now only a dark patch of ground.[55]

NOT EVEN THE *WAPATO* WERE SPARED. Captain John Harlow of Troutdale, Oregon, imported thirty-five European carp in May, 1880 and put them in his trout pond, near the Sandy River. He intended to sell them as human food, at one dollar apiece. By the end of the summer, the pond held seven thousand carp. The following spring Big River flooded just high enough to edge the pond, and three thousand juvenile carp slithered and jumped to freedom, polluting the Columbia River forever. Each would grow into a machine of riparian destruction. Carp feed by taking bottom soil into their mouths, then spritzing it out and picking from the edible bits floating there. This kills vegetation, clouds the water, and destroys the habitat of numerous native species. Within ten years carp could be purchased for five dollars a ton. Even at that price no one ate them, but the carp ate every *wapato* out of every marsh the fish could reach, which was every one that ever flooded. There remain a few tiny patches of *wapato*, but the vast beds disappeared and with them people's memory of this excellent and flavorful bulb.[56]

THE CHINOOK JARGON, on the other hand, survived a little longer and even expanded. The first Jargon vocabulary was published by Samuel Parker in 1835. By 1838 the Jargon was developed enough for the Catholic priests to learn four hundred words, which they listed in their Jargon dictionary. More than fifty dictionaries and word lists would eventually be published, ranging from a few sheets to books of nearly two hundred pages.[57] Spelling varied as widely as the ear or imagination of the authors allowed. One word was spelled nineteen different ways. Even English words in dictionaries for English readers came to be spelled many different ways, each author to his own orthography.

Horatio Hale listed 250 words in 1841.[58] In 1863 Gibbs listed over 500, of which he thought 230 Chinook, 67 English, 90 French, 24 Nootka, 32 Chehalis, and ten or less from each of six other languages.[59] In 1894 Myron Eells compiled a list of 1,402 words. English was up to 570, French to 147, Chehalis had doubled, Nootka and Chinook held constant. Eells' list was from Puget Sound, and included words from many local languages as well as 662 obsolete words and many localisms. Only 288 words were in current use there.[60] Hale conjectured,

> Could the state of things which exists here be suffered to remain a century longer, the result might be the formation of a race and idiom whose affinities would be a puzzle to ethnographers.[61]

The state of things did not remain. The Jargon's use retreated northward from the centers of white population. Long after it was forgotten in Astoria and Vancouver, the Jargon was still much used in British Columbia. At its height, it would be understood by one hundred thousand people,[62] three times as many as ever spoke the Chinook languages, across a vast area from northern California to Alaska and far inland. On reservations where people of different languages had been placed together it was how neighbors spoke to each other. Its use long continued at the Grand Ronde reservation. In 1866 a teacher there noted that the children could understand English, but "they will use that barbarous jargon, the Chinook."[63]

Though the Jargon facilitated communication, its effects were not all good. By providing an easy means of communication, the

Jargon kept Europeans from learning the native languages, some of which disappeared without a trace. It kept the native-speakers from learning English, which might have helped them save their lands and protect their rights.

Some words of Jargon came into general use; a few are even heard occasionally today. *Chuck* for water; *cultus* for bad or worthless; *illahee* for land or country; *kinickinick* for a smoking mixture; *klahowya* is occasionally revived as a greeting; *memaloose* for dead or graveyard; *olallie* for berries; *potlatch*, to give away; *siskiyou*, from Cree for a bobtail horse, now a mountain range; *siwash*, French for savage, a derogatory term for Indian (some people would come to think it was a specific tribe); *skookum* for strong or powerful; *tahmahnawis* for spirit or luck; *tillicum*, which at first meant people and later friend; and *tyee* for chief.

After the Hudson's Bay Company left Vancouver many of the French words dropped from the Jargon there. French words lasted longer near Catholic missions than near Protestant ones.[64] In British Columbia a newspaper in Jargon, called *Kamloops Wawa*, began publication in 1891, and was issued intermittently for four years. Missionaries translated various prayers, scriptures, and sermons into Chinook Jargon.

As to the question of whether the Chinook Jargon predated the coming of the Europeans, J. K. Gill, author and publisher of one dictionary, wrote in 1891,

> Within the year I have talked to an Indian who was a man grown when Lewis and Clark came to this country, and have his assurance that the Klickitat, Multnomah, Clatsop, Chinook, and other tribes all talked to each other in this ancient *Volapuk* [folk language] upon matters of business and other intertribal affairs.[65]

THE INDIAN Gill talked with was probably Indian John or Old John, thought to be the last Multnomah, who died in 1893. John said he recalled Lewis and Clark, and had received a small skillet from them. He lived on the Columbia Slough and around the Sandy River, until in his old age he was taken into the Multnomah County Poor Farm, where he died and was buried in the ground. Newspaper stories estimated his age at over one hundred years.[66]

The last flattened head along the river probably rested on the neck of Alice Slim Jim Charley, a Shahala born in 1880, who lived in Hood River before her death in 1973.[67]

The Cascades were flooded out of existence by Bonneville Dam in 1937, the June hogs eliminated by Grand Coulee Dam around the same year. The Long Narrows, Petroglyph Canyon, and Celilo Falls were drowned by The Dalles Dam in 1957. The petroglyphs were pried and dynamited off the walls of Petroglyph Canyon. They lean neglected now against the dam that drowned them, as people pass in the other direction to see the fish ladders.

Chinook became the name of a warm *foehn* wind off the Pacific, which in the middle of winter occasionally melts the snow all the way to Saskatchewan or Minnesota. Chinook became the pink-fleshed salmon the river people called *igunat*. Chinook became slang for all the canoe people of the coast. Chinook became a kind of Japanese-made truck camper vehicle.

THE CHINOOK had been living there peacefully, eating fish. They had no agriculture because the land provided vegetables for the digging. They had no herds of animals because fish swam freely into their nets. They did not require government leaders to tax them and order them around, priests to stage ceremonies interposing themselves to invoke a distant God, or great wars in which to be gloriously slain or mutilated. They bettered everyone at trade, and had time to lie in the sun when it shone.

Naked Against the Rain

Then strangers came, never asking their permission. The Chinook treated them equitably, aided them, and traded with them. These strangers built their houses, and traveled freely about the land. They sought no individual spirits, believing there to be only one central spirit. They were better at neither trade nor canoeing, and their houses were not larger or more comfortable than Chinook ones, but they carried terrible diseases with them wherever they went. The former people were utterly decimated and the newcomers took their country.

During the winter dances, "When a woman bends her head, another one goes and raises it. Then she pays her for having made her head straight."[68] Now there was no one to raise their heads. Now it was ended. *Tsagiglalal* had seen it all. In 1856 the floats-ashores had burned the town Coyote set her to watch. She watches still, but now she watches us. In 1989 someone copyrighted her image for a trademark.[69] In 1993 the authorities fenced her off, to protect her from vandals who had painted red handprints on nearby rocks.

COMCOMLY'S SKULL lay in the stacks of the Royal Navy Museum near Portsmouth for more than a century. In 1940 the museum and most of its collection were destroyed by Hitler's bombers, but Comcomly's skull, now minus its lower jaw, was spared. In 1953, after a lengthy correspondence between Astoria and England, the skull was returned to Astoria, where it was displayed in a glass case at the Clatsop County Historical Museum. Its journey was not over. In 1956 it traveled to the Smithsonian Institution for anthropometrical study.[70] In 1972 persons claiming descent from Comcomly appeared at the Clatsop County Historical Museum, demanding the skull's return. They said a Chinook's spirit could not be peaceful while its skull remained above ground.[71] The skull was relinquished, and after 138 years returned to earth, in Ilwaco Community Cemetery,[72] a town named after Comcomly's daughter Elowaka.

IT HAD BECOME someone else's turn to live along Big River. Whether *God* swept them away, like crumbs from a dinner table, to prepare the table for us, or this world is a manifestation of myriad more-or-less equivalent spirits, a swarm of which slew the Chinook because that is plasmodium's nature, we cannot know for certain this side of that final river. But surely the dead of August 1830 were fortunate. They died in their own high-gabled cedar-plank houses, practicing their own ancient ways, fishing their own drifts, speaking their own language. They did not linger to suffer the humiliation of living in little shacks and being sent to jail for fishing, of being forbidden to speak their own languages or perform their own ceremonies.

The Myth People who had been so close for so long were not the Chinook themselves after all, and the Myth People had finally come. The Chinooks must have laughed when they found that out.

Gone, four thousand years of knowledge about every river and marsh and mountain in my homeland, gone lore of trees, animals, and spirits, gone memories of all that happened. Gone their knowledge of herbs, gone their unbound society, gone names, families, whole bodies of knowledge and experience. Gone.

NOW COYOTE WAS MADE TIRED. Now the spirits of the Chinooks went off to live in rivers, mountains, and air.[73]

> *Kani,*
>   The Myth;
> *Kani,*
>   The true nature of things.

Tomorrow, good weather.[75]

"Homeward." *Prize-winning photograph by Edward Curtis, courtesy of the University of Washington Library, Special Collections,* NA 327.

Notes

Most of the references in these notes are to works listed in the bibliography, beginning on page 409. Citations in the notes give the author's last name, the year of publication, and page numbers of the reference where appropriate. Full details of publication will be found in the bibliography. For references to works not found in the bibliography, details of publication are supplied in the notes.

Epigraphs

Gibbs, 1955–56, 294.

Ursula K. Le Guin, 1985, *Always Coming Home* (New York: Harper & Row Publishers), 4.

She Who Watches

1. Statements in this introduction that may seem questionable but have no end note are documented where the subjects are covered more fully.

2. Boit, 1921, 311, entry for May 18, 1792.

3. Wilkes, 1845–48, 9:25.

4. Curtis, 1911, 8:180, n.1.

5. Jacobs, 1959, 36, 197; Hale, 1846, 6:199-200; Simpson, 1931, 102; Gibbs, 1955–56, 295-97.

6. Curtis, 1911, 8:145-46; Butler, 1957, 160, 162-63.

7. Dell Hymes suggested this solution in a letter to the author, Sept. 29, 1990.

8. Curtis, 1911, 8:85. See also French, 1961, 361.

9. Charles Winick, 1964, *Dictionary of Anthropology* (Paterson, New Jersey: Littlefield, Adams & Co.), 546.

10. Hymes, 1981, 27.

11. Hymes, letter to the author, Sept. 29, 1990.

CHAPTER 1: The People of Olden Times

1. Sapir, 1909, 7.

2. Isaac H. Whealdon, 1913, "Stories and Sketches from Pacific County," *Washington Historical Quarterly* 4:187-190.

3. Boas, 1901, 214.

4. Gibbs, 1955–56, 325.

5. Swan, 1857, 203-04.

6. Phebus and Drucker, 1979; Pettigrew, 1990, 7:523.

7. Pettigrew, ibid.

8. Swan, 1857, 104; Ray, 1938, 108.

9. Swan, 1857, 107.

10. Boas, 1894, 92-106.

11. Ibid., 94, line 5; 97, line 1.

12. Boas, 1901, 45-49; Silas Smith, 1901, 258.

13. Boas, 1901, 49.

14. Boas, 1894, 216-23. The upper Chinook *Itcixyan* replaces the lower Chinook *Icxian*, for consistency.

15. Jacobs, 1958, 395-96; Boas, 1901, 12.

16. James C. Strong, 1893, 134-35.

17. Franchère, 1967, 121.

18. Ross, 1923, 93-94.

19. Lewis R. Williams, 1924, 31.

20. Ray, 1938, 63.

21. Comcomly: This spelling is correct according to every person who heard his name firsthand. It is also the family spelling. See Ranald McDonald, 1923, 74-79 for list. Silverstein, 1990, 7:541, spelled it Concomly, evidently following Ray, 1938, 63. Historical records deny this, and there is no Chinook linguistic reason for the sound to be *n*. (Hymes, letter to the author, Dec. 27, 1991), but many examples in the language of repeated syllables, e.g. Komkomis, his father; Quasquas, his eldest son; and Carcumcum, his sister; and the names of almost all the birds.

CHAPTER 2: *Tlohonnipts* Float Ashore

1. Gibbs, 1877, 237-38.

2. Boas, 1894, 275-76; Gibbs, 1877, 236; Silas Smith, 1900, "Tales of Early Wrecks," 444-45.

3. See Barry, 1933, 296-301.

4. Sapir, 1909, 229-31.

5. Lewis and Clark, *Journals,* April 3, 1806; Cox, 1957, 169; Larsell, 1947, 22-23; Boyd, 1990, 7:137-38.

6. Dunn, 1845, 117.

7. Frederick F. Cartwright, 1972, *Disease and History* (New York: Thomas Y. Crowell). See also Erwin H. Ackernecht, 1965, *History and Geography of the Most Important Diseases* (New York City: Hafner Publishing Co.).

8. Cartwright, ibid.

9. Scouler, 1905, 203-04.

10. Lewis and Clark, *Journals,* April 3, 1806; Curtis, 1911, 8:180-83.

11. Lewis and Clark, *Journals*, Feb. 7 and April 3, 1806.

12. Boyd, 1990, 7:137-38.

13. Ames et. al., 1992, 275-90; Ames, May 9, 1991, "Indians constructed wooden houses"; Ames, remarks at Scapoose dig site, July 28, 1990. See also Ray, 1938, 124-26; Sapir and Spier, 1930, 202-05; Curtis, 1911, 8:90-92; Lieutenant William Broughton in Vancouver, 1798, 2:77.

14. Henry, 1897, 754; Henry, 1992, 613; Parker, 1967, 243; Vancouver, 1798, 3:129.

15. Henry, 1897, 805; Henry, 1992, 649-50.

16. Ames, remarks at Scapoose dig site, July 28, 1990; Hajda, 1984, 143; Lewis and Clark, *Journals*, April 3, 1806 (Moulton, 7:64-65).

17. Hajda, 1984, 80.

18. Tolmie, 1932, 17; Ray, 1938, 72; Jacobs, 1958, 497; Claude R. Warren, 1960, 27.

19. Ross, 1923, 98-99.

20. Thompson, 1962, 357. See also Townsend, 1970, *Narrative of a Journey*, 310.

21. Hunt, 1973, 305.

22. Jacobs, 1958, 67.

23. Emory Strong, 1960, 90.

24. Lewis and Clark, *Journals*, Clackstar, 28 houses, March 29, 1806; Quathlapootle, 14 large houses, March 29, 1806; Nihduilih, 18 houses, Oct. 24, 1805.

25. Curtis, 1911, 8:146.

CHAPTER 3: The Geography of Chinook *Illahee*

1. See in general, Curtis, 1911; Hodges, ed., 1907–10; Silverstein, 1990; Lewis and Clark, *Journals*, during the period Oct. 4, 1805 through April 21, 1806; Gibbs, 1967; Gibbs, 1877; Ray, 1938; Sapir and Spier, 1930, ; Emory Strong, 1960; Simpson, 1931; Barry, 1927, "The Indians of Oregon"; Barry, 1927, "The Indians of Washington."

2. Boas, 1894, 275, line 5.

3. Lewis and Clark, *Journals*, Clark, Jan. 8, 1806.

4. Boas, 1894, 101.

5. Lewis and Clark, *Journals*, Clark, April 3, 1806.

6. Boas, 1894, 101-06; Boas, 1901, 45-49.

7. Hymes, letter to the author, Dec. 27, 1991.

8. Gibbs, 1877, 171; Edward Curtis, 1911, 8:154; Krauss, 1990, 7:530.

9. Gibbs, 1877, 164, 171, 241.

10. Franchère, 1968, 74-75.

11. Hymes, in a letter to the author, Sept. 17, 1990, stated that Silverstein agreed that Kathlamet was a different language than Kiksht. The language spoken in the Wapato Lowlands will be forever in doubt, but was probably Kiksht.

12. Nakwaii dialect: Curtis, 1911, 8:181.

13. Nayagogo: "noisy place" according to Curtis, ibid. Michael Silverstein, nd, "Historical Sites of Chinookans" (unpublished), translated it, "Where there are blows."

14. Lewis and Clark, *Journals*, March 30, 1806; Emory Strong, 1960, 16. See also Seton, 1935, 191; Franchère, 1967, 51.

15. Seton, 1935, 190.

16. Hymes, letter to the author, Sept. 17, 1990. See also Boas, 1901, 240.

17. H. S. Lyman, 1900, 320. See also Lewis L. McArthur, 1974, *Oregon Geographic Names* (Portland: Western Imprints), under "Willamette River."

18. Lyman, ibid.

19. Henry, 1897, 811; Henry, 1992, 656-57. See also H. S. Lyman, 1900, 316-26; Slacum, 1972.

20. Curtis, 1911, 8:180, n. 1.; Sapir, 1909, 205, n. 2.

21. Sapir and Spier, 1930, 165-66.

22. Ibid., 164; Curtis, 1911, 8:180 n. 2.

23. Emory Strong, 1959.

24. Lewis and Clark, *Journals*, Oct. 27, 1805.

CHAPTER 4: Chinook As They Spoke It

1. See in general, Boas, 1891; Boas, 1904; Boas, 1911; Jacobs, 1937; Hymes, 1955; Silverstein, 1974; Gibbs, 1877; Pilling, 1893.

2. Hymes, 1981, 27-28.

3. Hajda, 1984, 155; Hymes, letter to the author, Sept. 17, 1990.

4. Kane, 1971, *Columbia Wanderer*, 25.

5. "Someone maligned" is anonymously quoted in John Hussey, 1957, *Chinook Point and the Story of Fort Columbia* (Tacoma: Washington State Park System), 8.

6. Swan, 1857, 142.

7. Wilkes, 1845–48, 4:318.

8. Hale, 1846, 6:134. See also Kane, 1925, 93.

9. Boas, 1911, 1:627-33, 655-56.

10. Ibid., 1:576, with addition of the parenthetical phrase at the end of line 6, suggested by Hymes in a letter to the author, Sept. 17, 1990.

11. Boas, 1911, 1:63.

12. Ibid., 1:635.

13. Boas, 1894, 153-60.

14. Jacobs, 1958, 366-69.

15. French, 1958, 258-63.

16. Swadesh, 1949; Swadesh, 1956.

17. Silverstein, letter to the author, Sept. 18, 1974; Hymes, letter to the author, Sept. 17, 1990.

18. Hymes, letter to the author, Sept. 17, 1990.

19. Hymes, letter to the author, Sept. 17, 1990; Silverstein, letter to the author, Oct. 24, 1974; R. L. Benson, interview by the author, Aug. 31, 1974.

20. Irving, 1836, ch. 60; Stuart, 1953, 42-43.

21. Penutian: consult Swadesh, 1949; Swadesh, 1956; Bruce Rigsby, 1965, "Linguistic Relations on the Southern Plateau," Ph.D. thesis, University of Oregon; Rigsby, 1969, "The Waiilatpuan Problem," *Northwest Anthropological Research Notes* 3(1):68-146; A. L. Kroeber, 1955, "Linguistic Time Depth Results So Far and Their Meaning," *International Journal of American Linguistics* 21:91-104; Hymes, 1957; Hymes, 1964, "Evidence for Penutian in Lexical sets with Initial *c- and *s-," *International Journal of American Linguistics* 30(3):213-42; Michael Silverstein, 1965, "Penutian: the Grammatical Dimensions of Sapir's Hypothesis," B.A. thesis, Harvard University.

22. Luther S. Cressman, 1962, 23.

23. Mexican interpretation is from displays at the National Museum of Anthropology, Mexico City, 1990.

24. Greenberg, 1987, 143-45, 331-17.

CHAPTER 5: Mountains Eat People

1. Emory Strong, interview by the author, Oct. 24, 1974.

2. *Glossaire du Parler Français au Canada*, 1968 (Quebec: Les Press d'University Laval), "dalle"; *Shorter Oxford English Dictionary*, "dalles." The historic definition has been flagstones; see Lewis L. McArthur, 1974, *Oregon Geographic Names* (Portland: Western Imprints), under "The Dalles." Flagstone is the continental French meaning, but the boatmen who named the formation were from Canada, where the word meant water chute, etc., the space between the stones.

3. Ames, Jan. 23, 1992, "Archaeologists fish for clues."

4. Warren, 1958–59; Warren, 1960; Tuohy and Bryan, 1958–59; Minor, et. al., 1989.

5. Emory Strong, 1959.

6. Silverstein, letter to the author, March 20, 1975.

7. Butler, 1957.

8. Lewis and Clark, *Journals*, Oct. 24, 1805.

9. John Eliot Allen, 1984, *The Magnificent Gateway* (Forest Grove, Oregon: Timber Press), 52-57.

10. Emory Strong, 1973.

11. Minor, et al., 1989.

12. Clarence Orvel Bunnel, 1935, *Legends of the Klickitat* (Portland: Binfords and Mort).

13. Hale, 1846, 6:199-200; Jacobs, 1959, 36, 197; Simpson, 1931, 102; Gibbs, 1955–56, 295-97.

14. Lewis and Clark, *Journals,* April 14, 1806; John Eliot Allen, 1984, *The Magnificent Gateway* (Forest Grove, Oregon: Timber Press), 56; Wilkes, 1845–48, 4:381; Parker, 1967, 140.

15. University of Michigan, 1958, carbon 14 test from a sample submitted by D. B. Lawrence.

16. W. Duncan Strong, et. al., 1930.

17. Lewis and Clark, *Journals,* Clark, Oct. 25, 1805 (Moulton, 5:339).

18. Sapir, 1909, 201-05.

19. Kelly, 1955.

20. Curtis, 1911, 8:146-47.

21. W. Duncan Strong, et. al., 1930; Cressman, 1960; Butler, 1959.

22. Sapir and Spier, 1930, 224-28; Curtis, 1911, 8:93-94; Lewis and Clark, *Journals,* April 21, 1806; Ross, 1923, 117-18; Irving, 1836, ch. 61; James A. Teit, 1928, "The Middle Columbia Salish," *University of Washington Publications in Anthropology* 2(4):121-22.

23. Bumming: Sapir, 1909, 187; Curtis, 1911, 8:95. French had heard it described by Wasco, interview by the author, June 13, 1974. See Harold Wentworth and Stuart Berg Flexner, 1967, *Dictionary of American Slang* (New York: Crowell) for "bum."

24. Sapir and Spier, 1930, 228.

25. Lewis and Clark, *Journals,* April 1, 1806.

26. Gibbs, 1877, 187.

27. Lewis and Clark, *Journals,* Jan. 3, 1806.

28. Henry, 1897, 833; Henry, 1992, 677.

29. Lewis and Clark, *Journals,* April 11, 1806 (Moulton, 7:101).

30. Gustavus Hines, 1851, *Oregon, its History, Condition and Prospects* (Buffalo: George Derby Co.), 158.

31. Elizabeth Derr Jacobs, 1959, *Nehalem-Tillamook Tales* (Eugene: University of Oregon), 118.

32. Sapir and Spier, 1930, 228.

33. Boas, 1891, 27.

34. Ross, 1923, 95; Franchère, 1968, 244; Ray, 1938, 100-01. Accounts of the value vary.

35. Ray, 1938, 100, n. 7.

36. Geometrical designs: Emory Strong, 1960, 196-97, with picture. Burial of valuables: Jacobs, 1958, 490, 609 n. 61. Ground up for medicine: source lost.

37. Simpson, 1931, 98.

38. Ross, 1923, 117-18.

39. Simpson, 1931, 96.

40. Butler, 1957, 61-62.

41. Roy F. Jones, 1872, 186, shows Sauvie Island example. See also Curtis, 1911, v. 8, opposite title page, 145-6, and n. 1; Emory Strong, 1960, 107-09, 125; Rubin, 1986.

42. Curtis, 1911, 8:145-46.

43. Greg Bettis and Timothy Brady, 1989, "Images From the Past" (unpublished), 3; Keyser, 1989, 2; both referring to Butler.

44. Research and consultation at Oregon Health Science University library, 1990. No known disease is even close.

45. Keyser, 1992, 101-02; interview by the author, Oct. 17, 1989.

46. Ames, remarks at Scapoose dig site, July 28, 1990.

47. W. Duncan Strong, 1945.

48. See various issues of *Screenings* (the journal of the Oregon Archaeological Society); Emory Strong, 1960; Seaman, 1946; Butler, 1957.

49. Walker, ed., 1998, classifies Chinook groups from the Cascades to the Long Narrows as plateau people. A. L. Kroeber, 1939, distinctly shows the Wasco-Wishram as within the coastal cultural area; he describes "an unusually sharp cleavage at The Dalles, where alone Pacific Coast and Plains Culture met in a conspicuous non-conformity." The non-conformity was noted by every early European visitor. Sapir and Spier, 1930, likewise show the Wishram to be a coastal culture. Verne F. Ray, 1936, "Native villages and groupings of the Columbia Basin," *Pacific Northwest Quarterly* 27, does not mention the upper Chinook as plateau dwellers. Driver and Coffin, 1975, show the Wishram as isolated and not closely correlated with their plateau neighbors. See also French, 1961; Barry, 1927, "The Indians of Oregon"; Berreman, 1937; H. G. Barnett, 1937, "Culture Element Distributions VII: Oregon's Coast," *University of California Anthropological Records* 1(3):155-204; none of which suggest such a cultural separation of the Chinook. In any case, we are attempting to follow the whole Chinook experience. The Celts, who once occupied most of Europe, ended as Irish, Iberian, Bretons, Welch, Manx, and Cornish, but were still Celts.

50. Thompson, 1962, 368-70; Thompson, 1971, 305ff.

51. Boas, 1891, 27-28.

CHAPTER 6: The Skulls of Free People

1. I have compared the bills for outfitting the *Columbia Rediviva* listed in F. W. Howay, ed., 1941, "Voyages of the 'Columbia' to the Northwest Coast, 1787–1790," *Massachusetts Historical Society Collections* (Boston), no. 79, 448-65 ("Expenditures for the Columbia's Outfit and Cargo, Sept. 1790"), with comparable prices two centuries later, and found increases of 15 to 112 times, averaging 54 times the 1790 cost.

2. Boit, 1921, 309.

3. Stuart, 1953, 42. The Chinook told Stuart it was Captain Gray, but the stories clearly differ.

4. Wilkes, 1845–48, 9:27

5. Bishop, 1927, 276.

6. Boas, 1891.

7. Morton, 1854, 2:321.

8. Boit, 1921, 311.

9. Simpson, 1931, 96.

10. Ross, 1923, 89-93.

11. See also descriptions in Swan, 1857, 154; Cox, 1957, 115, 303-04; Irving, 1836, ch. 60; Ross, 1923, 89-93; Townsend, 1970, *Narrative of a Journey*, 178; Franchère, 1967, 240-41; Lewis and Clark, *Journals*, Nov. 21, 1805; Scouler, 1905, 164; Thompson, 1962, 357; Kane, 1925, 93.

12. Franchère, 1967, 109.

13. Simpson, 1931, 96.

14. Ray, 1938, 68-71; Sapir and Spier, 1930, 255-56; Dunn, 1845, 122-23, 128-30; Ross, 1923, 99-101; Swan, 1857, 167-68; Cox, 1957, 302; Parker, 1967, 142-43, 251-52; Franchère, 1968, 241-42.

15. Lewis and Clark, *Journals*, Jan. 6, 1806.

16. Hunt, 1935, 305.

17. Simpson, 1931, 96.

18. Townsend, 1970, *Narrative of a Journey*, 303. See also Kane, 1925, 93.

19. Hale, 1846, 6:216.

20. Joseph Campbell, 1959, *The Masks of God* (New York: Viking), 38.

21. Olson, 1936.

22. Ernest Hooton, 1940, "Skeletons from the Cenote of Sacrifices at Chichen Itza," in *The Maya and their Neighbors* (New York, London: Appleton-Century Publishing), 280.

23. Julian Haynes Steward, ed., 1956, *Handbook of South American Indians* (Washington, D. C.: Government Printing Office), v. 6; Morton, 1851–57, 2:325-28.

24. Bishop, 1927, 276. See also Ross, 1923, 99-100; Swan, 1857, 167-68; Cox, 1832, 302; Parker, 1967, 142-43, 251-52.

25. Lewis and Clark, *Journals*, Oct. 17, 1805, March 19, 1806 (Moulton, 6:433, 6:437), April 20, 1806.

26. Silas Smith, 1901, 156.

27. Hajda, 1984, 151-53. See also Chapter 16.

28. Curtis, 1911, 8:139; Sapir and Spier, 1930, 143.

29. Jacobs, 1958, 344-45. See also Chapter 10.

30. Franchère, 1967, 110.

31. Ross, 1923, 91.

32. Swan, 1857, 155; Broughton, reported in Vancouver, 1798, 2:77.

33. Broughton, ibid.

34. Curtis, 1911, 8:93.

35. *Screenings* (the journal of the Oregon Archaeological Society), various issues; Emory Strong, 1960; Seaman, 1946.

36. Cox, 1957, 70-71.

37. For Broughton's exploration see Barry, 1932, 31-42, 143-55; Barry, 1926, 387-411; Sherriff, 1992, 53-59; Howay and Elliott, 1942, 318-27.

38. Barry, 1926, 400-08.

39. Swan, 1857, 156. The next naval officer we know of would be Captain Black of H.M.S. *Racoon*, in 1813, and one must assume that some Chinook had tasted alcohol before that.

CHAPTER 7: Skunk Cabbage Holds the People's Breath

1. Curtis, 1911, 8:203; Sapir and Spier, 1930, 208.

2. Boas, 1901, 50-58, combined with Jacobs, 1958, 75-80 (where Coyote leads the procession). The Kathlamet version was retranslated and analyzed by Hymes, 1985, 397-400.

3. Henry, 1897, 859; Henry, 1992, 703; Franchère, 1967, 107.

4. Analysis of Chinook diet is by Chedwah Stein, Oregon Public Health Division, interview by the author, Nov. 27, 1974.

5. Wilkes, 1845–48, 4:345.

6. Ray, 1938, 112; Sapir and Spier, 1930, 248. See also Erna Gunther, 1926, "An Analysis of the First Salmon Ceremony," *American Anthropologist* 28:605-17; Gunther, 1928, "A Further Analysis of the First Salmon Ceremony," *University of Washington Publications in Anthropology* 2(5).

7. Lewis and Clark, *Journals*, April 9, 1806.

8. Esther Warren, 1977, 49.

9. Sapir, 1909, 185.

10. Wilkes, 1845–48, 4:380; Douglas, 1904–05, 5:267-68.

11. Curtis, 1911, 8:203; Sapir and Spier, 1930, 208. H. L. Davis, 1935, *Honey in the Horn* (Cardinal paperback reprint, 1952, New York: Pocket Books Inc.), 184, ascribes May birth to Indians at an unnamed coast town. The book, while fiction, is deeply based on fact, though Davis' experience with Indians was at The Dalles.

12. Ray, 1938, 64. Qwalwanxu is the Chinook name of Emma Millet Luscier, Ray's informant.

13. Boas, 1894, 241-43.

14. Ray, 1938, 67.

15. Gairdner, 1841, 253.

16. Sapir and Spier, 1930, 259. A fudge: this is the ceremony for a Wishram child. See also Ray, 1938, 66-67; Curtis, 1911, 8:179.

17. Sapir, 1909, x-xi, 224 (fn).

18. Ibid., 189-91.

19. Swan, 1857, 197.

20. Emory Strong, 1960, 49, 51.

21. Swan, 1857, 197.

22. Lewis and Clark, *Journals*, Jan. 6, 1806.

23. *Atatalia*, or Basket Ogress: see Jacobs, 1958, 388-409; Sapir, 1909, 165-73, 274-87 (five stories); Boas, 1894, 9-19.

24. Gibbs, 1955–56, 313-14; Silas Smith, 1901, 261. Yes, *Tsiatko* does sound a lot like Bigfoot.

25. Boas, 1894, 151.

26. Jacobs, 1958, 313-15.

CHAPTER 8: What Coyote Did in This Land

1. Sapir, 1909, xi.

2. Hymes, 1981, 264.

3. Ibid.; Jacobs, 1958, 7.

4. Hymes, 1981, 309-41; Hymes, 1975, "Folklore's Nature."

5. Gibbs, 1955–56, 289.

6. Sapir, 1909, 75. But Jacobs, 1959, 21-24, disagrees.

7. Sapir, 1909, 101; Curtis, 1911, 8:124.

8. Rubin, 1981, 168-69.

9. The Coyote epic: Jacobs, 1958, 80-105; Sapir, 1909, 3-48; Curtis, 1911, 8:107-16. Jacobs, 1959, 215-16, comments on structure. Much of the commentary here is Rubin, 1981.

10. The Story Concerning Coyote: Jacobs, 1958, 95-96; Sapir, 1909, 31-33; not included in Curtis' epic. French had an unpublished Wasco version. Hymes, 1981, 91-118, gives several versions, compares and analyzes the style, and discusses the feather. See also Hymes, 1996, 110-14, 121-31. Bowdlerized but recognizable pioneer versions include Fred Lockley, 1928, *History of the Columbia River Valley* (Chicago: S. J. Clark), 1:92-93; William D. Lyman, 1910, 289-90.

11. Curtis, 1911, 8:113-14.

12. Ibid., 8:145-46.

13. Ending: Sapir, 1909, 49.

CHAPTER 9: The Chinook Invent a Language

1. Henry R. Wagner, "The Last Spanish Exploration of the Northwest Coast," *California Historical Quarterly*, 10:326-37.

2. Swan, 1857, 423.

3. George I. Quimby, 1948, "Culture Contact on the Northwest Coast, 1785-95," *American Anthropologist* 50:247ff.

4. Bishop, 1927, 268.

5. Ibid., 258-80. See also Bishop, 1967.

6. Bishop, 1927, 267.

7. Ibid., 277.

8. Ibid., 269.

9. Ibid.

10. Ibid., 270-71.

11. Ibid., 272.

12. The Chinook Jargon: see Parker, 1967; Blanchet, 1853; Gibbs, 1863; Hale, 1846; Hale, 1890; Boas, 1933; Jacobs, 1932; Silverstein, 1972; Hymes and Zenk, 1987; etc. See also dictionaries: Thomas, 1935; Shaw, 1909; Eells, 1894; and numerous others. See also Chapter 19, pages 302-03; Chapter 23, pages 369-71.

13. Jacobs, 1958, 557, 660, n. 536.

14. *Did not* predate whites: Howay, 1943; Bancroft, 1883, 3:631; Hale, 1846, 6:635. *Did* predate whites: J. K. Gill, in an 1891 letter to James Pilling, quoted in Pilling, 1893; Jacobs, 1932; Thomas, 1935, 22-23; Bancroft, 1883, 3:632-33; Ray, 1938, 36, n. 9; Jacobs, 1956, "Review of E. H. Thomas, *Chinook*," *Pacific Northwest Quarterly* 27:180-81.

15. Hale, 1846, 6:562. Evidently this was Michel LaFramboise, see Wilkes, 1845–48, 4:349.

16. Jacobs, 1932.

17. Hale, 1846, 6:643.

18. Jacobs, 1964.

19. Bishop, 1927, 277-78.

20. Boas, 1901, 53, 57.

21. Bishop, 1927, 277.

22. Ibid., 278-79.

23. Ibid., 273.

24. Lewis and Clark, *Journals*, Jan. 1, 1806.

25. Franchère, 1967, 57; Corney, 1965, 154; Ruby and Brown, 1976, 123-24.

26. Lewis and Clark, *Journals*, Feb. 7, 1806. See also Boyd, 1990, 7:137-38.

CHAPTER 10: A Tyrant Is Overthrown

1. Jacobs, 1958, 342-48: *Idyabixwasxwas*; Sapir, 1909, 248-53: *Diabexwasxwas*; Boas, 1901, 155-65: *Tiapexwasxwas*; Curtis, 1911, 8:150-53: *Kihlktagwah*. See Jacobs, 1959, 108-16, for analysis.

2. Boas, 1911, 1:655, gives heron, the important year-around resident of the river, as *qulqul*, and crane, an occasional visitor to some locals, as *qoasqoas*. Jacobs, 1959, 110, noted that it was "unfortunately not translated."

3. Hymes, 1981, 264.

4. Jacobs, 1959, 110-16, gives a full, mostly Freudian, analysis of this myth.

5. French, 1961, 362; Ray, 1938, 48-50; Sapir and Spier, 1930, 211-13; Curtis, 1911, 8:83.

6. Simpson, 1931, 170; Gibbs, 1877, 188-89; Tolmie, 1932; Kane, 1971, *Frontier*.

7. Ray, 1938, 49, 55; Boas, 1894, 268-69; Hajda, 1984, 200.

8. Lewis and Clark, *Journals*, Jan. 19, 1806 (Moulton, 6:222, 223).

9. Parker, 1967, 253.

10. Gibbs, 1877, 185.

11. Sapir and Spier, 1930, 213.

12. Gibbs, 1877, 185.

13. French, 1958.

14. Curtis, 1911, 8:116.

15. Simpson, 1931, 97.

16. Thompson, 1962, 362.

17. Comcomly: see Ray, 1938, 63; Ranald McDonald, 1923, 75, n.; Irving, 1836; Thompson, 1971; Simpson, 1931, 97, 104; Ross, 1923; Corney, 1965; Saylor, 1900, "Nations No More"; Scouler, 1905; *Oregonian*, 1899.

CHAPTER 11: Clothmen Pass

Most of this chapter is from the journals of Lewis and Clark. There being many published versions, references are identified by the date of the journal entry, in most instances with page numbers from Gary E. Moulton, 1983, provided in parentheses. See also Private Joseph Whitehouse, "Journal" in Reuben Gold Thwaites, ed., 1905, *Original Journals of the Lewis and Clark Expedition* (New York: Dodd Meade); Gass, 1958.

1. French, 1961, 421-23.

2. Ibid., 350.

3. Hymes, letter to the author, Sept. 17, 1990.

4. Lewis and Clark, *Journals*, Clark, Oct. 23 and 24, 1805 (Moulton, 5:328, house; 5:333, canoe).

5. Lewis and Clark, *Journals*, Lewis, Jan. 3, 1806, April 13, 1806, and others. Clark was not yet reconciled to dog flesh, see entries same dates.

6. Lewis and Clark, *Journals*, Nov. 21, 1805 and Jan. 6, 1806.

7. Ibid., Nov. 11, 1805.

8. Donald McKenzie, source of quote lost. If found, please return.

9. Canoes: much of this section is from Durham, 1960, 47-82. See also Lewis and Clark (Moulton, 6:162-71).

10. Durham, 1960, 77.

11. Ibid., 56.

12. Henry, 1897, 835; Henry, 1992, 679.

13. Duflot de Mofras, 1937.

14. Lewis and Clark, *Journals*, April 2, 1806.

15. Lewis and Clark, *Journals*, April 2, 1806 (Moulton, 7:57).

16. Ibid., Feb. 1, 1806, with drawings (Moulton, 6:198-99, lost canoe; 6:262, 6:267 largest canoe).

17. Boas, 1894, 53, 57.

18. Swan, 1857, 248.

19. Lewis and Clark, *Journals*, Nov. 20, 1805.

20. Ibid., Nov. 21, 1805.

21. Ibid., Nov. 21, 1805, March 15, 1806.

22. Ibid., March 1, 1806 (Moulton: Lewis, 6:365; Clark, 6:367).

23. Ibid., March 19, 1806.

24. Ibid., Nov. 21, 1805.

25. Ibid., Nov. 20, 1805.

26. Ibid., Jan. 6, 1806.

27. Ibid., Dec. 29, 1805.

28. Ibid., March 6, 1806 (Moulton: Lewis, 6:384).

29. Ibid., Dec. 9, 1805 (Moulton, 6:118).

30. Ibid., houseboards, Nov. 15, Dec. 19, 1805; canoe, March 17, March 24, 1806.

31. Ray, 1975.

32. Lewis and Clark, *Journals*, Dec. 9, 1805 (Moulton, 6:121). Word origins from Thomas, 1935. See also Thomas, 19-20. Additionally, the Nootka word *peshak* was heard: Lewis and Clark, *Journals*, Jan. 7, 1806 (Moulton, 6:178).

33. Nicholas Biddle, 1814, *History of the Expedition Under the Command of Captains Lewis and Clark* (Philadelphia: Bradford and Inskeep).

34. Lewis and Clark, *Journals*. Spoke like Clatsop: Nehalem, Clark, Jan. 8, 1806 (Moulton, 6:184); Kathlamet, Lewis, Nov. 7, 1805 (Moulton, 6:192); Skillute, Lewis, March 27, 1806 (Moulton, 7:18); Quathlapootle, Lewis, March 28, 1806 (Moulton, 7:26-27); Cashooks (of Willamette Falls), Clark, April 2, 1806 (Moulton, 7:54-55). Clark, coming downriver on Nov. 7, 1805 (Moulton, 6:31-32), described the Wahkiacum as speaking "a language different from the natives above with whom they trade for the wapato roots," perhaps crossing the border between Kathlamet and the language of the Wapato Lowlands, which was probably Kiksht.

35. Gass, 1958, 204 (entry for Nov. 23, 1805).

36. Lewis and Clark, *Journals*, Dec. 31, 1805.

37. Ibid., Jan. 4 (Moulton, 6:164).

38. Ibid., Feb. 12, 1806.

39. Ibid., Jan. 8, 1806.

40. Ibid., Dec. 3, 1805.

41. Ibid., Feb. 22, 1806.

42. Ibid. (Moulton, 6:483-87; in the version edited by James K. Hosmer, Appendix, 498-505). Whether Clackstar was Chinook or Clatskanie remains unresolved, but its size and location sound Chinook.

43. Ibid., Clark (Moulton, 6:484). I think Chinook.

44. Ibid., March 24, 1806; (Moulton: Clark, 7:10).

45. Ibid., March 30, 1806 (Moulton, 7:33).

46. Ibid., March 30, 1806. Soto-Shoto: Emory Strong, 1960, 16. See also Chapter 17.

47. Ibid., April 2, 1806.

48. Ibid., April 3, 1806.

49. Ibid., Clark, April 3, 1806; Lewis, March 31, 1806.

50. Ibid., April 10, 1806 (Moulton: Lewis, 7:102; Clark, 7:103).

51. Ibid., March 31, 1806 (Moulton, 7:38-39). Jargon scholar Henry Zenk, interview by the author, Sept. 28, 1994, and letter to the author, Feb. 6, 1995, called this evidence but not proof that Lewis and Clark heard "something like Jargon," that "doubtless gave rise to the later Chinook Jargon."

52. Ibid., Lewis, April 11 (Moulton, 7:107).

53. Ibid., April 11, 1806 (Moulton, 7:104).

54. Ibid., April 11, 1806.

55. Ibid., April 11, 1806 (Moulton, 7:106).

56. Ibid., April 10, 1806 (Moulton: Lewis, 7:102; Clark, 7:103).

57. Ibid., April 11, 1806.

58. Ibid., April 19, 1806 (Moulton: Lewis, 7:142; Clark, 7:144).

59. Ibid., April 21, 1806. See also Gass, 1958, 244 (entry for the same date).

CHAPTER 12: Salmon Come Thickly

1. Fish names are from Boas, 1911.

2. Dunn, 1845, 114-15.

3. Hajda, 1984, 91-95.

4. Suttles, 1968.

5. Curtis, 1911, 8:49; Wilkes, 1845–48, 4:383.

6. Chedwah Stein, Nutrition Section, Oregon State Public Health Division, interview by the author, Nov. 27, 1974. See also Oregon State University circular no. 808, "Foods of the Warm Springs Indians."

7. Rivera, 1949, 19-36.

8. Dr. George Barton, interview by the author, Oct. 31, 1974; Stein, interview by the author, Nov. 27, 1974.

9. Lewis and Clark, *Journals*, Nov. 1, 1805.

10. See particularly Henry, 1897; Henry, 1992; Corney, 1965; Lewis and Clark, *Journals*; Cox, 1957.

11. Chinook: Henry, 1897, 750; Henry, 1992, 610. Clowewalla: Henry, 1897, 819; Henry, 1992, 664; Clatsop: Henry, 1897, 772; Henry, 1992, 623-24.

12. Bishop, 1967, 128. See also Lewis and Clark, *Journals*, Jan. 8, 1806.

13. Miller, 1958, 14.

14. Jacobs, 1958, 499-500. See also Thomas Nelson Strong, 1906, 64-68.

15. Boas, 1894, 220-22; Ray, 1938, 78-80; Sapir and Spier, 1930, 239-40.

16. Boas, 1894, 211-16.

17. Jacobs, 1958, 280, n. 121.

18. See Chapter 19, note 7.

19. Sapir, 1909, 257-59.

20. Jacobs, 1959, 10.

21. Curtis, 1911, 8:175-79. See also Sapir and Spier, 1930, 262.

22. Ray, 1938, 71-72; Boas, 1894, 246-47.

23. Boas, ibid., 247.

24. Boas, 1901, 244-47.

25. Swan, 1857, 83.

26. Corney, 1965, 146.

CHAPTER 13: Blue Jay Knocks a Hole in a Rotten Log

1. Jacobs, 1958, 366-69; Boas, 1894, 153-60.

2. Jacobs, ibid., 367-68.

3. Mostly Durham, 1960, 67-72. See also Lewis and Clark, *Journals*, Feb. 1, 1806; Swan, 1857, 79-82.

4. Chief Lelooska (Don Smith), interview by the author, Dec. 2, 1973.

5. Swan, 1857, 82.

6. Ibid., 81.

7. Stuart, 1953, 41.

8. Simpson, 1931, 113-14.

9. Ray, 1938, 38.

10. Ames, lecture at Portland State University, April 1, 1990; Ames, remarks at Scapoose dig site, July 28, 1990; Ames et. al., 1992; Ames, 1991.

11. Winship party: Henry, 1897, 795, 828; Henry, 1992, 641, 673; Bancroft, 1883, 1:325, 2:132-35; Anna Jersyk, 1940, "Winship Settlement in 1810 was Oregon's Jamestown," *Oregon Historical Quarterly* 41:175-81; Stuart, 1935, 44-45. The Gales account is in M. Philps, nd, "Solid Men of Boston in the Northwest," unpublished, 29-51. See Ruby and Brown, 1976, 119-24.

12. Lamsay as pilot: conjecture, backed by Lamsay's subsequent career as pilot and interpreter from 1811 through 1846. They may not have used a pilot, but there is mention of using one in Ruby and Brown, 1976, 120, 122-23.

13. Stuart, 1935, 44-45.

14. Lisa Graumlich, 1985, "Long Term Records of Temperature and Precipitation in the Pacific Northwest Derived From Tree Rings," Ph.D. dissertation, University of Washington.

15. Gales, in Philps, nd, "Solid Men of Boston," 47.

16. There is also mention of a Captain Eayers who may have carried off Chinooks in Ruby and Brown, 1976, 123-24. Sounds like "Ayres": see Chapter 9, page 135.

17. Ross, 1923, 96.

18. Swan, 1857, 177-80; Ross, 1923, 97.

19. Thomas Nelson Strong, 1906, 64-68.

20. A. T. W. Simeone, 1962, *Man's Presumptuous Brain* (New York: E. P. Dutton), 3.

21. Kane, 1971, *Columbia Wanderer*, 45-46. See also Swan, 1857, 180-85; Thomas Nelson Strong, 1906, 59-63; Simpson, 1931, 100.

22. Hajda, 1984, 196.

23. Curtis, 1911, 8:105.

24. Jacobs, 1958, 205, 289 n. 214.

25. Franchère, 1967, 119.

26. Lewis and Clark, *Journals*, March 19, 1806 and Jan. 24, 1806.

27. Wilkes, 1845–48, 5:114-15, of Lamsay and his brother Jack.

28. Boas, 1901, 247-51.

29. Sapir and Spier, 1930, 252; Curtis, 1911, 8:174-75.

30. Gibbs, 1877, 187.

31. Gibbs, 1955–56, 315.

32. Silas Smith, 1901, 26; Boas, 1894, 161-71.

33. Boas, 1894, 167-71.

34. W. Duncan Strong, 1945.

CHAPTER 14: The *Bahsten* Make a Fort

1. Ross, 1923, 67. The visit to Qwatsamts is from Irving, 1836, ch. 8.

2. Ross, 1923, 70, but he gives a more balanced view on p. 274. See also Irving, 1836, 3, ch. 4. Franchère, 1967, 45, gives a friendlier view.

3. Gairdner, 1841, 255.

4. Franchère, 1967; Ross, 1923, 159; Barry, 1933, 299. See, however, Robert F. Jones, 1997, published as this book was being readied to go to press, from a manuscript of McDougall's "Post Log," where the interpreter was named Joseachal.

5. Simpson, 1931, 46.

6. Astoria: see Henry, 1897; Henry, 1992; Ross, 1923; Ross, 1956; Franchère, 1967; Hunt, 1973; Irving, 1836; Seton, 1993; Thompson, 1971; Thompson, 1962; Corney, 1965; Cox, 1832; Cox, 1957.

7. Franchère, 1967, 120-21.

8. Corney, 1965, 154.

9. Ross, 1923, 77.

10. Ibid.

11. Ibid., 150.

12. Henry, 1897, 881; Henry, 1992, 716-17.

13. Franchère, 1967, 47-52.

14. Seton, 1935, 191. See also Franchère, 1967, 51; Lewis and Clark, *Journals*, March 30, 1806.

15. Ross, 1923, 82.

16. Barry, 1933, 296 fn. lists twenty-seven sources on the *Tonquin* massacre, including Ross, 1923; Townsend, 1970, *Narrative of a Journey*; White, 1848; Lee and Frost, 1968; Silas Smith, 1900; Wilkes, 1845–48; etc. Barry concluded all devolved from Lamsay's account. But see note 4, above, for the possibility that it was a Quinault named Joseachal who guided and interpreted.

17. Cox, 1832, 170; Irving, 1836, ch. 12.

18. Thompson, 1962, 367.

19. Ibid., 368-70.

20. Corney, 1965, 175-77; Hunt, 1973, 4.

21. See Hunt, 1973.

22. Corney, 1965, 155.

23. Franchère, 1967, 69-71.

24. Seton, 1993, 185-87; Seton, 1935, 192-95, 265-67. See also Irving, 1836, ch. 53. Ross, 1923, 197, offers a more heroic version.

25. French, 1961, 351-54; Seton, 1935, 194; Cox, 1957, 257.

26. Ross, 1923, 110-11.

27. Irving, 1836, ch. 53; Ross, 1923, 215-17.

CHAPTER 15: Coyote Visits the Spring of Abundance

1. Franchère, 1967, 100; McLoughlin, 1941, 15, Oct. 6, 1825. Ray, 1938, 116-18, thinks otherwise.
2. Wilkes, 1845–48, 5:131.
3. Thomas, 1935, 172.
4. Douglas, 1904–05, 5:269-70.
5. Ibid., 5:254.
6. Jacobs, 1958, 507.
7. Lewis and Clark, *Journals*, Jan. 8, 1806; Wilkes, 1845–48, 5:131.
8. Lewis and Clark, *Journals*, Jan. 8, 1806; Sapir and Spier, 1930, 269-70; Emory Strong, 1960, 133-41.
9. Sapir, 1909, 246-48.
10. William D. Lyman, 1910, 5-6.
11. Kane, 1925, 94; Spencer, 1950, 16.
12. Boas, 1901, 142-44; Jacobs, 1958, 423-30.
13. Jacobs, ibid., 265-66; Boas, 1901, 103-4.
14. Douglas, 1904–05, 5:269.
15. Henry, 1897, 858; Henry, 1992, 701.
16. Ray, 1938, 94-95.
17. Ibid., 55.
18. Gibbs, 1877, 185.
19. Ray, 1938, 128.
20. Lewis and Clark, *Journals*, Lewis, Jan. 6, 1806 (Moulton, 6:168).
21. Ibid.
22. Ray, 1938, 73.
23. Ibid.
24. Sapir and Spier, 1930, 216.
25. Ibid., 216-17.
26. Simpson, 1931, 98.
27. Franchère, 1967, 111.
28. Corney, 1965, 147.
29. Bishop, 1927, 277. See also Franchère, 1967, 111; Thomas Nelson Strong, 1906, 17-19.
30. Cox, 1957, 172-73.
31. Jacobs, 1959, 70-82.
32. Hajda, 1984, 137-38 (from Henry, 1897, 820; Henry, 1992, 664).
33. Jacobs, 1959, 158-61.
34. French, interview by the author, June 13, 1974.

35. Ross, 1923, 93.

CHAPTER 16: The Gossip of Two Cultures

1. Thompson, 1962, 362.
2. Ibid.
3. Henry, 1897, 750; Henry, 1992, 610.
4. Irving, 1836, ch. 61, called it an act of policy.
5. Henry, 1897, 901; Henry, 1992, 732.
6. Gibbs, 1877, 199.
7. Simpson, 1931, 99.
8. Bishop, 1927, 77.
9. Ray, 1938, 72-73; Sapir and Spier, 1930, 217-21; Boas, 1894, 248-52.
10. Sapir and Spier, 1930, 217.
11. Gibbs, 1877, 197.
12. Sapir and Spier, 1930, 218.
13. Swan, 1857, 170.
14. Sapir, 1916, "Terms of Relationship and the Levirate," *American Anthropologist* (ns) 18:327-37.
15. Irving, 1836, ch. 60; Kane, 1971, *Frontier*, 92; Ranald McDonald, 1923, 88-91.
16. Irving, 1836, ch. 56.
17. Scouler, 1905, 166; Kane, 1971, *Columbia Wanderer*, 41.
18. Simpson, 1931, 103.
19. Henry, 1897, 849; Henry, 1992, 693.
20. Franchère, 1967, 121.
21. Irving, 1836, ch. 56.
22. Henry, 1897, 789; Henry, 1992, 637.
23. Ibid., both.
24. Henry, 1897, 901; Henry, 1992, 732.
25. Henry, 1897, 891; Henry, 1992, 723.
26. Ibid., both.
27. Henry, 1897, 906; Henry, 1992, 736.
28. Ross, 1923, 83-84.
29. Henry, 1897, 902-03; Henry, 1992, 733.
30. Saum, 1965.
31. Cox, 1832, 296-97.
32. Swan, 1857, 209-10. Gibbs, 1877, 236, agreed.
33. Thompson, 1962, 368.

34. Ibid., 362.

35. White, 1848, 56-57.

36. Ross, 1923, 247, 252; Irving, 1836, ch. 60.

37. Ross, 1956, 17.

38. Ross, 1923, 256.

39. Ibid., 257-58.

40. Irving, 1836, ch. 60.

41. Ross, 1923, 259.

42. Franchère, 1968, 358.

43. Gibbs, 1955–56, 297.

44. Ibid., 299.

45. Henry, 1897, 878; Henry, 1992, 713.

46. Henry, 1897, 893.

47. Cox, 1957, 157-58. Henry, 1897, 896, calls her Jane Burns, which is corrected to Barnes, in Henry, 1992, 728. See also Henry, 1897, 908; Henry, 1992, 739.

48. Avery, 1951, 331. Avery quotes from Hudson's Bay Company Archives, File F 3/1, 1791–99, Leaf 194.

49. Franchère, 1968, 242; Simpson, 1931, 109.

50. Franchère, 1967, 110; Cox, 1957, 173; Irving, 1836, ch. 40.

51. Cox, 1957, 173; Franchère, 1967, 110.

52. Henry, 1897, 914-15; Henry, 1992, 747-48.

53. Henry, 1897, 836; Henry, 1992, 679-80; Lewis and Clark, *Journals*, Jan 27, 1806.

54. Henry, 1897, 825; Henry, 1992, 679.

55. Henry, 1897, 912; Henry, 1992, 742.

56. Henry, 1897, 917; Henry, 1992, 743-44.

57. Henry, 1897, 910; Henry, 1992, 739-40.

58. Ruby and Brown, 1976, 145.

59. Cox, 1957, 172; Franchère, 1967, 195; Thomas Nelson Strong, 1906, 73; Ross, 1956, 195.

60. Simpson, 1931, 101.

CHAPTER 17: The *Kin Chautch* Make a War

1. Sapir and Spier, 1930, 214-15; Franchère, 1967, 115; Gibbs, 1877, 189-90; Tolmie, 1932, 218.

2. Kane, 1971, *Columbia Wanderer*, 41.

3. Sapir and Spier, 1930, 214; Ray, 1938, 57.

4. Tolmie, 1932, 218-19.

5. Boas, 1894, 258; Curtis, 1911, 8:100.

6. Curtis, ibid., 8:89.

7. Henry, 1897, 880-81; Henry, 1992, 716.

8. Boas, 1901, 182-86, two versions.

9. Henry, 1897, 879; Henry, 1992, 715.

10. Barry, 1932, 143-44.

11. Franchère, 1967, 116.

12. Scouler, 1905, 167.

13. Ross, 1923, 90.

14. Corney, 1965, 149. See also Bishop, 1927, 279.

15. Butler, 1959; Cressman, 1960; W. Duncan Strong, et. al., 1930; Emory Strong, 1960; Seaman, 1946; *Screenings* (the journal of the Oregon Archaeological Society), various issues.

16. Pettigrew, 1990, 7:523.

17. Nayagogo: The theory that the name refers to battles is the author's. See Chapter 3, note 13.

18. Henry, 1897, 911; Henry, 1992, 715-16. See also Gibbs, 1877, 190-91.

19. Boas, 1894, 270.

20. Franchère, 1967, 116.

21. Lewis R. Williams, 1924, 30-36; Boas, 1894, 270.

22. Hajda, 1984, 180; Ray, 1938, 49, 55.

23. Boas, 1894, 271-74.

24. Curtis, 1911, 8:179.

25. Sapir, 1909, 205-27.

26. Thompson, 1962, 307; Henry, 1897, 808-09; Henry, 1992, 654.

27. James A. Teit, 1928, "The Middle Columbia Salish," *University of Washington Publications in Anthropology* 2(4):92-109; Berreman, 1937; Sapir and Spier, 1930, 160.

28. George Peter Murdock, 1939, "Tribal Distribution in Eastern Oregon," *American Anthropologist* 40:98-99; Berreman, 1938, "A Review of 'Tribal Distribution in Oregon.'" *Pacific Northwest Quarterly* 29(3):316-17; Bruce Rigsby, 1965, "Linguistic Relations on the Southern Plateau," Ph.D. dissertation, University of Oregon, 28, 58-59.

29. Stuart, 1935, 11.

30. Lewis and Clark, *Journals*, April 11 and 21, 1806; Thompson, 1962, 305, on July 28–29, 1811; Ross, 1923, 112-13, in July 1811.

31. Ross, ibid., 185.

32. Ibid., 120.

33. Ibid., 90, shows toll was the object.

34. Ross, 1956, 73.

35. Henry, 1897, 789; Henry, 1992, 636.
36. Henry, 1897, 853; Henry, 1992, 698; Ross, 1923, 267-71.
37. Henry, 1897, 784-855; Henry, 1992, 633-34; Ross, 1923, 263.
38. Henry, 1897, 792; Henry, 1992, 638-39.
39. Franchère, 1967, 94-95; Ross, 1923, 256.
40. Henry, 1992, 666.
41. Henry, 1897, 792-810; Henry, 1992, 639-56; Ross, 1923, 12-16; Franchère, 1967, 96-99; Cox, 1957, 173-74.
42. Henry, 1897, 821; Henry, 1992, 666.
43. Chickelos by Corney, 1965, 144; a Clatsop by Henry, 1897, 793, and Henry, 1992, 639; a Wahkiacum by Franchère, 1967, 47; a Shoalwater by Hunt, 1973.
44. Simpson, 1931, 104.
45. Ross, 1956, 13.
46. Ibid.
47. Henry, 1897, 796-97; Henry, 1992; 643.
48. Henry, 1897, 794; Henry, 1992, 640.
49. Henry, 1897, 798-79; Henry, 1992, 644-45.
50. Henry, 1897, 800; Henry, 1992, 645.
51. Franchère, 1967, 96.
52. Henry, 1897, 804; Henry, 1992, 648.
53. Henry, 1992, 651.
54. Henry, 1897, 806; Henry, 1992, 650; Franchère, 1967, 97.
55. Ross, 1956, 15.
56. Henry, 1992, 821.
57. Ross, 1956, 15.
58. Henry, 1992, 668-69; Franchère, 1967, 98.
59. Henry, 1897, 822-23; Henry, 1992, 668-70.
60. Ross, 1923, 267.
61. Simpson, 1931, 63, 95.
62. Ross, 1956, 78, 81; Simpson, 1931, 63.
63. Ross, 1956, 79.
64. Ibid., 108.
65. Ibid., 90-94.
66. Simpson, 1847, 1:164-67.

CHAPTER 18: Comcomly Buys Secrets

1. Ray, 1938, 90.
2. Ibid., 90-92. See also Olson, 1936.

3. Sapir and Spier, 1930, 236.

4. Dunn, 1845, 128.

5. Ray, 1938, 91.

6. Sapir and Spier, 1930, 222-23.

7. Fort George Census, in Simpson, 1931, 170; Gibbs, 1877, 188-89 (Puget Sound figure). See also Tolmie, 1932, 205-27. The only work on slavery in the area, H. F. Hunt, 1918, "Slavery Among the Indians of Northwest America," *Washington Historical Quarterly* 9:277-83, gives only two quotes from Franchère on Chinook practices.

8. Hajda, 1984, 206. However, Boas, 1901, 55-56, and Boas, 1894, 262-63, suggests otherwise.

9. James A. Teit, 1928, "The Middle Columbia Salish," *University of Washington Publications in Anthropology* 2(4):113.

10. Ray, 1938, 51-54.

11. Swan, 1857, 166-68.

12. Franchère, 1967, 241; Parker, 1967, 247; Kane, 1971, *Columbia Wanderer*, 36.

13. Simpson, 1931, 101.

14. Curtis, 1911, 8:88-89.

15. Irving, 1836, ch. 40.

16. Boas, 1901, 166.

17. Jacobs, 1958, 479; Ray, 1938, 52.

18. Sapir and Spier, 1930, 223; Curtis, 1911, 89; Ray, 1938, 54.

19. Morton, 1854, 2:321.

20. Boas, 1894, 206; Gibbs, 1955–56, 137-38.

21. Gibbs, ibid., 137; he heard this from James C. Strong.

22. Ray, 1938, 83.

23. Curtis, 1911, 8:92.

24. Ray, 1938, 83.

25. Paul Wingert, 1952, 9.

26. Townsend, 1970, Oct. 1835.

27. Ross, 1923, 96.

28. Curtis, 1911, 8:92.

29. Franchère, 1967, 119.

30. Corney, 1965, 145.

31. Parker, 1967, 193-94; Spencer, 1950, 21.

32. Wilkes, 1845–48, 5:128 has pictures of power boards. Wingert, 1952, has pictures of batons. See also Silas Smith, 1901, 260-61; Norman Feder, 1971, *Two Hundred Years of North American Indian Art* (New York: Praeger).

33. Boas, 1893, 40.

34. Boas, 1894, 205-10.

35. Ray, 1938, 86.

36. Boas, 1894, 209.

37. Sapir and Spier, 1930, 241.

38. Boas, 1894, 209.

39. Sapir and Spier, 1930, 245.

40. Jacobs, 1958, 511, 512.

41. Boas, 1894, 197.

42. Jacobs, 1958, 651, n. 464.

43. Jacobs, ibid., 513.

44. Sapir and Spier, 1930, 248.

45. Boas, 1894, 200-11.

46. Ray, 1938, 87.

47. Ray, ibid., 89.

48. Boas, 1894, 209.

49. Lee and Frost, 1968, 64.

50. Corney, 1965, 114-40.

51. Henry, 1897, 759; Franchère, 1967, 178.

52. Ruby and Brown, 1976, 145.

53. Thomas Nelson Strong, 1906, 93-96.

54. Corney, 1965, 144; Scouler, 1905, 165-66, 168.

55. See Chapter 24, note 10.

CHAPTER 19: Where Conjurers Assemble

1. Jacobs, 1958, 534.

2. Cox, 1957, 166.

3. Ray, 1938, 80-85; Curtis, 1911, 8:101-04.

4. Boas, 1894, 147-48; Alvord, 1855, 5:652.

5. Boas, 1894, 262-63.

6. Ibid.

7. Gibbs, 1955–56, 125-27, 304; Thomas, 1935, 104; Blanchet, 1853, 28; Swan, 1857, 173.

8. Boas, 1901, 245-46.

9. Jacobs, 1959, 200-208.

10. Jacobs, 1958, 153-55; Boas, 1901, 126-28.

11. Hajda (Phillips), 1955.

12. Jacobs, 1962, 90-99

13. Boas, 1894, 24-25.

14. Hymes, 1958, 238.

15. Hymes, 1981, 309; and in general.

16. Jacobs, 1958, 241-46.

17. Ibid., 106-12.

18. Jacobs, 1959, 73, 80-81.

19. Elizabeth Derr Jacobs, 1959, *Nehalem-Tillamook Tales* (Eugene: University of Oregon), 47, n. 3.

20. Boas, 1894, 112; Boas, 1901, 117, 128, 141, 154.

21. Sapir, 1909, 65, 93, 103, 117, 139, 145, etc.

22. Jacobs, 1958, 226.

23. Boas, 1894, 223-24.

24. Ogden, 1933, 49.

25. Kane, 1971, *Frontier*, 123.

26. Jacobs, 1958, 109.

27. Sapir, 1909, 223.

28. Jacobs, 1958, 109.

CHAPTER 20: **Fort Vancouver Rules**

1. Henry, 1897, 827; Henry, 1992, 671-72.

2. Sapir and Spier, 1930, 222; Emory Strong, 1960, 33 (CL-9 in his list of village sites), the name quoting *Oregon Native Son*, Oct. 1899. Paul Kane rendered it Katchutequa.

3. Simpson, 1931, 122.

4. Boas, 1901, 182-86.

5. Alfred A. Cleveland, 1903, "Social and Economic History of Astoria," *Oregon Historical Quarterly* 4:131-49.

6. McLoughlin, 1941, 28; Simpson, 1931, 253.

7. Simpson, ibid., 98, 253.

8. Work, 1914.

9. See Chapter 8, note 12.

10. Hale, 1846; Hale, 1890.

11. Gilbert M. Sproat, quoted in Bancroft, 1883, 3:632-33.

12. Boas, 1933.

13. Ranald McDonald, 1923, 76-79.

14. Ibid., 76.

15. Ibid., 78.

16. Boas, 1911, 598.

17. Thomas, 1935, 160.

18. Swan, 1857, 55.

19. Simpson, 1931, 104; Scouler, 1905,176, 203.

20. Ruby and Brown, 1976, 178; attributed to Josiah Sturgess.

21. Scouler, 1905, 276-77.

22. Boyd, 1990, 7:138.

23. Simpson, 1931, 170.

24. Slacum, 1972.

25. Kane, 1971, *Frontier*, 104, 106, in May 1847.

26. Simpson, 1931, 97, 104.

27. Ibid., 104.

28. Jacobs, 1945, *Kalapuya Texts* (Seattle: University of Washington Press), 161.

29. Ibid.

30. Simpson, 1931, 87.

31. Franchère, 1968, 109.

32. Spencer, 1933.

33. Franchère, 1967, 109.

34. See Ross, 1923, 106; H. S. Lyman, 1900; Emory Strong, 1960, 29.

35. Spencer, 1933.

36. Simpson, 1931, 187; Kane, 1971, *Columbia Wanderer*, 21.

37. Kane, ibid., 23.

38. Simpson, 1931, 95.

39. Saylor, 1900, "Nations No More"; *Oregonian*, 1899; Ranald McDonald, 1923, 74-77 n.; Ermatinger, 1914.

40. Douglas, 1904–05, 5:254.

41. McLoughlin, 1941, 48, in 1827.

42. Simpson, 1931, 109.

43. Ibid., 110.

44. Kane, 1925, 111; Douglas, 1904–05, 6:223-24.

45. Kane, ibid.

46. White, 1848, 60-61; Townsend, 1970, *Narrative of a Journey*, 21:338-39.

47. Townsend, ibid., 21:361.

48. Simpson, 1931, 99.

49. Ibid.

50. Ibid., 101.

CHAPTER 21: Now They Were Sitting on Their Frog's Croak

Title: Jacobs, 1958, 313-14.

1. Kelly, 1955.

2. James C. Strong, 1893, 134-35.

3. Swan, 1857, 169-70.

4. Gibbs, 1877, 210.

5. Ranald McDonald, 1923, 78.

6. Parker, 1967, 247.

7. Howay, 1933; Howay, 1934.

8. Scouler, 1905, 277.

9. McLoughlin, 1941; McLoughlin, 1958. Various dates in both collections.

10. McLoughlin, 1958, 47.

11. Samuel A. Clarke, 1902, *Pioneer Days of Oregon History* 1:232-33 (Portland); Chuck Williams, 1980, 88.

12. McLoughlin, 1941, 71-73, 81, 82; Johanson, 1946; Silas Smith, 1900, "Wreck of the Bark *William and Ann*"; Howay, 1934.

13. Corney, 1965, 148.

14. McLoughlin, 1958, 31, entry for Aug. 5, 1829. See also Reid, 1994, 86 n. 3.

15. Howay, 1934, 11.

16. Simpson, 1931, 110.

17. William C. Sturtevant, gen. ed., 1998. *Handbook of North American Indians.* (Washington, D. C.: Smithsonian Institution), 15:421.

18. Boyd, 1990, 7:136. But see also Eugene Arima and John Dewhurst, "Nootka of Vancouver Island," in Suttles, 1990, 7:408 for a far higher estimate.

19. Lewis and Clark, *Journals* (Moulton, 6:483-87).

20. Mooney, 1928, 15-17.

21. Russell Thornton, Tim Miller, and Jonathan Warren, 1991, "American Indian Population Recovery Following Small Pox Epidemics, *American Anthropologist* 93:28-45.

22. Morse, 1822, 368-70.

23. Simpson, 1931, 170.

24. Ibid., 94.

25. Kalama, Skilloot, Multnomah, Clackamas, Clowewalla and Charcowah, and Shahala and White Salmon by Lewis and Clark, *Journals* (Moulton, 6:498-505); Clatsop, Shoalwater, Wahkiacum, Kathlamet, Quathlapootle, and Wasco by Morse, 1822, 371; Wishram by Stuart, 1935, in 1812, shown as 300 fighting men, which I have multiplied by five for total population.

26. Swan, 1857, 156-58; Kane, 1971, *Columbia Wanderer*, 36-37; Ray, 1938, 96-97; Sapir and Spier, 1930, 267-68; Lewis and Clark, *Journals*, Clark, March 9, 1805, and April 18, 1806.

27. Sapir, 1909, 292-94.

28. Kane, 1971, *Columbia Wanderer*, 37.

29. Kane, 1971, *Frontier*, 96.

30. Simpson, 1931, 104. See also Franchère, 1968, 30-31.

31. Thomas Nelson Strong, 1906, 129-30.

32. Jacobs, 1958, 313-34.

33. Swan, 1857, 367-69.

34. Gibbs, 1877, 157-241.

CHAPTER 22: Tales of Hunger, Fears of Dying

1. Sapir, 1909, 244-45.

2. Jacobs, 1958, 458-61. See also Boas, 1901, 207-15.

3. Curtis, 1911, 8:96-99.

4. Ibid., 8:98.

5. Boas, 1894, 13. Bishop, 1927, also noted this position.

6. Canoe burial was described by all sources. Box burial was described by Bishop, 1927, 278; and by Edward Bell, clerk of Broughton's ship, quoted in Barry, 1932, 38.

7. W. Duncan Strong, 1945.

8. Lewis and Clark, *Journals*, October 31, 1805.

9. Thefts: Curtis, 1911, 8:99; Fish bones: W. Duncan Strong, et al., 1930, 40.

10. Scouler, 1905, 279-80.

11. Sapir and Spier, 1930, 272.

12. Swan, 1857, 189.

13. Butler, 1957.

14. Boas, 1894, 256-58.

15. Jacobs, 1958, 483.

16. Boas, 1894, 258.

17. Jacobs, 1958, 141-42.

18. Wilkes, 1845–48, 5:117-18.

19. Sapir, 1909, 95-99.

20. Dunn, 1845, 114-15, 135.

21. Boas, 1901, 241-44. See also Swan, 1857, 83-85; Henry, 1897, 857-58; Henry, 1992, 701.

22. Boas, 1901, 244.

CHAPTER 23: *Cole Sik, Waum Sik*

1. Wasusgani references are from Jacobs, 1958, 546-47. She was the mother of his respondent, Elizabeth Howard.

2. McLoughlin, 1958, 145; McLoughlin, 1941, 92, Sept. 25, 1830.

3. Simpson, 1931, 323; McLoughlin, 1958, 100.

4. Simpson, 1931, 325; McLoughlin, 1941, 83-85, Aug. 5, 1830.

5. Simpson, 1931, 323-24.

6. Lee and Frost, 1968, 108-09; Wilkes, 1845–48, 5:104.

7. See Chapter 14, note 17.

8. Wilkes, 1845–48, 5:140.

9. Kane, 1971, *Frontier*, Portrait Log no. 25, Appendix 2, among others. Plowing began in 1826, see McLoughlin, 1941, 31.

10. Lee and Frost, 1968, 132.

11. Douglas, 1904–05, 192. On October 11 he wrote that the epidemic started eleven weeks earlier.

12. Jacobs, 1958, 546-47.

13. Townsend, 1970, *Narrative of a Journey*, 333.

14. Mcloughlin, 1941, 88.

15. Kane, 1971, *Columbia Wanderer*, 21.

16. Douglas, 1904–05, 292, 303.

17. McLoughlin, 1941, 88.

18. Fort George Report, in Simpson, 1931, 170.

19. Wilkes, 1845–48, 4:370.

20. Ogden, 1853, 102.

21. Source lost. If found, please inform author.

22. Ranald McDonald, 1923, 76.

23. Cook, 1955, 303-15, 321-22.

24. McLoughlin, 1941, 96; McLoughlin, 1958, 163-64, 166.

25. McLoughlin, 1958, 153; McLoughlin, 1941, 150.

26. Sapir, 1909, 139-45; Jacobs, 1958, 409-17.

27. McLoughlin, 1941, 100; McLoughlin, 1958, 217.

28. McLoughlin, 1941, 104; Townsend, 1970, *Narrative of a Journey*, 333.

29. McLoughlin, 1941, 115.

30. Townsend, 1970, *Narrative of a Journey*, 333.

31. Ibid.

32. Alice Bay Maloney, ed., 1945, *Fur Brigade to the Bonaventure: John Work's California Expedition, 1832–33*, (San Francisco: California Historical Society).

33. Douglas, 1904–05, 306-07; McLoughlin, 1941, 104.

34. John Work, in Maloney, ed., 1945, *Fur Brigade to the Bonaventure*, cited in Cook, 1955. See also Ogden, 1853, 103.

35. Ogden, 1853, 71.

36. Cook, 1955; Larsell, 1947; H. H. Stage and C. M. Gjullin, 1935, "Anopheles and Malaria in the Pacific Northwest," *Northwest Science*, 9:5-11; Edward W. Twichell, 1925, "The California Pandemic of 1833," *California and Western Medicine*, May, 7; Scott, 1928; Boyd, 1990.

37. Tolmie, 1932.

38. Townsend, 1970, *Narrative of a Journey*, 343. See also Virgil J. Vogel, 1970, *American Indian Medicine* (Norman: University of Oklahoma Press); Eric Sloan, 1965, *A Reverence for Wood* (New York: Funk & Wagnalls).

39. Kane, 1971, *Frontier*, Portrait Log no. 25, Appendix 2.

40. Cook, 1955.

41. Larsell, 1947.

42. Jack Warren, Oregon State Vector Control biologist, interview by the author, April 21, 1983.

43. Ibid.

44. Lewis and Clark, *Journals*, Dec. 26, 1805.

45. David Kittleson, University of Hawaii Library, letter to the author, Oct. 19, 1973.

46. McLoughlin, 1941, 88.

47. *Isabella*, May 2: McLoughlin, 1958, 117. *Eagle*, June 10: ibid., 119.

48. Jack Warren, interview by the author, April 21, 1983.

49. Ibid.

50. Wyeth, 1899, Jan. 10-23, 1832.

51. McLoughlin, 1941, 232-33.

52. Wyeth, 1899, 149.

53. They were lucky: author's unsubstantiated opinion.

54. Thomas Nelson Strong, 1906, 80.

55. Landerholm, 1956, 84.

CHAPTER 24: Comcomly's Skull

1. Fred W. Powell, 1917, "Hall J. Kelley in Oregon," *Oregon Historical Quarterly* 18:326.

2. See drawing, Wilkes, 1845–48, 4:343.

3. Townsend, 1970, *Narrative of a Journey*, 338-39, 361; White, 1848, 60-61; Kane, 1925, 111; Kane, 1971, *Columbia Wanderer*, 40; Harvey, 1939.

4. Stewart, 1960.

5. Ibid.

6. *Oregonian*, 1899.

7. Thomas Nelson Strong, 1906, 5.

8. McLoughlin, 1941, 128-29.

9. Ranald McDonald, 1923.

10. Parker, 1967, 253-55; Kane, 1971, *Columbia Wanderer*, 40-41; Townsend, 1970, *Narrative of a Journey*, 339-41.

11. Townsend, ibid., 339-41; Parker, 1967, 253-55.

12. Parker, 1967, 255.
13. Wilkes, 1845–48, 4:369-70.
14. Kane, 1971, *Columbia Wanderer*, 40; Kane, 1925, 98.
15. Spencer, 1933.
16. *Oregon City Free Press*, Dec. 12, 1848.
17. Boyd, 1994; Boyd, 1990.
18. Barry, 1933.
19. Kane, 1971, *Frontier*, 104, 106.
20. Saum, 1965, quoting a letter from Archibald McDonald to a friend in the East, April 1836. See also Ross, 1923, 196-98.
21. Parker, 1967, 250.
22. Swan, 1857, 102. Lucile McDonald, 1966, 38, supplies his name.
23. Jacobs, 1958, 563.
24. Blanchet, in Landerholm, 1956, 83.
25. Swan, 1857, 295.
26. Jacobs, 1958, 539, 542-43.
27. Swan, 1857, 108.
28. Ibid., 167. See also 156-57.
29. Gibbs, 1967, 35.
30. Curtis, 1911, 8:86.
31. Parker, 1967, 274.
32. Lee and Frost, 1968, 314.
33. Ibid., 283-85, 321.
34. Thomas Nelson Strong, 1906, 143-45.
35. Landerholm, 1956, 84.
36. Jacobs, 1958, 539-42.
37. Wilkes, 1845–48, 4:388.
38. Joseph Lane, first territorial governor of Oregon, quoted in Henry R. Schoolcraft, ed. 1851–7. *History, Conditions and Prospects of the Indian Tribes of the United States* (Philadelphia: Bureau of Indian Affairs), 1:66.
39. Kane, 1971, *Columbia Wanderer*, 21.
40. Gibbs, 1967, 35.
41. Joseph Drayton, the artist with United States Exploring Expedition, quoted in Wilkes, 1845–48, 4:382.
42. Chuck Williams, 1980, 104.
43. Jacobs, 1958, 548-50.
44. Gustavus Hines, 1851, *Oregon, its History, Condition and Prospects* (Buffalo: George Derby Co.), 91-92.

45. Gibbs, 1967, 35.

46. Lucile McDonald, 1966, 55-56.

47. Herman, et al., 1900.

48. Ranck, 1926.

49. Jacobs, 1958, 550-53.

50. Ibid., 553.

51. See Terrence O'Donnell, 1991, *An Arrow in the Earth: General Joel Palmer and the Indians of Oregon* (Portland: Oregon Historical Society Press).

52. French, 1961, 421-23.

53. Wilkes, 1845–48, 5:121.

54. Kane, 1925, 98.

55. John Donovan, 1962.

56. Rubin, 1984, "Something to Carp About," *Oregonian*, "Northwest Magazine," May 27, 12-13.

57. Thomas, 1935.

58. Hale, 1846; Hale, 1890.

59. Gibbs, 1863.

60. Eells, 1894.

61. Thomas, 1935, 27.

62. Hale, 1846, 6:644.

63. Hajda, 1991, 99.

64. Eells, 1894.

65. J. K. Gill, quoted in Pilling, 1893.

66. George H. Himes, 1905, "Origin of Word 'Multnomah," *Orchard and Farm*, Aug.; Sharon Nesbit, 1976, "Indian John: Last of the Multnomahs," *Gresham Outlook*, May 24; Oregon Historical Society vertical file, "Indian John" (see OHS photograph, "Chief John," ORHI 26175, loc/orig. 0333P137).

67. Chuck Williams, 1980, 53. Her name comes from a display at the Wanapum Museum, Vantage, Wash.

68. Boas, 1894, 268.

69. Rubin, 1989.

70. Stewart, 1960, 563-76.

71. Mae Miller, Clatsop County Historical Society, interview by the author, 1974.

72. Stephen A. Meriwether, 1972, Ilwaco, Washington, *Tribune*, Sept. 20, 1972.

73. Jacobs, 1958, 166, 375.

74. Cultee sometimes used this ending. See Boas, 1894, 112; Boas, 1901, 17, 128, 141, 154.

A Select Bibliography of the Chinook

Adams, Barbara. 1958. "The Cascade Indians." B.A. thesis, Reed College.

Alvord, Major B. 1855. "Concerning the Manners and Customs, the Superstitions etc. of the Indians of Oregon." In *History, Conditions and Prospects of the Indian Tribes of the United States*, ed. Henry R. Schoolcraft, 5:651-57. Philadelphia: Bureau of Indian Affairs.

Ames, Kenneth. 1990-92. "The Past Revealed," a series of articles in the *Oregonian*:

> May 9, 1991. "Indians constructed wooden houses." 3F.

> May 30, 1991. "Archaeologists hunt economic answers in food." 2E.

> Jan. 23, 1992. "Archaeologists fish for clues to when salmon took key role." 3B.

> March 26, 1992. "Art of northwest coast had distinctive style." 2D.

Ames, Kenneth M., Doria F. Raetz, Stephen Hamilton, and Christine McAffee. 1992. "A Southern Northwest Coast Plank House." *Journal of Field Archaeology* 19(3):275-90.

Avery, Mary W. 1951. "An Additional Chapter on Jane Barnes." *Washington Historical Quarterly* 42:330-32.

Bancroft, Hubert Howe. 1883. *The Native Races of the Pacific States of North America*. 1:150-54, 222-49. See also 3:155-57, 519-20, 626-32. San Francisco: A. L. Bancroft & Co.

Barry, J. Neilson. 1926. "Broughton on the Columbia in 1792." *Oregon Historical Quarterly* 27:397-411.

———. 1927. "The Indians of Oregon—Geographic Distribution of Linguistic Families." *Oregon Historical Quarterly* 28:49-61.

———. 1927. "The Indians of Washington—Geographic Distribution of Linguistic Families." *Oregon Historical Quarterly* 28:147-162.

———. 1932. "Columbia River Exploration, 1792." *Oregon Historical Quarterly* 33:31-42, 143-155.

———. 1933. "Astorians Who Became Permanent Settlers." *Washington Historical Quarterly* 24:296-301.

Berreman, Joel. 1937. "Tribal Distribution in Oregon." *Memoirs of the American Anthropological Association* no. 47.

Bishop, Captain Charles. 1927. "Journal of the Ship Ruby." Ed. T. C. Elliott. *Oregon Historical Quarterly* 28:258-80.

———. 1967. *The Journal and Letters of Capt. Charles Bishop on the Northwest Coast of America, etc. 1794–1799.* Ed. Michael Roe. Hakluyt Society. England: Cambridge University Press.

Blanchet, Father François Norbert. 1853. *Pronouncing Dictionary and Jargon Vocabulary to speak the Chinook Jargon.* Portland: S. J. McCormick. Reprinted as an appendix in Paul Kane, 1971, *Columbia Wanderer.*

Boas, Franz. 1891. "Physical Characteristics of the Indians of the North Pacific Coast." *American Anthropologist* 4:25-32.

———. 1893. "Doctrine of Soul and Disease Among the Chinook." *Journal of American Folklore* 6:39-43.

———. 1893. "Notes on the Chinook Language." *American Anthropologist* 6:56-63.

———. 1894. *Chinook Texts.* Bureau of American Ethnology Bulletin 20. Washington, D. C.

———. 1901. *Kathlamet Texts.* Bureau of American Ethnology Bulletin 26. Washington, D. C.

———. 1904. "The Vocabulary of the Chinook Language." *American Anthropologist* (ns) 6:118-47.

———. 1911. "Introduction" and "Chinook." In *Handbook of American Indian Languages*, Bureau of American Ethnology Bulletin 40, 1:1-79 and 563-677. Washington, D. C.

———. 1933. "Notes on the Chinook Jargon." *Language* 9:208-13.

Boit, John. 1921. "Log of the Columbia Rediviva." In "Voyages of the Columbia to the Northwest Coast," ed. F. W. Howay, *Oregon Historical Quarterly* 22:306-312. See also *Oregon Historical Quarterly* 22:352-58, "Remnant of Official Log of the Columbia," annotated by T. C. Elliot.

Boyd, Robert T. 1975. "Another Look at the 'Fever and Ague' of Western Oregon." *Ethnohistory* 22(2):135-53.

———. 1990. "Demographic History, 1774–1874." In Wayne Suttles, ed., *Northwest Coast*, Volume 7 of *Handbook of North American Indians*, gen. ed. William C. Sturtevant, 7:135-49. Washington, D. C.: Smithsonian Institution.

———. 1994. "The Pacific Northwest Measles Epidemic of 1847–1848." *Oregon Historical Quarterly* 95:6-47.

———. 1998. "Demographic History Until 1990." In Donald E. Walker, Jr., ed., *Plateau*, Volume 12 of *Handbook of North American Indians*, gen. ed. William C. Sturtevant, 12:467-83. Washington, D. C.: Smithsonian Institution.

Boyd, Robert T. and Yvonne P. Hajda. 1987. "Seasonal Population Movement Along the Lower Columbia River: The Social and Ecological Context." *American Ethnologist* 14(2): 309-26.

Broughton, Lieutenant William. See Captain George Vancouver, 1798, *A Voyage of Discovery to the North Pacific Ocean and Round the World.* See also J. Neilson Barry, 1926, "Broughton on the Columbia in 1792"; and 1932, "Columbia River Exploration, 1792."

Butler, B. Robert. 1957. "Art of the Lower Columbia Valley." *Archaeology* 10:158-65.

———. 1959. "Lower Columbia Valley Archaeology." *Tebiwa* (publication of the Idaho State College Museum) v. 2.

Carver, G. M. 1899. "Poisoned Arrows: How the Indians Secured the Venom." *Oregon Native Son* 1:307-8.

Clark, Ella. 1952. "The Bridge of the Gods in Fact and Fancy." *Oregon Historical Quarterly* 53:29-38.

Clark, William. See Meriwether Lewis and William Clark, *Journals of the Lewis and Clark Expedition.*

Cook, S. F. 1955. *The Epidemic of 1830–33 in California and Oregon.* Berkeley: University of California.

Corney, Peter. 1965. *Early Voyages in the North Pacific.* Fairfield, Wash.: Ye Galleon Press. Originally published in 1821 as "Voyages to the North Pacific, 1813–18," in *London Literary Gazette.*

Cosminsky, Sheila Claire. 1964. "An Analysis of Wasco-Wishram Mythology." M.A. thesis, Washington State University.

Cox, Ross. 1832. *Adventures on the Columbia.* New York: privately published.

———. 1957. *The Columbia River.* Eds. Edgar I. Stewart and Jane R. Stewart. Norman: University of Oklahoma Press.

Cressman, Luther S. 1948. "Lower Columbia Indian Weapons." *Oregon Historical Quarterly* 49:297-98.

———. 1960. *Cultural Sequences at The Dalles, Oregon.* Philadelphia: American Philosophical Society.

———. 1962. *The Sandal and the Cave.* Portland: Beaver Books.

Curtin, Jeremiah. See Edward Sapir, 1909, *Wishram Texts.*

Curtis, Edward. 1911. *The North American Indian,* 8:85-154, 172-83, 198-205. Norwood, Mass.: Plimpton Press.

Dennis, Elsie F. 1930. "Indian Slavery in the Pacific Northwest." *Oregon Historical Quarterly* 31:69-81, 181-95, 285-96.

Donovan, John. 1962. "Mt. Coffin history." *Screenings* (Journal of the Oregon Archaeological Society) 11:3. January.

Douglas, David. 1904–05. "Journal and Letters of David Douglas: Second Journey to the Northwest Parts of the Continent of North America, 1829–33." *Oregon Historical Quarterly* 5:215-71, 325-69; 6:76-97, 206-27, 288-309, 417-49.

———. 1914. *Journal, 1823–27, 1833–34.* London: Royal Horticultural Society.

Driver, Harold Edson and James L. Coffin. 1975. "Classification and Development of North American Indian Cultures: a Statistical Analysis of the Driver-Massey Sample." In *Transactions of the American Philosophical Society.* Philadelphia.

Drucker, Philip. 1965. "The Mercantile Chinook." In *Cultures of the North Pacific Coast,* 168-74. San Francisco: Chandler Publishing Co.

Duflot de Mofras, Eugène. 1844. *Exploration du Territoire De L'Oregon, California . . . .* Paris: Arthur Betrand.

————. 1937. *Travels on the Pacific Coast.* Ed. and trans. Marguerite Eyer Wilbur. Santa Ana, California: Fine Arts Press.

Dunn, John. 1845. *History of the Oregon Territory and British North-American Fur Trade.* Philadelphia: G. B. Zieber.

Durham, Bill. 1960. *Canoes & Kayaks of Western America.* Seattle: Copper Canoe Press.

Dye, Eva Emery. 1899. "The Chinook Jargon." *Oregon Native Son* v. 1, Aug.

Eells, Myron. 1886. "Stone Age in Oregon." *Smithsonian Report* 283-95.

————. 1894. "The Chinook Jargon." *American Anthropologist* 7:300-12.

Elliott, T. C. 1917. "The Log of HMS *Chatham*," *Oregon Historical Quarterly* 28:231-43.

————. 1932. "The Chinook Wind." *Oregon Historical Quarterly* 33:243-49.

Emmons, George Falconer. 1854. "Replies to Inquiries Respecting the Indian tribes of Oregon and California." In *History, Conditions and Prospects of the Indian Tribes of the United States,* ed. Henry R. Schoolcraft, 3:200-225. Philadelphia: Bureau of Indian Affairs.

Ermatinger, C. O. 1914. "The Columbia River Under HBC Rule." *Washington Historical Quarterly* 5:192-206.

Fee, Chester Anders. 1941. "Oregon's Historical Esperanto—The Chinook Jargon." *Oregon Historical Quarterly* 42:176-85.

Franchère, Gabriel. 1967. *Adventure at Astoria, 1810–14.* Trans. Hoyt Franchère. Norman: University of Oklahoma Press.

————. 1968. *Narrative of a Voyage to the Northwest Coast of America in the Years 1811, 1812, 1813 and 1814, or the First American Settlement on the Pacific.* Ed. Milo Milton Quaife. New York: Citadel Press. The original 1854 edition was translated and edited by J. V. Huntington. (New York: Redfield).

French, David H. 1958. "Cultural Matrices of Chinookan Non-Casual Languages." *International Journal of American Linguistics* 24(4):258-63.

————. 1961. "Wasco-Wishram." In *Perspectives in American Indian Cultural Change,* ed. Edward H. Spicer, 337-430. Chicago: University of Chicago.

French, David H. and Katherine S. French. 1998. "Wasco, Wishram and Cascades." In Donald E. Walker, Jr., ed., *Plateau,* Volume 12 of *Handbook of North American Indians,* gen. ed. William C. Sturtevant, 12:360-77. Washington, D. C.: Smithsonian Institution.

Gairdner, Dr. Meredith. 1841. "Notes on the Geography of the Columbia River." *Journal of the Royal Geographical Society.* 11:250-57. London.

Gass, Patrick. 1958. *Journal of Patrick Gass.* Minneapolis: Ross & Haines.

Gibbs, George. 1863. *A Dictionary of the Chinook Jargon.* Smithsonian Miscellaneous Collection 161. Washington, D. C.

———.1877. "Tribes of Western Washington and Northwestern Oregon." *Contributions to North American Ethnology* 1:157-241.

———.1955–56. "George Gibbs' Account of Indian Mythology of Oregon and Washington Territory." Ed. Ella E. Clark. *Oregon Historical Quarterly* 56:293-325, 57:125-67.

———.1967. *Indian Tribes of Washington Territory.* Fairfield, Wash.: Ye Galleon Press.

Greenberg, Joseph Harold. 1987. *Languages of the Americas.* Palo Alto: Stanford University Press.

Hajda, Yvonne P. (Phillips). 1955. "A Study of the Distribution of the Wishram Indian Myths." B.A. thesis, Reed College.

———.1984. "Regional Social Organization in the Greater Lower Columbia, 1792–1830." Ph.D. dissertation, University of Washington.

———.1990. "Southwestern Coast Salish." In Wayne Suttles, ed., *Northwest Coast*, Volume 7 of *Handbook of North American Indians*, gen. ed. William C. Sturtevant, 7:503-17. Washington, D. C.: Smithsonian Institution.

———.1991. "The Confederated Tribes of the Grand Ronde Community of Oregon." In Carolyn Buan and Richard Lewis, eds., *The First Oregonians*, 95-100. Portland: Oregon Council for the Humanities.

Hale, Horatio. 1846. *Ethnography and Philology.* Volume 6 of Lieutenant Charles Wilkes, USN, *Narrative of the U. S. Exploring Expedition During the Years 1838–42.* Philadelphia: Lea & Blanchard.

———.1890. *An International Idiom: A Manual of the Oregon Trade Language or Chinook Jargon.* London: Whittaker & Co.

Harvey, A. G. 1939. "Chief Comcomly's Skull." *Oregon Historical Quarterly* 40:161-67.

Henry, Alexander. 1897. "The Manuscript Journals of Alexander Henry, Fur Trader of the Northwest Company, and of David Thompson, Official Geographer of the Same Company." In Elliott Coues, *New Light on the Early History of the Greater Northwest*, 747-916. Minneapolis: Ross & Haines.

———.1992. *The Journal of Alexander Henry the Younger, 1799–1814*, vol. 2, *The Red River and the Journey to the Pacific.* Ed. Barry M. Gough. Toronto: The Champlain Society.

Herman, J. H., L. W. Coe, and Robert Williams. 1900. "The Cascade Massacre." *Oregon Native Son* 1:495-505.

Hodges, W. A., ed. 1907–10. *Handbook of the American Indian North of Mexico.* Washington, D. C.: Bureau of American Ethnography.

Howay, F. W. 1933. "Brig *Owhyhee* in the Columbia, 1827." *Oregon Historical Quarterly* 34:324-29.

———.1934. "Brig *Owhyhee* in the Columbia, 1829–30," *Oregon Historical Quarterly* 35:10-21.

———.1943. "Origin of the Chinook Jargon." *Oregon Historical Quarterly* 44:25-55.

Howay, F. W. (introduction and biographic note) and T. C. Elliott (footnotes), 1942. "Vancouver's Brig *Chatham* in the Columbia." *Oregon Historical Quarterly* 43:318-19, 326-27.

Hunt, Wilson Price. 1973. *The Overland Diary of Wilson Price Hunt.* Ed. Hoyt C. Franchère. Ashland: Oregon Book Society.

———.1935. *The Discovery of the Oregon Trail: Robert Stuart's Narratives and Account of the Tonguin's Voyage and Events at Astoria, 1811–12 and Wilson Price Hunt's Diary of his Overland Trip, 1811–12.* Ed. Philip Ashton Rollins. Translated from the 1821 Paris edition. New York: Charles Scribners' Sons.

Hymes, Dell H. 1955. "The Language of the Kathlamet Chinook." Ph.D. dissertation, University of Indiana at Bloomington.

———.1957. "Some Penutian Elements and the Penutian Hypothesis." *Southwest Journal of Anthropology* 13:69-87.

———.1958. "Linguistic Features Peculiar to Chinookan Myths." *International Journal of American Linguistics* 24:253ff.

———.1975. "Folklore's Nature and the Sun Myth." *Journal of American Folklore* 8:345-68.

———.1975. "From Space to Time in Tenses in Kiksht." *International Journal of American Linguistics* 41:313-30.

———.1981. *"In Vain I Tried To Tell You," Essays in Native American Ethnopoetics.* Philadelphia: University of Pennsylvania Press.

———.1983. "Poetic Structure of a Chinook Text." In *Essays in Honor of Charles Hocket,* 507-25. Leiden: E. J. Brill.

———.1985. "Language, Memory and Selective Performance in Cultee's 'Salmon Myth' as Twice Told to Boas." *Journal of American Folklore* 98:391-434.

———.1996. "Coyote, the Thinking (Wo)man's Trickster." In *Monsters, Tricksters, and Sacred Cows: Animal Tales and American Identities,* ed. A. James Arnold, 108-137. Charlottesville: University Press of Virginia.

Hymes, Dell and Henry Zenk. 1987. "Narrative Structure in Chinook Jargon." In *Pidgin and Creole Languages,* ed. Glenn G. Gilbert, 445-65. Honolulu: University of Hawaii.

Irving, Washington. 1836. *Astoria.* New York: G. P. Putnam. (There being many editions, end notes are referenced by chapter.)

Jacobs, Melville. 1932. "Notes on the Structure of the Chinook Jargon." *Language* 8:27-50.

————.1937. "Historical Perspectives in Indian Languages of Oregon and Washington." *Pacific Northwest Quarterly* 28:55-74.

————.1952. "Psychological Inferences from a Chinook Myth." *Journal of American Folklore* 65:121-37.

————.1955. "A Few Observations on the World View of the Clackamas Chinook Indians." *Journal of American Folklore* 68:283-89.

————.1958. *Clackamas Chinook Texts.* Bloomington: University of Indiana.

————.1959. *The Content and Style of an Oral Literature: Clackamas Chinook Myths and Tales.* Chicago: University of Chicago.

————.1960. *The People Are Coming Soon: Analysis of Clackamas Chinook Myths and Tales.* Seattle: University of Washington Press.

————.1962. "The Fate of Indian Oral Literature in Oregon." *Northwest Review* 5:90-99.

————.1964. "Indications of Mental Illness Among Pre-Contact Indians of the Northwest States." *Pacific Northwest Quarterly* 55:49-54.

Johanson, Dorothy O. 1946. "McLoughlin and the Indians." *The Beaver* 277:18-21.

Jones, Robert F. 1997. "The Identity of the *Tonquin*'s Interpreter." *Oregon Historical Quarterly* 98:296-314.

Jones, Roy F. 1872. *Wappato Indians, their history and prehistory.* Privately printed.

Kane, Paul. 1855. "The Chinook Indians." *Toronto Daily Colonist.* Aug. 6–9.

————.1925. *Wanderings of an Artist Among the Indians of North America.* Toronto: The Radisson Society of Canada.

————.1971. *Paul Kane's Frontier.* Austin, Texas: J. Russell Harper. Includes *Wanderings of an Artist.*

————.1971. *Columbia Wanderer.* Ed. Thomas Vaughan. (Includes "Lecture on the Chinook," 1855, and Fr. François Norbert Blanchet's "Pronouncing Dictionary and Jargon Vocabulary to speak the Chinook Jargon," reprinted as an appendix). Portland: Oregon Historical Society Press.

Kelly, Gail. 1955. "Themes in Wasco Culture." B.A. thesis, Reed College.

Keyser, James D. 1989. "Tsagaglalal: She Who Watches." Unpublished.

————.1992. *Indian Rock Art of the Columbia Plateau.* Seattle: University of Washington Press.

Krauss, Michael E. 1990. "Kwalhioqua and Clatskanie." In Wayne Suttles, ed., *Northwest Coast*, Volume 7 of *Handbook of North American Indians*, gen. ed. William C. Sturtevant, 7:530-32. Washington, D. C.: Smithsonian Institution.

Kroeber, A. L. 1934. "Native American Populations." *American Anthropologist* 36:1-25; table, 3.

————.1939. "Cultural and Natural Areas of Native North America." *University of California Publications in American Archaeology and Ethnography* v. 38 (map 6, accompanying). Berkeley.

LaBonte, Louis. 1900. "Reminiscences of Louis Labonte." Ed. H. S. Lyman. *Oregon Historical Quarterly* 1:169-88.

———. 1900. "Reminiscences of a Native Son." Ed. H. S. Lyman. *Oregon Native Son* 2:253.

Landerholm, Carl. 1956. *Notices and Voyages of the Famed Quebec Mission to the Pacific Northwest.* (Contains Blanchet, Demers, Bolduc, and Langlois journals). Portland: Oregon Historical Society Press.

Larsell, Olof. 1947. *The Doctor in Oregon.* Portland: Binfords & Mort.

Lee, Daniel, and Joseph H. Frost. 1968. *Ten Years in Oregon.* Fairfield, Wash.: Ye Galleon Press. The original edition was published for the authors in 1844. (New York).

Lewis, Albert Buell. 1906. *Tribes of the Columbia Valley and the Coast of Washington and Oregon.* American Anthropology Association v. I, part 2. Lancaster, Pennsylvania: New Era Printing Co.

Lewis, Meriwether and William Clark. *Journals of the Lewis and Clark Expedition.* The most comprehensive version is Gary E. Moulton, ed., 1983 (Lincoln: University of Nebraska); there are numerous other versions, including Reuben Gold Thwaites, ed., 1905; James K. Hosmer, ed., 1924; and a host of one-, two-, and three-volume editions. Because there are so many versions, end notes are referenced by the date of the journal entry, in most instances with page numbers in Moulton provided in parentheses.

Lyman, H. S. 1900. "Indian Names." *Oregon Historical Quarterly* 1:316-26.

Lyman, William D. 1910. *The Columbia River.* Portland: Binfords & Mort.

———. 1915. "Indian Myths of the Northwest." *Proceedings.* American Antiquarian Society. Worchester, Massachusetts. October.

McChesney, Charles E., et al. 1969. *The Roles of Certain Indian Tribes in Washington and Oregon.* Fairfield, Wash.: Ye Galleon Press.

McDonald, Lucile. 1966. *Coast Country.* Portland: Binfords & Mort.

McDonald, Ranald. 1923. *Ranald McDonald, 1824–1894.* Ed. William S. Lewis and Naojiro Murakami. Spokane: Eastern Washington Historical Society.

McLoughlin, Dr. John. 1941. *McLoughlin's Fort Vancouver Letters, 1st series: 1825–38.* Ed. E. E. Rich. London: HBC Record Society.

———. 1958. *Letters of Dr. John McLoughlin Written at Fort Vancouver, 1829–32.* Ed. Burt B. Barker. Portland: Binfords & Mort.

Mayer, Nancy. 1994. "Ilchee returns to river as 7-foot bronze." *Oregonian.* Oct. 30. C7.

Miller, Emma Gene. 1958. *Clatsop County, Oregon: A History.* Portland: Binfords & Mort.

Minor, Rick. 1983. "Columbia Estuary Chronology." In "Aboriginal Settlement and Subsistence at the Mouth of the Columbia River." Ph.D. thesis, University of Oregon.

Minor, Rick, Katherine Anne Toepel, and Stephen Dow Beckham. 1989. *Overview of Investigation at 45SA11, Archaeology of the Columbia River Gorge.* Eugene: Heritage Research Associates.

Mooney, James. 1928. "The Aboriginal Population of America North of Mexico." *Smithsonian Miscellaneous Collection* 80(7). Washington, D. C.

Morse, Reverend Jedidiah. 1822. *Report to the Secretary of War on Indian Affairs.* New Haven, Conn.: S. Converse.

Morton, Dr. Samuel George. 1854. "Physical Type of the American Indian" (with photographs of Chinook skulls). In *History, Conditions and Prospects of the Indian Tribes of the United States,* ed. Henry R. Schoolcraft, 2:315-35. Philadelphia: Bureau of Indian Affairs.

Ogden, Peter Skene. 1933. *Traits of American Indian Life and Character, by a Fur Trader.* San Francisco: Grabhorn Press. The original 1853 edition was published in London.

Olson, Ronald L. 1927. *Adze, Canoe & House Types of the Northwest Coast.* Seattle: University of Washington Press.

———. 1936. *The Quinault Indians.* Seattle: University of Washington Press.

Ordway, Sgt. John. 1916. *The Journal of Sergeant John Ordway.* Ed. Milo M. Quaife. Madison: State Historical Society of Wisconsin.

Oregonian. 1899. "Comcomly's Followers." Dec. 17.

———. 1905. "Tsin-is Tom, Last of Clatsops." Feb. 26. 22.

———. See also Kenneth Ames, Nancy Mayer, Glen Ranck, George H. Roberts, and Rick Rubin.

Oregon State University Extension Service. 1972. "Nutritive Values of Native Foods of the Warm Springs Indians." Circular 809. Corvallis.

Parker, Samuel. 1967. *Journal of an Exploring Tour Beyond the Rocky Mountains (1835–7).* Minneapolis: Ross & Haines. Originally published in 1838.

Pettigrew, Richard M. 1977, "Portland Basin Chronology." In "A Prehistoric Culture Sequence in the Portland Basin of the Lower Columbia Valley." Ph.D. thesis, University of Oregon.

———. 1990. "Prehistory of the Lower Columbia and Willamette Valley." In Wayne Suttles, ed., *Northwest Coast,* Volume 7 of *Handbook of North American Indians,* gen. ed. William C. Sturtevant, 7:518-29. Washington, D. C.: Smithsonian Institution.

Phebus, George E., Jr. and Robert M. Drucker. 1979. *Archaeological Investigations at Seaside Oregon.* Seaside, Oregon: Seaside Museum and History Society.

Phillips, W. S. 1913. *The Chinook Book.* Seattle: R. L. Davis Printing Co.

Pickering, Charles. 1863. *The Races of Man; and Their Geographic Distribution. New Edition to Which is Prefixed an Analytical Synopsis of the Natural History of Man, by John Charles Hall.* London: H. G. Bohn.

Pilling, James Constantine. 1893. *Bibliography of the Chinookan Languages Including the Chinook Jargon.* Bureau of Ethnology Bulletin 15. Washington, D. C.

Ramsey, Jarold W. 1977. *Coyote was Going There: Indian Literature of the Oregon Country.* Seattle: University of Washington Press.

Ranck, Glen. 1926. "Tribal Lore of the Wishram." *Oregonian.* Feb. 7, sec. 3, p. 9.

Ray, Verne F. 1937. "Historical Position of the Lower Chinook." *Pacific Northwest Quarterly* 28:363-72.

———. 1938. *Lower Chinook Ethnographic Notes.* Seattle: University of Washington Press.

———. 1975. "The Chinook Indians in the Early 1800s." In *The Western Shore, Oregon Country Essays*, ed. Thomas Vaughan, 120-50. Portland: Oregon Historical Society Press.

Reid, John Phillip. 1994. "Restraints of Vengeance: Retaliation In Kind and the Use of Indian Law in the Old Oregon Country." *Oregon Historical Quarterly* 95:48-92.

Rivera, Trinita. 1949. "Diet of a Food Gathering People." In *Indians of the Urban Northwest*, ed. Marian W. Smith, 19-36. New York: Columbia University Contributions to Anthropology.

Roberts, George H. 1880. "Sauvie Island." *Oregonian.* July 9.

Ross, Alexander. 1923. *Adventures of the First Settlers on the Oregon or Columbia River.* Reprint, ed. Milo Milton Quaife. Chicago: Lakeside Press. Originally published in 1849. (London: Smith & Eider).

———. 1956. *Fur Hunters of the Far West.* Ed. Kenneth A. Spaulding. Norman: University of Oklahoma Press.

Rubin, Rick. 1981. "Coyote on the Columbia." In *The Northwest Experience* 2:166-79. Seattle: Madrona Publishers.

———. 1983. "Deadly August." Portland: *Oregonian*, "Northwest Magazine." Aug. 14. 12-14.

———. 1985. "In Search of an Oregon Religion." *Sweet Reason* 4:20-26. Portland: The Oregon Commission for the Humanities.

———. 1986. "She Who Watches." Portland: *Oregonian*, "Northwest Magazine." Sept. 28. 4.

———. 1989. "Who Does She Belong to?" *Oregonian*, "Forum." Oct. 9. B7.

Ruby, Robert Holmes and John A. Brown. 1976. *The Chinook Indians: Traders of the Lower Columbia River.* Norman: University of Oklahoma Press.

Santee, J. J. 1932. "Comcomly and the Chinooks." *Oregon Historical Quarterly* 33:271-78.

Sapir, Edward. 1907. "Preliminary Report on the Language and Mythology of the Upper Chinook." *American Anthropologist* 533-44.

————. 1909. *Wishram Texts.* (Includes "Wasco Tales and Myths," collected by Jeremiah Curtin). Washington, D. C.: American Ethnological Society.

Sapir, Edward and Leslie Spier. 1930. *Wishram Ethnography.* Seattle: University of Washington Press.

Saum, Lewis O. 1965. *The Fur Trader and the Indian.* Seattle: University of Washington Press.

Saylor, F. H. 1900. "Bridge of the Gods." *Oregon Native Son* 1:417-23.

————. 1900. "Nations No More." *Oregon Native Son* 1:463-68.

————. 1900. "Legendary Lore of the Indians." *Oregon Native Son* 2:116-20, 198-202, 315-17, 417-21.

Schaeffer, Claude E. 1963. "William Brooks, Chinook Publicist." *Oregon Historical Quarterly* 64:41-54

Scharbach, Alexander. 1962. "Aspects of Existentialism in Clackamas Chinook Myths." *Journal of American Folklore* 75:15-22.

Scott, Leslie M. 1928. "Indian Diseases as Aids in Pacific Northwest Settlement." *Oregon Historical Quarterly* 29:144-61

Scouler, Dr. John. 1905. "Journal of a Voyage to Northwest America 1824–26." *Oregon Historical Quarterly* 6:162-77, 276-88.

Seaman, Norma G. 1946. *Indian Relics of the Pacific Northwest.* Portland: Binfords & Mort.

Seton, Alfred. 1835. "Life on the Oregon." *American Monthly.* May-July.

————. 1935. "Life on the Oregon." Ed. Fred S. Perrine. *Oregon Historical Quarterly* 36:187-204.

————. 1993. *Astorian Adventure: The Journal of Alfred Seton 1811–1815.* Ed. Robert F. Jones. New York City: Fordham University Press.

Shaw, George C. 1909. *The Chinook Jargon and How to Use It.* Seattle: Rainier Printing.

Sherriff, John. 1992. "John Sherriff on the Columbia, 1792." Ed. Andrew David. *Pacific Northwest Quarterly* 83:53-59.

Silverstein, Michael. 1972. "Chinookan Jargon: Language Contact and the Problem of Multi-Level Generative Systems." *Language* 48:378-406, 596-625.

————. 1974. "Dialectal Developments in Chinookan Tense-Aspect Systems: An Areal-Historical Sketch." *International Journal of American Linguistics* Memoir 29. 545-99.

————. 1990. "Chinookans of the Lower Columbia." In Wayne Suttles, ed., *Northwest Coast,* Volume 7 of *Handbook of North American Indians,* gen. ed. William C. Sturtevant, 7:533-46. Washington, D. C.: Smithsonian Institution.

Simpson, George. 1847. *Narrative of a Journey Round the World, 1841–42,* 1:164-77, 244-60. London: Henry Colburn.

————. 1931. *Fur Trade and Empire: George Simpson's Journal.* Ed. Frederick Merk. Cambridge: Harvard University Press.

Slacum, William A. 1972. "Memorial of William Slacum Praying Compensation for his Services in Obtaining Information in Relation to the Settlements on the Oregon River." *25th Congress, Senate Document #24.* (Dec. 18, 1837). Reprint. Fairfield, Wash.: Ye Galleon Press.

Slocum, Robert G. and Kenneth H. Matsen. 1968. *Shoto Clay: A Description of Clay Artifacts from the Herzog Site in the Lower Columbia Region.* Oregon Archaeological Society Publication 4. Portland: Binfords & Mort.

Smith, Harlan I. 1906. "Noteworthy Archaeological Specimens From the Lower Columbia Valley." *American Anthropologist* 8:298-307.

Smith, Marian W. 1943. "Columbia Valley Art Style." *American Anthropologist* (ns) 45:158-60.

———. 1949. "Basketry Design and the Columbia Valley Art Style." *Southwest Journal of Anthropology* 8:336ff.

———. 1949. *Indians of the Urban Northwest.* New York: Columbia University.

Smith, Silas. 1900. "Tales of Early Wrecks on the Oregon Coast." *Oregon Native Son* 1:443-46.

———. 1900. "Wreck of the Bark *William and Ann.*" *Oregon Native Son* 2:40-411.

———. 1901. "Primitive Customs and Religious Beliefs of the Indians of the Pacific Northwest Coast." *Oregon Historical Quarterly* 2:255-65.

Spencer, Omar C. 1933. "Chief Cassino." *Oregon Historical Quarterly* 34:19-30.

———. 1950. *The Story of Sauvie Island.* Portland: Oregon Historical Society Press.

Stewart, T. D. 1960. "The Chinook Sign of Freedom: A Study of the Skull of the Famous Chief Comcomly." *Smithsonian Report for 1959.* Washington, D. C. 563-76.

Strong, Emory. 1959. *Wakemap Mound.* Portland: Oregon Museum of Science and Industry.

———. 1960. *Stone Age on the Columbia.* Portland: Binfords & Mort.

———. 1972. "Earthquake & Landslide on the Columbia." *Geological Newsletter* v. 38, no. 10. Portland: Geological Society of the Oregon Country.

———. 1973. "Archaeological Evidence of Land Subsidence on the Northwest Coast." *Ore Bin* 35:109-14.

Strong, James C. 1893. *Wah-Kee-Nah and Her People.* New York: Putnams.

Strong, Thomas Nelson. 1906. *Cathlamet on the Columbia.* Portland: Binfords and Mort.

Strong, W. Duncan. 1945. "The Occurrence and Wider Implications of a 'Ghost Cult' on the Columbia River Suggested by Carvings in Wood, Bone and Stone." *American Anthropologist* 47:244-61.

Strong, W. Duncan and W. Egbert Schenck. 1925. "Petroglyphs Near The Dalles of the Columbia River." *American Anthropologist* 27:76-90.

Strong, W. Duncan, W. Egbert Schenck, and Julian H. Steward. 1930. "Archaeology of The Dalles-Deschutes Region." *University of California Publications in Anthropology* 29:1-154. Berkeley: University of California Press.

Stuart, Robert. 1935. *The Discovery of the Oregon Trail: Robert Stuart's Narratives and Account of the Tonguin's Voyage and Events at Astoria, 1811–12 and Wilson Price Hunt's Diary of his Overland Trip, 1811–12.* Translated from the 1821 Paris edition. Ed. Philip Ashton Rollins. New York: Charles Scribners' Sons.

———. 1953. *On the Oregon Trail.* Ed. Kenneth A. Spaulding. Norman: University of Oklahoma Press.

Suttles, Wayne. 1968. "Coping With Abundance—Subsistence on the Northwest Coast." In *Man the Hunter,* ed. Richard B. Lee and Irven Devore, 56-68. Chicago: Aldine Publishing Co.

———, ed. 1990. *Northwest Coast.* Volume 7 of *Handbook of North American Indians,* general ed. William C. Sturtevant. Washington, D. C.: Smithsonian Institution.

Swadesh, Morris. 1949. "The Linguistic Approach to Salish Prehistory." In *Indians of the Urban Northwest,* ed. Marian W. Smith, 161-71. New York: Columbia University Contributions to Anthropology.

———. 1956. "Problems of Long Range Comparison in Penutian." *Language* 32:17-41.

Swan, James G. 1857. *The Northwest Coast.* New York: Harper & Bro.

Taylor, Herbert C., Jr. 1963. "Aboriginal Populations of the Lower Northwest Coast." *Pacific Northwest Quarterly* 55:158-65.

Taylor, Herbert C., Jr., and Lester L. Hoaglin, Jr. 1969. "The 'Intermittent Fever' Epidemic of the 1830s on the Lower Columbia River." In Charles E. McChesney, et al., 1969, *The Rolls of Certain Indian Tribes in Washington and Oregon.* 160-78. Fairfield, Wash.: Ye Galleon Press.

Thomas, Edward Harper. 1935. *Chinook, A History & Dictionary.* Portland: Binfords & Mort.

Thompson, David. 1962. *Narrative, 1784–1812.* Ed. Richard Glover. Toronto: Champlain Society.

———. 1971. *Travels in Western North America, 1784–1812.* Ed. Victor G. Hopwood. Toronto: Macmillan of Canada.

Tolmie, Dr. William F. 1932. "Diary of William F. Tolmie." Ed. Edward Huggins. *Washington Historical Quarterly* 23:205-27.

Townsend, John Kirk. 1970. *Narrative of a Journey Across the Rocky Mountains to the Columbia River.* Reprint (first published in 1839 in Philadelphia). Fairfield, Wash.: Ye Galleon Press.

———. 1970. In *Early Western Travel, 1748–1846,* ed. Reuben Gold Thwaites, 21:121-369. Reprint (first published in 1905). Fairfield, Wash.: Ye Galleon Press.

Tuohy, Donald R. and Alan L. Bryan. 1958–59. "Southwest Washington Archaeology: an Appraisal." *Tebiwa* (publication of the Idaho State College Museum) 2:27-58.

Vancouver, Captain George. 1798. *A Voyage of Discovery to the North Pacific Ocean and Round the World.* 3 vol. London. 3:85ff. See also J. Neilson Barry, 1926, "Broughton on the Columbia in 1792;" and 1932, "Columbia River Exploration, 1792."

Walker, Donald E., Jr., ed. 1998. *Plateau.* Volume 12 of *Handbook of North American Indians,* general ed. William C. Sturtevant. Washington, D. C.: Smithsonian Institution.

Warre, Captain Henry. 1970. *Sketches in North America and the Oregon Territory.* Barre, Massachusetts: Imprint Society.

Warren, Claude R. 1958–59. "A Re-evaluation of Southwest Washington Archaeology." *Tebiwa* (publication of the Idaho State College Museum) 2:9-26.

———. 1960. "Housepits and Village Patterns in the Columbia Plateau and Southwest Washington." *Tebiwa* (publication of the Idaho State College Museum) 3, no. 1, no. 2.

Warren, Esther. 1977. *The Columbia Gorge Story.* Newport, Oregon.

White, Elija. 1848. *Ten Years in Oregon.* Ed. A. J. Allen. Ithaca, New York: Mack, Andrus Co.

Whitehouse, Private Joseph. 1905. "Journal." In *Original Journals of the Lewis and Clark Expedition,* ed. Reuben Gold Thwaites. New York: Dodd, Mead.

Wilkes, Lieutenant Charles, USN. 1845–48. *Narrative of the United States Exploring Expedition During the Years 1838–1842.* Philadelphia: Lea & Blanchard.

Williams, Chuck. 1980. *Bridge of the Gods, Mountains of Fire.* White Salmon, Washington: Elephant Mountain Arts.

Williams, Lewis R. 1924. *Chinook by the Sea.* Ridgefield, Wash: Privately printed.

Wingert, Paul S. 1949. *American Indian Sculpture, a Study of the Northwest Coast.* New York: Hacker Art Books.

———. 1952. *Prehistoric Stone Sculpture of the Pacific Northwest.* Portland: Portland Art Museum.

Work, John. 1914. "Journal of John Work, June-Oct. 1825." ed. T. C. Elliott. *Washington Historical Quarterly* 5:83-115.

———. 1920. "Journal of John Work, 1828." ed. William S. Lewis and Jacob A. Myers. *Washington Historical Quarterly* 11:104-14.

Wyeth, Captain Nathaniel. 1899. *Correspondence and Journal of Captain Nathaniel J. Wyeth's Expedition to the Oregon Country.* Ed. F. G. Young. Eugene: University of Oregon.

Zenk, Henry. 1990. "Kalapuyans." In Wayne Suttles, ed., *Northwest Coast,* Volume 7 of *Handbook of North American Indians,* gen. ed. William C. Sturtevant, 7:547-53. Washington, D. C.: Smithsonian Institution.

Index

Childhood, 101-03; boy's first deer, elk, bear celebrated, 105; girl's first berries, roots celebrated, 105; toys and games, 103-4

Chinini, 125, 132

Chinook Jargon, 128-32, 358; antiquity of, 390 n. 14; evolved, 302-303; expanded and died, 369-71; heard by Lewis & Clark, 157-158, 161-62, 393 n. 34;

Chinook language, 5, 51-59, 150, 231; orthography, 7-8; Penutian connection, 58-59; slang, 181-82

Chinook (name), 4-5

Chinook, people described, 22, 80-84, 88, 151, 236; different from whites, 324

Clackamas Chinook, 45, 95, 321, 359; ground burial, 333-34; to reservation, 367

Clatskani Athabasca, 41, 159-60; killed Astorians, 203, 278

Clatsop Chinook, 17-18, 39-40, 156-60; after epidemic of 1830, 345; last Clatsop, 312; raided by Quileute, 252; response to missionaries, 358-59; took smelt, 337; *William and Ann* murders of, 319

Clothing, 86-87; Wishram, Wasco wore Plateau clothes, 76

Clowewalla Chinook, 45, 95

Coalpo, guided Astorians, 201-03, 256-57; ranked by Simpson, 307

Coalpo's wife, at Cascades battle, 256-57, 259-260; offered daughter to Simpson, 307

Coastal culture, 76-77, 385 n. 49

Cobaway, Clatsop headman, 156, 305; three daughters married whites, 242, 278, 307

Cole sik, waum sik, 342-50

Columbia River, *Wimahl,* 3, 15-16, 313-14; duration of Chinook occcupancy, 4-5, Columbia River Bar, 39, 197

Comcomly, 23, 146-47, 250-51; at Astoria, 227, 232, 234-35; bought secrets, 263; died, 344; distressed by floats-ashore move to Fort Vancouver, 300; four daughters married clothmen, 307; friendship with Captain Bishop, 125-127, 134-35; greeted Astorians 198-199; had four wives, 231; lost eight family members in 1824–25, 304-05; lost eye conjecture, 250-51; name, 23; 231, 378-79, n 21; offered help against British, 237-38; passed leadership to second son, Shalapau, 278-79; pilot to Fort Vancouver, 310; resisted alcohol, 240; his skull, 353-54, 373; traded with Lewis and Clark, 154; visited Makah, perhaps Nootka, 307; in Winship incident, 186. *See also* bibliography, 393 n. 34

Confrontations, at the Cascades, in 1806, 162-63, in 1812, 206; in 1813, 255; in 1814, 255-56; at the Long Narrows in 1811, 204-05; in 1812, 206-208; in 1829, 261; at Oak Point in 1810, 185-87; pattern of confrontations, 208-09. *See also* Battle of 1814

Conjurers, 287-288. *See also* Shaman

Cooniac Chinook, 41, 337; Winship incident, 185-86

Cosmology, 5, 21; Astorians' view, 239; Coyote's role, 107

Cowlitz Salish, 42; 345; took best smelt, 337

Coyote, 17-18, 106-21, 239, 374; announced coming of people, 11, 108; announced fishing taboos, 17-18; compared to Christ, 107-08; in art, 50, 75-76, 106; Coyote on

Hudson's Bay Company (HBC), 299-301, 317, 319-20, 341; blamed Dominis for *cole sik*, 342, 349; merged with North West Company, 299. *See also* Fort Vancouver

Hunting, mammals and birds, 211-12; sea lions, 337-38

Ice Age, 12-13

Illchee (Moon Girl), daughter of Comcomly, 315; born, 146; called "The Princess," 237; first menstruation, 174-78; married Cassino, 355-56; met, married McDougall, 99, 27-28, 232-35, 277-78; survived *cole sik*, 348

Infanticide, 242, 311, 361

Itcixyan (water spirit), 18-20, 119-120

Joseachal, Quinault, 199, 203

Kahatlau, daughter of Comcomly, 147; called "Princess Margaret," 237

Kalama Chinook (Tlakalama), 42; epidemic of 1830, 345

Kalapuya (neighboring non-Chinooks), 46, 52, 301, 308, 346

Kamac Tualatin Kalapuya, 308

Kanakas (Hawaiians), 302; "Kanaka Village," 303

Kathlamet Chinook, 18, 40-41, 45, 89; epidemic of 1830, 345; villages, 41-42, 160; movement of villages, 185

Kawok (spirit helpers), 171-74, 281-84; strongest, 263; slaves sought, 269; *tahmanawis* men, 287; revealed before death, 295-96. *See also Yuhlma*, wild spirits

Kennedy, Alexander, 300, 307, 309

Kiasno, Comcomly's Scapoose first wife, 126; bore Chenamus, Illchee, 146, 175

Kiksht (upriver Chinook language), 57, 150, 161-62

Kilakota, married, deserted by Mathews, 242, 278

Kin Chautch, 123

Klallam, 318

Klamath (neighboring non-Chinooks), 67; myth of the Klamath Eagle, 322

Klickitat (neighboring non-Chinooks), 45, 47-48; Bridge of the Gods myth, 63-64; trade, 67, 69

Komkomis, Comcomly's father, 23, 250

Konapee, floats-ashore, 27, 90, 305. *See also* Soto

Lamsay (George Ramsay), 27, 185; aboard Tonquin, 199, 203; Chinook messenger, 240; fathered son, Yellow-cum, 307, 358; pilot, 301, 310; with Wilkes party, 358

Land of the dead, 191-95

Legend, differ from myth, 142; exaggeration five times in, 133; of four cousins, 18-20; of girl who broke menstrual taboos, 176-77; of going with the ghosts, 247-48; of starvation, 327-29; of Tiapexwasxwas, 137-42; of Wishram dispute and migration, 65-66; of youth who killed too much game, 173

Lewis and Clark party, 39, 148-63; Chinook census by, 320-21; saw larger mosquito, 349

Long Narrows, 65, 73, 97; Lewis and Clark visited, 150, 163; incidents at, 204-5, 206-8, 254, 261

Love, 228; between slaves and free persons, 269-70

Elk withdrew powers, 173

Four Cousins, 18-20

Frogs, 105, 313, 324

Grizzly Woman announced trees, 288-89

Klamath Eagle came to gamble, 322

Origin Myths: fire men, 13; Gitlapshoi (Shoalwater), 11-12; of landforms, 21; Southwind and Thunderbird, 13-14; Wishram, 66; Wishpoosh and Coyote, 215-16

Salmon came up the river, 93-95

Skunk invited the people, 285-86

Tsagiglalal, 74

Wild Woman and Crane (Tillamook), 293

Nakwaiih village, 43

Names, naming, 100-101, 231

Nayagogo, "Where There are Blows," 43, 89, 248, 249

Neahcoxie village, 39

Neahkeluk village, 40; burned by Hudson's Bay Company, 317-19; secret society, 263

Neerchokioo village, 89, visited by Lewis and Clark, 161

Nemalquinner village, 45

Netul (Fort Clatsop), 157

Nez Perce Sahaptin (neighboring non-Chinooks), attacked Nixluidix, 255; trade, 67-68

Nixluidix village (Wishram), 48, 64; Lewis and Clark visited, 149-50; Nez Perce attacked, 255; smallpox ended trade, 364; soldiers leveled, 367

Nobles, 142-43, 145

Norcarte, 156

North West Company (Nor'westers), 237-243; bought Astoria, 237-38; fought a battle, 255-61; merged with Hudson's Bay Company, 299

Old age, 294

Old John, last Multnomah, 372

Ornamentation, 87-88, 133, 166

Pacific Fur Company, 198, 237. *See also* Astorians

Paiute. *See* Shoshone

Passissiuks, passiuks, "cloth men," 149-50

Penutian language phylum, 58-59

Political life, 142-46

Population statistics, 1805–06 by Lewis and Clark, 159; 1824, 306; after 1830s epidemics, 344-46; summary of estimates, 320-21

Pregnancy and childbirth, 97-99

Prophesies, of battle, 253; of *cole sik,* 341; of end, 315; of death of oysters, 277; of white people coming, 28

Puberty rites. *See* First ceremonies

Quathlapootle village, 44, 160, 345

Quatqos. *See* Shalapau

Quileute (neighboring non-Chinooks), 187, 307; raid Clatsop 251-52

Qwalwanxu, 97-98; had coyote power, 99

Qwasqwas. *See* Chenamus

Qwatsamts (Comcomly's Shoalwater village) 4, 23, 80, 186; described, 38-39; epidemic of 1830 at, 344, 365; first menstruation ceremony at, 175; secret society, 263

Qwayaq, Comcomly's Chehalis second wife, 97-99; bore Shalapau, Kahatlau, 147

Ramsay, George. *See* Lamsay

Ramsay, Jack Sr., floats-ashore, 27

Ramsay, Jack Jr., 27, 158, 358

Raven, Comcomly's second daughter, 147; married Archibald McDonald, bore Ranald McDonald, died, 304; "Princess Sunday," 237. *See also* Toole

Reservations, 366-68, 370

Ritual number five, 133, 291

Sachla, 307

Sahaptin (neighboring non-Chinooks), 49, 120-21, 163

Salmon, Chinook, king or tyee (*igunat*), 95-96, 102, 160, 163, 165; dog or calico (*utsiya*), 178; dried, 47 102, 168-69; June hogs, 102, 372; Myth of, 93-5; silverside or coho (*oowun*), 178; salmon head soup, 219; sockeye (*otsui-ha*), 165. *See also* Fish, Foods

Sanitation, 170

Secret societies, 263-66

Sexual relations, adultery, 223-24; chastity, 228; sex roles, 221-25; struggle between sexes, 363; women offered freely, 125, 155, 228

Shahala Chinook (Cascades), 46-47, 63-67; atrocity of 1856, 366; charnel houses, 151, 332; epidemic of 1830, 344-46; feared smallpox in 1811, 204; fishing at, 97; Lewis and Clark passed, 151, 162; population, 306, 320-21; Ross incident at, 208; seer predicted coming of whites, 28; sent to reservations, 367; skirmishes at, 162-63, 206, 208-9, 254-56, 258-60; strategic portage, 64, 366; battle of 1814, 256-61

Shalapau (Quatqos), Comcomly's second son, 97-103, 304; "Duke of York," 237; named heir, 278-79

Shaman, 29, 145, 246; curing, 188-90, 275-77; training, 274-75

Shelathwell, Shoalwater headman, 125-27, 134, 228; seen by Lewis and Clark, 154, 156

Ship captains, Ayres, 135; James Baker, 89; Charles Bishop, 124-28, 132-35; Lt. William Broughton, 88-91, 300; John O. Dominis, 316-17, 342, 349; Robert Gray, 79; Swippton, 163; D. W. Thompson, 316, 319; Jonathon Thorn, 197-99, 203; Nathan Winship, 185-87

Ships, *Albatross*, 185; *Chatham*, 89; *Columbia Rediviva*, 4, 79-81; *Convoy*, 316-17, 319, 341; *Dolly*, 200, 203; *Eagle*, 341; *Isaac Todd*, 240; *Isabella*, 341; *Jenny*, 89, 123, 126; *Mexicana*, 123; *Owhyhee*, 316-17, 341-42; *Phoenix*, 123; *Racoon*, 237-238; *Ruby*, 124, 125, 135; *Tonquin*, 197-200, 203; *William and Ann*, 317, 341

Shipwrecked sailors, Japanese, 25, 354; Konapee, 25-27; Jack Ramsay, 27

Shoalwater Chinook, 37-39; disputed with Skilloot, 160; lost culture after epidemic of 1830, 351, 365, 367; missionaries found difficult, 358-59; offended Lewis and Clark; 156-57; origin myth, 13-14; trade, 72. *See also* Qwatsamts

Shoshone, Paiute, (neighboring non-Chinooks), 49; attacked, 252-54

Simpson, George, 301, 307

Skilloot Chinook, 40, 42, 160. 337

Slaves, 142-43, 266-70, in Fort George Report of 1824, 306; killed at owner's death, 270, 333; trade, 67-69, 135, 267-68

THE TYPEFACE USED IN THIS BOOK is Minion, a contemporary face based upon classical, old-style typefaces of the late Renaissance, created for electronic composition by Robert Slimbach.

Chinook Illahee, the land of the Chinook-speakers, around AD 1260, from the northwest. Mount St. Helens is in one of its frequent eruptions. The sand spit (lower right) is the twenty-seven-mile Long Beach Peninsula, which encloses Willapa or Shoalwater Bay. South of the Columbia River, the Chinook lived to Tillamook Head, the first rocky cape. The villages of the Chinook lined the great river for two hundred miles upstream, the tributary Willamette for twenty-seven miles to Willamette Falls (upper right), and halfway up Shoalwater Bay.